# TORT LAW AND HOW IT'S TIED TO OUR CULTURE

M. Stuart Madden, Esq.

DORRANCE
PUBLISHING CO
EST. 1920
PITTSBURGH, PENNSYLVANIA 15238

Dorrance Publishing Co
585 Alpha Drive
Suite 103
Pittsburgh, PA 15238
Visit our website at *www.dorrancebookstore.com*

ISBN: 978-1-4809-8978-8
eISBN: 978-1-4809-9465-2

# Contents

1. The Cultural Evolution of Tort Law . . . . . . . . . . . . . . . . . . . . . . .1

2. Graeco-Roman Antecedents of Western Law . . . . . . . . . . . . . . . .35

3. Paths of Western Law after Justinian . . . . . . . . . . . . . . . . . . . . . .87

4. Myth, Folklors, and Ancient Ethics . . . . . . . . . . . . . . . . . . . . . .151

5. The Vital Common Law: Its Role in a Statutory Age . . . . . . . . .191

6. A Comparitive Analysis of United States
    and Colombia Tort Law: Duty, Breach, and Damages . . . . . . . .259

7. Tort's Law Themes of Economic Efficiency . . . . . . . . . . . . . . . .291

# CHAPTER 1:

# THE CULTURAL EVOLUTION
# OF TORT LAW

## I. INTRODUCTION

Countless years before the coalescence of human groupings into civil societies, kinship groups, and later tribes and cultures, people needed norms by which individual conduct could be ordered. The primary stimulus for such norms was group survival, and the ancillary motivations were the achievement of civil peace and the protection of one's person and property from wrongful harm. The means by which normative behavioral impositions operated took countless shapes, but the avenues taken could be classified, in roughly chronological order, as spiritualism, folk tales, folk law, mythology, religion, and customary law.[1]

The application of such sources as justification for modern civil justice decision-making has largely disappeared, although perhaps not entirely. An electronic search within state and federal legislative databases for "I cannot tell a lie" or "Horatio Alger" would surely reveal a cluster of allusions, and the cyclical debate over religion in public affairs without more betrays the tenacity of religion's

---

[1] For the purposes of this Chapter, the terms "ancient" and "primitive" are distinguished in this way: "ancient" is a designation that the example existed in recorded antiquity, and "primitive" connotes that the example can be identified or hypothesized as existing in pre-symbolic society.

influence on our public life. Withal, even though the sources of contemporary civil law have changed, the needs of modern society for a similar order and predictability in human civil affair remain very similar to the needs confronting our ancestors. It is therefore unsurprising that ancient examples of normative beliefs, practices, and customary law reveal sprawling similarities with modern tort law.

At the core of tort norms, and later tort law, has always been a group desire that disputes be resolved without retaliation and escalation with norms

> provided to [ensure]…that homicide should not be committed,…but [that] there should be a legal case for each of these, and they should not be decided by the individual's anger or whim.[2] Islamic law too is clear cut in its differentiation between excusable self-defense and culpable retaliation.[3]

Nevertheless, dissimilarities between ancient and modern approaches to civil justice are apparent at almost every turn to this inquiry. Some primitive remedies for conversion might offer not only restitution to the wronged party but also the opportunity to exact a fine, to be collected by the complainant himself, a double recovery by today's standards.[4] Other pairings of right and remedy might at first seem suggestive of the modern action in public nuisance, but, upon closer evaluation can be seen to depart from that rule in the designation of who may bring the claim. And a very large number of disputes are resolved not by fact-finding, application of governing norms, and an adjudicatory declaration, but rather by mediation and conciliation, which although a goal in numerous modern state and federal precincts in the United States, cannot be described as a general rule.

As suggested, over the ages the nature of offenses that have stimulated

---

[2] DOUGLAS M. MACDOWELL, THE LAW IN CLASSICAL ATHENS 123 (Cornell 1978) (quoting Demosthenes, *Against Konon* 54.17-19).

[3] *See infra* text discussing THE KORAN.

[4] *See, e.g.*, Shih-Yü Yü Li, *Tibetan Folk-Law*, J. Roy. Asiatic Soc. G.B. & Ireland Parts 3, 4, pp. 127-48 (1950), reprinted in 1 ALISON DUNDES RENTELN & ALAN DUNDES, FOLK LAW 513-26 (1995).

identification as redressable wrongs has become mostly settled. The designations of the subsections in Part II to this Chapter largely comprise them: (1) public and private nuisance and disturbing the peace; (2) unintentional killing; (3) assault and battery; (4) trespass to land and chattels; (5) conversion; (6) negligence; (7) strict liability; (8) deceit and false report; (9) defamation and false witness; and, in some cultures, (10) covetousness and hoarding.

Describing with confidence the range of remedies for such wrongs, much less their varied justifications, is a more difficult task. Or at least it seems so due to the diverse ways tort objectives are described often in terminology that seems not so much a dispassionate description than an argument for a polemical position. The more interesting groupings of tort objectives can be found in a source one would not at first think of—Friedrich Nietzsche. In his GENEALOGY OF MORALS, Nietzsche identifies a core cluster of the objectives of punishment.[5] Winnowed of punishments suited to criminal actions, what remains are the more classically civil, or only quasi-criminal, responses, i.e., the types of remedies associated with torts. These include:

> Punishment consisting of the payment of damages to the injured party, including affect compensation.[6] 3. Punishment as the isolation of a disequilibrating agent, in order to keep the disturbance from spreading further.[7]. . . 8. Punishment as a means of creating memory, either for the one who suffers it—so-called "improvement"—or for the witnesses. 9. Punishment as the payment of a fee, exacted by the authority which protects the evil-doer from the excesses of vengeance. 10. Punishment as a compromise with the tradition of vendetta...[8]

---

[5] FRIEDRICH NIETZSCHE, THE BIRTH OF TRAGEDY AND THE GENEALOGY OF MORALS 213 (Francis Golfing, trans., Anchor Books 1956).

[6] "Affect compensation" may be understood to mean damages for emotional distress.

[7] Particularly among indigenous peoples, a person refusing to follow community norms was perceived, as is true in some instances today, to destabilize the community. As will be seen in the discussion to follow, for lesser offenses, the response might be temporary shunning. For more serious or more sustained delicts, the individual might be banned from the group.

It is noteworthy that primitive and ancient law contain numerous examples in which the society has seemingly concluded that simple corrective justice is insufficient to reach the joint objectives of redressing the harm done and of deterring the actor and others from the same or similar conduct. For example, throughout the Rules of Punishment for Tibetans, published by the Manchu Imperial Court in 1733, the burden imposed by the restitutionary interest of the rule, i.e., the return of the animal, and elsewhere the property, etc., is seemingly ancillary to, the punishment dimension of the rule.[9] It might be surmised that over time a culture's collective wisdom was that simple restorative justice had insufficient gravitas as a deterrent if unaccompanied by a fine payable to the wronged party.[10] In cases of incorrigibility, though, the penalty might be shunning or even banning from the community.[11]

As a general proposition, spiritualism, folk tales, folk law, mythology, reli-

---

[8] NIETZSCHE, *supra* at 213. *See also* HENRY SUMNER MAINE, ANCIENT LAW 358 (Charles M. Haas ed., Beacon Press 1963) (1861) (emphasis in original):

> *Now the penal Law of ancient communities is not the law of Crimes; it is the law of Wrongs, or, to use the English technical word, of Torts. The person injured proceeds against the wrong-doer by an ordinary civil action, and recovers compensation in the shape of money-damages if he succeeds. . . . [All such Torts] gave rise to an Obligation or vinculum juris, and were all requited by a payment of money.*

To Maine's account it is worthwhile to add that in addition to or as an alternative to money damages, and as will be described below, both primitive and ancient communities might require other remedies. Replacement of any goods or animals damaged or injured is one example.

[9] In this sense, the diverse fines provided for in Tibetan folk law operated as punishment bearing similarities to today's punitive damages. *See, e.g.*, Rules 20-21, Rules of Punishment for Tibetans; Yü Li, *supra* note 4, at 525.

[10] *Id.*

[11] Few societies today maintain gulags to which persons may be banished, although with the passing of opportunities to send persons to entirely different continents such as Australia, prisons and jails sufficed.

Excommunication in the Catholic Church harkens to such themes. In the early church, excommunication carried with it the revocation of other ordinary rights in civil society. This deterrent cannot be seen to have worked terribly well, as in the year 1337 it is estimated that half of Christendom was under sentence of excommunication. 1 ERNST TROELTSCH, THE SOCIAL TEACHING OF THE CHRISTIAN CHURCHES 234 n.100a (Olive Wyon trans., Harper & Brothers 1960) (1911).

gion, and customary law underlay most ancient law. The import of spiritualism and its more formal successor, religion, is self-revealing. So too is mythology with its gods, demigods, pantheism, and anthropomorphism. Customary law, sometimes called the "living law," has reflected norms to which a particular society has assigned epochal and steadfast adherence; rules that a culture has followed so unflaggingly and consistently as to permit the application of no inconsistent rule. To Sir John Salmond, customary law embraces "any rule of action which is actually observed by men—any rule which is the expression of some actual uniformity of voluntary action," irrespective of whether it is obligatory and enforceable or exists by reason of de facto observance.[12]

The ancient Babylonian *Code of Hammurabi* endeavored to gather, rationalize, and organize already extant customary law. For all that is apparent, Hammurabi himself intended that his law would reconcile wrongs and bring justice to those aggrieved.[13] His unmistakable goal was the economic stability and enhancement of the people.[14] In a further example, the ancient Rules of Punishment for Tibetans have been interpreted as "an attempt to standardize… folk-law by removing authority from the local chieftains and monasteries."[15] It is therefore not surprising that the antecedents of customary law have often included folk law, folk custom, and folk tales. In the many examples of primitive and ancient law to follow, it is seen that the norms of conduct, be they characterized as folk law, custom, or otherwise, were enforced not by any leadership of the community but rather by the whole.

Sometimes in literate societies, and invariably in preliterate ones, folk laws and customs, as well as folk tales, were dispersed and preserved orally. A culture's oral tradition has been described as a tradition that "represents the complete information deemed essential, retained and codified by a society, primarily in oral form, in order to facilitate its memorization and ensure its dissemination to present and future generations."[16]

---

[12] JOHN SALMOND, JURISPRUDENCE 30-31 (8th ed.)(Sweet & Maxwell, Ltd. 1930).

[13] *See generally* RUSS VERSTEEG, EARLY MESOPOTAMIAN LAW (2000).

[14] *Id.*

[15] Yü Li, *supra* at 520.  ·

[16] A. Raphael Ndiaye, *Oral Tradition: From Collection to Digitization 1* (65th Interna-

Man's capacity for symbolic communication accelerated the development and communication of norms. The characteristic of all such norms was that they confined the realm of permissible behaviors.[17] This higher level capacity of man to communicate in endurable form was more than a boon; with increasing populations and social complexities attendant thereto, it was an absolute essential to survival.[18] Without symbolling, the communication of norms could only survive in a state of enduring retardation, confined to the lumbering and limited means of oral communication. And without norms human life would fall into chaos. As put by Langer, "[Man] can adapt himself somehow to anything his imagination can cope with, but he cannot deal with Chaos."[19] Increasingly, therefore, without symbolling the generational and geographic transmittal of norms would lag behind societies' expanding needs.

Thus, early man needed norms and proscriptions to permit his very survival. Even before the advent of kingdoms, there was a premium on keeping the "king's peace," even in large human groupings, which could be described as units of the earliest proto civilizations. These norms and proscriptions have been described loosely as "natural law," and form the foundation of all modern law. Hobbes placed the source of natural law as "reason," writing in LEVIATHAN: "Reason suggesteth convenient Articles of Peace, upon which men may be drawn to agreement. These Articles are they which otherwise are called the Laws of Nature."[20] T.E. Holland describes the rights conferred by natural law as these: "I. To personal safety and freedom[;] II. To society and control of one's family and dependents[;] III. To reputation[;] IV. To advantages open to the community generally; such as the free exercise of one's calling[;] V. To possession and ownership [; and ] VI. To immunity from damage by fraud."[21]

The discussion to follow validates Hobbes recitation in that it will show that the norms and customs to which man turned his attention from the ear-

---

tional Federation of Library Associations & Institutions Conference) (1999).

[17] CLIFFORD GEERTZ, THE INTERPRETATION OF CULTURES 67-68 (1973).

[18] Id.

[19] Id. (quoting Susanne K. Langer, PHILOSOPHY IN A NEW KEY 287 (1942)).

[20] THOMAS ERSKINE HOLLAND, THE ELEMENTS OF JURISPRUDENCE 34 (10th ed. 1910) (quoting THOMAS HOBBES, LEVIATHAN 63 (Univ. Press 1904) (1651)).

[21] Id. at 169.

liest times bear a similarity—regular if not perfect—to the natural law described by Hobbes and other later theorists.

# II. PARTICULAR APPLICATIONS OF ANCIENT TORT LAW

## A. NUISANCE AND DISTURBING THE PEACE

Throughout primitive and ancient law are examples of strictures suggesting that the social group placed a greater premium on restoring order and good will than it did on determining that one disputant was right and the other was wrong. In Australian aboriginal customary law, for example, the objective of resolution of a dispute would more often be the quieting of temper and the restoration of a placid community rather than any strict identification of which party was at fault.[22]

Tibetan folk law demonstrates numerous examples of remedies for what today might be termed "public nuisance." In the *Rules of Punishment for Tibetans*, Rule No. 26, titled "Making Fire to Burn Wild Animals Out of Their Lairs," vests in the individual who discovers the infraction the remedy of fining the hunter "1 'nine.'"[23] Reposing the remedy in the person discovering the delict might at first seem like an example of the "special injury" rule in public nuisance, in that an individual may bring the claim. Yet in this "Fire Rule," there is no articulated need that the reporting individual/claimant have suffered any injury at all.[24] Perhaps the rule simply stands as an example of a pub-

---

[22] KENNETH MADDOCK, ABORIGINAL CUSTOMARY LAW, in ABORIGINES AND THE LAW 212, 232 (Peter Hanks & Bryan Keon-Cohen eds., 1984). Maddock references the effect of "community opinion about the merits of a case as helping to decide the outcome through its influence on both the disputants and their potential supporters...." *Id.* (citing L. R. HIATT, KINSHIP AND CONFLICT: A STUDY IN AN ABORIGINAL COMMUNITY OF NORTHERN ARNHEM LAND 146-47 (1965)).

[23] Yü Li, *supra* at 526.

[24] *Id.*

lic nuisance proceeding that can be brought not only by public officials but also by individuals, with the inclusion of individuals seen as a prudential device to increase deterrence by increasing detection.

Penalty provisions referencing one or more "nines" or one or more "animals" were enforceable with reference to Rule No. 39, which detailed how these terms correlated with livestock:

> One 'nine' means a combination of nine animals such as 2 horses, 2 *dso*, 2 three-year-old cows, 1 two-year-old cow. 'Five animals' means 1 *dso*, 1 cow, 1 three-year-old cow, and 2 two-year cows. The person who comes to demand these fines is entitled to receive as his fee 1 three-year-old cow from the guilty. In places where horses are not plentiful *dso* may be offered in their stead.[25]

Further to the theme of norms directed principally at maintaining peace and quiet, among the Pygmies living in the Ituri Forest of the former Congo, there has long been a saying that "a noisy camp is a hungry camp."[26] This proposition is so because the Pygmies are hunters, and as is self-evident, unnecessary noise drives the game deeper into the forest.[27] As it might be today, and yet for different reasons, noise that is unreasonable in its volume, timing, or location may be treated as a nuisance.

Anthropologist Colin Turnbull records an incident in which the father of an attractive village girl chased away a suitor and persisted in his tirade by taking a position in the middle of the village, calling for others to support him. That failing, the father took to rattling the roofs of the surrounding huts.[28] An elder interceded in a calm voice: "You are making too much noise— you are killing the forest, you are killing the hunt. It is for us older men to sleep at night and not to worry about the youngsters. They know what to do

---

[25] *Id.* at 529.

[26] COLIN M. TURNBULL, THE FOREST PEOPLE 120 (1962).

[27] *Id.*

[28] *Id.* at 119.

and what not to do."[29] Evidently displeased, the father nevertheless accepted the resolution.[30]

Under Roman Law, the Institutes of Justinian included rules that reveal numerous restrictions against the imposition of one's will over the rights of a neighbor. Specifically as to urban estates is Book II, Title III, para. 1, in which there is a prohibition on the obstruction of a neighbor's view.[31] In another notable example, pertaining to what would today be called the law of private nuisance or trespass, a provision goes so far as to detail a preference that adjoining landowners bargain in advance for agreement as to contemporaneous uses of land that might trigger dispute. In Book III, Title III, para. 4, the Institutes provide that one wishing to create such a right of usage should do so by pacts and stipulations.[32] A testator of land may impose any such agreements reached upon his heirs, including limitations upon building height, obstruction of light, introduction of a beam into a common wall, the construction of a catch for a cistern, an easement of passage, or a right of way to water.[33] These last examples reflect a clear preference for ex ante bargaining over economically wasteful ex post dispute resolution. The provision permitting the testator to bind his heirs to any such agreement is additionally efficient in a manner akin to the approach that was taken later and famously by Justice Bergen in the cement plant nuisance case of Boomer v. Atlantic Cement Co.,[34] who ensured that the award of damages would be indeed a one-time resolution of the dispute by requiring that the disposition of the claim be entered and recorded as a permanent servitude on the land.

As codified, the customary law of private nuisance in ancient Mesopotamia provided specifically for redress should one's irrigation waters overflow onto another's property or crops. Particularly harsh legal consequences might be visited upon the landowner who failed to contain his irrigation canals, as flooding of the water might "result not only in leaving

---

[29] *Id.*

[30] *Id.*

[31] *The Institutes of Justinian* bk. 2, tit. 3, para. 1 (JAC Thomas trans. 1975).

[32] *Id.* at bk. 2, tit. 3, para. 4.

[33] *Id.*

[34] 257 N.E.2d 870 (N.Y. 1970).

crops and cattle dry and parched in one part, but also widespread floods in another part of a district."[35] In a simple case only involving damaged grain, replacement of a like amount might give sufficient remedy.[36] But an unmistakable message of potentially severe penalties would be clear to those knowing that should the careless farmer be unable to replace the grain, the neighbors might be permitted to sell his property and sell him into slavery to achieve justice.[37]

## B. MANSLAUGHTER OR WRONGFUL DEATH

At Surah 4, the Koran prohibits, unsurprisingly, the intentional killing of a believer.[38] In traditional Islamic law, the unintended killing of another would warrant payment of a full *diyet*, or blood-money, set at 3.8 grams of silver.[39] Should a believer be killed by "mischance," i.e., accident, the responsible party "shall be bound to free a believer from slavery; and the blood-money shall be paid to the family of the slain, unless they convert it into alms."[40] Killing in self-defense would be unpunished. Lawrence Rosen gives an example of the limitations on the defense with the example of one Zeyd, who attacked Amr. Reviewed by the mufti, it was noted that Amr could have rescued himself by calling for help, thus denying him the privilege of self-defense.[41]

There are numerous Eastern examples of the treatment of unintentional killing as an offense redressable in money or other damages. In ancient India, if a person were accidentally killed by an animal-drawn vehicle, the driver

---

[35] VerSteeg, *supra* note 14, at 136 (quoting G.R. Driver & John C. Mills, The Babylonian Laws 152 (1952)).

[36] *Id.* (citing *Laws of Hammurabi* § 53).

[37] *Id.* (citing *Laws of Hammurabi* § 53); *see also* Raymond Westbrook, *Slave and Master in Ancient Near Eastern Law*, 70 Chi.-Kent L. Rev. 1631, 1644 (1995).

[38] The Koran, 4:93 (J.M. Rodwell trans., Everyman 1994).

[39] Haim Gerber, State, Society, and Law in Islam 33 (1994).

[40] The Koran, *supra* at 4:93.

[41] Gerber, *supra* at 52 (citing Lawrence Rosen, Responsibility and Compensatory Justice in Arab Law and Culture, in Semiotics, Self, and Society 101-19 (Benjamin Lee & Greg Urban eds., 1989).

would be subjected to the same monetary liability as would be imposed upon a thief of a chattel of equivalent value.[42] In China, for injuries resulting in death, traditional law distinguished between intentional killing and accidental killing. T'ang Code Article 339 provided that "[a]ll cases of accidentally *(kuo shih)* killing or injuring someone follow the manner in which the death occurs and is treated as redeemable."[43] By "redeemable" it is meant that the offense may be expiated by the payment of money to the victim's family.[44] The analogous provision in the Ch'ing Code describes accidental killing *(wu sha)* in the context of hunting for game *(hsi sha)*. It states that for an accidental killing the punishment should be the same as for a killing in a fight, except that "redemption is permitted." The Ch'ing Code gives examples of an accidental death such as: "where one is shooting wild animals or for some reason is throwing bricks or tiles"; climbing and one's fall causing others to fall; navigating a boat by sail, riding a horse that becomes frightened, driving a cart downhill, or lifting an object when "[one] lacks the strength to sustain it and someone else is harmed." In each such instance, when "there has been no intention to harm," the Code provides that "the sentence is to conform to the punishment for killing or injuring in a fight," except that redemption is permitted, with "the money to be given to the family of the person killed or injured as a contribution to funeral or medical expenses."[45]

## C. ASSAULT AND BATTERY

Historically, intentional battery has been an offense that creates a high risk of retaliation, or self-help, or "blood feud" between kinship groups. Even so, some native American Indian groups even while making allowance for such violent responses, provided simultaneously for the peaceable intercession of

---

[42] The Law Code of Manu 145 (Patrick Olivelle trans., Oxford University Press 2004) [hereinafter Code of Manu].

[43] Geoffrey MacCormack, The Spirit of Traditional Chinese Law 38 (1996).

[44] *Id.* at 39.

[45] *Id.*

the village council.[46] In the Asian context, numerous Indian groups, in contrast, demonstrate, without exceptions, "a general disapproval of retaliation as a means of obtaining justice."[47]

Putting aside its punishment of death for one who strikes his mother or father, [48] under the Torah one who inflicts a direct non-mortal blow to another will not be liable if the victim is able to get up and about, "even with a stick," providing an interesting early invocation of the principle *de minimis non curat lex*.[49] If, however, the injury is sufficiently serious that the victim is temporarily incapacitated, the aggressor "must compensate him…for his enforced inactivity, and care for him until he is completely cured."[50] This approach contemplates not only recovery for what is today termed economic loss (compensation for "enforced inactivity"), but also rehabilitation expenses.

In Islamic law, compensatory justice for injurious battery might provide for damages according to a schedule keyed to the severity of the harm, rather as does modern workers compensation. Liability might be according to *diyet*, or blood-money.[51] Full blood-money due for the unintentional death of the victim was set at 10,000 *dirham*, or 3.8 grams of silver.[52] Serious injury to the hand, the leg, or the eye was compensable with half blood-money.[53] Loss of a tooth might warrant 1/20 blood-money.[54]

The Koran is not pacifistic by any means, and does not feign to offer remedies to persons who may avoid injury by resort to self-help, or by means of re-

---

[46] Upendra Baxi, People's Law in India - The Hindu Society, in Asian Indigenous Law: In Interaction with Received Law 251 (Masaji Chiba ed., 1986) [hereinafter Asian Indigenous Law] (addressing indigenous law governing the Konyak Nagas of India).

[47] *Id.*

[48] "Anyone who strikes his father or mother must die. Anyone who abducts a man— whether he has sold him or is found in possession of him—must die. Anyone who curses father or mother must die." Exod. 21:15-17 (The Jerusalem Bible).

[49] *Id.* at 21:19.

[50] *Id.* at 21:18-19.

[51] Gerber, *supra* at 33.

[52] *Id.*

[53] *Id.* at 35.

[54] *Id.*

taliation. While the Koran explains that God does not countenance attacking others first, Muslims may "fight for the cause of God against those who fight against you[.]"[55] Is it then paradoxical that it may be true that, as some scholars claim, "the function of law in Islam is merely to get people back on a negotiating track"?[56] This perception pertains to an objective that the state attend to affairs of government, not religion. Islam, in turn, attends to religion, and not to the state, and that it is in these subject matters that the "negotiating" ideal obtains.[57] Within the tribal customary law of the Awlad Ali of Egypt, for battery resulting in injury, *diyah* or blood-money, would be paid to the family of the victim, together with *kebara*, calculated in money and animals.[58]

Under the *Rules of Punishment for Tibetans*, battery could incur variable fines depending upon the severity of injury. A fine of three "nines" would be levied for a fight resulting in an injury to the eye, hand, or foot. If the injury was such as could be cured, the fine was one "nine," as was true also for a fight causing broken teeth, or an abortion.[59] When hair would be torn off, the fine was five animals.[60]

In ancient Indian law, the "low born" were treated very differentially than were the Brahmins. For injurious assaults against one of a superior caste, punishment ranged from amputation of the limb used by the assailant to banishment or exile, or for spitting on one's superior, the cutting off of the assailant's lips.[61] Other aggression causing injury and pain to another (or to an animal) called for the king to "impose a punishment proportionate to the severity of the pain."[62]

---

[55] THE KORAN, *supra* at 2:186.

[56] LAWRENCE ROSEN, THE ANTHROPOLOGY OF JUSTICE 61 (1989), quoted in GERBER, *supra* at 59. "In the classical Islamic theory of the state .... [T]he state was seen not as the instrument for the application of law, nor were the courts ... envisioned as vehicles for economic redistribution or the construction of a particular political order." *Id.*

[57] *Id.*

[58] ASIAN INDIGENOUS LAW, *supra* at 65.

[59] Yü Li, *supra* at 526 (citing Rule 28, *Rules of Punishment for Tibetans*).

[60] *Id.*

[61] *Code of Manu, supra* at 144.

[62] *Id.*

Under Greek law, striking another gave rise to a private cause of action in battery *(dike aikeias)*.[63] If liability was found, it was ordinarily against the one striking the first blow. The penalty was an amount payable in money damages as assessed by a jury.[64]

## D. TRESPASS TO LAND AND CHATTELS

In the ancient work *Manu*, entitled alternatively *The Law Code of Manu* or *Mana.va Dharmasastra*, the text references ancient Indian law governing the trespass of animals.[65] For such fields surrounding a settlement as are left open, any farm animal damage to crops should not be punished. To receive any protection for one's fields, a person "should erect there a fence over which a camel cannot look and cover every hole through which a dog or pig could poke its head." For damage caused by herded livestock to such fenced land, a fine of 100 *panas* should be imposed—and if the livestock are unherded, they should be impounded. For livestock damage to other fields, "one and a half *[p]anas* should be assessed for each animal," and the owner of the land should be compensated for any crop loss.[66]

Prior to the *Laws of Hammurabi*, the *Laws of King Ur-Nammu* and the *Laws of Lipit-Ishtar* were published.[67] Read together as principal sources of the law of ancient Babylonia, there is seen an emphasis on the protection of person, property, and commerce from forced divestiture of a right or a prerogative.[68] Regarding navigation, a collision between two boats on a body of water having a perceptible upstream and downstream would trigger a presumption of fault on the part of the upstream captain, on the logic—faulty or not—that the upstream captain had a greater opportunity to reduce avoidable accidents than did his counterpart, as the former would be traveling at a slower speed.[69]

---

[63] MACDOWELL, *supra* at 123 (citing Demosthenes, 47.45-7, 47.64; Isokrates, 20.19).

[64] *Id.*

[65] *Code of Manu, supra* at 141.

[66] *Id.*

[67] *See* VERSTEEG, *supra* at 18.

[68] *Id.* at 22-26.

Anglo-American common law trespass includes numerous instances in which a landowner is held liable in trespass if a structure or an activity on the first individual's property causes damages, by diversion of water or otherwise, to the land of another. The account *Against Kallikles* is found in Athenian law, recorded by Demosthenes, in which it appears that Kallikles and a neighbor both lived on a hillside.[70] Kallikles's neighbor constructed a wall to protect his land from water runoff from rainfall, which served this purpose, but also diverted water onto his Kallikles's property. Kallikles brought a suit because his property was damaged due to his neighbor's wall.[71] By Demosthenes' account, if found guilty for this trespass, Kallikles would be fined in damages *(dike blabes)* a sum of 1000 *drachmas*.[72]

In ancient Athens, an action for destruction of, or damage to, chattels was defined in a way as to merge the modern notions of trespass to chattels and conversion. An action for "damage" could be brought for any "physical damage to a piece of property, such as to destroy it or make it useless or less valuable than before, but without taking it away ... [.]"[73]

Tibetan folk law includes methods of economic recovery, recovery in kind, and punitive consequences that bespeak strong deterrence objectives.[74] Should one's trespassing cattle damage another's field, the owner of the field may seize the cattle pending payment for the damage.[75] Should the land at issue not be a field but instead a pasture utilized by nomads for the grazing of their animals, Tibetan folk law proscribes the trespassing of one nomadic tribe's cattle on the pasture of another tribe. Again, the trespassing cattle may be seized pend-

---

[69] *Id.* at 130 (referencing G. R. DRIVER AND JOHN C. MILES, THE BABYLONIAN LAWS 431-32 (1952)). The author questions the reliability of this, as to the author's limited knowledge, in an encounter with an upstream boat, the downstream boat is the boat fighting the current. Irrespective, the point made is the same. *Id.*

[70] MACDOWELL, *supra* at 136-37 (citing H. J. Wolff, *The Dikh Blabhs in Demosthenes*, O.R., LV., 164 AM. J. PHILOLOGY 316 (1943)).

[71] *Id.*

[72] *Id.* at 136-37.

[73] *Id.* at 149 (quoting Demosthenes, *Against Kallikles* 21:50).

[74] *See generally* Yü Li, *supra.*

[75] *Id.* at 516.

ing payment for the harm done. Should the grazing be done in the course of a caravan's passage through the territory of another tribe, a pristinely market-based transaction is expected. The traveling tribe offers to the local tribal chieftain a gift of "grass money," to compensate for the grass the herd is expected to graze.[76]

The *Rules of Punishment for Tibetans* contains provisions for the conversion of another's animals.[77] Rule No. 30, "Injury to Other People's Animals," states that should the animal of another be killed, the perpetrator is fined one "nine," and also must pay the full value of the animal to the owner. If a horse is shot and killed, two horses must be given in compensation. If the horse is only injured, a fine of a two-year-old cow is levied.[78]

In ancient India, should a cart or coach kill a large animal (such as a cow or an elephant), its owner (if the driver was unskilled) would be fined half the amount that would be applicable if the offense had been theft.[79] For the similar death of a small farm animal, the fine would be 200 *panas*; for a "beautiful animal" or a bird, the fine would be 50 *panas*, and for a donkey, a sheep or a goat, 5 *m sas*.[80]

## E. CONVERSION OR THEFT

During the Egyptian Sixth Dynasty, from approximately 2460 to 2200 B.C., the law bled together the notions of theft as a criminal action as opposed to conversion, to be prosecuted by a civil complainant.[81] During the reign of Pepi I, c. 2325, a prosecutor named Weni was appointed, and he presided over these and other matters.[82] His recitations of the suits brought before him gives evi-

---

[76] *Id.* at 516-17.

[77] *Id.* at 57.

[78] *Id.*

[79] CODE OF MANU, *supra* at 145.

[80] *Id.*

[81] *See* RUSS VERSTEEG, LAW IN ANCIENT EGYPT 151-52 (2002) [hereinafter LAW IN ANCIENT EGYPT]. This absence of a distinction between which rules might be criminal, and enforced by the state, and which would be civil, leaving the wronged individual to pursue a claim for damages, continued through Roman law and beyond.

dence of the law employed and the remedies exacted.[83] Weni recounts being sent by the king "to prevent [the army] from taking bread or sandals from a wayfarer, to prevent any one of them from taking a loin-cloth from any village, [and] to prevent any one of them from taking any goat from any people."[84] Upon a finding of responsibility, the remedy exacted would typically be that of requiring the thief to return any stolen goods to the victim, and also payment to the victim of money damages in the amount of two to three times the value of the property stolen.[85]

For the wrong of conversion, ancient Greece followed an approach consistent with that of so-called "civilized" societies and pre-literate societies alike throughout the world. That approach was a two-pronged response to conversion of chattels.[86] First, the wrongdoer must give up the wrongfully gained property. Second, the perpetrator should be punished.[87] Following successful prosecution of a claim for theft *(dike klopes)*, the punishment might be the payment of a fine gauged at twice the value of the property.[88] In egregious instances, an additional penalty of time in public stocks might be imposed.[89] For some theft, the remedy would be restitution in some fixed amount, or in a multiple of the value of what was stolen.[90] The same would be required of any knowing receiver of any such stolen goods.[91] In comparison, among American Indian indigenous groups, cash fines might be levied for petty thefts.[92]

---

[82] LAW IN ANCIENT EGYPT, *supra* at 85, 161.

[83] *Id.* at 161.

[84] *Id.* (quoting SIR ALAN GARDINER, EGYPT OF THE PHARAOHS 96 (1961)).

[85] *Id.* at 162 (citing ANDREA MCDOWELL, JURISDICTION IN THE WORKMEN'S COMMUNITY OF DEIR EL-MEDINA 230 (1990)).

[86] MACDOWELL, *supra* at 147-48.

[87] *Id.*

[88] *Id.* at 148 (citing Demosthenes, *Against Timocrates* 24.105.24.114; Lysias, *Against Philokrates* 29.11).

[89] *Id.*

[90] RAYMOND WESTBROOK, THE CHARACTER OF ANCIENT NEAR EASTERN LAW, IN A HISTORY OF ANCIENT NEAR EASTERN LAW 1, 81 (Raymond Westbrook ed., 2003).

[91] *Id.*; MACDOWELL, *supra* note 2, at 148.

[92] ASIAN INDIGENOUS LAW, *supra* note 50, at 216-39.

As with Native Americans, among certain African tribes theft is rare.[93] One anthropologist assigned one reason to be that the tribal members have few individual possessions.[94] However, other delicts resembling theft might be treated with great seriousness. Among the Pygmies living in the Ituri Forest, mentioned earlier, of the former Congo, the men hunted as groups, with some acting as beaters to drive game in a certain direction, and the others setting nets at agreed-upon locations.[95] As Colin Turnbull describes it, "In a small and tightly knit hunting band, survival can be achieved only by the closest co-operation and by an elaborate system of reciprocal obligations which insures that everyone has some share in the day's catch. Some days one gets more than others, but nobody ever goes without."[96] In one incident that Turnbull recorded, a member of the hunting party set up his nets in a place that garnered for him a comparative advantage over the others. Brought to task, the hunter returned to camp and "ordered his wife to hand over the spoils." Interestingly, the wrongdoer's amenability to accept this result might have been affected by his recognition that he could not, as a practical matter, defy it. He likely recognized that he was not in a position to break away from his group, as "his band of four or five families was too small to make an efficient hunting unit."[97] More generally, for theft among the Pygmies, the punishment for the frustrated nocturnal theft of food from a neighbor's pot, might include public whipping or shunning.[98]

All bodies of folk law reveal norms against conversion. For Tibetans, pursuant to the *Rules for Punishment of Tibetans*, a theft of domestic animals such as "dogs [or] pigs" could result in a fine, recoverable by the wronged party, of five animals.[99] Theft of other domestic animals, such as fowl, was treated variously, with conversion of fowls punishable by a fine of a three-year-old cow.

---

[93] Turnbull, *supra* at 120.

[94] *Id.*

[95] *See id.* at 97-101.

[96] *Id.*

[97] *Id.*

[98] *See id.* at 120-21.

[99] Yü Li, *supra* at 525.

Additionally, in each instance the stolen animal had to be returned. This latter requirement converts the restitutionary objective of the rule into a hybrid rule that is at once restitutionary and punitive. For theft of personalty ("gold, silver, sable, otter-skin, hides, money, cloth, food, etc."), the malefactor was required to return property "of equal value." In addition, fines would be imposed, keyed to the value of the stolen goods, e.g., three "nines" for the theft of a two-and-one-half-year-old cow; one "nine" for a sheep; and a three-year-old cow for the theft of an animal of lesser value than a sheep.[100]

Conversion or theft by Muslims is prohibited in Surah 7: "Give…the full in measures and weights; take from no man his chattels, and commit no disorder on the earth after it has been made so good."[101] Muslims on pilgrimage are instructed to kill no game in the lands through which they journey. If such game is purposefully killed, the person responsible shall compensate for it "in domestic animals of equal value (as determined by two persons in the group), or feed the poor, or fast "that he may taste the ill consequences of his deed."[102] Although hunting is prohibited for pilgrims,[103] it is lawful for them "to fish in the sea."[104] The same approach, with variations, is found in the customary law of other populations. Among the agricultural community of the Konyak Nagas of India, conversion might be punished by fines, but the stricter penalty of banishment might be reserved for chronic offenders.[105]

Folk stories, too, have long carried social norms from generation to generation. Joel Chandler Harris, in his writing of the Uncle Remus stories, comments upon how story and fable transport the listener from the common reality of known things into the emotive state of feeling—wherein lay the enduring power of oral history and fable.[106]

---

[100] *Id.*

[101] The Koran, *supra* at 7:83.

[102] *Id.* at 5:96.

[103] *Id.; see also id.* at 5:97.

[104] *Id.* at 5:97.

[105] Asian Indigenous Law, *supra* at 251.

[106] In the course of one story in which Uncle Remus finds himself obliged to feint and weave in response to a boy's inquiry, Harris writes:

Indeed, one of the queerest results of the old man's manner of telling his sto-

One example might be that of an Indian folk tale, in which even the theft of a mason's services creates an opportunity for some sanctimonious advice on victim responsibility.[107] The story, entitled *The Burglar's Gift*, describes a mason who found himself so in need of work that he agreed to build a cellar for a man of suspicious character; indeed, "he was reported to be a thief and burglar."[108] The mason completed the work and was invited to the burglar's home to receive "his humble reward." Arriving the following morning, the mason was distressed to see that he was the only guest, and his alarm only grew greater as the burglar's tone grew hostile and he began to beat the mason. "I shall return to you every piece taken in wages," said [the mason,] "and the greatest reward for me is to let me go." But the appeal fell on deaf ears and the host relished every lash he gave to the mason. The latter invoked all the holy angels, the Holy Book and God to rid himself of the present misfortune. At last the burglar seemed to have got tired and stopped.

The beating suspended, the mason gathered himself to go home, only to have the burglar bid him to sit down. After a fine meal, the burglar presented the mason "a malmal (turban) and a five rupee note by way of reward." While confused at "this paradoxical behaviour of the burglar," the mason accepted these gifts and asked again to go. "'I shall be most happy to bid you good-bye after I place a valuable and an everlasting gift at your feet,' said the burglar... The burglar continued, 'You did not ask me why I belaboured you so heartlessly?'" To both of these declarations, the mason did not respond.

"Look," said the burglar, "what I gave you as tokens of my appreciation will last a short while and disappear. What I want to give you now will last forever and is sure to pass from one generation to another, and why I gave

---

ries—the charm of which cannot be reproduced in cold type—was that all the animals, and all of the various characters that figured therein, were taken out of the reality which we know, and transported bodily into that realm of reality which we feel: the reality that lies far beyond the commonplace, everyday facts that constitute not the least of our worries.

Joel Chandler Harris, Uncle Remus Returns 62- 63 (1918).

[107] S. L. Sadhu, *Folk Tales From Kashmir, The Burglar's Gift*, Chap. 10, http://www.koausa.org/Folk/Sadhu.

[108] *Id.*

you a beating thus was to imprint the lesson indelibly on your mind and body so that you never lose sight of the great truth. The lesson I want you to learn is that you need not fear thieves and burglars as long as your doors and windows are well bolted and hasped. On the basis of my professional experience my advice to you is that you should always keep your windows and doors properly hasped and bolted at night to be free of the fear of thieves. You will please excuse me for the beating but the lesson had to be rubbed in thoroughly."[109]

## F. NEGLIGENCE

Some scholars assert that the concept of "the reasonable man" has been common to all ancient cultures.[110] The historical record seems to provide support for this. For example, under ancient Mesopotamian law, a wrongdoer that negligently caused personal injury might be responsible for the person's medical expenses, with provision too that the duration of the remedy take into account for the time the victim was invalided.[111] This rule, it is seen, is quite similar to that contained in the *Code of the Covenant* referenced above.[112]

Further evidence in early Mesopotamian law of the negligence concept of duty is found in the identification of a neighbor's duty as it might pertain to discourage neighbors from permitting their unoccupied land to elevate a risk of trespass or burglary to the nearby property. The *Law of Lipit-Ishtar* provided that should a robbery occur, the inattentive neighbor, who had notice that his unattended property provided access to the complainant's prop-

---

[109]   *Id.*

[110]   GERBER, *supra* at 34. The author therein references the administration of Islamic law of the Byzantine Empire, a codification of ancient customary law, which contains reference to a dispute arising from a claim of a coachman who was alleged to have beaten his horses so severely that they bolted and injured a child. From the record it appears that the coachman was permitted to interpose the defense that he had acted reasonably, and the disputants were permitted to present evidence that he had not. *Id.*

[111]   WESTBROOK, *supra* at 82 (discussing the *Laws of Hammurabi* § 202, the Hittite Law § 10, and Exod. 21:18-19).

[112]   EXOD., *supra* at 21:18-19.

erty by potential robbers, would be liable for any harm to the complainant's home or property.[113]

The *Rules of Punishment for Tibetans* No. 26, referenced earlier regarding its public nuisance implications,[114] also provided that witnesses (those "in sight") of a "fire[] caused by carelessness" would be "entitled to fine the guilty [five] animals."[115] If the carelessly started fire killed an individual, the fine was one "nine."[116] Those carelessly handling firearms "without justifiable causes," and irrespective of injury, could be fined "[two] nines for *Ch'ienhu*, [one] nine for *Paihu*, [seven] animals for centurions, [five] animals for lesser centurions, and [three] animals for lesser elders and commoners."[117] The logic of the "failure to cover a ditch" cases that are a mainstay of modern torts casebooks is reflected in *Code of the Covenant* provisions declaring that should one leave a ditch uncovered and an ox or a donkey fall into it, he must pay the owner (although he would be permitted to keep the dead animal as his own!).[118]

Again with reference to harms done due to an actor's breach of a duty of reasonable care, in the law of ancient India, there were rules for accidents caused by animal-drawn vehicles.[119] If the driver was unskilled and the accident was "due to the driver's incompetence," the owner of the vehicle "should be fined 200"; and "all the riders should be fined 100."[120] If the driver was skilled, he would sustain the fine.[121]

---

[113] VerSteeg, *supra* note 14, at 135 (discussing *Lipit-Ishtar* para. 11).

[114] Yü Li, *supra* at 526.

[115] *Id.*

[116] *Id.* For definitions of "nines," *see supra.*

[117] *Id.*

[118] Exod., *supra* at 21:33-34.

[119] *Code of Manu, supra* at 144-45.

[120] *Id.*

[121] *Id.*

## G. STRICT LIABILITY

A commonly cited provision of the *Laws of Hammurabi* treats the imposition of strict liability when one's animal injures another in this manner: "If an ox gores an ox and causes its death, the owners of both oxen shall divide the value of the live ox and the carcass of the dead ox."[122] Mosaic law provides similarly, and even more forcefully if the incident results in the death of a person: "If an ox gore[s] a man or a woman that they die, then the ox shall be surely stoned and his flesh shall not be eaten."[123] The proscription on eating the animal, which is permitted when an ox gores another ox, has been described as a recognition that "the animal has killed a superior in the cosmic order, namely a human being."[124] The entire remedy reveals the premium placed on (1) the cathartic importance of some civil remedies (not to mention modern criminal penalties), in this case the stoning of the animal; and (2) the importance invested in nature's order, i.e., forbidding eating the animal, surely an orderly and "dignified" end for such beasts, in that it offended such order.

The *Code of the Covenant* addresses the issue more particularly. There is no strict liability if the ox has not gored before. The penalty will be that the ox be stoned, and its flesh uneaten. If, on the other hand, the ox "has been in the habit of goring before," and its owner is aware of this, if the ox kills "a man or woman, the ox must be stoned and its owner put to death."[125] In a seeming endeavor to ameliorate such harsh consequences, the *Code* also states that if instead the careless owner has assigned to him a "ransom," he must "pay whatever is imposed, to redeem his life."[126] Deaths of children are treated with markedly less severity, as the payment of a ransom is the sole prescribed punishment, and the goring of a slave presumptively even less severely—the stoning of the ox and the payment of thirty shekels.[127]

---

[122] WESTBROOK, *supra* at 17.

[123] SALMOND, *supra* at 431 (quoting Exod., *supra* at 21:28).

[124] WESTBROOK, *supra* at 77.

[125] EXOD., *supra* at 21:28-30.

[126] *Id.* at 21:30-31.

[127] *Id.* at 21:31-32.

Such forms of strict liability have persisted to this day. Using an example of Salmond's: "If my horse or my ox escapes from my land to that of another man, I am answerable for it without any proof of negligence."[128] While this application of strict liability for trespass may be based on a reasonable presumption of negligence upon such occurrences, Salmond suggests that its truer origins may be in a vicarious liability, placing upon the owner of property responsibility for injuries caused by such property, such as a master's responsibility for the actions of his slaves under Roman law.[129]

## H. DEFAMATION AND FALSE WITNESS

In the speech Against Konon, Demosthenes gives a very clear public order rationale for a civil action for slander in these words: "For instance, there are cases of slander; these, they say, were instituted in order that men who are abused should not be induced to hit one another."[130] Several ancient cultures evidently considered defamation or false witness to have such a corrosive effect on the public peace and order as to require the most severe penalties. In ancient Egypt, one tried for defamation could, as today, interpose truth as a defense. Interestingly, if found liable, the libelant was not punished for this first transgression. Instead, he or she was required to take an "oath of mutilation," covenanting that they would submit to amputation of their nose, ears, or both should they engage in a further transgression.[131] In THE KORAN, Surah 104 condemns "every backbiter, defamer."[132] Though the believer may, as is common to cultures old and new, trust in amassed wealth, the defamer is admonished to bear in mind "being flung into the Crushing Fire."[133]

---

[128] SALMOND, *supra* at 430-31 (citing Ellis v. Loftus Iron Co., L. R. 10, C. P. 10 (1874)).

[129] *Id.* at 431.

[130] MACDOWELL, *supra* note 2, at 123 (quoting Demonsthenes, *Against Konon* 54.17-19).

[131] LAW IN ANCIENT EGYPT, *supra* at 179 (citing Ellen Bedell, *Criminal Law in the Egyptian Ramesside Period* 138 (1973) (unpublished Ph.D. dissertation, Brandeis University).

[132] THE KORAN, *supra* at 104:1.

[133] *Id.* at 104:4.

Elsewhere, THE KORAN condemns anyone defaming a "virtuous" woman unless the author of the writing or utterance has four witnesses who support the account.[134] Without the witnesses, in which Surah 24 is seemingly more interested than whether or not the account is true, the responsible party will receive "fourscore stripes," and is barred in perpetuity from giving testimony.[135] Should a husband accuse his wife, the word of God was to pay no heed to the testimony of witnesses and instead required the husband to first testify four times as to the truth of the accusation.[136] When the husband repeated the accusation the fifth time, should he be untruthful, "the malice of God be upon him."[137] If in his fifth oath the husband speaks the truth, it will "call down the wrath of God" upon the wife.[138] Republishers of a defamation too would face a "sore" punishment.[139]

Variations in the severity of the response to a delict might turn upon the status of the victim. Under ancient Indian law, defamation of a Brahmin by one of a lesser caste might be punished corporally.[140] For more prosaic libel and slander between social equivalents, a fine would be the suitable punishment.[141] This differentiation seems to be the exception that tests the rule of equal protection often, but not invariably, represented throughout ancient law.[142]

---

[134] *Id.* at 24:4.

[135] *Id.*

[136] *Id.* at 24:6.

[137] *Id.* at 24:7.

[138] *Id.* at 24:9.

[139] *Id.* at 24:18.

[140] *Code of Manu, supra* at 143.

[141] If a man arrogantly makes false statements about someone's learning, country, caste, occupation, or physical features, he should be fined 200. If a man calls someone 'one-eyed,' 'lame,' or some other similar name, he should be fined at least [one] karsapana, even if what he says is true. *Id.*

It is noteworthy that these examples hew to the modern limitation upon defamation as relating solely to false statements of fact, and excluding opinion, such as, *e.g.,* "miserly" or "stupid."

[142] For example, inscribed on the tomb of the Egyptian Vizier Rekhmire (1479-1425 B.C.) is: "I judged both [the insignificant] and the influential; I rescued the weak man from the strong man; I deflected the fury of the evil man and subdued the greedy man in his hour .... I was not at all deaf to the indigent." LAW IN ANCIENT

Pursuant to Mesopotamian law, should the slander pertain to the sexual honor of another, the punishment might be shaming or flogging.[143] This was true also of the Torah.[144] Later scholars, including Locke, would describe such rules as those of "positive morality,"[145] or "the law of opinion or of reputation."[146] These rules "consist[] of the rules imposed by society upon its members and enforced by public censure or disapprobation."[147]

## I. DECEIT AND FALSE REPORT

In our time, we can refer to the children's expression "Cross my heart and hope to die" as an affirmation of the community's disapproval of deceit.[148] The proscription of trespass to chattels or conversion, the occurrence of which has always been common to the playground, remains imbedded in several children's rhymes that indicate a strong community aversion to any initiative by a giver of goods to engage in self-help to regain possession. One such folk axiom is found in a French children's rhyme, reduced in writing as "[o]nce given, stays given; [t]aking away is stealing!"[149] More severe consequences are suggested in a saying attributed to Dutch, Flemish, German and French children, to this effect: "Once given, taken away, [g]o to Hell three times."[150]

---

EGYPT, *supra* at 23 (quoting T.G.H. JAMES, PHARAOH'S PEOPLE: SCENES FROM LIFE IN IMPERIAL EGYPT 57 (1984)).

[143] WESTBROOK, *supra* at 81 (citing the *Laws of Hammurabi* § 127 and the *Middle Assyrian Laws* §§ 17-19).

[144] DEUT. 22:13-19 (THE JERUSALEM BIBLE).

[145] SALMOND, *supra* at 21.

[146] *Id.* (referring to John Locke, *An Essay Concerning Human Understanding*, bk. 2, ch. 28 § 7 (5th ed. 1848)). The inclusion here of a potential punishment for opinion may be explained by the sanctity accorded one's reputation for sexual probity. This would in later times be manifest is such rules of law defining slander per se as including false statements as to another's sexual conduct.

[147] JOHN SALMOND, JURISPRUDENCE 47 (2d ed. 1907).

[148] *See* A.F. Chamberlain, *Legal Folklore of Children*, 16 J. AM. FOLKLORE 280 (1903), reprinted in FOLK LAW, *supra* at 417-19.

[149] CHAMBERLAIN, *supra* at 419.

[150] *Id.*

Prohibitions upon the making of false reports have been quite common throughout legal systems or groupings of legal norms. THE KORAN provides that one committing a crime or an "involuntary fault" (suggesting negligence or even blamelessness), but who then "layeth [the blame] on the innocent" will be punished by being required to "bear the guilt of calumny and of a manifest crime."[151]

In Tibetan folk law, deceit regarding the ownership of animals was punishable more severely than even the intentional killing of an animal. Within its rules regarding lost animals, Rule 31 of the *Rules of Punishment for Tibetans* provided for a fine of three "nines" for anyone "falsely claim[ing] possession of such an animal," and one "nine" for anyone attempting to hide them.[152] In other instances, too, the punishment of deceit exceeded that applicable to delicts involving arguably less economic dislocation. An individual falsely reporting a theft could be fined three "nines," with the fine distributable equally "between the elder in charge and the person falsely charged."[153] Vigilance against deceit is manifest further in Rule 19, pertaining to land transfers. For any new transferee who discovers "traces" of another's pasturage within three days of the vesting of the transferred interest, the new transferee must so report within three days. The transferor must thereupon "swear an oath" that no competing pasturage or third-party rights exist on the land.[154] The acceleration of the "limitations" period for a claim arising from this wrong seems sensible in a setting in which the effect of grazing will disappear within days, and with it, the possibility of proof.

The Koran reflects God's prohibition of deceit, as followers are enjoined to "be not false in your own engagements, with your own knowledge…"[155] Additionally, in the circumstance of a death, THE KORAN details the testimony that must be sworn and the accompanying safeguards against deceit. Two "just" men are to be chosen to swear as to the circumstances of the death, and included in that oath should be words to the effect that "We will not take a bribe though the party be of kin to us…"[156] Importantly, any oath of the first two

---

[151]  THE KORAN, *supra* at 4:110-120.

[152]  Yü Li, *supra* at 527.

[153]  *Id.* at 526.

[154]  *Id.* at 524.

[155]  THE KORAN, *supra* at 8:27.

men selected can be challenged "if it shall be made clear that both have been guilty of a falsehood..."[157] Should this occur, two other men "nearest in blood" to the first affiants will speak to the truth.[158] The scripture notes with satisfaction that the prospect of a challenge to the veracity of the first oaths will facilitate truth telling in the first instance: "Thus will it be easier for men to bear a true witness, for fear lest after their oath another oath be given."[159]

Differing from but related to deceit, an act of "imposture" is interpreted to mean taking undue advantage of another through the device of being an "imposter." It is logical that in defense of the faith adherents to THE KORAN would be sensitive to claims that they themselves were imposters for proclaiming Muhammad's words as those of God. To this potential claim, Surah 10 reinforces the confidence of believers in declaring what they believe to be true in matters of faith with the suggestion that "if they charge thee with imposture, then say: My work for me, and your work for you. Ye are clear of that which I do, and I am clear of that which ye do."[160] Elsewhere at Surah 22 believers castigated as imposters are reminded that they can recall to their accusers that so many of the great and accepted prophets, including Abraham, Noah, and others, were so charged and ultimately prevailed.[161]

## J. COVETOUSNESS AND HOARDING

Among certain Aleutian groups, cultural and economic norms developed to protect limited resources and to deter non-cooperative appropriation or hoarding.[162] The indigenous tribes considered natural resources such as wildlife not the subject of private, but rather of common ownership, a form of distributional necessity among subsistence cultures.[163] The harsh subsistence environ-

---

[156]  *Id.* at 5:106.

[157]  *Id.* at 5:107.

[158]  *Id.*

[159]  *Id.* at 5:108.

[160]  *Id.* at 10:42.

[161]  *Id.* at 22:42-44.

[162]  DENNIS LLOYD, THE IDEA OF LAW 236-37 (1976).

ment in which the Aleuts dwelt generated rules adhering to strict efficiency norms.[164] Among such groups, in the words of one scholar, "'life is hard and the margin of safety small, and unproductive members of society cannot be supported.'"[165] It will be seen that to the characterization of "unproductive" can be added those whose conduct disrupts the allocative efficiencies of the group.[166] Thus, these norms penalize resource overreaching and the arrogation of resources beyond one's needs.[167]

Similarly, the Aleutians considered the treatment of land as commonly held, rather than susceptible of private ownership, to be the most efficient manner of maximizing hunting resources. Further, although captured game and hunting instruments might be considered private property, the community was "strongly hostile to the idea of anybody accumulating too much property for himself[,] and thereby limiting the amount of property that [could] be effectively used in the community."[168] The ordinary remedy might be confiscation.[169] The influential anthropologist Hoebel identified one Aleutian grouping that considered keeping an excess amount of goods as a "capital crime."[170] Muslims are warned against the vice of covetousness in such language as is found in Surah 113:

> "Say: I betake me for refuge to the Lord of the DAY-
> BREAK…against the mischief of the envier when he envi-

---

[163] This approach is carried forward today in the United States' recognition of collectively held aboriginal rights to certain fish, wildlife, and marine mammals. Along kindred lines, the protection of similar collective rights is the very essence of the law of public nuisance, both antiquarian and modern, providing, in different circumstances, remedies against interference with rights held jointly by the public in matters of health, safety, and welfare. *See generally* JOHN L. DIAMOND ET AL., UNDERSTANDING TORTS (2d ed. 2001).

[164] *See* LLOYD, *supra* at 237.

[165] *Id.* (quoting E. ADAMSON HOEBEL, THE LAW OF PRIMITIVE MAN (1954)).

[166] *See id.*

[167] *See id.*

[168] *Id.*

[169] *Id.*

[170] *Id.*

eth."[171] Further, "Covet not the gifts by which God hath raised some of you above others. The men shall have a portion according to their deserts. The women shall have a portion according to their deserts.

An Indian folk tale relates the travails that may follow one who covets the wife of another. The story is titled The Village Teacher,[172] and is told in this way:

> Following the passing of a village's old and respected teacher, there arrived a new teacher "gifted with all those qualities which make us look wistfully on our departed youth: energy, health, ambition, hope and vanity." The vanity of the young school teacher and his condescension together prompted him to desire female companionship, and, in particular, a pretty and prosperous housewife. The woman's son attended the school teacher's school, and at the closing of school he would tell the boy: "Remember me to your mother." The mother, being both intelligent and perceptive, deduced the teacher's motives, and planned her response. One day, the boy told the teacher that his mother would like a word with the teacher at her home, and, further, that her husband was expected to be away. Quite excited and dressed at his best, he arrived at the woman's house, where he was received warmly.
>
> As he drank the proffered tea, a call came from the yard. It was the husband. The wife began to tremble. "I am undone," she said, "if he discovers you here he will kill me and not spare you either." "Have no fear," the teacher said, "he cannot be so harsh." "I know better how ruthless he is," she quickly corrected the increasingly anxious teacher. "Would to God I were dead rather than be surprised in this compromis-

---

[171] THE KORAN, *supra* at 113:1-5.

[172] Sadhu, "The Village Teacher," Chap. 25, in FOLK TALES FROM KASHMIR, *supra* note 122.

ing situation," she said as she began to beat her breast. "Is there no other exit?" the teacher asked. "No, none," she replied "[and if] [h]e sees you here [then] I am killed....Nothing can save me unless..." "Unless what?" he interjected. "Unless," she said, "you disguise yourself to escape his suspicion." The teacher answered that he would do anything for her sake. She gave him a working woman's cloak and scarf, and placed him in front of a basket of maize and two millstones.[173]

When the husband entered the home, he asked "What is that grinding sound upstairs?" His wife told him it was the sound of "[a] deaf woman turning out maize flour." As the husband and his wife passed time "in the kitchen garden and in the barn," the teacher wore his hands to blisters pretending to be a working woman. Revealing his awareness of the ruse, the husband said, finally, "The fellow must be tired now and feeling bitter...[y]ou had better dismiss him now. The lesson must have gone home to him." The housewife gave the teacher his clothes and he left hurriedly. The wife and her husband preserved the secret. The people in the village remarked the next day that the teacher had lost a great deal of his spirit and liveliness. Sometime later, the housewife sent a message to the teacher asking if he should like to visit again. This time he simply responded: "Ask her if she has consumed the flour ground previously."[174]

# K. CONCLUSION

H.G. Wells offered a vision of the history of law as "based upon a confused foundation of conventions, arbitrary assumptions,...and [constituting] a very imprac-

---

[173] *Id.*

[174] *Id.*

ticable and antiquated system indeed"[175] Every observer must reach his or her own determination. To this observer, the preponderant evidence is that law, taken as a whole, demonstrates a tropism towards rationality and progressive values.

Tort law is at once discrete into its faces and yet sprawling in its reach. The above discussion of ancient and primitive law confirms what Gregory C. Keating wrote:

> "[Tort law] curbs the freedom of prospective injurers and en-
> hances the security of potential victims. Risk impositions thus pit
> the liberty of injurers against the security of victims and the law
> of accidents sets the terms on which these competing freedoms
> are reconciled. Its task is to find and fix terms that are fair."[176]

The goal of the review contained in this Chapter cannot be to amuse with examples of how more efficient, transparent, humanitarian, or behaviorally expert modern Western law is when contrasted to its ancient counterparts. How another culture responded to a social need cannot be fairly done only after removing the subject from its context, taking it, in a sense, by forceps and removing it from its naturally constructed diorama. All of us have mused at one point or another as to how incomprehensible certain modern affairs would appear to visitors—of this world or another—who might themselves, a thousand years hence consider such phenomena to be stranded, non-contextual relics. As is true today was true also in ancient times: very few legal rules have no social bona fides; very few rules are per se meritless.

It is premature to congratulate ourselves that modern Western legal systems have seemingly achieved consistent levels of efficient and moral norms. For example, for every arguably progressive initiative one state of this nation may take, such as the implementation of social host liability for permitting an inebriated guest to say good evening and drive away, there is a setback, such

---

[175] H. G. WELLS, THE OUTLINE OF HISTORY 536-37 n.1 (3d ed., Garden City Publishing Co. 1929) (1920).

[176] GREGORY C. KEATING, *A Social Contract Conception of The Tort Law of Accidents*, in PHILOSOPHY AND THE LAW OF TORTS 23 (Gerald J. Postema ed., 2001).

as the decisions of courts to disallow public nuisance claims to be brought against the manufacturers of small concealable handguns that by their marketing drown counties surrounding large metropolitan areas with these weapons well knowing that the guns will end up on the city streets.

The objective of this review is to unveil examples of how other cultures in distant times responded to a social imperative of finding how social groups responded to the need to cabin individual behavior to advance common wellbeing, to deter behavior that saps the wellbeing of the larger group, and to increase the incidence of behavior conducing to the public good.

Prominent among the consistencies between and among the cultures referenced is a standard of egalitarianism and equal application of law that typically characterizes primitive groups deriving sustenance from hunting or agriculture.[177] Additionally, there is impressive congruence in proscriptions of unconsented-to taking. Whether the delict involved deprivation of another's right to their own reputation or the theft of goods, no human group, even in the earliest time, permitted one individual to take from another simply because he was stronger, crueler, faster or less principled, i.e., simply because he could otherwise get away with it. The collective was better served by deterring such behavior with such remedies as requiring the return of what was owed, be it the return of the object or its equivalent, or its money equivalent, or, in the case of a dignitary harm, the rendering of an apology or its symbolic equal, or alternatively suffering the penalty that would accompany the false allegation had it been true.

A similarity can also be seen in the treatments of trespass to land or private nuisance. If the harm to the property, or the interruption of the occupant's right to profitably exploit it, could be quantified in lost crops or otherwise, the amends would be in kind. Otherwise the injured party could be made whole by money damages. In turn, under the law of public nuisance, which in all times has been described as behavior that detracted from good of the general community, a culprit might first receive a sound thrashing, in the hope that it would deter continued deleterious behavior.

It is also seen that the remedies available under numerous law systems were quite sophisticated in the rectificatory quality of permissible awards, and

---

[177] Asian Indigenous Law, *supra* at 251.

included not only compensation in rough equivalence to the immediate severity of the harm suffered, but also, when appropriate, costs of care and rehabilitation, as well as lost income.

Importantly, certain humanitarian progress is also evident. At the most ancient end of the cultural timeline investigated, the penalty for delicts ranging from manslaughter to battery to kidnapping might be corporal punishment or even death. Or the transgression might result in vendetta, or in a blood oath, binding the parties and their families to a violent continuation of the dispute. With the passage of time, there were introduced alternative means of remedying such wrongs, to wit, the payment of money to the victim or to his or her family—developments that brought the rectificatory norms into greater alignment with modern standards of corrective justice.

While providing some fact and the lore of ancient normative treatment of civil wrongs, this Chapter is also a précis to a longer inquiry into the where's, the when's, and the who's of the origins of our modern tort law. It can been seen that the carbon dating of the roots of modern common law reach back further than the rise of a lawyer class in pre-empire England, and with regard to the modern civil code treatments for extra-contractual harm, antedate even the Roman law that underlies the Napoleonic Code.

# CHAPTER 2

# THE GRÆCO-ROMAN ANTECEDENTS
# OF MODERN TORT LAW

## I. INTRODUCTION

All legal systems, and the norms and mores that preceded them, originate in a cultural context. The distinctive form of each system reveals a symbiotic relationship with the society and the social order it serves. The law of ancient Greece, and that of ancient Rome, developed in cultural environs that were strongly status based, with the factors of such status associated with land, lineage, sex and condition of servitude. At least as far as their respective contributions to systematization of Western law in general, and the law of delict in particular, there is no bright line at which point the Grecian influence disappeared and the Roman *sequelae* came to dominance. As the vitality of Athenian legal contributions came to wane, their codes, and even their living jurists, were in personal contact with, and were an acknowledged influence upon, Roman "law givers". Indeed, the Grecian philosophical influences of dialectical reasoning, and the legal codifications Draco and Solon, were contemporaneous with important developments in Roman law, and available to study by Roman Jurisconsuls.

This Chapter tracks the laws of early Greece and early Rome from their respective origins in myth and legend, through their primitive and customary laws, concluding with their initial written legal recordations and their later comprehensive codifications. The review reveals significant similarities and disparities between the respective approaches. At the most primary level and at the earliest times, we see the cohering of norms, and then laws, that give order and security to society. Over time, and through revisions that are quite literally millennial, we see developed a corpus of the law of civil liability for wrongs. As importantly, the combined Graeco-Roman developments created and bequeathed to modern Western law a taxonomy of civil causes of action, the remedies presented and valuable proto-procedural approaches that inform the Western law of delict, or tort, to this day. Throughout, in an evolution that most would describe as progressive, we see (1) the cohering of laws giving security to society; (2) the movement from vengeance as a remedy to compensation; (3) the identification of a great array of wrongs for which civil remedies might be sought; (4) the introduction of fault-based liability for certain harms; and (5) the introduction of equity so as to permit the rendition of justice in circumstances in which existing law or its absence might preclude it.

It is recognized commonly that our modern Western law derives linearly from that of early Greece and early Rome. That "body" of law is sometimes referred to in the conjunctive as "Graeco-Roman" law, a characterization that does no disservice to history provided it is accompanied with certain clarifications. As mentioned, the law of early Greece and the law of early Rome represent distinctive juridical bodies. The law of early Greece largely but not entirely preceded Roman law, and must be examined as a particular onto its own. Second, the use of the term "law" itself should be appreciated as originating almost totally, in myth, transmitted through the poetry and other literature of the ancients, axioms of conduct offered by wise men, tradition, customs, and a mixture of each of these. This was true of both the Greek and the Roman experience. Only eventually would efforts be made to consolidate the norms from these differing sources and from the disparate regions of the respective nations, render them into a written form. In the Greek experience, the pressure came first from the respective kings, and later from democratic assemblies. In Rome, the impetus was exclusively imperial.

Analyses of this type have sometimes sought philosophical characterizations of the law of ancient Greece and that of ancient Rome and its fluid empire. Through imposition of a modern taxonomy onto cultural-legal norms of these ancients, inquiries have posed such questions as "Can the law of Rome be characterized as having adopted an approach of instrumentalism in its senatorial and lesser mandates?"[1] There is no fault to be found in such inquiries. However in my view they reap little benefit, as one can presuppose that *any* written law by virtually any society has had and continues to have an objective of modifying the behavior of those subject to it.[2]

In the discussion to follow we will encounter examples of civil recourse that will seem to us today primitive and even barbaric. Indeed it was not until the Third Century A.D. that Roman Law took a decided turn away from its principal goals of sanction and deterrence and adopted increasingly an emphasis on compensation and rectification. Throughout, however, we will also find quite progressive forms of dispute resolution, including many that as modified are today employed throughout civil code and common law justice systems alike. Particularly as these norms and laws are preserved for us, as they were for the ancients themselves, in the form of classical literature, we will find law and logic accompanied by poetry that has on its own merits endured through the ages.

A strictly Roman definition of delict (*maleficia*) is "acts involving what dominant opinion regards as wrong, and as [such] the law punished them or allowed them to be punished on this ground."[3] For the purposes of this

---

[1]  *See, e.g.,* Abraham Bell, Gideon Parchomovsky, *A Theory of Property*, 90 CORNELL L. REV. 531 (2005), in which the authors, writing of *in rem* jurisdiction, state: "Some conceptualists advance instrumental reasons for certain ancient rules, but they fail, or do not bother, to explain the institution . . . in its entirety." *Id.* at 535.

[2]  The exceptions would be quite limited, and would include such rules as bills of attainder or certain *ex post facto* laws, and these, in any event, would only be exceptions that test the rule. The former has had as its typical purpose the punishment of particular individuals or their families, and are not laws of general applicability. The latter may fail in any test as to whether they operate to correct the behavior of persons who have already committed the acts that are now proscribed, but yet do operate as a prophylaxis against the future unwanted behaviors of others.

[3]  J. DECLAREUIL, ROME THE LAW GIVER 194-95 (Greenwood, Westport, Ct.

Chapter I will approach and describe delict more narrowly to mean a civil, non-contractual harm.[4] This definition is not very noteworthy, and indeed will be recognized as a standard contemporary definition of "tort". In the context of ancient Greek and Roman law, however, there is yet another benefit to my chosen definition of delict, and it is that in the periods in question there had yet to be made the distinction between civil wrongs and certain wrongs that would be later defined as criminal. The various forms of homicide (intentional, accidental, etc.) or mayhem or serious battery are the primary examples of this.[5]

The effect of the absence of a criminal treatment of even intentional homicide in early Greek and Roman law was that these "crimes" were subject to "civil" trial or other resolution, that is, a dispute between the victim or his survivors and the perpetrator, rather than a trial in which the state was the party bringing the action against the alleged actor. In the descriptions and discussion to follow we will see much corroboration for the suggestion of Sir Henry Sumner Maine that ancient law is more akin to the law of civil delict than it is to criminal law.[6] Thus the definition of delict as a civil non-contractual wrong is further refined by the understanding that "civil" means, as pertinent to the times, only that the action was between private parties, and adjusts without more for the fact that in the earlier periods of the Grecian and the Roman legal development under discussion, distinctions had yet to be made between what would today be considered criminal wrongs, or civil wrongs, but not both.

---

1970)(citing *Institutes of Gaius* 3, 181; *Institutes of Justinian* 4, 1-pr.). Hans Kelsen took the approach of defining any breach of a legal norm as a delict. M. D. A. Freeman, Lloyd's Introduction to Jurisprudence (7th ed.) 2612 (Sweet and Maxwell 2001).

[4] As is evident from the discussion that follows, there was not then, any more than there is today, a concensus as to just what breaches or wrongs ought properly be characterized as delictual.

[5] *See particularly* the Code of Draco and the Code of Solon, described below.

[6] Henry Sumner Maine, Ancient Law 217 (1861).

# II. THE LAW OF ANCIENT GREECE

## A. GENERALLY

It is today widely supposed that the ancient Greeks had adopted some organizing principles of substantive and procedural civil law prior to any written recordation, or at least any surviving written evidence. Instead, the earliest moments of a Greek political order sufficient to sustain civil law, or the law relating to resolution of disputes between one citizen and another, comes to us in largely literary form. These forms include Homeric and other poetry, and the historo-literary recitations of the mythological origins of many ancient norms. To the Greeks, Zeus was the giver of law (*dike*) to men, and such laws or norms of behavior (*themistes*) as were explicit or implicit in the mythical accounts were described as the gifts of Zeus. It was an age that predated society of sufficient internal coherence to generate "law" as the product of communal human deliberation, or even law as the edict of a ruler or rulers with sufficient dominion to have regal declarations give order to any realm of significance. As importantly, it was also an age still a captive of the conclusion that phenomena ranging from natural forces to the consequences of human behavior were guided by edicts of gods and not men.

## B. MYTHICAL ORIGINS

For the purposes of this chapter a description of early Greek themes of justice and judging ought naturally precede any description of more particular law. The great poet Hesiod (~700 B.C.) wrote of the earliest concepts of justice, and recited how at this early time in Grecian cultural awareness, those who transgressed the will of a god or gods were answerable not to man but to such god(s). As would be expected, such legal tenets as can be identified in Greek mythology are revealed in mythic stories or fables, rather than in a narrative form that contains an "if" clause (the *prostasis*), and end with a "then" clause (the *apodasis*) that is characteristic of law codes.[7] Thus the *prostasis* identifies a

---

[7] RUSS VERSTEEG, EARLY MESOPOTAMIAN LAW 3 (2000) (describing as illustrative the *Code of Hammurabi*). Thus the prostasis identifies a circumstance or activity that the

circumstance or activity that the lawmakers concluded need a legal rule, while the *apodasis* describes the legal consequences the creation of such a circumstance or the engagement in such activity.[8] This approach bears the most significant markings of code-based law throughout the ages and followed today, while not, of course, exclusively, throughout the world.

This inquiry will emphasize the contributions of Hesiod, the influential, earliest and enduring interlocutor for the most ancient concepts of Greek justice. His contribution is most pronounced for its substantial telling of tales of right, wrong, and the norms that the ancient Greeks adopted and adapted in their path from diffuse tribal groupings to the great, if small, Athens. Hesiod was an historian and poet, and his work survives as authoritative in its recitation (or interpretation) of myth as then subscribed to by Greeks of his day. He wrote that he would often visit a particular mountain known to be habitated by the Muses, from whom he took much of his inspiration. The motivation for his copious treatment of normative and proto-delictual concerns has been tied by some to a story in which Hesiod and his brother were denied justice in a matter of inheritance.

It is in Hesiod's WORKS AND DAYS that we find the recitation that in Greek mythology, or more properly, in the beliefs of the ancient Greeks, "justice" itself, or herself, was assigned a place in the pantheon and named "virgin Justice", who sits beside her father Zeus.[9] It is usually vain to try to identify the first wrong recognized by a culture, although certain among them seem to invite the effort.[10] While Greek mythology does not insist upon this designation, it does seem as though violence of man against man for might well be the "original" proscription, with robbery, deceit and defamation rounding out the group.

---

lawmakers concluded need a legal rule, while the apodasis describes the legal consequences the creation of such a circumstance or the engagement in such activity. *See generally* M. Stuart Madden, Tort Law Through Time and Culture: Themes of Economic Efficiency, EXPLORING TORTS 22 (M. Stuart Madden, ed.) (Cambridge 2005).

[8] Id at 11.

[9] HESIOD, WORKS AND DAYS 11. 248-264, in HESIOD AND THEOGONIS (Dorothy Wender, transl.)(Penguin 1976). Alternative sources of Hesiod's work are available on search engines such as *www.wikipedia.org*, and Project Guttenberg, The translations will vary unimportantly.

[10] For example, the "original sin" of the Judeo-Christian BOOK OF GENESIS.

At the earliest of moments, to the mind of the ancient Greek, the gods ordained that man would occupy an elevated place among living creatures, and that this unique entitlement was a function of man's capacity for reason. An early and signal virtue that such reason was made available to man but not to the baser worldly inhabitants was his ability to abstain from violence against other men. It is Cronos, the father of Zeus, who declares that a singular attribute of man's elevation over beasts is that man can and should follow the "right" and foreswear violence.[11] Here regarding an injunction of the greatest generality, to wit, avoid violence, the punishment for man's departure from Cronos's mandate is harsh indeed, as transgressors invite not only their own punishment but also potentially the punishment of their entire communities.[12] This theme of theatrical over-deterrence is repeated throughout the era's normative presentations.

As is seen similarly in Judeo-Christian scripture, in the mythos of ancient Greece deceit was the original sin, and it was amply punished by the sovereign god Zeus. The story as recounted by Hesiod is of a time in which the gods hid

---

[11] Works and Days, *supra* at 11.238-247.

> But for those who practise violence and cruel deeds far-seeing Zeus, the son of Cronos, ordains a punishment. Often even a whole city suffers for a bad man who sins and devises presumptuous deeds, and the son of Cronos lays great trouble upon the people, famine and plague together, so that they wash away, and their women do not bear children, and their houses become few, through the contriving of Olympian Zeus. And again, at another time, the son of Cronos either destroys their wide army, or their walls, or else makes an end of their ships on the sea.
>
> * * *
>
> [T]he son of Cronos has ordained this law for men, that fishes and beasts and winged fowls should devour one another, for right is not in them; but to mankind he gave right which proves far the best. For whoever knows the right and is ready to speak it, far-seeing Zeus gives him prosperity; but whoever deliberately lies in his witness and forswears himself, and so hurts Justice and sins beyond repair, that man's generation is left obscure thereafter. But the generation of the man who swears truly is better thenceforward.

Hesiod, Works and Days, *supra* at 11, 274-285, Hesiod and Theogonis 67 (Dorothy Wender, transl.)(Penguin 1976).

[12] *Id.*

from man "the means of life", and principally, fire, on the logic that with such tools man would provide for himself in one day enough to sustain him for a year.[13] However, the clever Prometheus stole fire from the gods, with later help from Iapetus, and Zeus, furiously, "planned sorrow and mischief against men."[14] He bade Hephaesteus to mix earth and water to make the form of a woman, in a lovely "maiden-shape", and then instructed Athena and Aphrodite to weave into the human experience "cruel longing and cares that weary the limbs."[15]

Much of Hesiod's writing is devoted not so much to mythos as to ethos, which is to say, it can be understood as a recitation not only of fable but rather also of extant norms. References to gods abound even in the absence of a governing myth, for in the absence of a civil society positioned to enforce proto-legal norms, the Greeks adverted to the power of gods to smite wrongdoers. Hesiod gives these observations regarding both robbery by violence and theft by deceit:

> Wealth should not be seized: god-given wealth is much better;
> for if a man take great wealth violently and perforce, or if he
> steal it through his tongue, as often happens when gain de-
> ceives men's sense and dishonour tramples down honour, the
> gods soon blot him out and make that man's house low, and
> wealth attends him only for a little time.[16]

Hesiod writes of also of ex ante precautions against later disputes as the prefereable means of handling money, employment and other matters of business, to the point of advising persons to secure witnesses for corroboration of agreements as to wages.[17]

---

[13] The notion of the raw efficiency of such a situation was troubling to the gods, the story relates, as in the midst of such abundance they predicted that man would put away his oxen and tools and "the fields would run to waste." Hesiod, Works and Days 11. 42-53, in Hesiod and Theogonis, id. at 6.

[14] Hesiod, Works and Days 11. 42-53, in Hesiod and Theogonis, supra at 60.

[15] Hesiod, Works and Days 11. 60-68, in Hesiod and Theogonis, id. at 61.

[16] Hesiod, Works and Days 11. 320-341, in Hesiod and Theogonis, id. at 68-69.

[17] "Let the wage promised to a friend be fixed; even with your brother smile — and get a witness; for trust and mistrust, alike ruin men." Hesiod, Works and Days

Hesiod devotes several passages to the delict of libel and slander, suggesting an early recognition that traficking in harmful untruths was an invitation to a physical and even violent response. He advised: "Do not get a name either as lavish or as churlish as a friend of rogues or as a slanderer of good men."[18] When a libel or a slander occurs in the context of a legal proceeding, what today might be called "false utterance," not only is the target of the falsity injured, but Justice herself: Should "virgin Justice" suffer "hurt" by "lying slander", Hesiod writes, her report of this to Zeus, together with any other incidents of "mens' wicked heart" will result in an undesignated retribution.[19]

## C. OF JUDGES AND JUSTICE

The historian Herodotus, better remembered for his defining history of the Persian War, also wrote stories of the integrity (or its want) of the earliest judges and the process of judging. As a starting off point, historian Michael Gagarin chooses Herodotus's story of Deices, the first king of Medes.[20] As Gagaran relates the story: "Deioce, a wise man... [who] already had a high reputation in his village,... practiced *dikaiosyne* ("justice")... zealously. There was considerable lawlessness (anomie) throughout the country, and when the people of Deioces own village observed his qualities. 'they chose him (repeatedly) to be their judge.' Since he was 'straight' (*ithys*) and 'just' (*dikaios*) he rapidly gained a reputation as the only one who judged cases 'correctly' (*kata to orthon*)."[21] At this stage from what appears a "formal" res-

---

11. 370-372, in HESIOD AND THEOGONIS, *supra* note 9 at 70.

[18] HESIOD, WORKS AND DAYS 11. 715-716, *id.* at 82.

[19] *See also* HESIOD, WORKS AND DAYS 11. 717-721: "Never dare to taunt a man with deadly poverty which eats out the heart; it is sent by the deathless gods. The best treasure a man can have is a sparing tongue, and the greatest pleasure, one that moves orderly; for if you speak evil, you yourself will soon be worse spoken of." *id.* at 82.

Of gossip, Hesiod continues, at 11 760-63: "So do: and avoid the talk of men. For Talk is mischicvous, light, and easily raised, but hard to bear and difficult to be rid of. Talk never wholly dies away when many people voice her: even Talk is in some ways divine." HESIOD AND THEOGONIS, *supra* at 84.

[20] HERODOTUS, 1.96-98, in MICHAEL GAGARIN, EARLY GREEK LAW 20 (U. Cal. 1986).

olution of a civil dispute depended upon the agreement of both parties to present their cases to a particular respected and "straight" man willing to undertake this task.

This premium placed on the rectitude of the judge, be he a patrician or a plebian, but always a wise man, is repeated frequently in the literature, and with such a frequency as to suggest that that the early Greeks were more concerned with false judges than they were with false idols. In his THEOGONY Hesiod reemphasized the need for the "straight" over the "crooked" in dispute resolution, admonishing his brother Perces to follow the path of the "straight" and to avoid the "crooked" (*hybris*). He warns of the consequences of crooked judgments, and he employs as a metaphor for the risk to a just society of corrupt judge the vivid image of justice being dragged of by "gift devouring" [corrupt] kings.[22] Not only would be authors of just resolutions of disputes be rewarded, but also their communities, with prosperity and peace.[23] Surely no more direct encomium to justice can be imagined.[24]

---

[21] *Id.* at 20-21 (references omitted).

[22] But you, Perses, listen to right and do not foster violence; for violence is bad for a poor man. Even the prosperous cannot easily bear its burden, but is weighed down under it when he has fallen into delusion. The better path is to go by on the other side towards justice; for Justice beats Outrage when she comes at length to the end of the race. But only when he has suffered does the fool learn this. For Oath keeps pace with wrong judgements. There is a noise when Justice is being dragged in the way where those who devour bribes and give sentence with crooked judgements, take her. And she, wrapped in mist, follows to the city and haunts of the people, weeping, and bringing mischief to men, even to such as have driven her forth in that they did not deal straightly with her.

HESIOD, THEOGONY 11 213-18, 220-24, in HESIOD, THE THEOGONY (Thomas Cook, transl.) (1740), available at Literature Online. *See also* HESIOD AND THEOGONIS, *supra* note 9 at 30.

Hesiod refers to Perses as his brother, but it is supposed by some that Perses is a literary character Hesiod has created to be a foil for certain of his dialogues.

[23] [T]hey who give straight judgements to strangers and to the men of the land, and go not aside from what is just, their city flourishes, and the people prosper in it: Peace, the nurse of children, is abroad in their land, and all-seeing Zeus never decrees cruel war against them...

HESIOD, WORKS AND DAYS 11 225-37, in HESIOD AND THEOGONIS, *supra* at 30.

[24] Conversely, judges, princes and others who author corrupt justice are reminded that

What are the qualities or aptitudes that permit a man or a ruler to not only do justice fairly but also have the parties and the populace concur in the (overall) fairness of the justice dispensed? Hesiod is content to explain that a King's skill in resolving disputes turns upon the with the favor of the Muses. If a King has been so favored, "soothing words flow from his mouth." Hesiod continues: "And he, speaking surely, quickly and intelligently puts an end to even a great dispute. Therefore there are intelligent kings, in order that in the *agora* [public meeting place] they may easily restore matters for people who have suffered damages, persuading them with gentle words."[25] A third and final example of dispute resolution is from the Illiad, found in the trial scene on Achilles shield. The dispute is over a killing, for which a reparation has been offered but rejected, and the disputants have brought the matter for argument before a public forum for settlement:

> A crowd, then, in a market place, and there
> Two men at odds over satisfaction owed
> For a murder done: one claimed that all was paid,
> And publicly declared it; his opponent
> Turned the reparation down, and both
> Demanded a verdict from an arbiter,
> As people clamored in support of each,
> And criers restrained the crowd. The town elders
> Sat in a ring, on chairs of polished stone,
> The staves [skeptra] of clarion criers in their hands,
> With which they sprung up, each to speak in turn,
> And in the middle were two golden measures
> To be awarded to him whose argument
> Would be the most straightforward.[26]

---

the "deathless gods" are omnipresent and all knowing, and should there be evidence of tainted justice that "oppress their fellows" . . . "the people [will] pay for the mad folly of their princes who, evilly minded, pervert judgement and give sentence crookedly." HESIOD, WORKS AND DAYS 11 248-264, *id.* at 31.

[25] HESIOD, THEOGONY 11. 84-90, in HESIOD AND THEOGONIS, *id.* at 25-26.

[26] HOMER, THE ILIAD 18. 497-508 (Robert Fitzgerald, trans.) (Garden City, N.Y. 1974).

Often the means and the effect of the settlement of a dispute could be as reveal-ing of the underlying dignitary norms they might would be of the strictly com-pensatory matter. In the CATALOGUE OF WOMEN, dated as early as 580 B.C., and attributed, perhaps erroneously, to Hesiod, there is the story of Sysiphus's payment of Aithon money and cattle to take Aithion's daughter, Mestra, as his bride. After going to Sysiphus's home, the daughter thinks the better of the arrangement and returns to her father. Sysyphus demands the return of either Mestra or his cattle. The dispute is lain before a goddess, and the poem relates: "And straightaway strife and dipute arose between Sysiphus and Aithon over the slim-ankled girl. No mortal was able to judge the case, and so they referred it to a goddess. And she unerringly settled the matter." In the course of deciding the dispute, the goddess is credited with describing the applicable norm: "[W]hen one wishes to recover the price one has paid for something [without giving up the object]," one must lose both the object and the payment, "for once payment is made, it cannot be reclaimed."[27] In analyzing this story Gagarin references authority suggesting that the goddess's resolution reflects an implicit conclusion that "Sysiphus was trying to use Mestra for the same purpose as Aithon was, namely cheating others out of a sale, so he rightly loses both her and the cattle."[28] Further to the theme of love's labors lost, a recitation from myth assigned to Hesiod and Acusilaus, and involving the seduction by Zeus of Io, the daughter of Peiren, makes clear that pursuant to the mythic norm, at least, there should be no "heart balm" remedy for a disappointed suitor.[29]

A core theme of many mythic dispute resolutions was seemingly the need to repose in an individual the authority to resolve a dispute in order that the

[27] HESIOD, CATALOGUE OF WOMEN frag. 43a31-40 (580 B.C.).

[28] GAGARIN, *supra* note 20 at 36 n. 1, referencing J.T. Kakridis, Mestra: zu Hesiods frg. 43a M-W, ZPE 18-25 (1975).

[29] AEGIMIUS, Fragment #3, Apollodorus, ii. 1.3.1:

Hesiod and Acusilaus say that she (Io) was the daughter of Peiren. While she was holding the office of priestess of Hera, Zeus seduced her, and being discovered by Hera, touched the girl and changed her into a white cow, while he swore that he had no intercourse with her. And so Hesiod says that oaths touching the matter of love do not draw down anger from the gods: 'And thereafter he ordained that an oath concerning the secret deeds of the Cyprian should be without penalty for men.

agitated disputants not resort to self help. In so proceeding, it was accepted that the decision maker was enjoined to hear both disputants before entering a judgment.[30] In THE ILIAD Book 2 we read the tale of the chariot race. Emulus, who was in actuality the fastest charioteer, comes in last, due to the intervention of Athena. Achilles at first proposes to give Eumelus second prize, to rectify the wrong done to him, leaving Diomedes, the actual first place winner, with his first place prize. All are content save Antilochus, who had finished second in actuality, and who proposes to Achilles that the order of finishing remain as it was in fact, and that the compensation due Emulus be his award of a special prize as "the best man in the race."[31] It is a result that in the finest Aristotelian logic "makes straight" a wrong, and in not dislodging either Diomedes or Antilochus from their true order of finish, is probably also Pareto Optimal.[32]

## D. PHILOSOPHICAL EXEGESIS

As lay speakers for a philosophical epoch of greater significance than any other, the Hellenist philosophers defined virtue, morality and ethics in terms that remain the bedrock of Western philosophy. Putting aside only a few proponents of distracting philosophic anomalies, the Greek philosophers first identified an ideal of individual behaviors that accented study, modesty in thought and deed, and respect of law. Secondly, the Hellenist thinkers envisioned a society (at that point a city state) of harmony, accepted strata of skill and task, and, naturally again, respect of law.

The Hellenist image of a society and its individual participants was one of harmony, rewards in the measure of neither more nor less than one's just deserts,

---

[30] "Decide no suit until you have heard both sides speak.", from THE PRECEPTS OF CHIRON Fragment #2 — Plutarch Mor. 1034 E. (http://omacl.org/Hesiod/frag2.html.)

[31] HOMER, THE ILIAD Book 23, verses 287-351, *supra* note 26 at 458-465 (Richard Lattimore, trans.) (U. Chicago 1967).

[32] A rule is Pareto Optimal when its effects benefit all parties, in essence, a win-win proposition. MARK SEIDENFELD, MICROECONOMIC PREDICATES TO LAW AND ECONOMICS 49 (1996). For a general description of Pareto Optimality principles, *see generally*, ROBIN PAUL MALLOY, LAW AND ECONOMICS: A COMPARATIVE APPROACH TO THEORY AND PRACTICE (1990).

and subordination to law. Even as it is recognized generally that a democracy better fulfills the goals of a just, a moral, and an efficient polity, for a pre-democratic ideal, evaluated in recognition of its era, measures up respectably.

Hints of the political circumstances in which Stoics found themselves can be found in the graphics handed down to us from antiquity that portray the various philosophers either speaking to small groups or, from all that appears, to no one at all. There are no representations of them speaking in political groups, or advising political representatives. The reason for this seeming isolation of the philosophers from the political process is that by the time much of much of the most enduring work of the most influential Greek philosophers, political power in the Greek mainland had passed over to the Macedonians. This political powerlessness necessarily affected the focus of many of the philosophers. As Bertrand Russell explained, with the imposition of Macedonian rule, "Greek philosophers, as was natural, turned aside from politics and devoted themselves more to the problem of individual virtue and salvation. They no longer asked: how can men create a good state? They asked instead: how can men be virtuous in a wicked world, or happy in a world of suffering."[33]

Russell's observation, true to a point, proves too much, as the writings of the philosophers of that era cannot be cabined so severely. Indeed, when writing not of virtue but instead, or also, of government in general or law in particular, Hellenist thinkers turned directly to such themes as (1) the justification underlying the identification and imposition of law governing civil and other wrongs; (2) the proper forum for and conduct of law givers; and (3) the essential justice of certain remedies for particular wrongs.

# 1. THE JUSTIFICATION FOR IMPOSITION OF LAW GOVERNING WRONGS

Socrates (-399 B.C.) commended abidance of existing law, a commitment that ultimately led to his rejection of opportunities to flee his death sentence. To

---

[33] Bertrand Russell, A History of Western Philosophy 230 (1945).

the Thinker, a life of virtue and ethics could only be sustained in a secure, orderly and law abiding society.

Hellenist thinking cannot be reduced to the aphorism "virtue is its own reward." Rather, there were specific rewards associated with a life of virtue, as well as real or imagined disincentives to the adoption of a baser life and the collateral degrading pursuits associated therewith. Time and time again the philosophers stated that a life of excess, be it eating, drinking or both, incapacitated the actor from realization of the contributions available to and expected of citizen's of virtue.[34] To both Plato and Socrates, the just man would be content, if not happy, and the unjust man miserable.[35] In addition, and more specifically, such excesses invited physical illness and impairment, a certain departure from God's, or a god's, charge to mankind. To employ only two examples from Socrates: (1) The entire structure of Socrates' ethics is permeated by the principle of avoidance of doing harm[36]; and (2) in parts of his lectures Socrates hypothesizes that perhaps the identifying marker of all acts of "justice" was simply "returning what was owed".[37]

In Plato's version of Socrates' words, individual good and justice were, in fact, profitable. The point could not be put more plainly if Socrates were to be described as so stating, and indeed Socrates states just this:[38] "On what ground, then, can we say that it is profitable for a man to be unjust or self indulgent or to do any disgraceful act which will make him a worse man, though he can gain money and power?" Happiness and profit inure to the man who, alternatively, "tame[s] the brute" within, and is "not be carried away by the vulgar notion of happiness being heeping up an unbounded store [,]" but instead follows the rule of wisdom and law encour-

---

[34] To Protagoras Socrates spoke of the physical dangers of excess, stating that "pleasure for the moment ... lay[s] up for your future life diseases and poverty, and many other similar evils[.]" PLATO'S LYSIS, in SOCRATIC DISCOURSE BY PLATO AND XENOPHON 288 (J. Wright transl., A.D. Lindsay, ed. 1925).

[35] ANTHONY GOTTLELB, THE DREAM OF REASON: A HISTORY OF PHILOSOPHY FROM THE GREEKS TO THE RENAISSANCE 64 (2000).

[36] *Id.* at 164.

[37] *Id.* at 159-160.

[38] THE REPUBLIC OF PLATO 318-320 (Francis McDonald Cornford, transl.) (1969).

aging "support to every member of the community, and also of the government of children[.]"[39]

Less well known than his other major works, in THE LAWS Plato (428 -347 B.C.)[40] created a dialogue between three speakers, each elderly: an unnamed Athenian, Clinias, a Cretan, and Megillus, a Spartan. He wrote in a time when public law, or legislation, was distinguished from private law, but within private law, no clear line existed between delict and crime. Plato believed that in the main man desired to do what was right, but that he needed guidance as to what "right" was, and encouragement to pursue it. Accordingly, in THE LAWS Plato expanded upon the simple recitation of legal or moral imperatives by giving to the different sections of his "specimen" laws discussion that included both "direction and encouragement" to the audience,[41] including Plato's view of what constituted the worthier choices a man might make.

In THE LAWS Plato does not essay to write comprehensively of his view of an ideal corpus of law, and indeed there is no showing that it aspired to such. Rather, as he surely intended it, as a treatise accessible to the quite literate Athenian population from which could be drawn representative examples of rules of conduct and the reasons therefore. For what was not included, we can only suppose that the author intended that the organizing ethic revealed therein would encourage right-minded people to make the correct choices, guided by ethics if not law.[42]

To Plato's mind, many of the wrongs to which man might be drawn did not even need the attention of the law. Incest, for example, was within a class of wrongs so base that acculturated norms alone should suffice to eliminate it.[43] Regarding obligations that were, in contrast, suited to external obligations,

---

[39]  *Id.*

[40]  PLATO, THE LAWS (A.E. Taylor, transl.)(Everyman, 1966).

[41]  *Id.* at xv.

[42]  For the distinction between ethics, and acting from ethics, and law, see below.

[43]  Ath: Well, then, you see how all such lusts are extinguished by a mere phrase.

Meg.: Phrase? What phrase?

Plato placed several rules that might represent tort-property or tort-contract hybrids under the rubric of Agriculture. Here the Athenian suggests a statute that would forbid the moving of a neighbor's landmark, be the neighbor friend or foe. He adds ominously that one violating this rule risks the wrath of Zeus, the "protector of the stranger to the other[.]..."[44]

Plato warns against "little repeated torts between neighbors" that might created ill will.[45] Persons will be held strictly liable to others for personal harm or invasion of property.[46] Throughout THE LAWS Plato's Athenian describes a regimen in which the ownership rights to land are protected as sedulously as they would come to be in English law a millennium later in its laws of trespass and nuisance. One working the soil of another "shall make the damage god to him, and shall moreover, by way of medicine for his churlish behavior, pay a further sum of double the amount of the damage to the sufferer."[47] For the creation of a nuisance such as the planting of trees in too close a proximity to the land of another, the actor must pay such a fine as is set by the magistrate.[48] For some wrongs to land, Plato's Athenian seems to introduce an element of *culpa*. Thus the man who "in making a bonfire... take[s] no precaution for the timber of his neighbor's land" must likewise pay the fine imposed.[49] With regard to the conversion of personal property, such as the "humouring" of the bees on one owner's land so that they migrate to the other's property, he must pay damages.[50]

---

Ath: The saying that they are all unhallowed, abominations to God, deeds of black shame. The explanation must surely be that no one holds a different language about them; all of us, from our very cradles, are hearing the same report of them from all quarters[.]...

PLATO, THE LAWS, *id.* at 224.

[44] *Id.* at 230.

[45] *Id.* at 231.

[46] [N]eighbor must take every care to do nothing exceptional to neighbor; must keep himself strictly from all such acts, and above all from encroachment on a neighbor's lands[.]" *Id.* at 231.

[47] PLATO, THE LAWS 231 (A.E. Taylor, transl.)(Everyman, 1966).

[48] *Id.*

[49] *Id.*

[50] *Id.*

Plato returns repeatedly to the issue of water in terms of its potential for damaging the land of another. He describes the duties of landowners both to others possessing land either higher in gradient or lower to their own. To his up-gradient neighbor the landowner owed a duty not to impede the outflow of rainwater; to the down gradient neighbor a duty not to cause damage "by careless discharge of the efflux" from the higher property. In the event of a breach of these obligations, an affected neighbor might seek an order from a magistrate directing the appropriate party to commence compliances.[51]

In his TREATISE ON GOVERNMENT Aristotle recognizes that absent a circumstance in which "we suppose a set of people to live separate from each other... and that there were laws subsisting between each party, to prevent their injuring one another[,]" they still require, for those instances in which commerce requires that they aggregate in one place, "alliances subsisting between each party to mutually assist and prevent any injury." It is noteworthy that Aristotle writes here of "alliances", or agreements, and to "prevent[ing]" harm, as distinct from providing remedies for harm that has already occurred. This suggestion of the potential superiority of *ex ante* agreements permitting accords between neighbors before disputes may arise will be evident anew in Roman law codes and their several and copious interpretations.[52]

## 2. THE PROPER FORUM FOR AND CONDUCT OF "LAW GIVERS"

As had Hesiod before him, Aristotle deliberated at length regarding the proper forum for and conduct of "law givers". To Aristotle, great moral responsibility attaches those who would so organize a city that is prepared to live under the rule of law; "[W]hosoever endeavours to establish wholesome laws in a state, attends to the virtues and the vices of each individual who composes it; from

---

[51] PLATO, THE LAWS, *supra* at 232 (A.E. Taylor, transl.)(Everyman, 1966) Again the Athenian suggests that liability is not strict, but instead applies only to "careless discharge".

[52] *See* notes below.

whence it is evident, that the first care of him who would found a city...must be to have his citizens virtuous[.]...[L]aw is an agreement and a pledge, as the Sophist Lycophron says, between the citizens of their intending to do justice to each other, though not sufficient to make all the citizens just and good[.]"[53]

Aristotle wrote of the application of unwritten law when he referenced the approach taken by the Ephors of Sparta "using their own judgement."[54] Again, as Hesiod had ascribed to Muses his inspiration for many of his statements of law, so too does a figure in Aristotle's account of early law, an unlikely law giver, Zaleucus, a shepard. Aristotle wrote: "[W]hen the Locians asked the oracle how they might find relief from the considerable turmoil they were experiencing, the oracle responded that they should have laws enacted for themselves, whereupon a certain Shepard named Zaleucus ventured to propose to the citizens many excellent laws, When they learned of these and asked him where he had found them, he replied that Athena had come to him in a dream."[55] It appears that attribution of early law to the intervention of a god or a goddess was not unusual, and perhaps served to lend weight to the instructive power of any law thus derived. In analogous stories the Cretans assigned the origins of certain laws to the mythic figure Minos and others, while the Spartans believed that Lycurgas's laws came from the Delphic Oracle.[56]

## 3. THE ESSENTIAL JUSTICE OF CERTAIN REMEDIES FOR PARTICULAR WRONGS

External law may coerce or induce man to act in accordance thereto. Ethics, in contrast, comprise "laws for which external legislation is impossible".[57] Ethics concerns man's act, or omission to act, and by the exercise of his free

---

[53] ARISTOTLE, A TREATISE ON GOVERNMENT bk. III, ch. 9, at 80 et. seq.
[54] ARISTOTLE, POLITICS BOOK III, 1.1270 B 30, at 578 (Ernest Barker, trans.) (Oxford: Clarendon 1946).
[55] F.E. Adcock, *Literary Tradition and Early Greek Code-Makers*, 2 CAMB. HIST. J. 95 (1927), referenced in GAGARIN, *supra* at 57.
[56] PLATO, THE LAWS, *supra* at 624A-625A.
[57] T.E. HOLLAND, JURISPRUDENCE 27 (11th ed)(1910).

will or choice, not in furtherance of external legislation but rather pursuant to mans' "will as its [ethics'] objects and aims. ... [pursuant to] the free choice of the individual."[58]

Returning what was owed, in effect giving up the actual or conceptual unjust enrichment associated with a wrongful taking, is of course part and parcel to the analysis of Aristotle, in NICOMACHEAN ETHICS Book V, ch. 2, in which "The Thinker" is credited with laying the cornerstone of the corrective justice principles of today's common law,[59] although the logic has equivalent bearing upon economic considerations. Under the Aristotelian principle of *diorthotikos*, or "making straight," at the remedy phase the court will attempt to equalize things by means of the penalty, taking away from the gain of the wrongrdoer. Whether the wrongdoer's gain is monetary, or measured in property, or the community's valuation of a personal physical injury consequent to the defendant's wrongful act, by imposing a remedy approximating the actor's wrongful appropriation and "loss" to the sufferer, "the judge restores equality..."[60] This justice should be meted out equivalently to all, irrespective of whether the sufferer is a good man or a bad one. [61] As Book V Chapter 4 is paraphrased by Joachim: "If, for example, the thief was a gentleman and the injured party a beggar - - a member of an inferior class in the state - - this difference of rank is nothing to the law.... All that the law is concerned with is that, of two parties

---

[58]  *Id.* (citations omitted).

[59]  "[T]he law . . . treats the parties as equal, and asks only if one is the author and the other the victim of injustice or if the one inflicted and the other has sustained an injury. Injustice in this sense is unfair or unequal, and the endeavor of the judge is to equalize it." ARISTOTLE, NICOMACHEAN ETHICS 154 (J. Welldon trans., 1987), discussed in David G. Owen, *The Moral Foundations of Punitive Damages*, 40 ALA. L. REV. 705, 707-08 & n.6 (1989). *See alternatively* ARISTOTLE, NICOMACHEAN ETHICS, bk. V, ch. 3, at 400-02 (Richard McKeon ed., 1947) in INTRODUCTION TO ARISTOTLE (Richard McKeon, ed.)(Modern Library 1947)

[60]  "[T]he judge tries to equalize things by means of the penalty, taking away the gain of the assailant. For the term "gain" [*kerdos*] is applied generally to such cases - - even if it is not a term appropriate to certain cases, *e.g.*, to the person who inflicts the wound - - and "loss" [*zemia*] to the sufferer; at all events, when the suffering has been estimated, the one is called loss and the other gain... Therefore the just... consists in having an equal amount before and after the suffering."

[61]  2 THE COMPLETE WORKS OF ARISTOTLE 786 (Jonathan Barnes ed., 1984).

before it, one has got an unfair advantage and the other has suffered an unfair disadvantage. There is, therefore, a wrong which needs redress - - an inequality which needs to be equalized."[62]

Aristotle classified among the divers "involuntary" transactions that would invite rectification "clandestine" wrongs, including "theft, adultery, poisoning,... false witness[;]" and "violent" wrongs, including "assault, imprisonment, ... robbery with violence, ... abuse, [and] insult." [63] Importantly, Aristotle does not promise distributive justice, in the sense that a man may remedy his antecedent unequal position *vis a vis* another.[64] Rather, corrective justice will only work to rectify the marginal inequality that the wrongdoing has imposed.[65]

Aristotle understood corrective justice to enable restoration to the victim of the status quo ante major, insofar as a monetary award or an injunction can do so.[66] Importantly, he proceeds to distinguish between excusable harm and harm for which rectification could appropriately be sought. For an involuntary harm, such as when "A takes B's hand and therewith strikes C[,]" an act that

---

[62] SAUL LEVMORE, FOUNDATIONS OF TORT LAW 60 (1993).

[63] ARISTOTLE, NICOMACHEAN ETHICS Bk. 5, Ch. 2 in INTRODUCTION TO ARISTOTLE 402 (Richard McKeon, ed.) (1947).

[64] To Aristotle:

> Justice (contrary to our own view) implies that members of the community possess unequal standing. That which ensures justice, whether it is with regard to the distribution of the prizes of life or the adjudication of conflicts, or the regulation of mutual services is good since it is required for the continuance of the group. Normativity, then, is inseparable from actuality.

PRIMITIVE, ARCHAIC AND MODERN ECONOMIES: ESSAYS OF KARL POLANYI 96 (George Dalton, ed.)(1968).

[65] *Id.* at Ch. 3, p. 403:
" [A]wards should be made "according to merit"; for all men agree that what is just in distribution must be according to merit in some sense, though they do not all specify the same sort of merit, but democrats identify it with the status of the freemen, supporters of oligarchy with wealth (or noble birth) and supporters of aristocracy with excellence."

[66] "Therefore the just is intermediate between a sort of gain and a sort of loss, viz, those which are involuntary; it consists in having an equal amount before and after the transaction." Ch. 4, *id.* at 407.

was not "within [A's] power[,]" or for acts pursuant to "ignorance", a more nuanced legal response is indicated.[67] Even for such involuntary acts as "violat[e]
proportion or equality", Aristotle suggests opaquely, some should be excused,
while others should not be excused.[68]

In his hypothetical laws, Aristotle's writings presage distinctions that
would eventually form the basis for dividing absolute liability from innocent
causing of harm. As to voluntary and harmful acts attributable to ignorance,
Aristotle distinguishes between acts acts in which the ignorance is excusable
and acts in which the ignorance is not.[69] The former, which we might today
characterize as innocent, would not prompt remediation, while the latter
would. Thus Aristotle describes an act from which injury results "contrary to
reasonable expectation" as a "misadventure", and forgivable at law.[70] To Aristotle, an unintentional act[71] that causes harm, but where such harm "is not
contrary to reasonable expectation[,]" constitutes not a misadventure but a
"mistake". To Aristotle, "mistake" is a fault-based designation. The example
used is redolent of what would be termed "negligence" in today's nomenclature: a man throwing an object "not with intent to wound but only to prick[.]"
This man, although not acting with an intent to wound another in any significant way, would nonetheless be subject to an obligation in indemnity, for to
Aristotle, when "a man makes a mistake ... the fault originates in him[.]"[72]

## E. THE CODES OF SOLON AND OTHERS

With the end of the hereditary monarchy, political power in Greece passed
to the nobility, who in turn sat in the Supreme Council of State on a hill
known as Areopagus. Administration of the law was vested in magistrates,
all of whom were drawn from the nobility. The law that was in fact admin-

---

[67] ARISTOTLE, NICOMACHEAN ETHICS CH. 8, *supra* note 63 at 414.

[68] *Id.*

[69] *Id.*

[70] ARISTOTLE, NICOMACHEAN ETHICS CH. 8, *supra* note 63 at 415.

[71] An act that "does not imply vice[.]" *Id.*

[72] *Id.*

istered was customary law, and indeed the Greek for law was *nomos*, or custom.[73] It was largely unwritten, and as its divination, articulation and application rested in the noble classes, the lower classes viewed it with and understandable mistrust.

It is probable that the Greeks began to inscribe their laws in the middle of the Seventh Century, B.C. In about 621 B.C., in response to popular turmoil, the nobility agreed to reduce customary law to writing, and produced the first Greek-written legal code, the Code of Draco. Draco was Greece's first law scribe, at the time he enjoyed the position of *archon eponymous*. Draco's law concerning homicide, variously 620 B.C. or 621 B.C., set exile as the penalty, and included other provisions such as pertain to the seeking of a pardon and the protection of the perpetrator from retaliation by the victim's family.[74] It provided: "Even if a man unintentionally kills another, he is exiled. The kings are to adjudge responsible for the homicide either the killer or the planner[.]... If anyone kills the killer or is responsible for his death, as long as he stays away from the frontier markets, games and Amphictyonic sacrifices, he shall be liable to the same treatment as the one who kills an Athenian[.] ... It is allowed to kill or arrest killers, if they are caught in the territory.... If a man defending himself straightaway kills someone forcibly and unjustly plundering or seizing him, the killer shall pay no penalty."[75] A borrower in default could be sold into slavery if his social status was less than his lender.[76]

Zaleucus and Charondas undertook to set down in written form penalties for other delicts, surely a valuable endeavor to the extent that it would serve

---

[73] *See generally*, Cathleen Freeman, *Legal Code and Procedure*, in J. C. SMITH, DAVID N. WEISSTUB, THE WESTERN IDEA OF LAW 296 (Butterworths 1983).

[74] Demosthenes 23, GAGARIN, *supra* at 64. In his POLITICS Aristotle describes the proof associated with a judgment of homicide as involving the testimony of relatives who were witnesses to the killing: "There is a homicide law *(pen ta phonika nomos)* that if the plaintiff provides a certain number of his own relatives as witnesses to the killing, the defendant is guilty of homicide." ARISTOTLE, POLITICS 1269A1-3 (Ernest Barker, transl.) (Oxford:Clarendon 1946) *See also id.* at 1274B23-26.

[75] RONALD S. STROUD, DRAKON'S LAW ON HOMICIDE (Berklley 1968) in MICHAEL GAGARIN, EARLY GREEK LAW 86 (U. Cal. 1986).

[76] May be found at http://en.wikipedia.org/Draco

to lessen the then extant uncertainty of results at the penalty phase of a dispute. Charondas differentiated "minutely" the numerous types of assaults,[77] but such was the tenor of the time,[78] as Aristotle relates the "lawgiving" endeavors of others as incidental and not collectively significant.[79]

In its employment of the penalty of death for a wide range of offenses, even for offenses as minor as petty theft, Draco's Code, even as revised, was extraordinarily harsh by today's standards - whither today's expression of "Draconian" as an equivalent of "harsh". Even not so very long after its era, Aristotle wrote dismissively of the significance of Draco's codification, characterizing it merely as derivative and harsh.[80] In Draco's defense, though, his charge was not to reform the law, but rather to codify existing customary law, and that he did.[81]

Nevertheless, as Greek cultural mores evolved, an ever increasing number of Greeks concluded that Draco's Code in written form betrayed a harshness that invited, if not demanded reform, and the task of the first major revision fell to Solon, who was appointed to the task in 594 B.C.[82] He was given one

---

[77] GAGARIN, *supra* at 64-65. Prof. Gagarin cites the parody in HERONDAS, MIMES 2.46ff, as well as Aristotle's characterization of Charonsas's laws in POLITICS 1274 B 8. *Id.* at n. 56.

[78] ARISTOTLE, POLITICS 1274 B 19-20, *supra* note 54.

[79] "Pittacus was the author of some laws, but never drew up any form of government; one of which was this, that if a drunken man beat any person he should be punished more than if he did it when sober; for as people are more apt to be abusive when drunk than sober, he paid no consideration to the excuse which drunkenness might claim, but regarded only the common benefit. Andromadas Regmus was also a lawgiver to the Thracian [T]alcidians. There are some laws of his concerning murders and heiresses extant, but these contain nothing that any one can say is new and his own. And thus much for different sorts of governments, as well those which really exist as those which different persons have proposed." ARISTOTLE: A TREATISE ON GOVERNMENT (William Ellis, A.M., transl.) (J.M. Dent. & Soncs, Ltd. 1928).

[80] "As for Draco's laws, they were published when the government was already established, and they have nothing particular in them worth mentioning, except their severity on account of the enormity of their punishments." ARISTOTLE: A TREATISE ON GOVERNMENT bk. II, ch. 7, at 65.

[81] ARISTOTLE: A TREATISE ON GOVERNMENT at *id.*

[82] Solon could be described as dour. An aphorism attributed to him is this: "Let no man be called happy until his death. Till then, he is not happy, only lucky." Available at *http://www.QuoteFox.com/Solon* page 3 (2005).

year to reform the Athenian constitution, as well as its legal code, and its law courts.[83]

Under the laws of Solon, the penalty for rape was 100 drachmas.[84] The penalties for theft depended upon the value of the goods stolen.[85] Penalties were also imposed for libel,[86] and for a favorite topic of students of common law tort, the dog bite. For the lattermost, the penalty was the giving over of the dog, with the dog wearing a large wooden collar.[87] In one provision that would suggest revision of the established legal maxim *de minimus non curat lex*, Solon's laws contained a penalty for conversion of cow dung.[88]

Solon's law also contained regulations regarding matters that would today sound in nuisance, including rules for the minimum distances between homes, and the permissible interposition of walls, ditches, wells, beehives, and certain trees.[89] Demosthenes contains an account of one such dispute involving one neighbor's claim of damage arising from the placement of a wall on his neighbor's property.[90] Solon's revisions also introduced the jury court (*heliaca*), which came to be employed in most disputes save suits involving bloodshed and arson. The juries reached remarkable numbers, some as large as 500 members, although the law provided that any number be uneven in order to preclude a tie. The jury would be the finder of fact in accordance with the applicable law, at which point, if the finding was one of guilt or responsibility, the law provided for the penalty. Jurors swore to hear both sides of a dispute impartially, but

---

[83] Such was the respect afforded Solon's work that when the Romans in 454 B.C. turned to the task of their own first and great legal codification, the TWELVE TABLES, they sent commissioners to Athens to study the laws of Solon. *See generally*, Kathleen Freeman, *Legal Code and Procedure*, in J. C. SMITH, DAVID N. WEISSTUB, *supra* note 73 at 297. The Roman Twelve Tables are discussed below at Parts III A, B.

[84] Fragment 26, from GAGARIN, *supra* note 20 at 65 (U. Cal. 1986).

[85] DEMOSTHENES 24.105; Fragment 23, at GAGARIN, *id.* at 65.

[86] Fragments 32-33, *id.* at 65.

[87] Fragment 64, *id.* at 65.

[88] Fragment 64, *id.* at 65.

[89] Fragment 60-62, *id.* at 65.

[90] DEMOSTHENES 11. 55, in Ugo Enrico Paoli, La loi de Solon sur les distances, 27 REVUE HISTORIQUE DU DROIT FRANCAIS ET ETRANGER 505-517 (1949), reprinted in ALTRI STUDI DI DIRITTO GRECO E ROMANO 571-83 (Milan 1976).

after that, the trials themselves could be extraordinary affairs in which litigants and jurors might end up in shouting matches, showing behavior more like today's town meeting than a modern trial.[91]

Thus from the time of Solon's revisions onward, the law applied in Greek courts was the Code of Solon, as it might be amended or clarified from time to time by decree of the Assembly of the People. In order to preclude casual alteration or repeal of the Code, a specific and laborious procedure was followed for any proposed changes.[92] In the end, however, the laws of the Greek "democracy" could not under any circumstances fulfill the ideal of Kantian social contract theory. That social contract theory in particular contemplates "the idea of society as a system of cooperation between free and equal persons[.]"[93] And Greece, for its advances in the democratic ideal, never freed itself from the restrictions of slavery and status based upon land ownership and gender.

# III. ROMAN LAW

## A. EARLY ROMAN LAW

It is received wisdom that together with Anglo-American common law, Roman Law is one of the two foundations of the civil law now observed throughout much of the Western world.[94] The law today characterized as Roman Law had its sources in statutes, plebicites,[95] constitutions, and praetorian orders, among

---

[91]  *See generally*, Kathleen Freeman, *supra* note 73 at 297-98.

[92]  Kathleen Freeman, *supra* note 73 at 298.

[93]  Gregory C. Keating, Chapt. 1, *A Social Contract Conception of the Tort Law of Accidents*, in Philosophy and the Law of Torts at 27. Keating continues, at *id.*:

> [A] fundamental task of principles of justice on this account is to find terms of cooperation that express the freedom and equality of democratic citizens, recognizing that these citizens hold diverse and incommensurable conceptions of the good.

[94]  *See generally*, Julius Wolff, Roman Law 3-5(Norman: U. Oklahoma 1951).

[95]  The plebiscite (*plebes scitum*) was comparable to what today, at the state-wide level,

other stimuli. However, as J. Declareuil points out: "The most ancient law was entirely customary."[96] The pronounced and continuing effect of customary law was recognized in theistic and secular societies alike. In the earliest Roman Law codification, that of the Twelve Tables, we see the greatest incidence of rules that reflect the norms of an agricultural society. These rules must, of course, make provision for the protection of the individual and family from the wrongful interruption of others with their personal safety and the preservation of their property. Due, if preliminary, attention is also given to subjects that pertain to the preservation of individual rights against the potential predations of the wealthier, landed and more politically powerful nobility. Finally, early Roman Law sets forth a framework of proscriptions and penalties for the types of conflicts that would be predictable in the agricultural setting, which is to say, protection of crops and livestock.

While early Greek Law evidenced the textures of philosophy and jurisprudence to which its famous philosophers contributed, Roman Law was practical and elementary.[97] After much public pressure for a compilation and rationalization of the disparate sources of law as enforced by the consuls, in 451 B.C. a commission of 10 jurists (*Decemviri*) was appointed to consolidate the laws. Within a year they produced 10 "Tables", and then, upon reappointment, wrote the additional two tables, constituting together the famous "Twelve Tables". It is uncertain to what

---

are called "initiatives". Originally it would be a decision by the plebs of approval or disapproval of a proposal of a tribune, and binding only the plebs; later it would represent one of a variety of statutory and more broadly applicable forms. J. DE-
. CLAREUIL, ROME THE LAW GIVER 19 (Greenwood, Westport, Ct. 1970).

[96] J. DECLAREUIL, *id.* at 16. "Law has always had much to do with customs and precedents, which derived their authority from various facts established by our ancestors since times immemorial." WILLIAM S. H. JUNG, OUTLINES OF MODERN CHINESE LAW (1934). Jung continues: "To trace the laws of a nation with a history of over four thousand and six hundred years, or, in other words, to delineate those customs and precedents by which our daily dealings of our early ancestors were regulated, therefore, is without question a matter of extreme difficulty." *Id.*

[97] "The Roman genius was essentially practical; to the speculative and theoretical side of Jurisprudence it made no contribution; indeed, such was its poverty in this respect that it was constrained to import from Greece elementary notions in respect to the foundations of law." WILLIAM A. HUNTER, INTRODUCTION TO ROMAN LAW 2 (F. H. Lawson, rev.) (Sweet & Maxwell 1955).

extent the Twelve Tables were a simple, if for the first time coordinated, exposition of customary law, or whether they reflected a reform reflecting the a need to reconcile customary law with new Republican constitutional authority. Nor is there any clear reflection within the Twelve Tables of any purposeful endeavor to adopt the progressive jurisprudence of Greece or any other of its neighbors.[98]

Under Roman law of this early era, criminal and delictual wrongs were most often correlative, but of course distinguishable. An array of delicts included some prohibitions which tracked religious or patriarchal values, and still others relying in whole or in part upon legend.[99] For the fluidity of the concept of delict, in Rome as was true as well in Greece, civil wrongs or *maleficia* were "acts involving what dominant opinion regarded as wrong, and the law punished them on this ground."[100] R. W. Lee summarized the Roman Law of delict in words that resonate in today's law of tort: "A few simple principles covered the whole ground, and adopted in modern codes, have been found sufficient to provide for the complexities of modern life. A man must see that he does not willfully invade another's right, or, in breach of a duty, willfully or carelessly cause him pecuniary loss. If he does either of these things, he is answerable in damages."[101]

## B. THE TWELVE TABLES

The Twelve Tables, dated at approximately 450 B.C., represent the Roman's first recorded effort at a comprehensive recitation of existing customary and nascent statutory law. It was reduced originally to 12 wooden tablets, and as these, together with the original language, were lost in episodic conflict with the Celts, even the most ancient of the surviving were doubtless modernized.[102]

---

[98] Of the Decemvirs William A. Hunter writes: "They were dictated by the rigid and jealous spirit of the aristocracy, which had yielded with reluctance to the just demands of the people. But the substance of the Twelve Tables was adapted to the state of the city[.] ..." WILLIAM A. HUNTER, *id.* at 4.

[99] J. DECLAREUIL, *supra* note 3 at 195.

[100] J. DECLAREUIL, *id.* at 194.

[101] R. W. LEE, AN INTRODUCTION TO ROMAN-DUTCH LAW 319 (3d ed. 1953), quoted in THE ROMAN LAW READER, *supra* note 92 at 146.

[102] *See generally* WOLFGANG KUNKEL, AN INTRODUCTION TO ROMAN LEGAL AND

The Italic community that generated the ambitious Twelve Tables was in no sense egalitarian. Political power and the ownership of land resided in the nobility (*patricii*), from whose ranks were drawn the knights (*equites*) of the Roman army. Below these were the common people (*plebs*), who tended to such land of the nobility as was not attended to by the sons of the nobility or their slaves. Such land as was not so allotted would be occupied by *plebs*, who in return for this generosity were by law clients of the nobility and obligated to take arms at the behest of their *patricii*. Plebs could not marry *patricii*, could not hold state office, and could not occupy the priesthood.[103]

The actual writing of the Twelve Tables was undertaken by an elite group of jurists, patricians of course, called *decemvirs*. They presented ten tables of laws, inscribed most probably on wood but perhaps on bronze. Within a short while it was concluded that the work fell short of the comprehensive treatment desired, and a second group of *decemvirs*, this one including plebian representation, was appointed. This second group prepared the final two tables.

In the Twelve Tables the legislators did not dedicate themselves to the description of civil government, as might the drafters of a constitution. Rather, they essayed to codify the *ius civile*, i.e., those rules which were applicable to the rights and duties of the individual citizen, but to do so as completely as possible.[104] For its plentiful strengths and limitations, the Twelve Tables gave a written unity Roman Law that would last for hundreds of years. Cicero (106-43 B.C.), of whom more is said below, noted the continuing primacy and influential potency of the Twelve Tables as a resource among students of the law, lawyers and jurists.

In early Rome, slavery existed, but in no means at the robust level as would be manifest in a later epoch. As Kunkel relates: "The unfree serf ate the same bread as his master, and at the same table, and was protected against personal inury by a statutory compensation of half the amount prescribed for the case of a free man[.]"[105]

---

CONSTITUTIONAL HISTORY (J. M. Kelly, trans.) 23 et seq. (Oxford-Clarendon 1973).

[103]  *Id.*

[104]  *Id.* at 24-25.

[105]  *Id.* at 8, referencing TWELVE TABLES, Viii. 3.

With only incidental variations, the TWELVE TABLES represented an absorbtion prior customary law. It was not by chance that the consolidation of that customary law into written form corresponded inexactly with the Roman community's ascension, in terms of size, political organization and legal structure, so as to permit it to publish law and provide mechanisms for its enforcement. The lack of coincidence is attributable to these two truths held generally to be necessary, but neither in themselves sufficient, predicates of law. First, to be considered law, be it private or public, the norms thus published must be rules of generally applicability as to the population cohorts to which they purport to be applicable. Second, the law must be accompanied by the means of its application and enforcement. As to this latter proposition, at the time of the TWELVE TABLES and at other junctures in the law of early Rome, the populace certainly welcomed the effect that codification would have on arbitrary and unpredictable actions by the judges. At the same time, they showed no great alacrity in abandoning the sum total of the tradition-based prerogatives, including the rights of blood vengeance and retaliation. This was particularly so in the early years in which the consolidation of families, kinships groups, freed men and slaves was yet to assume the size that would permit it to take on the responsibility of ensuring just resolution of disputes, or even, for that matter, defend its own borders.

THE LAWS OF THE TWELVE TABLES, Table II, *Concerning Judgments and Thefts*, is sufficiently concise as to invite setting it out in full:.

> Law IV. Where anyone commits a theft by night, and having been caught in the act is killed, he is legally killed.
>
> Law V If anyone commits a theft during the day, and is caught in the act, he shall be scourged, and given up as a slave to the person against whom the theft was committed. If he who committed the theft is a slave, he shall be beaten with rods and hurled from the Tarpeian Rock. If he is under the age of puberty, the praetor shall decide whether he shall be scourged and surrendered by way of reparation for the injury.

Law VI. When any persons commit a theft during the day and the light, whether they be freemen or slaves, of full age or minors, and attempt to defend themselves with weapons, or with any kind of implements; and the party agains whom the violence is committed, raises the cry of thief, and calls upon other persons, if any are present, to come to his assistance; and this is done, and the thieves are killed in the defence of his person and property, it is legal and no liability attaches to the homicide.

Law VII. If a theft be detected by means of a dish and a girdle, it is the same as manifest theft, and shall be punished as such.

Law VIII, Whenever anyone accuses and convicts another of theft which is not manifest, and no stolen property is found, judgment shall be rendered to compel the thief to pay double the value of what was stolen.

Law IX. Where anyone secretly cuts down trees belonging to another, he shall pay 25 asses for each tree cut down.

Law X. Where anyone, in order to favour a thief, makes a compromise for the loss sustained, he cannot afterwards prosecute him for theft.

Law XI. Stolen property shall always be his to whom it formerly belonged; nor can the lawful owner ever be deprived of it by long possession, without regard to its duration; nor can it ever be acquired by another, no matter in what way this may take place.[106]

As was true of the Greeks,[107] at the time Roman legislators turned their attention to the TWELVE TABLES, there existed no complete distinction between civil and criminal transgressions. The TWELVE TABLES were intended princi-

---

[106] THE LAWS OF THE TWELVE TABLES, THE CIVIL LAW 58-65 (New York: AMS Press 1973), in J.C. SMITH, DAVID N. WEISSTUB, *supra* note 73 at 317-18.

[107] *See* PLATO, THE LAWS xiv, xv (A.E. Taylor, trans.)(Everyman 1966).

pally to consolidate comprehensively, and in written form, the *ius civile*, thought traditionally as an endeavor at "safeguarding... the small man in particular against the arbitrary behavior of the patrician nobility in legal relations and the administration of justice."[108] Specific measures follow largely the form of other ancient and modern codifications, i.e., a predicate act or omission is identified by a description beginning with the word that can be translated as "If', then the act or the omission is described, and finally the legal consequences thereof.[109] After this, and despite the brevity of the sentences, lack of clarity pervades, with frequent ambiguity in the subject and the object of the chosen verb form.[110]

The rustic form of early Roman law contained no provisions for the compulsory attendance of the defendant, and accordingly, the Twelve Tables described a protocol that the plaintiff was obliged to follow. As translated: "If [plaintiff] summons [defendant] to law, and if [defendant] does not go, [plaintiff] shall call up witnesses. Then [plaintiff] shall seize [defendant]. If [defendant] resists [plaintiff] shall lay hands on (seize) him. If sickness or age is a weakness, [plaintiff] shall provide a beast to carry [defendant]."[111]

As Kunkel suggests, it is in many of the particular provisions of the Twelve Tables that the role of the code in Early Rome's "cultural history" is revealed.[112] Recalling that at the time of its scrivening there were no clear markers delineating between what would be the realm of crime and the realm of delict, it appears that capital punishment was enforced by the state only in instances of treason, and also perhaps for particularly grave religious transgressions, the relation between the two being that each was considered an offense not against another individual but rather against the commonwealth.[113]

Even for intentional murder (*oarrucudas*), the punishment would be de-

---

[108]  Kunkel, *supra* note 103 at 24-25.

[109]  *See generally* M. Stuart Madden, Chapter 1, *Tort Law Through Time and Culture: Themes of Economic Efficicy*, in Exploring Tort Law (M. Stuart Madden, ed.) (Cambridge 2005).

[110]  Wolfgang Kunkel *supra* note 103 at 25.

[111]  *Id.* at 25 n. 2.

[112]  *Id.* at 26-27.

[113]  Kunkel, *supra* at 27.

termined by the victims survivors (*agnates*). The family could seek blood vengeance, after a judicial finding of intent and malice. For unintentional homicide and for delicts more generally, payment of a prescribed number of cattle to the victim's *agnate* might suffice. For example, the TWELVE TABLES describes an unintentional slaying, and its compensatory remedy, in this way: "[I]f the spear has rather flown from the hand than been thrown", the killer would surrender to the victim's family a ram. The ram might then be slaughtered in ritual vengeance, thus the term "scapegoat" attributed to Augustinian period jurist Labeo.[114]

Certain acts other than intentional homicide would warrant the victim or the victim's family putting the perpetrator to death, in each instance a revelation of the strong theme of legitimized vengeance found throughout the TWELVE TABLES. This countenanced vengeance can be seen as the very "self help" that the law of civil delict would require another millennium or more to dispatch. Interesting as well, in many instances the manner permitted for the execution of the punishment would bear a conceptual similarity to the nature of the offense. The intentional arsonist could be burned alive. One who stole crops at night could be hung at the location of the theft as a sacrifice to Ceres, goddess of the harvest. A false accuser could be thrown into an "abyss".[115]

The victim's prerogatives against certain transgressors revealed a liberality not shown even in instances of alleged intentional homicide. An individual encountering a thief "red handed" by night was permitted to kill him if the burglar was armed.[116] If the theft occurred during the day, slaying the perpetrator was approved if the victim first cried out to neighbors for help (*endoplorare* = *implorare*) so as to permit corroboration as to the permissibility of killing the thief.[117] Alternatively, the victim could take the thief to the magistrate, who could then return him to the victim. The recourse then was as before, as the victim could kill the thief. Or, he could sell the thief as a slave, or demand ransom from the thief's family or others. For thieves not caught in the act, super-

---

[114]  *Id.* at 27.

[115]  *Id.* at 28

[116]  TWELVE TABLES T., 8, 1, 2, 13; 9, 6, cited in J. DECLAREUIL, *supra* at 196 n. 2.

[117]  KUNKEL, *supra* at 28.

compensatory damages might be imposed in the form of moneys amounting to twice the value of what was stolen.[118]

Pursuant to the TWELVE TABLES, accidental personal injury triggered specific remedies. For breaking the bone (*os factum*) of a free man, the remedy was retaliation in kind,[119] although the authority as to this differs, with another source indicating that the breaking of a bone of a freedman the defendant was required to pay 300 as.[120] The latter penalty seems more in keeping with the tendency of the TWELVE TABLES to influence the customary law in the direction away from the blood feud dimensions of customary law and in the direction of a system in which penalties would be assessed in money, livestock, or goods. For breaking the bone of a slave, the penalty was 150 as[121], and for less severe injuries. 25 as.[122] The wrongful cutting down of a tree was likewise penalized by a payment of 25 as.[123]

Numerous fines were set at multiples of the proved harm. They included, without limitation, double the value of the wrong for usury, for a depositary who failed to repay the deposit, a seller of land who misrepresented the area of land, or a guardian responsible for misadministration. A threefold multiple of the plaintiffs loss would be due for the misadministration of a receivership.[124]

*Damages*—The severity of the penalties associated with certain delicts can be seen to relate directly to the gravity of the offense as it might be evaluated in an early agricultural society. As mentioned, the intentional arsonist could be dispatched by burning. Also considered capital offenses were the noctural theft of another's crops or permitting one's animals to graze on another's crops. If, however, one set fire to another's house by accident, he was responsible only in damages to be assessed at the level of the value of the home, or if he was too poor to pay, he would be "lightly chastised."[125] For what would later be

[118]  *Id.* at 28.

[119]  XII T., 8, 1, 2, 13; 9, 6, cited in J., *supra* at 196.

[120]  TWELVE TABLES VIII 3, discussed in KUNKEL, *supra* at 28.

[121]  TWELVE TABLES VIII 3, referenced in KUNKEL at *id.*

[122]  TWELVE TABLES VIII. 4, referenced in KUNKEL at *id.*

[123]  CICERO, DE LEGIS 3, 11, cited in J. DECLAREUIL, *supra* at 197 n. 1.

[124]  J. DECLAREUIL, *supra* at 197.

[125]  H. F. JOLOWICZ, HISTORICAL INTRODUCTION TO ROMAN LAW quoted in THE

termed either intentional torts or negligence-based torts, it has been urged that at this early stage of Roman Law neither, as to the former, the actor's frame of mind nor the level of care employed were of any moment.[126]

While numerous delicts against property, if proven would garner the victim a percuniary award in the amount of the value of the property, still others would permit recovery of two or even three times the actual loss suffered. As review of these instances demonstrates that these multiple awards were resesrved for circumstances in which either the conduct of the accused was more blameworthy, or the loss to the victim could not be remedied with a simple compensatory award. For the wrongdoer discovered to have in his home the possessions of the accuser, the penalty was three times the value of the goods.[127]

## C. THE LEX AQUILIA AND CICERO

The TWELVE TABLES treatment of damage to property (*damnum injuria datum*) was superceded by the *Lex Aquilia* (286-195 B.C.), advanced by the Tribune of the Plebians Aquilius (-286 B.C.).[128] The *Lex Aquilia*, a Plebiscitum, was stimulated most probably by a popular movement and an ensuing plebiscite.[129] Its three chapters reflected an important step in synthesis of the evolving law for the securing of damages for private wrongs, and it replaced all prior law regarding injury to persons or things.[130] Reflective significantly of modifications, some legal and some equitable, to the TWELVE TABLES at the instance of a succession of Praetors, the *Lex Aquilia* preserved the general rule that one was strictly liable

---

ROMAN LAW READER, *supra* at 148.

[126] "I do not know of any very satisfactory evidence that a a man was generally held liable either in Rome or England for the accidental consequences of his own act." OLIVER WENDELL HOLMES, JR., THE COMMON LAW 4 (Little Brown 1881) (Dover Books edition 1991).

[127] H. P. JOLOWICZ, *supra* at 146.

[128] While some authorities state that there exists no certain date for this development, H. F. JOLOWICZ, HISTORICAL INTRODUCTION TO ROMAN READER, quoted in THE ROMAN LAW READER, *supra* at 146, William A. Hunter dates Is development at approximately 286 B.C. WILLIAM A. HUNTER, *supra* at 145.

[129] J. DECLAREUIL, *supra* at 199.

[130] GAIUS Dig. 9, tit. 2.

for one's actions. The most noteworthy exception pertained to murder, with the *Lex Aquilia* differentiating between the intentional and the unintentional taking of life.[131] Its structure and substance became the most typical means of proceeding in a matter of *damnum injuria datum*.[132]

In its general and specific sections together, the *Lex Aquilia* provided for remedies for wrongs ranging from simple damage (*damnum injuria datum*) to fraudulent defenses in legal proceedings (*infitiatio*).[133] It is also credited with the introduction of elements of fault (culpa), including absence of due care (today's negligence) to the law of delict. Should the actions of the wrongdoer (*corpore*) result directly or indirectly in harm to another thing, the action would be *directa actio Legis Aquiliae*.[134] If the injury was to a slave or to a quadriped (*quae pecu*, i.e., cattle, sheep, etc.), the wrongdoer could be obligated to pay as damages the highest value that the property had held over the preceding year.[135] The law included provisions intended to stimulate truth telling, for if a person were to be found responsible, and to have willfully denied the claim against him, his payment for the wrong could be doubled. If the injury was not lethal, the damages owed would be the highest value of the injured slave (or damaged property) within the month previous to the injury. An *action factum* arise if a person intentionally drove his neighbor's animal(s) into water, and they drowned.[136]

Under the *Lex Aquilia*, if property was damaged by direct contact, or by an agency directed by the wrongdoer, and if the value of the property was diminished thereby, the cause of action would be in *directa actio Legis Aquiliae*. If a slave or a quadriped was killed, the actor could be bound to pay the highest

---

131 THE ROMAN LAW READER 151 (F. H. Lawson, ed.)(Oceana 1969).

132 WILLIAM SMITH, A DICTIONARY OF GREEK AND ROMAN ANTIQUITIES (John Murray, London 1875), available at http://penelope. uchicago.edu/thayer/e/roman/texts/secondary/smigra/home.html.

133 J. DECLAREUIL, *supra* at 199, citing D. 9. 2, 2-¶ 11-6, 27-5.

134 WILLIAM SMITH, A DICTIONARY OF GREEK AND ROMAN ANTIQUITIES (John Murray, London 1875), available at http://penelope.uchicago.edu/ Thayer/ E/RomanfTexts/secondary/SMIGRA/home.html

135 GAIUS iii. 211

136 Dig. 9 tit. 2 §§ 7, 9.

value of the slave or the animal during the preceding year.[137] The third chapter provided for the case of a slave or quadruped (*quae pecudum*) being damaged, or any thing else being damaged or destroyed. In this case he had to pay the highest value that the thing had within the thirty days preceding the unlawful act. If the damage was done to a thing (*corpus*), but not by a *corpus*, there was an *actio utilis Legis Aquiliae*, which is also an *action in factum or* on the case. Such a case would occur when, for instance, a man should purposely drive his neighbour's beast into a river and it should perish there.[138]

Later Roman law drew a distinction between injuries to the person and injuries to property. The former were termed, and the later *damnum injuria datum*. A wrong involving theft of property was termed *furtum*. When violence accompanied such a wrong, it was termed *rapina*, or *vi bona rapta*.[139] The protections afforded by the action in injuria addressed directly the interests protected by today's torts focusing on personal physical injury: the right to be free of physical interference with one's own person. The wrong would be redressable whether it was intentional or merely negligent, and could include "a multifarious variety of wrongs", such as, without limitation, striking, whipping, kidnapping, or falsely imprisoning. It could also include wrongs that involve no physical contact, such as insult in the presence of others (*convicium facere*), defamation by spoken word, writing or deed,[140]or importunings to unchastity.[141]

Cicero (106-43 B.C.) wrote of the truth of an ethic that sounded simultaneously in terms of corrective justice and deterrence-efficiency. In his ON MORAL DUTIES he wrote that even after "retribution and punishment" have

---

[137] GAIUS ii I 211.

[138] Dig. 9 tit. 2 s 7 ss 3, 9.

[139] WILLIAM A. HUNTER, *supra* at 139-40.

[140] *E.g.*, taking the property of a solvent man as though in the course securing compensation for a debt of an insolvent man. *Compare Nader v. General Motors Co.*, 25 N.Y. 2d 560 (n.y. 1970), for an example of deeds as defamation. In that case, the automobile manufacturer was found liable for, inter alia, defamation for its acts of having the consumer advocate followed by private detectives as though he was suspected of wrongdoing, and also of contriving to have Mr. Nader be witnessed or photographed in unsavory settings.

[141] HUNTER, *supra* at 140.

been dealt to the transgressor, the person who has been dealt the wrong owes a duty to bring a close to any such misadventure by permitting a gesture such as repentance or apology.[142] From the extension to the wrongdoer of the opportunity to apologize or to repent could be reaped the immediate good of reducing the likelihood that he would "repea[t] the offense.", as well as the broader and eventual good of "deter[ing] others from injustice."[143]

As did Plato in The Laws, Cicero in his De Legibus included lengthy perorations that contain sample ethical or legal models. The work was probably completed in 45 B.C., following interruptions in Cicero's literary activity during his provincial governorship and the Civil War (49-48 B.C.). In De Legibus Cicero adopts the approach of Plato in The Laws, as Plato was the Athenian in The Laws, Cicero in De Legibus plays himself, with Quintus and Atticus as the two others. Cicero was pronouncedly bound to a vision of natural law, writing in his De Legibus: "Law is the highest reason, implanted by Nature, which commands what ought to be done, and forbids the opposite."[144] With Law as the perfection of Nature, and since man's "right reason" leads him to law, in Cicero's "learned men", nature, reason, virtue and justice coalesced to form Law that for reason of its perfection man shared with the gods.[145] Cicero was, of course, not naive, and he recognized as well man's capacity for "evil tendencies".[146] Cicero commends Socrates for his criticism of those who segregate considerations of utility from Justice,[147] for this separation, Cicero claimed, "is the source of all mischief."[148]

At what level do justice and morality serve to deter persons from wrongdoing? As to the latter, Cicero suggests that the man tempted to wrongdoing

---

[142] On Moral Duties 16, in Basic Works of Cicero 16 (Moses Hadas, ed.)(1951)

[143] Id.

[144] Cicero, De Re Publica; De Legibus (Clinton Walker Keyes, transl.)(Harvard, 1952).

[145] Id. at 321, 323.

[146] "The similarity of the human race is clearly marked in its evil tendencies as well as in it goodness. For pleasure also attracts all men; and even though it is an enticement to vice, yet it has some likeness to what is naturally good." Id. at 331.

[147] Id. at 341.

[148] Id. at 333, 335.

is given pause not so much by an apprehension that he will be pursued by the Furies as by a recognition that he will be beset "with the anguish of remorse and the torture of a guilty conscience."[149] Reemphasizing the superiority of ethics to law in the fashioning of just behavior, Cicero comments that the man who moderates his wrongful impulses solely for reasons external to himself, i.e., the apprehension of punishment by law, or "some consideration of utility and profit", is "merely shrewd, not good."[150] To Cicero, Justice and Morality were not fixed by opinion but rather by Nature[;].[151] And good men would cleave to equity, fairness, generosity and the discharge of duty just as Justice herself and "all the other virtues are also to be cherished for their own sake." True disinterested pursuit of good is the proper goal, writes Cicero, of duty, equity and generosity "sought for its own sake." If man is motivated not by inner desire but rather by anticipated gain (or for that matter the prospect of eluding punishment) his work is not just but rather for hire.[152]

Writing of duties extending beyond the family, Cicero subscribed to a species of distributive justice that endorsed a concept that, insofar as possible, no one ought be left behind. In his words: "Whether we bestow or requite a favor, duty requires, if other things are equal, that we should help those who need our help most[.]"[153] Nonetheless, Cicero conceded, "[T]hat is not the way of the world."[154]

As to persons beyond a benefactor's core family or kinship group, to Cicero there existed a duty to the entire world as to such things "we receive with profit and give without loss."[155] Thus in order that we may receive such blessings as are identified in the maxims such as "Keep no one from a running

---

[149] CICERO, DE RE PUBLICA; DE LEGIBUS, *id.* at 341.

[150] *Id.* at 343.

[I] It is not merely Justice and Injustice which are distinguished by nature, but also are without exception things which are honourable and dishonourable... [V]irtue is reason completely developed; therefore everything honourable is likewise natural.

[152] DE LEGIBUS XVIII, *id.* at 351.

[153] ON MORAL DUTIES 16, in BASIC WORKS OF CICERO 22 (Moses Hadas, ed.) (1951).

[154] *Id.*

[155] *Id.* at 23.

stream[;]" or "Let anyone who pleases take a light from your fire[;]" or "Give honest advice to a man in doublt[;]" Cicero writes, it follows that if we receive blessings we must be willing to give likewise of the same in order to "contribute to the common weal."[156]

The Licinian Laws of 367 B.C. led to the creation of a role of administrators of the law, officials who were elected for terms of one year, and who bore the title of Praetor. Although the task of the Praetor was to administer, rather than to make the law, beginning in 242 B.C. the Praetor with urban jurisdiction, *Praetor Urbanis*, was permitted to enlarge upon or otherwise shape existing law or custom when fairness so dictated. Herein arose over time powers that would approximate those that at a later time would be termed the powers of equity. Such offense as might be given by vesting in the Praetor this authority was tempered with the knowledge that the risk of protracted abuse of office was lessened due to the fact that he was subject to annual election. Upon his assumption of office, each Praetor would issue a proclamation called an *Edictum Perpetuum*, which purported to define the laws and remedies he would apply, but the one-year term of an *Edictum Perpetum* made the phrase oxymoronic. Moreover, the liberty afforded the Praetor was constricted even more by the *Lex Cornelie* (67 B.C.) that forbade a Praetor from violating his own *Edict*.[157] The *Lex Cornelia* also, due to the inflation experienced since the publication of the Twelve Tables, worked upward modifications in the sums assigned as monetary remedies.[158]

A considerable amount of the Praetor's influence over the development of equity was brought to a close with the *Edictum Perpetuun*, by Salvius Julianus (~129-138 A.D.) at Hadrian's command, that served to freeze the Praetor's interpretative flexibility by requiring the enunciation of the law he intended to

[156] *Id.*

[157] William A. Hunter, Introduction to Roman Law (9th ed.) 11-13 (F. A. Lawson rev.) (Sweet & Maxwell 1955). The date of the *Lex Cornelia* is elsewhere put at approximately 81 B.C. F.H. Lawson, The Roman Law Reader 151 (F.H. Lawson, ed.) (Oceana 1969)

[158] The Roman Law Reader, at *id.* A story, perhaps apocryphal, gained currency, if you will, of a man who came to walk the streets of Rome handing out freely the 25 as. that were the original penalty for diverse offenses, but which sum had become over time no more than pocket change.

follow at the outset of the one-year praetorship, and proscribing any departure therefrom.[159] Of greater importance, at this time, four centuries before the reign of Justinian I, Hadrian assumed complete legislative power, with the effect of making all law, public and private alike, at the will of the Emperor.

## D. LATER ROMAN LAW-THE INSTITUTES AND INTERPRETATIONS

Numerous codifications or collections of the law preceded the 533 A.D. Code of Justinian. A collection of Imperial statutes was prepared by the jurist Papirius Justus in the latter part of the Second Century A.D. Under Diocletian there was prepared a *Codex Gregorianus* that recorded constitutions to the approximate date of 295 A.D. There followed a *Codex Hermogenianus* that compiled constitutions up to approximately 365 A.D., and then a *Codex Theodosianus* under the auspices of Theodosius II that pertained to the Eastern Empire, which was completed in 439 A.D. at the instance of Valentinian III for the Western Empire.[160]

The later Roman Law of delict derived from the TWELVE TABLES, and of course the customary law that preceded the TWELVE TABLES, as further designed at the warp and woof of jurists and praetors to produce as complete as possible structure of civil liability.[161] It is recognized now as a major development "from archaic formalism to rationalism[.]"[162]

Of the sources of later Roman law the Institutes of Justinian (483-562 A.D.) proclaim: "Our law comes either from written or unwritten sources, just as among the Greeks; some laws are written, others unwritten. Written law comprises legislation, *legis* (enactments of the *comitia*), plebiscites, resolutions of the Senate, the will of the Emperor (in its various manifestations, the edicts of magistrates, and the answers of the learned."[163] Today in civil

---

[159] *See generally* J. DECLAREUIL, *supra* at 21-22.

[160] *See* WILLIAM A. HUNTER, *supra* at 18; *see also* THE ROMAN LAW READER, *supra* at 10.

[161] *Id.* at 146.

[162] *Id.*

[163] THE INSTITUTES OF JUSTINIAN, BOOK 1, TITLE II (*Concerning Natural Law, the*

code nations courts place repeated reliance upon the interpretations of the law by legal scholars, and this practice originated in Roman law, where involvement of jurists was pervasive and practically plenipotentiary. Participation of jurists in identification of the appropriate interpretive law was a pressing need in the setting of voluminous legal sources in the near millennium since the Twelve Tables and competing interpretations thereof. In 426 A.D. Theodosiums II enacted "The Law of Citations," which appointed the writings of five jurists, Papinian, Paulus, Gaius, Ulpian and Modestinus, as the principal heuristic devices for the interpretation of the law, and further declared that the writings of these Jurisconsuls would, if in agreement, be conclusive on any matter of interpretation. In the event of a tie, the conclusion of Papinian would be adopted. The act of Theodosiums II of incorporating the learned work of this finite group of revered jurists as a necessary part of legal interpretation and jurisprudential application continued and elevated the role assigned the Decemvirs in the creation of the Twelve Tables, and was followed, predictably, by Justinian I in his publication of his later Code, Institutes, and Digests.

The Code of Justinian was one part of a three-part presentation of Roman Law. Published in 533 A.D. and the two years immediately following, the first part, the Code, was intended as a succinct manual for study by lawyers, jurists and students of law. The Institutes of Justinian comprised the second part, and were a reduction and modernization into twenty volumes of the literally thousands of volumes interpreting, codifying and analyzing Roman law since the time of the Twelve Tables, quite a millennium before. The third part were the Digests, or *Pandects*, which were the works Rome's most celebrated jurists. Their work did not represent commentary on the compilation of Justinian, as some of the work of these jurists preceded the Code and the Institutes by hundreds of years. Yet as the work of revered jurists charged in their own time with interpretation of the evolving Roman Law, Justinian identified the Digests as a principal and enduring source to which contemporary jurists and

---

*Law of Nations, and the Civil Law*) par. 3, M J. C. Smith, David N. Weisstub, *supra* at 353, from The Institutes of Justinian 3-5 (J.A.C. Thomas, trans.) (Juta & Co. 1975).

lawyers ought turn in understanding the Code of Justinian and the Institutes of Justinian. Together, the Code, the Institutes, and the Digests comprised the *Corpus Juris* of 533 A.D., the great compilation of Roman Law credited with systematizing classic Roman Law. It is in the *Corpus Juris* that scholars now identify that in Roman Law "the goal of compensation of damage began to prevail over the goal of punishment and sanction."[164]

For this undertaking Justinian employed the assistance of Tribonian,[165] who thereupon enlisted the help of nine jurists to the task of editing the combined compilations, referenced above, of Gregorian, Hermogenian and Theodosian. This Code of Justinian was presented, as had been its predecessor a millennium before, in 12 books or tables. Then Tribonian and seventeen lawyers set about the task of extracting from, rationalizing and modernizing perhaps 2000 treatises, the work of the finest jurists in Roman law. They reduced this body of jurisprudence to approximately fifty books that would be called the Digests or *Pandects*. Most conspicuous among the contributions to the Digests were the works of Gaius, Ulpianus, Paulus and Marcianus.

The Institutes and the Digests of the Jurisconsuls urged strongly a natural law orientation of Roman Law. "All peoples who are governed by law and customs use law which is in part particular to themselves, in part common to all men; the law which each people has established for itself is particular to that state and is styled civil law as being particularly of that state: by what natural reason has established among all men is observed equally by all nations and is designated *ius gentium* or the law of nations, being that which all nations obey. Hence the Roman people observe partly their own particular law, partly that which is common to all peoples."[166] Evidencing a similarly full-throated natural law commitment to principles of universal duty applicable to all men, the

---

[164] Ulrich Magnus, *Compensation for Personal Injuries in a Comparative Perspective*, 39 WASHBURN L.J. 348-49 (2000).

[165] For reason of his seemingly unsurpassed mastery of the law, culture and science of this era Tribonian has been described as the Francis Bacon of his day.

[166] THE INSTITUTES OF JUSTINIAN, BOOK 1, TITLE II (*Concerning Natural Law, the Law of Nations, and the Civil Law*) par. 1, in J. C. SMITH, DAVID N. WEISSTUB, *supra* at 352, from THE INSTITUTES OF JUSTINIAN 3-5 (J.A.C. Thomas, trans.) (Juta & Co. 1975).

Third Century jurist Ulpian, quoting Celsus, wrote: "Justice is a fixed and abiding disposition to give every man his rights. The percepts of the law are as follows: to live honorably, to injure no one, to give to every man his own. Jurisprudence is a knowledge of things human and divine, the science of the just and the unjust."[167]

Committed to the identification of the delineation between "what is "just and what unjust", The Institutes of Justinian and other sources of Roman law reflect an endeavor to "give each man his due right", and comprises "precepts" to all Romans "to live justly, not to injure another and to render to each his own."[168] Violation of a "personal action" not sounding in contract is in *delict*.[169] The Institutes include rules that reveal numerous strictures against the imposition of one's will over the rights of a neighbor, and strong deterrents for the disregard thereof. In one notable example, pertaining to what would today be called the law of private nuisance or trespass, a particular provision goes so far as to detail a preference that adjoining landowners bargain in advance for agreement as to contemporaneous uses of land that might trigger dispute. In Book III par. 4, the Institutes provide that one "wishing to create" such a right of usage "should do so by pacts and stipulations."[170] A testator of land may impose such agreements reached upon his heirs, including limitations upon building height, obstruction of light, or introduction of a beam into a common wall, or the construction of a catch for a cistern, an easement of passage, or a right of way to water.[171] To much the same

[167] ULPIAN, DIGEST 1, 1, 10, quoted in GEORGE SABINE, A HISTORY OF POLITICAL THEORY 163-73 (Holt Rinehart & Winston 1937), in SMITH & WEISSTUB, *id.*at 349.

[168] THE INSTITUTES OF JUSTINIAN BOOK I, Preamble; par. 1; par. 3, in SMITH & WEISSTUB, *id.* at 352, from THE INSTITUTES OF JUSTINIAN 84, 85 (J.A.C. Thomas trans., 1975).

[169] GAIUS, THE INSTITUTES OF ROMAN LAW, Fourth Commentary par. 3 in SMITH & WEISSTUB, id at 353, from THE INSTITUTES OF ROMAN LAW BY GAIUS 442- 443 (E. Post Trans. 1925).(J.A.C. Thomas trans 1975).

[170] THE INSTITUTES OF GAIUS continue: "He can also, by will, charge his heir not to build beyond a given height or not to obstruct the light of the neighbor's premises or to allow the latter to insert a beam into the wasll or to accept raindroppings; as also to allow the neighbor a right of passage over his land or to draw water there." THE INSTITUTES OF JUSTINIAN BOOK III par. 4, in SMITH & WEISSTUB, *supra* at 358, from THE INSTITUTES OF JUSTINIAN 84, 85 (J.A.C. Thomas trans. 1975).

[171] *Id.*

effect, and specifically as to urban estates, is Book III, Title II par. 2 as interpreted by Gaius in his Institutes of Roman Law,[172] to which Ulpianus, adds a prohibition on the obstruction of a neighbor's view.[173]

Just as today an emotional distress component to an award for personal physical injury may amplify the compensatory award received by the victim, so to in Roman Law the transgressor might be liable to the victim for greater damages when the wrong took place in circumstances that would worsen the harm's shame or degradation. Thus at the penalty phase, a penalty would be made greater if the *injuria* occurred in a public place. The same aggravation of penalty might accompany a battery in which a man is beaten with sticks, or scourged, or when parents are beaten by their children, or a patron struck by a freedman, or where the injury is to a particularly valuable part of the body, such as the eye.[174]

Slaves *qua* slaves had no redress in *injuria*. Indeed, masters were permitted to flog their own slaves. Conceptually, the slave was not a being in any entire sense, but instead a unit of labor that could lose value if mistreated. However, if another were to injure a master's slaves, the action in *injuria* was deemed to devolve to the master, as an action in insult, irrespective of whether the actor intended any insult. This would be so even when no severe injury was involved. Should the slave's injury be severe, the Praetor could grant to the master an action in *injuria*.[175] The imputation of an injury suffered by a slave to the master has been described as a progenitor to the later law of agency. The reasoning given is that under Roman Law the slave had no legal standing, and in a juridical sense was absorbed into his master's family, and represented before the law by his master. In later eras of freed men or freed servants, it would be a substantial but measured step to visualize the free servant as enjoying a relation to the master (employer) similar to that of the ancient slave to his master. The final step to this analysis is the identification of circumstances, be they broad or narrow, in which the actions of the servant are treated in a legal sense as

---

172 *Gaius, On the Provincial Edict, Book VII*, THE DIGEST (or PANDECTS) BOOK VIII TITLE II par. 2., *id.* at 359.

173 ULPANIUS, ON SABINUS, BOOK XXIX, *id.* at Title II par 3, at 359.

174 HUNTER, *supra* at 140-41.

175 HUNTER, at 141.

the actions of the master. In Holmes' words: "This is the progress of ideas as shown us by history; and this is what is meant by saying that the characteristic feature which justifies agency as a title of the law is the absorbtion *pro hac vice* of the agent's legal individuality in that of his principal."

If a wrongful injury was inflicted upon a child (persons under p*otestas*), the remedy in *injuria* would lay in the father (*paterfamilias*), who could bring an action both on his behalf and on behalf of his child.[176] From what appears, this approach partakes at least in half measure of that taken for injuries to slaves, with the damage to the father being essentially in insult and/or lost services.

[—*Theft*—] Originally, Roman Law treated theft as delictual, or a civil wrong, with accompanying penalties, as referenced below. Only later would theft be catalogued as criminal. Thus for the purposes of the present description, theft can be compared to the various later common law delicts of conversion, trover *di bonis asportatis*, etc.

[—*Wrongs to Moveable Property*—] Roman law regarding injury to property was sufficiently supple to recognize variations of injury. The actor could interfere with property by two means: (1) deprive the owner of possession by (a) stealth (*furtum*), or (b) by violence (*vi bona rapta*). The wrongdoer might also interfere with the occupier's rights without dispossessing him of the property by damaging the property or otherwise impairing its usefulness (*damnum injuria datum*).[177] A man suspecting that his property had been asported to another's house was permitted to search for it, but only upon seeking entry dressed only in a loin-cloth (*licium*), and carrying a plate. The origins of the requirement of a loin cloth are thought to predate the separation of the Indo-Germanic, and most probably have a common sense rationale of minimizing the potential that the accuser would contrive to hide goods beneath his clothes and later claim that they had been found in the accused's home. No similar explanation of the requirement of the plate is apparent.[178]

Other provisions reflective of the slaveholding era are not of central sig-

---

[176]  *Id.*

[177]  *Id.*

[178]  H. F. JOLOWICZ, HISTORICAL INTRODUCTION TO ROMAN LAW, in THE ROMAN LAW READER, *supra* at 147.

nificance to this treatment but nevertheless worthy of mention as an early example of a commitment that the substance of the law be favored over its formal requisites if such an approach was necessary to the imposition of justice. One delict that occurred with sufficient frequency as to prompt its inclusion in the Institutes was the third-party's seduction of another's slave to steal from its master for the benefit of the third party. In order to catch the perpetrator, the law permitted the master to carry out what would today be termed a "'sting" operation, in which the slave would take some goods to the wrongdoer to permit the completion of the wrong. While some jurists were uncertain if the action for theft by stealth (*action furti*) or action for corruption of a slave (*actio servi corrupti*) could be brought, as the owner had consented to the movement of the goods, and the slave had not in fact succumbed to corruption, Justinian disagreed that "such subtlety" should preclude the bringing of both actions.[179]

## 2. PERSONAL ACTIONS

Gaius, in his Fourth Commentary to his Institutes of Roman Law, differentiated personal actions from real actions. A "personal action" was "an action which seeks to enforce an obligation imposed on the defendant by his contract or delict", with delict, for the purposes of the Commentary, confined to contracts, transfers of property, or promises of performance. It is in his description of "real" actions that we find the description of modern delict, with a strong emphasis on the torts that today fall into the categories of nuisance and trespass. A "real" action was "an action by which one claims as one's own in the *intentio* some corporeal thing or some particular right in the thing, as a right of use or usafruct of a thing belonging to a neighbor, or the right of a horse's way, of carriageway through his land, of raising one's house above a certain height, or having the prospect of one's windows unobstructed; or, when the opposite party (that is the owner) brings the negative action, asserting that there is no such right in the thing."[180]

---

[179]  HUNTER, *supra* at 142.

[180]  GAIUS, THE INSTITUTES OF ROMAN LAW, Fourth Commentary par. 3 in SMITH & WEISSTUB, *supra* 353, from THE INSTITUTES OF ROMAN LAW BY GAIUS 442- 443

## 3. DEFENSE OF PERSON AND PROPERTY

A man was not free to defend his property with the same freedom as obtained in defending his person. An occupant of property could resist a burglar with non-lethal force. However, in what seems to be an equivalent of a modern (if not universal) rule, one discovering a burglar could not kill him unless he was unable to escape from peril without endangering himself.[181]

# IV CONCLUSION

As is true of tort law today is equivalently true of Græco-Roman law of delict, tort law has always represented a society's revealed truth as to its better self, and further to so doing, has identified the behaviors it wishes to encourage and the behaviors it wishes to discourage. The conclusion is inescapable that no organizing principle will be adequate to explain the entirety of the law of delict, and this is true of tort law today as it is of Græco-Roman Law. As expressed by Gerald W. Postema, "[T]ort practice appears to be too heterogenous to submit easily to the strictures of any single valued explanatory theory. Some part of the tort balloon seems to pop out, regardless of the shape of the explanatory box we construct."[182]

This Chapter has focused upon Western law, and more specifically upon the markers, some clear and some vague, within the experience of the ancient Greeks and the ancient Romans that informed our modern law of civil remedies for harm. More so with the Greek experience than with the Roman, the progress has not been invariably smooth. But in a Hegelian sense, progress it has nonetheless been. From the practices countenanced by the ancients, which focused upon kinship rights, retribution and vengeance, and which counte-

---

(E. Post Transl. 1925) (J.A.C. Thomas transl. 1975).

[181]  HUNTER, *supra* at 140.

[182]  *Introduction*, PHILOSOPHY AND THE LAW OF TORTS 15 (Gerald W. Postema, ed.) (Cambridge, 2001).

nanced self help as the primary remedy for wrongs, by the time of the *Corpus Juris Civilis* Western law had made a permanent commitment to peaceable resolution of disputes, often before juries, and the adoption of rectificatory justice in place of criminal or quasi-criminal proceedings for all but the most aggravated offenses.

In terms of civil justice generally, the Greeks and the Romans identified and effectuated protections in a sprawling array of delicts that would inform all of later Western law. For personal physical injury, a nonexclusive recitation would include intentional and unintentional battery, maiming, wrongful death, and defenses, if limited, including accident and mistake among them. For damage to personal property, causes of action were permitted for harms ranging from the killing or injury of animals to the converion of personal items. Fraud or deceit were penalized to the extent that such actions might induce an unfair sale of property or an unjust legal defense, among other potential distortions of justice. Personal dignitary wrongs from defamation to turning a citizen away from a public bath were prohibited, while there existed seemingly no cultural expectation that a "love balm" cause of action would be recognized. Limited powers of equity permitted the Praetor, even if by obvious contrivance, to avoid imposition or denial of legal remedies that offended the community sense of fairness. And the entirety of ancient Geek and ancient Roman law moved definably towards the remedies of compensatory justice over violent retribution.

Contemplating the respective contributions to modern Western law of the Greeks and the Romans of the eras under discussion, some have suggested that elegance and erudition of the Greeks represent juridical contributions that surpass those of the Romans. Those so proposing point to the lasting philosophical contributions of the Hellenist period, the philosophers' employment of dialectical and negative pregnant reasoning, and their appreciation that ethics should stand on an equivalence with law. The Greeks developed and conveyed ethics, the norms that might or might not eventually find there way into law, but which even if remaining simple ethics, obligated the adherent to examine individual questions of conscience and morality. Their great thinkers advanced philosophy and the engines of dialectical reasoning that power it. It would be Grecian ethics, philosophy and reasoning together that permitted the receptivity to re-analysis and to ongoing change that has preserved the intellectual importance of the ancient Hellenist period. What did the Romans bring to the table, the *quare* concludes, other than organization and systematization?

For the Greeks, at least from a philosophical and not necessarily a statutory perspective, the objective of the law giver was to give direction to people, which is to say, to identify the "right" objectives of desire and the most worthy objectives of man and society. In contrast, for the Romans, from the time of the TWELVE TABLES through and including that of Justinian, and even at the intellectual level of their Jurisconsuls, the premium was placed not upon theistic canon, the science of law, or intellectual education, but rather upon the written recitation of and organized body of law, suitable to its time.

By the close of the reign of Justinian I these advancements, among others, could be counted: (1) the adoption of money damages as the dominant remedy in resolving civil disputes; (2) the identification of instances in which strict liability for the consequences of one's actions might not apply, such as in the instance of action not voluntarily taken or taken without culpa; (3) the codification of numerous beneficial interests in land or its enjoyment, and the normalization of means for protecting them, including introduction of the preference for *ex ante* resolution of prospective disputes between neighboring landowners; (4) transparency in decision making, by dint of requiring successive Praetors to pronounce the law they would apply and to forgo application of any other; and (5), notwithstanding the noted limitation on the power of the Praetor, recognition that in instances where the application of a legal remedy, or the absence of one, would work a manifest unfairness, the implicit vesting in the Praetor not to defy the law but rather to find a means why the law should be inapplicable.[183]

Particularly taking into account their tradition-bound endeavors at codification, and that most of their leading philosopher's plied their ideas beyond the centers of political or judicial power, the Greek legal legacy was not so visionary as some might suppose, or at least have hoped. Nor for that matter

---

[183] WILLIAM A. HUNTER, *supra* at 6, 7.

were the Roman contributions so symbolic of stasis as some have claimed. Neither the Grecian nor the Roman contributions would, standing alone, provide the foundational support for later Western law that together they represent, and comparing the Greek contribution with that of the Roman is really nothing more than an intellectual diversion. In truth the two civilizations, and their respective comparisons, are *sui generis*, an no more suited to comparison than apples and oranges. It is unquestionably true that the ancient Romans never elevated issues of ethic, philosophy or self-challenging jurisprudence that might have been hoped for in the one thousand years between the TWELVE TABLES and the publication of the *Corpus Juris Civilis*. The Romans did produce, however, what the Greeks could never have, and it was this: A one thousand-year written, closely examined and regularly revisited experiment in a rule of law by civil and criminal code. In many ways picking up where the custom-bound endeavors of Greece's Draco and Solon left off, the Romans solidified the *terra firma* of Western law.

# CHAPTER 3

# PATHS OF WESTERN LAW
# AFTER JUSTINIAN

## INTRODUCTION

Preparation of the Code of Justinian, one part of a three-part presentation of Roman law published over the three-year period from 533-535 A.D., had not been stymied by the occupation of Rome by the Rugians and the Ostrogoths. In most ways these occupations worked no material hardship on the empire, either militarily or civilly. The occupying Goths and their Roman counterparts developed symbiotic legal and social relationships with the intruders, and in several instances, the new Germanic rulers sought and received approval of their rule both from the Western Empire, seated in Constantinople, and the Pope. Rugian Odoacer and Ostrogoth Theodoric each, in fact, claimed respect for Roman law, and the latter ruler held the Roman title *patricius et magister militum*. In sum, the Rugians and the Ostrogoths were content to absorb much of Roman law, and to work only such modifications as were propitious in the light of centuries of Gothic customary law.

By the middle of the Sixth Century A.D., Justinian I, Emperor of Rome's Eastern Empire, had completed the three-part *Corpus Juris Civilis.*[1]  The parts themselves, described more fully below, are referred to generally as the Code,

---

[1]   Naturally, the work itself was that of dozens of scholars and jurists of the day.

the Digests (or *Pandects*), and the Institutes. To Justinian, this classification, re-codification and modernization of Roman law was part of an over-all plan to militarily re-unite the Eastern Empire with the vestiges of the Western Empire, and to have his great legal work regulate the entire Empire. As it would happen, the legacy of Justinian would be the influence of the *Corpus Juris Civilis*. His military leadership was often ill-advised. He would preside a short period over a unified Empire, but upon his death the unified Empire soon fell apart, in a condition of social dislocation and poverty that was worse for Justinian's military efforts.[2]

With military control of Italy, Gaul, Iberia and Northern Africa in continuing ferment, it is understandable that the Roman law of Justinian I was not seamlessly conveyed to its recipients. Indeed, of the *Corpus Juris Civilis*, only the shortest of its three parts, the Code, enjoyed continuous use, if not application, after the fall of the Western Empire towards the end of the Sixth Century.[3] After the Western Empire was finally separated from the Eastern Empire, and even in the monarchies in which Roman law would have its most pronounced effect, the integrally important Institutes and the Digests (or *Pandects*) were lost or simply ignored until their reintroduction in the mid-Twelfth Century.

Following Justinian, in no nation-state or territory, even within the Italian peninsula, did Roman law endure as the principal source of law. Even before the final Germanic usurpation of the Western Empire, by means of force or assimilation, the Frankish, Ostrogothic and Visigothic populations with the greatest contact with the Roman Empire, as occupiers or commercial partners, had already blended their own and respective customary law with some of the structure, and some of the substance, of Roman law. This process continued throughout the Early Medieval era.[4] Following the epoch of Justinian, and upon the establishment of the great Italian university in Bologna and the renewed training of glossators and scholars to study and disseminate Roman

---

[2] Both Justinian's military and short term civil successes were undeniable success. However, only 17 years after he reunited Rome, it would fall again.

[3] Munroe Smith, The Development of European Law 80 (Columbia Univ.) (1928).

[4] In England, independently of earlier Roman rule and prior to the later Norman invasion, there had been established both a recognized customary law and early generations of courts empowered to advance it as a distinctly English common law.

Law, scholars and students would return to their countries of origin to teach Roman law. Nevertheless, the legal and political influence of Roman law would never resemble what it might have had its preservation and dissemination not been so hybridized, necessarily, by its contact with and adaptation to the customary law of the recipient states.

The results of these many marriages between Roman Law and the customary law and culture of the Goths, and the incremental changes in both sources wrought thereby, are identifiable today in the laws of common law nations and civil code nations alike. Three pronounced examples of Germanic law, those of the Lombards, the Burgundians, and the Salian Franks, are the subject of this section.

# II. THE FALL OF THE WESTERN EMPIRE, THE RUGIANS AND THE OSTROGOTHS

Before his imperial government could turn his attention finally to the publication and implementation of the *Corpus Juris Civilis,*[5] Emperor Justinian I had first to wrest control of Italy from the Ostrogoths of Theodoric (493-526 A.D.), his Rugian predecessor Odoacer (476 – 91 (A.D.), and also the Franks from Gaul, the Visigoths from Spain, and the Vandals of Northern Africa. Justinian's appetites to reunify the Eastern and Western Empires were whetted.

---

[5]  The *Corpus Juris Civilis* comprised three parts. The first part, the Code of Justinian, was intended as a succinct manual for study by lawyers, jurists and students of law. The Institutes of Justinian were the second part, a (if this can be imagined) twenty-volume distillation of literally thousands of volumes interpreting, codifying and analyzing Roman law since the time of the Twelve Tables, quite a millennium before. The third part was the Digests, or *Pandects*, which were the works of Rome's most celebrated jurists. The Digests did not represent commentary on the compilation of the Code or the Institutes, as some of the work of these jurist preceded the *Corpus Juris Civilis* by hundreds of years. Yet they represented sources to which the legal and the legislative communities had long turned, and it was Justinian's goal that they continue to be available for this function.

He reinvaded Italy in 534 A.D., and after divers foreign campaigns administered from Constantinople, in August, 554 A.D. Justinian proclaimed the reinstitution of Roman rule over the Western Empire.

However, the retaking of Italy, together with warfare against the Vandals in north Africa and the Visigoths in Spain, left the Empire generally enfeebled. Italy itself was probably in worse condition than it had been under Odoacer and Theodoric. Justinian's restored rule lasted only fourteen years. He died in 565 A.D. and by 568 A.D. Lombards again occupied large areas of Italy, and within decades their occupation was practically completed.[6]

In broad strokes, the aftermath of the Germanic invasions of Roman territory resulted in the creation of three states or "empires." The Ostrogoths ruled northern Italy, the Danubian territories and southeastern Gaul (or modern France). The Visigoths ruled southwestern Gaul and Spain. In these territories much of Visigothic law would merge with Roman law, with consequences that lasted through the later Islamic conquests and had a pronounced influence on later Spanish law. The third empire was that of the Franks. This encompassed of Italy and Spain, as well as, roughly speaking, modern Austria, Germany, Belgium and Holland.[7]

These Germanic intrusions, some peaceable but others not, are attributable to two primary imperatives: (1) the coming, for these groups, of the agricultural age, and the consequent need for arable farmland; or, or coincident with, (2) pressure upon these groups by the military advances from the East of other invaders, such as the Huns. In time, unable to turn back the encroachments, the Empire adopted such accommodations as it could with the Germanic groups. These agreements gave the newcomers permission to enter the Roman territory in peace, as *foerderati*, and to secure not only the relative safety they needed but also land for livestock and crops. And they gave to the Romans what they most needed and were increasingly unable to provide for themselves: security against other threats of invasion by more avaricious and violent tribes.

---

[6] THE LOMBARD LAWS ix (Katherine Fischer Drew, trans.) (U. Pa. Press.1973).

[7] *See generally* MUNROE SMITH, THE DEVELOPMENT OF EUROPEAN LAW xix (Columbia Univ.)(1928).

The Roman landholders were not out and out displaced, but instead adopted a general protocol for sharing their land with their Germanic neighbors. The nuances and operation of these agreements are unimportant for present purposes. One rationale underpinning this arrangement is that this new arrangement of host and guest between the Roman and the Goth was suited to the circumstances of the time, as the Goth might be called upon to join in the defense of the territory, and in his absence, the Roman could ensure that the farm would be attended to.

For only a short period of time, perhaps 460 to 530 A.D., did all of Italy function as an independent state. Nonetheless, even with the changes in capitals, relations of the crowns with the church, and cultural departures from *Pax Romana*, the peninsula remained in important ways the same state.[8] The most conspicuous vestiges of Roman rule would not be swept away until the Tenth Century.

The Goths comprised Germanic groups who in the earliest of ancient times had settled between the Elbe and the Vistula. They were pagan. In the early Christian era of the Roman Empire, they alternatively invaded or settled in today's Italy, and in Gaul, today's France and also parts of Northern Italy. As an entirety, they are often described as barbarians, which in its colloquial sense means violent, rapacious, and lacking in social refinement.[9] And it is true that the Germanic tribes of this epoch were in a state of transition from warrior societies to agricultural ones, and that some succeeded in this transition more rapidly than others. But it would be wrong to persist in an image of the Goths as a primitive and unruly lot preternaturally indisposed to cultural and legal advancement. The term "barbarian," after all, was never a characterization of the behaviors of the Germanic tribes, but rather was a simple description that they wore beards, or *barbas* in Latin.[10] Also, as the description of their law codes or compilations will reveal, the various Germanic groups were quite politically

---

[8] CHRIS WICKHAM, EARLY MEDIEVAL ITALY: CENTRAL POWER AND LOCAL SOCIETY 400-1000 (Barnes & Noble 1981).

[9] The second definition of "barbarian" contained in WEBSTER'S THIRD NEW INTERNATIONAL DICTIONARY (Merriam Webster 1993) is "marked by a tendency toward brutality, violence or lawlessness[.]"

[10] *Id.*, for definition of "barbs" or "barben" as the clipping of wool or the shaving of a beard.

self-aware. They were deft in their recognition that their rule of the kingdoms within the deteriorating, and then former, Western Empire, required a melding of Gothic customary law with the Roman law of their Roman subjects. This objective was accomplished by two principal means. Some of the Gothic rulers created two parallel statute books, one to be applied to the Germanic tribes and one, that would track imperfectly the laws of Justinian, applicable to the former Roman subjects. A second means was to create a unitary, hybrid body of law that combined a written recitation of Gothic customary law within which were woven precepts, for the most part progressive, of Roman law.

In general, unwritten customary law has always been a retardant to change. In contrast, written codes can be, and often were, modified to conform more closely to cultural expectations.[11] Thus the very rendering of Gothic customary law into written codes or constitutions was an advancement onto itself, and had resulted from the increased contact by each and all Germanic tribes with the written tradition of the Romans. After the death of Theodosius in 395 A.D., the Emperor ceased to lead the army. In the Fourth and the Fifth Centuries the civil government, represented by the Senate, was under the constant cloud of uncertainty concerning the army's commitment to civil rule. There followed Emperors such as Majorian (457-61 A.D.), but the true picture of the condition of the Western Empire was measured in the successes of military leaders such as Aetius (429-54 A.D.) and Ricimer (456-72 A.D.). Aetius was assassinated in 454, but not before continuing the Roman sphere of influence in Gaul, and more importantly, turning back barbarian invaders of the Empire.[12] The relationship between Gaul and Italy grew evermore tenuous.[13]

---

[11]  In the words of one scholar: "[T]he sanctity and inviobility of tribal custom remained fixed only as long as it was unwritten." LAWS OF THE SALIAN AND RIPUARIAN FRANKS 1 (Theodore John Rivers, transl.) (AMS 1986). The laws of the Franks are discussed specifically below.

As to Britain, only in the past century did there become available a fairly full record of the Anglo-Norman study of Roman law. The principal source would be the *Liber Pauperum* of Vicarius, together with Accursius's Gloss (*Glossa Ordinaria*).

[12]  Aetius enlisted mercenary Huns to turn back the Visigoths and Gothic allies to turn back the Huns. *See generally* CHRIS WICKHAM, EARLY MEDIEVAL ITALY: CENTRAL POWER AND LEGAL SOCIETY 400-1000 19 (Macmillan 1981).

[13]  Emperor Avitus (433-6 A.D.), formerly a Gallic senator and a transparent proponent

The Western Empire's slide into dissolution was accelerated by the army's revolt over pay, which brought Odoacer to the throne in 476 A.D. He elected to sit at Ravenna rather than Rome. At this period in time the Vandals controlled most of Northern Africa, and even Sicily, although Odaecer succeeded in recovering that island by treaty.

Following Recimer's brief ascension's to the leadership of Italy, serving as *patricius*, Odoacer, having declined the Eastern Empire's offer that he become Emperor of the West, instead became King in 476 A.D. There followed fourteen years of relative peace. Then, without dissent from Eastern Emperor Zeno, Theodoric's Ostrogoths invaded Italy and overthrew Odoacer, who was murdered in 493 A.D.,[14] which would end with the 489 A.D. invasion of the Ostrogoths under Theodoric. Although a barbarian and an Arian (a sect of Christianity rejected by the Pope), the northern bishoprics thought it prudential to place their support behind Theodoric. After four years of war, the Goths took Ravenna and Odoacer was slain in 493 A.D.[15]

The law that might have been available to the Germans in these early years would have been Theodoric's 508 *Edictum Theodorici*, the Ostrogoth's abbreviated law code intended for his Roman and Gothic subjects alike. The fall of that kingdom in 554 effectively extinguished the opportunity for Theodoric's code to enjoy any enduring influence.

Theodoric's success lay in part in his receiving recognition from the Eastern Empire, and his fall followed soon after that recognition was withdrawn in 535 A.D. in anticipation of Justinian's quest to reunify the Empire. However finite in time as was Theodoric's rule, its influence was due to his acumen in recognizing the need to maintain support within the Senate, seated in Constantinople, although the Senate was divided between anti-Gothic and pro-Gothic sentiment. The Senate itself continued its slide into ineffectuality, with

of an expanded role for that region, had his short reign ended after the defeat of part of the Gallic army at the hands of an Italian force under the leadership of Recimir. CHRIS WICKHAM, EARLY MEDIEVAL ITALY: CENTRAL POWER AND LEGAL SOCIETY 400-1000 20 (Macmillan 1981).

[14] GIBBON'S THE DECLINE AND FALL OF THE ROMAN EMPIRE 531 (D.M. Low, abridgement) (Chatto and Windus 1960).

[15] DECLINE AND FALL, at *id.*

little legislative activity of consequence, and even major public works projects, such as restoring the Coliseum, were carried out by the Church or the kings (in the case of the Coliseum, by Theodoric). Much of Italy was devastated by the Gothic wars, and Justinian's triumph would be limited, both in time and in effect. As to the latter, a Brecian landowner, Staviles, is quoted as stating that he "live[d] the law of the Goths."[16]

What followed was a drama of grand geo-political scope by any measure, past or present. Theodoric was succeeded by his grandson, Althalaric, and his regent, his mother Alalasuntha, was de facto ruler. Upon Althalaric's death, Amalasuntha married her cousin, Theodahad, who had her killed. At this, the Eastern Empire's Justinian declared war, inaugurating the Gothic Wars that would last nearly twenty years (535-554 A.D.).

Prior to its hybridization by contact with Roman law, ancient Germanic law was already imbued with markedly different themes. With allowances for variations between the different Gothic groupings, Germanic law typically included judicial and quasi-judicial practices that tolerated, or even contemplated, blood feud, with or without the alternative of compensation. This admixture has been described as one that "intermingle[ed] vengeance, compensation, and kinship liability [.]"[17] Due in substantial measure to the inopportunity of Germanic occupation, it is unsurprising that Justinian's work was not as immediately influential as it would surely have been had it been presented and disseminated in a stable empire. Only in the late Eleventh Century and early Twelfth Centuries would the full texts and interpretations (the *Pandects* and the Institutes) of Justinian be "found," and reemerge as a basis for civil code scholarship and application. During this interval of up to Five Centuries, however, the law of the territories within the old Western Empire had not remained in static expectancy of the return of Roman law. Rather, the formerly western Roman realms, now under Gothic rule, had developed their own bodies of law, relying principally upon tradition, customary law and politic obeisance to Roman law.

---

[16] Early Medieval Italy, *supra*.

[17] Alexander C. Murray, Germanic Kinship Structure 135 (Pontifical Institute of Medieval Studies 1983).

As suggested, for a substantial period of time before the fall, or disintegration, of the Western Empire, Rome had in fact relied for its protection and conquest upon armies within which fought a large number of barbarians. As to the latter, many Lombards served Justinian in war with Persia. In the former role, that of protection, during the Fourth Century, Germans assimilated into under-populated areas, aided by a practice in which Roman hosts would share land with barbarians. The efforts of the latter would then turn to both agriculture and defense. Germanic pressure for land made this consensual arrangement unstable, and eventually, with the approval of the Romans, the Visigoths settled in Gaul, and later into Spain. After the risks posed by the advances of the Huns from Asia, the Eastern Empire countenanced Ostrogothic settlements in Italy. Further crossings of the Rhine were accomplished by the Vandals, who settled in northern Africa, the Burgundians, who settled in southeastern Gaul, and the Franks, initially in northeastern and eventually in all of Gaul. At and during these times the Anglo-Saxons wrested control of Britain from the Romans.[18]

According to one historian, the Western Empire had ceased to exist even before the re- conquests of Justinian, and places the date at approximately 500 A.D. Even before this time, J.M. Roberts writes, the Western Empire could not feed itself without importations from Northern Africa and certain Mediterranean islands. In 476 A.D. Odoacer supplanted the last Western emperor, and Italy became, as the other western territories had or would become, functionally independent, although formally part of an Empire ruled from Constantinople. By 500 A.D., the increasingly unwieldy state apparatus, no longer able to govern efficiently its far flung empire, had simply "seized up" or collapsed of its own weight.[19]

Much of primitive law never fully escaped the pull of kinship groups.[20] It

---

[18] THE LOMBARD LAWS 4, 5 (Katherine Fischer Drew, trans.)(U. Pa. Press.1973). Justinian was able to reverse some but not all of these depredations, with victory over the Vandals in Africa, the overthrow of the Ostrogoths in Italy, and limited successes in Gaul.

[19] J.M. ROBERTS, THE NEW HISTORY OF THE WORLD 290, 293 (Oxford 2003).

[20] See generally M. Stuart Madden, The Cultural Evolution of Tort Law, 37 ARIZ. ST. L.J. 831 (2005).

can even be stated that Graeco-Roman law, from the *Grecian Code of Solon* through and including the laws of Justinian, remained snared in matters of family, because the wrongs of noble families were far fewer than those of ordinary birth, much less those of slaves. Also the remedies the nobility might seek when wronged were characteristically greater than those that might be obtained by those of lower birth. Still and all, the tendency of Graeco-Roman law for harm was an ever-increasing distancing from rules that tied the very definition of the harm as not being solely to the injured party, but also to the family, with the consequence that the family was both permitted to and expected to vindicate it.

The focus of this section is upon the paths of Roman law as it became administered by the new Gothic masters of former Roman territories. To create a context for these subjects, we must first visit briefly the status of Roman law as it was imposed by Justonian I upon the reunification, however short-lived, of the Eastern and the Western Roman Empire. After a final visitation with the body of law prepared at the direction of Justinian I, and to the extent that written recordation makes it now possible it, the article will turn to the mixture of Roman and Germanic law enforced by three major Gothic kingdoms: the Burgundians, the Lombards, and the Salacian Franks.

## III. THE LIMITED SURVIVAL OF THE LAW OF JUSTINIAN

The first part of the *Corpus Juris Civilis* prepared under the auspices of Justinian was the Code, and was intended as a succinct manual for study by lawyers, jurists and students of law. The Institutes of Justinian comprised the second part, and were a reduction and modernization into twenty volumes of the literally thousands of volumes interpreting, codifying and analyzing Roman law since the time of the Twelve Tables, quite a millennium before. The third part was the Digests, or *Pandects*, which were the works Rome's most celebrated jurists.

The *Pandects* did not represent a contemporaneous commentary on the compilations of Justinian. Indeed, some of the work of these jurists preceded the Code and the Institutes by hundreds of years. Yet as the work of revered jurists charged in their own time with interpretation of the evolving Roman law, Justinian identified the Digests as a principal and enduring source to which contemporary jurists and lawyers ought turn in understanding and interpreting the *Code of Justinian* and the INSTITUTES OF JUSTINIAN. Together, the Code, the Institutes, and the Digests comprised the *Corpus Juris Civilis* of 534 A.D., the compilation, classification and modernization of Roman law was credited with systematizing classic Roman law,[21] and more importantly, with inventing law as a science. It is in the *Corpus Juris Civilis* that scholars now identify that in Roman law "the goal of compensation of damage began to prevail over the goal of punishment and sanction."[22]

For this undertaking Justinian employed the assistance of Tribonian,[23] who thereupon enlisted the help of nine jurists to the task of editing the combined compilations, referenced above, of Gregorian, Hermogenian and Theodosian. This *Code of Justinian* was presented, as had been its predecessor a millennium before, in 12 books or tables. Then Tribonian and seventeen lawyers set about the task of extracting from, rationalizing and modernizing perhaps 2000 treatises, the work of the finest jurists in Roman law. They reduced this body of jurisprudence to approximately fifty books, which would be called the Digests or *Pandects*.

The Institutes and the Digests of the Jurisconsuls urged strongly a natural law orientation of Roman Law. "All peoples who are governed by law and customs use law which is in part particular to themselves, in part common to all men; the law which each people has established for itself is particular to that state and is styled civil, law as being particularly of that state: by what natural reason has established among all men is observed equally by all nations and is designated *ius*

---

[21]  *See generally* M. Stuart Madden, *The Graeco-Roman Antecedents of Modern Tort Law*, BRANDEIS L. REV. 867, 901-03 (2006) (at nn. and accompanying text.)

[22]  Magnus, Ulrich, *Compensation for Personal Injuries in a Comparative Perspective*, 39 WASHBURN L. J. 348-49, (2000).

[23]  For his seemingly unsurpassed mastery of the law, culture and science of this era Tribonian has been described as the Francis Bacon of his day.

*gentium* or the law of nations, being that which all nations obey. Hence the Roman people observe partly their own particular law, partly that which is common to all peoples."[24] Evidencing a similarly full-throated natural law commitment to principles of universal duty applicable to all men, the Third Century jurist Ulpian, quoting Celsus, wrote: "Justice is a fixed and abiding disposition to give every man his rights. The percepts of the law are as follows: to live honorably, to injure no one, to give to every man his own. Jurisprudence is a knowledge of things human and divine, the science of the just and the unjust."[25]

Here follow several representative examples of delictual liability under the Roman law of Justinian:

### Personal Actions, Generally

Committed to the identification of the delineation between "what is "just and what unjust," The INSTITUTES OF JUSTINIAN and other sources of Roman law reflect an endeavor to "give each man his due right," and comprise "precepts" to all Romans "to live justly, not to injure another and to render to each his own."[26] Violation of a "personal action" not sounding in contract is in *delict*.[27]

### Nuisance and Trespass

The Institutes include rules that reveal numerous strictures against the imposition of one's will over the rights of a neighbor, and strong deterrents for the

---

[24] THE INSTITUTES OF JUSTINIAN, BOOK I, TITLE II(*Concerning Natural Law, the Law of Nations, and the Civil Law*) par. 1, in J. C. SMITH, DAVID N. WEISSTUB, *supra* 352, from THE INSTITUTES OF JUSTINIAN 3-5 (J.A.C. Thomas, trans.)(Juta & Co. 1975).

[25] Ulpian, Digest1, 1, 10, quoted in GEORGE SABINE, A HISTORY OF POLITICAL THEORY 163-73 (Holt Rinehart & Winston 1937), in SMITH & WEISSTUB, *id.* at 349.

[26] THE INSTITUTES OF JUSTINIAN BOOK I, Preamble; par. 1; par. 3, in SMITH & WEISSTUB, *supra* 352, from THE INSTITUTES OF JUSTINIAN 84, 85 (J.A.C. Thomas trans., 1975).

[27] GAIUS, THE INSTITUTES OF ROMAN LAW, Fourth Commentary par. 3 in SMITH & WEISSTUB, *supra* note at 353, from THE INSTITUTES OF ROMAN LAW GAIUS 442-443 (E. Post Trans. 1925).(J.A.C. Thomas trans 1975).

disregard thereof. In one notable example, pertaining to what would today be called the law of private nuisance or trespass, a particular provision goes so far as to detail a preference that adjoining landowners bargain in advance for agreement as to contemporaneous uses of land that might trigger dispute. In Book III par. 4, the Institutes provide that one "wishing to create" such a right of usage "should do so by pacts and stipulations."[28] A testator of land may impose such agreements reached upon his heirs, including limitations upon building height, obstruction of light, or introduction of a beam into a common wall, or the construction of a catch for a cistern, an easement of passage, or a right of way to water.[29] To much the same effect, and specifically as to urban estates, is Book III, Title II par. 2 as interpreted by Gaius in his INSTITUTES OF ROMAN LAW,[30] to which Ulpianus, adds a prohibition on the obstruction of a neighbor's view.[31]

*Defense of Person and Property*

A man was not free to defend his property with the same freedom as obtained in defending his person. An occupant of property could resist a burglar with non-lethal force. However, in what seems to be an equivalent of a modern (if not universal) rule, one discovering a burglar could not kill him unless he was unable to escape from peril without endangering himself.[32]

---

[28]  The INSTITUTES OF GAIUS continue: "He can also, by will, charge his heir not to build beyond a given height or not to obstruct the light of the neighbor's premises or to allow the latter to insert a beam into the wall or to accept rain droppings; as also to allow the neighbor a rite of passage over his land or to draw water there." THE INSTITUTES OF JUSTINIAN BOOK III par. 4, in SMITH & WEISSTUB, *supra* note at 358, from THE INSTITUTES OF JUSTINIAN 84, 85 (J.A.C. Thomas trans 1975).

[29]  *Id.*

[30]  GAIUS, ON THE PROVINCIAL EDICT, BOOK VII, THE DIGEST (OR PANDECTS) BOOK VIII Title II par. 2., *id.* at 359.

[31]  Ulpanius, on Sabinus, Book XXIX, *id.* Title II par 3, *id.* at 359.

[32]  HUNTER, *supra* note at 140.

*Emotional Distress*

Just as today an emotional distress component to an award for personal physical injury may amplify the compensatory award received by the victim, so too in Roman law the transgressor might be liable to the victim for greater damages when the wrong took place in circumstances that would worsen the harm or cause its degradation. Thus at the penalty phase, a penalty would be made greater if the *injuria* occurred in a public place. The same aggravation of penalty might accompany a battery in which a man is beaten with sticks, or scourged, or when parents are beaten by their children, or a patron struck by a freedman, or where the injury is to a particularly valuable part of the body, such as the eye.[33]

*Theft*

Originally, Roman law treated theft as delictual, or a civil wrong, with accompanying penalties, as referenced below. Only later would theft be catalogued as criminal. Thus for the purposes of the present description, theft can be compared to the various later common law delicts of conversion, trover *di bonis asportatis*, etc.

Other provisions reflective of the slaveholding era are not of central significance to this treatment but nevertheless worthy of mention as an early example of a commitment that the substance of the law be favored over its formal requisites if such an approach was necessary to the imposition of justice. One delict that occurred with sufficient frequency as to prompt its inclusion in the Institutes was the third-party's seduction of another's slave to steal from its master for the benefit of the third party. In order to catch the perpetrator, the law permitted the master to carry out what would today be termed a "'sting" operation, in which the slave would take some goods to the wrongdoer to permit the completion of the wrong. While some jurists were uncertain if the action for theft by stealth (*action furti*) or action for corruption of a slave (*actio servi corrupti*) could be brought, as the owner had consented to the movement of the goods, and the slave had not in fact succumbed to

---

[33] Hunter, *supra* note at 140-41.

corruption, Justinian disagreed that "such subtlety" should preclude the bringing of both actions.[34]


*Wrongs to Moveable Property*

Roman law regarding injury to property was sufficiently supple to recognize variations of injury. The actor could interfere with property by two means: deprive the owner of possession by (a) stealth (*furtum*), or (b) by violence (*vi bona rapta*). The wrongdoer might also interfere with the occupier's rights without dispossessing him of the property by damaging the property or otherwise impairing its usefulness (*damnum injuria datum*).[35]

A man suspecting that his property had been asported to another's house was permitted to search for it, but only upon seeking entry dressed only in a loincloth (*licium*), and carrying a plate. The origins of the requirement of a loin cloth are thought to predate the separation of the Indo-Germanic, and most probably have a common sense rationale of minimizing the potential that the accuser would contrive to hide goods beneath his clothes and later claim that they had been found in the accused's home. No similar explanation of the requirement of the plate is apparent.[36]


*Injuries to Slaves*

Slaves *qua* slaves had no redress in *injuria*. Indeed, masters were permitted to flog their own slaves. Conceptually, the slave was not a being in any entire sense, but instead a unit of labor that could lose value if mistreated. However, if another were to injure a master's slaves, the action in *injuria* was deemed to devolve to the master, as an action in insult, irrespective of whether the actor intended any insult. This would be so even when no severe injury was involved. Should the slave's injury be severe, the Praetor could grant to the master an

---

[34]  HUNTER, *supra* note at 142.

[35]  *Id.*

[36]  H. F. JOLOWICZ, HISTORICAL INTRODUCTION TO ROMAN LAW in THE ROMAN LAW READER, *supra* 147.

action in *injuria*.[37] The imputation to the master of an injury suffered by a slave has been described as a progenitor to the later law of agency. The reasoning given is that under Roman law the slave had no legal standing, and in a juridical sense was absorbed into his master's family, and represented before the law by his master. In later eras of freed men or freed servants, it would be a substantial but measured step to visualize the free servant as enjoying a relation to the master (employer) similar to that of the ancient slave to his master.

The final step to this analysis is the identification of circumstances, be they broad or narrow, in which the actions of the servant are treated in a legal sense as the actions of the master.[38] If a wrongful injury was inflicted upon a child (persons under *potestas*), the remedy in *injuria* would lay in the father (*paterfamilias*), who could bring an action both on his behalf and on behalf of his child.[39] From what appears, this approach partakes at least in half measure of that taken for injuries to slaves, with the damage to the father being essentially an insult and/or lost services.

Following the fall of the Western Empire, the full three parts of the *Corpus Juris Civilis* simply disappeared from usage. Where apparent at all, only the Institutes and partial versions of the Code were available for study in the middle ages. Only in the first parts of the Twelfth Century would the resource in a largely entire form regain prominence, and this through the fortuitous discovery of a Sixth Century manuscript of the Digest, examined at Amalfi, then Pisa and Florence, and that became the basis for the study of Roman law at Bologna, the new and international center for political and legal study.[40] The work there performed with Roman law in the Twelfth Century and thereafter is the subject for another examinatino.

---

[37] Hunter, at 141.

[38] In Holmes' words: "This is the progress of ideas as shown us by history; and this is what is meant by saying that the characteristic feature which justifies agency as a title of the law is the absorption *pro hac vice* of the agent's legal individuality in that of his principal." Oliver Wendell Holmes, The Common Law (1880).

[39] *Id.*

[40] *See generally* Francis de Zulueta, Peter Stein, The Teaching of roman law in England around 1200 1 (Selden Society 2000).

# IV. THE BURGUNDIAN CODE (LEX GONDOBADA)

Prior to the hybridization of Germanic law occasioned by its contact with Roman law, blood feud had enjoyed centuries of observance among Gothic groups. In the customary law of Germanic tribes the victim's kinship group would be permitted to wreak retribution upon the slayer himself or his family. A remedy that might today seem unruly at best was simply a norm that was considered just, and not unduly disruptive of the community. The movement towards a *wergeld*[41] approach could naturally be seen as consistent with new Germanic kingdoms within contained domains, and with the stronger central authority appurtenant, predictably, thereto.[42]

The stronger the central authority, the logic continues, the more likely it is that the monarch and his constituents will come to consider pursuit of justice through blood feud to be, in the view of the king, a disturbance of the king's peace, a concept that would later underlay the doctrines of public nuisance and trespass *vi et armis*. For the society, now settled for the first time into stable agricultural and economic matrices, the blood feud resolution of murder or manslaughter would, logically, become increasingly unpopular. The rules for compensation, whether tied to lost life or to any other catalogued wrongdoing,

---

[41] *Wergeld* represented the value of a person's life, reduced to a money amount. The composition for an innocent or negligent homicide, or often even an intentional homicide, was the payment of the *wergeld* to the victim's family. Each of the Gothic codes examined here adopted a form of *wergeld* or *wergild*.

[42] The slave was unaccounted for in the calculation of *wergeld*, the early unwritten forms of Germanic customary law or the later hybridized and written versions. *See, e.g.*, MUNROE SMITH, THE DEVELOPMENT OF EUROPEAN LAW 12 (Columbia 1928):

"The slave…is a thing, not a person. In the earliest Germanic law he is constantly compared to an animal. If he is killed, no wergeld is paid to his master, but damages based on value, as in the case of animals. The master has the power of life and death over the slave. The slave acquires not for himself but for his master."

To Smith's account I would only add that in cases of *liability* for what a slave has done, the approach was one of two: either the master would be required to pay composition for the slave's acts, or the slave, who would have no money, would be physically punished.

were quantified in *soladi*, the value of which was measured in grains of gold.[43] Both before and after the widespread adoption of compensatory resolution of conflicts, responsibility or innocence for a wrong would be determined by oath taking. Fact witnesses had no opportunity to testify for or against a party. The claimant and the accused were both given an opportunity to state the basis for their claim or defense to the magistrate. Upon so doing, the respective parties would bring before the court oath takers. Under the *Burgundian Code* the requisite number was 12, and they could include relatives. What was sought from the oath takers was not an attestation as to what had occurred, but rather an affirmation as to the integrity and the honesty of the person on whose behalf they appeared.[44]

In or about 406 A.D., the approximate time of the Vandal invasion of Roman territory around the Rhine, the Burgundians too took arms against northern Germany. There they ruled from 413 to 436 A.D., when they were overrun by the Huns. But as would happen in many instances of Roman co-option of former enemies, by 443 A.D. the Romans granted to the Burgundians of certain territory in Savoy, between Lake Geneva, the Rhone and the Alps.[45] This Roman grant was in return for the Burgundian's assistance in safeguarding the Western Empire against Germanic and other groups deemed a greater risk to the Empire.

Provision of land to the Burgundians followed the logic and practice of *hospitalitas* between host and guest as mentioned above, as was the approach taken generally with other Germanic populations, including the Lombards. Land was allotted pursuant to a rule of "hospitality," and provided that the

---

[43] In the time of Constantine, a *solidus* was worth about 120 grains of gold. THE BURGUNDIAN CODE: LIBER CONSTITUTIONUM SIVE LEX GUNDOBADA: CONSTITUTIONES EXTRAVAGANTES 19 n.4 (Katherine Fischer, transl.)(U. Pa. Press 1949).

[44] In contrapuntal distinction to the Burgundian approach, western law would come to reject the relatives of the opposing party as being in any way acceptable on a jury. Even as witnesses, relatives will have their objectivity assailed, and of course testimony as to the general good reputation of a defendant is only permitted after the claimant has placed it in issue. *See also id.* (explaining with specificity the procedures for oath taking).

[45] E. A. THOMPSON, ROMANS AND BARBARIANS: THE DECLINE OF THE WESTERN EMPIRE 23-24 (Wisc. 1982).

land within the affected territory would be parceled out in a ratio of two-thirds to the Burgundian "guests" *(hospes)*, and one third to the Roman "host" *(hospes* as well). The Roman host would in turn keep two-thirds of the slaves, with one-third going to the Burgundian guest.

The logic of this arrangement was that it resolved three principal objectives of the Empire. First, the arrangement slaked, for the time, the Burgundian's thirst for new agricultural land. Second, it brought, and literally bought, a peaceable cessation of combat with the Burgundians. Third, insofar as the new role of the Burgundians was to aid Rome in the protection of the Western Empire, they could be expected periodically to be called to arms. In their absences, with the Roman host still *in situ*, the farms and livestock would not go unattended. This arrangement of hospitality with the Burgundians would typify accords that were similar, in both form and function, to Rome's relation with other Germanic groups.[46]

To the increasingly powerful Franks the Burgundian lands seemed a delectable prize, and they sought it by force of arms. The Salian Franks attacked the Burgundians in 500 A.D., but were unable to prevail. Not long thereafter, and as further to the reality that the concept of allies and enemies during these times was very fluid, the Salian Franks and the Burgundians joined forces to defeat the Visigoths in 507 A.D.[47]

Now custodians of land that had for centuries been ruled under Roman law, the Burgundians under King Gundobad, who ruled from 474 A.D. to 516 A. D.,[48] apparently thought it politic not to force feed Burgundian customary

---

[46] It bears mentioning that Rome had by this time centuries of experience in the assimilation of persons of other nations. In 212 A.D. it had granted citizenship "to all free subjects of the empire." J. M. ROBERTS, THE NEW HISTORY OF THE WORLD 250 (Oxford 2003).

[47] An excellent resource as to the Visigoths and their social structures is P. D. KING, LAW AND SOCIETY IN THE VISIGOTHIC KINGDOM (Cambridge 1972).

[48] These are the dates ordinarily assigned, although other scholars have differed. *E.g.,* E. A. THOMPSON, ROMANS AND BARBARIANS: THE DECLINE OF THE WESTERN EMPIRE 24 (Wisc. 1982), in which the author puts the dates at *c.* 480 -516 A.D.). The point here is not so much whether a particular royal reign was a few years longer or shorter, but rather that many of the dates contained in such histories are not entirely certain.

law to its Roman citizens. Instead the Burgundian's sought to merge their own customary law with Roman law in a way that would not prove unpalatable to either population. The books containing law applicable to Burgundians in affairs *inter se*, or in matters between Burgundians and Romans, had various names, in large part due to conflicting translations: *Lex Burgundionum; Liber Legum Gundobadi; Lex Gundobada, la Loi Gombette,* and *Gombata.* The laws applicable to Romans in their dealings with other Romans were collected in the book *Lex Romana Burgundionum.* These separate Constitutions (or Codes) were subject over time to numerous revisions during the reign of Gundobad, but it is estimated that in the aggregate they were compiled between 488 and 533 A.D. This approach was consistent with an ever widening practice among Germanic kingdoms to adopt two sets of law: one thought harmonious with the customary law of the new rulers, and the other to be applied to Romans. As to the former, it has been claimed that the laws published under Gundobad's reign relied in many ways to the *Lex Visigothorum,* published in 483 A.D. under Visigoth King Euric.[49]

The description to follow of the Burgundian Codes will reveal numerous similarities with the Roman law of the lands they were now to rule. This can be seen as an astute effort to harmonize the legal and cultural differences between two very distinct peoples. As did other Germanic Codes, the *Burgundian Code* provided that Roman citizens would be judged by Roman law, and ignorance of the law was no defense.[50] A principal Gothic contribution to the *Lex Gundobada* was its continuation of the Germanic customary law concept of *wergeld.*[51] By adopting this approach to resolution of disputes over intentional or innocent murder, payment of *wergeld* was in lieu of other and violent forms of response by the victim's kinship group, in forms such as blood feud. This is not to say that the Burgundians were definitionaly averse to the penalty of a life for a life. Section 1 of the Law of Gundobad provided for the ultimate penalty in cases of intentional murder.[52]

[49] *See generally* THE BURGUNDIAN CODE: LIBER CONSTITUTIONUM SIVE LEX GUNDOBADA: CONSTITUTIONES EXTRAVAGANTES 4 -5, 7 (Katherine Fischer, transl.)(U. Pa. Press 1949)

[50] *lex Gundobada* (First Constitution) Sect. I par. 8. Book of Constitutions par. 8.

[51] For an explanation of *wergeld* or *wergild, see* notes above.

In more general terms, the king's goal in setting forth the *Burgundian Code* is twofold. First, the objectives of the realm sound in the very reasoning that even today underlay a state's assertion of its police power as to matters affecting the health, safety and welfare of citizens. Second, the Code was intended to provide uniform rules of general applicability for administration by courts (*comites*) and the magistrates (*praeepositi*) who will be called upon to render judgment.[53]

### Negligence and Accidental Harm

The *Burgundian Code* assigned a different and lower level of culpability to harm caused by accident or negligence and that caused purposefully. In an example of an injury arguably inflicted by one man upon another, the *Burgundian Code* states that a purely accidental injury imports no liability. The Code uses the example of man with a lance. If a lance has been thrown upon the ground, or left there "without intent to do harm" (*simpliciter*), and "if by accident a man or an animal impales himself thereon," the injury is considered a simple accident and no legal consequences follow. The provision distinguishes a setting in which at the time of the injury the lance is being held by the man "in such a manner that it could cause harm to a man."[54] While the provision does not explicitly so state, there are two reasonable implications of the distinction drawn: (1) the man who is holding the lance at the time of the injury may have a higher level of culpability than does the man who is not in control of the

---

[52] "If anyone presumes with boldness or rashness bent on injury to kill a native free-man,…let him make restitution for the committed crime not otherwise than by the shedding of his own blood." *lex Gundobada* (First Constitution) Sect. II par. 1.

[53] In keeping with the Burgundian inattentiveness to the organization that characterized Justinian's Code, this language is found in a section pertaining to damage caused by animals:

> "This is established for the welfare and peace of all, that a general definition be set forth relevant to each and every case, so that the counts and magistrates of the localities, having been adequately instructed, may understand how matters should be judged."

*lex Gundobada* (First Constitution) Sect. XLIX par. 1.

[54] *lex Gundobada* (First Constitution) Sect. XVIII par. 2.

lance when the injury occur; i.e., he may be seen as being careless, rendering the mishap not attributable to pure accident; and (2) this distinction suggests that there may be some remedy in composition for the man holding the lance in what would be described today as a negligent manner.

Regarding animals, the Code expressly disposes of its "ancient rule of blame." With its specific references to animals, the provision rejects strict liability for injuries caused by one's animals. *lex Gundobada* Section XVIII par. 1. provides that if a horse accidentally kills another horse, or an ox an ox, or a dog, no money damages will be required, and the matter will be settled by having the owner of the animal that attacked the other simply hand the animal over to the owner of the injured animal. Even for the more serious loss of a dog's bite killing a man, no composition at all was required, "because what happens by chance ought not conduce to the loss or discomfiture of man."[55]

### Theft or Conversion Regarding Chattels

Compensation for other delicts, such as trover, would be provided for by replacement in kind of the animal or object stolen. For example, one stealing the little bell (*tintinnum*), and presumably the horse itself, would be required to "return another horse like it; and let like provision be observed concerning a lead ox."[56] Similar to today's distinction between trespass to chattels and conversion,[57] the *lex Gundobada* differentiated between significant disruption of ownership rights and lesser ones that might be characterized as mere intermeddling. If a freeman would ride off on another's horse, but return it within a day, he would be required to pay two *soladi* to the owner. If the interloper kept the horse for more than one day, he would be subject to the more stringent penalties governing the wrongful use of another's horse on journey.[58]

---

[55] *lex Gundobada* (First Constitution) Sect. VIII par. 1, titled "Of Those Things That Happen By Chance."

[56] *lex Gundobada* (First Constitution) Sect. IV par. 3.

[57] *E.g.*, CompuServe v. Cyber Promotions, 962 F. Supp. 1015 (S.D. Ohio 1997).

[58] *See* discussion below.

In some sections, the *Lex Gundobada* might ordain composition with a type of property different than that involved in the theft. For example, a freeman's theft of another's plowshare would warrant composition of "two oxen with yoke and attachments (harness)[.]"[59] This declaration of a remedy in seeming disproportion to the value of the personalty most probably reflects an agricultural community's strong antipathy towards theft of items so central to its means of livelihood.

Separate provision was made for the more serious crime of theft by violence. In a rule applicable to Burgundians and Romans alike, the Code provided that one who by violence took away from its possessor "anything, even a young calf," would be fined the value of the item or animal "ninefold." Introduced here is clearly an extra-compensatory provision that bears similarities to today's punitive damages. The ninefold penalty is nine times that which would be required for the purposes of compensatory justice; fully 8/9 ths of the award is intended to punish the perpetrator; and those throughout the community who learn of such a judgment are certain to consider it a deterrent against pursuing the same or similar conduct. While modest multiples of value were employed frequently throughout the several Gothic codes, a multiple of nine was preserved to serve a different purpose, to impose a more severe extra compensatory penalty and to convey a stronger deterrence message to the community.

Should an attempted theft be associated with a trespass, the rights inuring to the landholder enlarged substantially. The importance of vineyards to the persons of this era is evident in the uncompromising response the *Burgundian Code* took towards thieves who entered a vineyard by night. The owner could kill him without liability.[60] Should the thieves' trespass for the purpose of theft occur during the day, the matter could be remedied by the payment of three *soladi* to the owner and two *soladi* to the crown.[61]

Over centuries and across continents, severe punishment has attended a crime either resulting from a conspiracy or even the conspiracy itself. So too

---

[59] *lex Gundobada* (First Constitution) Sect. XXII par. 9.

[60] *lex Gundobada* (First Constitution) Sect. CIII par.2.

[61] *lex Gundobada* (First Constitution) Sect. CIII par 1.

in the *lex Gondobada*. For example, should a "native freeman and a slave commit a theft together," the freeman was required to pay three times the value of what was stolen, and the slave would be flogged. If, however, it was a "minor theft," *e.g.*, "a pig, a sheep, a goat, or a hive of bees," he would be liable in composition for six *soladi*. Bearing in mind the distinction between the operative words "together" and "with," a different rule applied to the freeman who committed a theft merely accompanied by (or "with") his slave. The freeman would be liable in composition for an amount "threefold" the value of what was stolen, and, it almost goes without saying, the slave would be flogged.[62]

In a most extraordinary provision, the *lex Gondobada* states that a person who steals a hound or a hunting or running dog must "kiss the posterior of that dog in the presence (*in conventu*) of all the people.." We can well imagine that most persons elected an alternative in which he would pay five *soladi* to the owner and a fine of two *soladi* to the state.[63] I will not impose my observations as to the rationale of this rule upon the reader.

### Disturbing the Peace, Battery and Wounds

All violence, even if only threatened, created the threat of disturbing the peace, and stimulated compensatory remedies therefor. Even if no blow was inflicted, one drawing a sword "for striking another" would be fined twelve *soladi* by the crown. If a blow were to fall, the fine to the king would be the same, and the amount of composition to the victim would turn upon the severity of the wound.[64]

In matters of battery the magistrate as fact finder was required only to decide whose version of events was to be believed, and then apply those facts to a schedule of penalties. Thus a person found liable for wounding another would be held responsible in composition depending upon the nature of the injury.

For example, one who would strike a freeman would be liable for a single *solidus* for each blow, plus an additional fine of six *solidi* to the king's treasury.[65]

---

[62]  *lex Gundobada* (First Constitution) Sect. XCI par. 1.

[63]  *lex Gundobada* (First Constitution) Sect. XCVII par. 1.

[64]  *lex Gundobada* (First Constitution) Sect. XXXCII par. 1

[65]  *lex Gundobada* (First Constitution) Sect. V par. 1.

One cutting off the arm of a freeman *or* a slave would be liable for half of the victim's *wergeld*. A wound of any lesser severity would be "judged according to the nature of his wound."[66] A wound to the face was dealt with more severely, with the penalty being three times the amount that would be due for an injury to a "[body] part which is protected by clothing."[67]

The wrongful breaking of bones received specific attention. The *Burgundian Code* stated that if one broke another's arm, or his shinbone, but the person regains the use of it, composition would be set at 1/10th of the victim's *wergeld*. If in contrast the victim were to suffer "a clear disability," the composition would be set by the magistrate's evaluation of the extent of the injury.[68] The knocking out of teeth also garnered separate treatment, with composition set according to the class of the victim. The assailant imprudent enough to knock out the teeth of a "burgundian of the highest class" or a Roman noble was required to pay fifteen *soladi*.[69]

*Homicide*

As to the defense to a charge of homicide, provision was made for justifiable homicide, such as in the case where a man is "injured by blows or wounds" and "pursues his persecutor" and slays the initial attacker while yet in a state of "grief and indignation" his potential liability for intentional murder will be tempered by evidence of his mental state (if, of course, supported by oath takers). Upon such proof, and if the fatal injury was that sustained by a man of the middle class (*mediocris*), the matter could be resolved by payment of 100 *soladi*.[70] While such quasi-excuse for justifiable homicide might at first be seen

---

[66] *lex Gundobada* (First Constitution) Sect. XI par. 1. Of course the slave, as chattel of its master, would not receive the damages, be it in *wergeld* or otherwise.

[67] *lex Gundobada* (First Constitution) Sect. XI par. 2.

[68] *lex Gundobada* (First Constitution) Sect. XLVIII par. 1, 2, 3, 4.

[69] *lex Gundobada* (First Constitution) Sect. XXVI par. 1. The composition set for the injured member of the middle class was ten *soladi*, and for "persons of the lowest classes" five *soladi*.

[70] *lex Gundobada* (First Constitution) Sect. II par. 2. As might be expected, the composition to be paid would be higher if the victim was a nobleman (*optimas nobilis*),

as an implicit acquiescence in violent retribution for homicide, it bears reiterating that a potential and substantial monetary penalty might await the initial victim who pursues and kills his assailant. Thus there remained a significant financial incentive for declining to engage in self-help and leaving justice to the magistrates. Moreover, the *lex Gundobada* is quick in its effort to deter a blood feud brought by the victim's family against the family of the killer, stating that "the relatives of the man killed must recognize that no one can be pursued *except the killer*[.]"[71] A provision of this type is an exemplar of the movement of Germanic codes away from kinship-based remedies of revenge and self-help and towards systems of rectificatory justice.[72]

Departures from this tendency would appear to have involved homicide in the course of robbery of a merchant or another. The perpetrator could be sentenced to death, and if the things or moneys stolen could not be located, the victim would be compensated for "in fee simple" from the wrongdoer's property.[73]

*Self Defense*

Under the *Burgundian Code* the privilege of defending one's self was not a complete, but only a partial, defense.[74] More precisely, if a man defends himself with violence against his assailant, even if any "acts of this sort [are] from necessity," he remains liable for "half the established payment according to the degree of blame."[75] By way of example, if a man defending himself were to

---

and smaller if he was of the lowest class (*minor persona*). *Id.*

[71] *lex Gundobada* (First Constitution) Sect. XI par. 1 (emphasis added).

[72] Slaves did not enjoy the benefits of this progressive sensibility, as capital penalties continued to exist for certain delicts of slaves. For example, a slave who was solicited to steal a horse, mare, ox or cow could be "handed over to death[.]" *lex Gundobada* (First Constitution) Sect. IV par. 1.

[73] *lex Gundobada* (First Constitution) Sect. XXIX par. 1

[74] Regarding only the limited privilege of self-defense with deadly force, *see* People v. Wilner, 879 P.2d 19 (Colo. 1994) (following rule permitting defense with deadly force where such defense is reasonable in response to the threat). *See also* discussion in Dan B. Dobbs, The Law of Torts 162 (West 2000).

[75] *lex Gundobada* (First Constitution) Sect. XLVIII par. 4.

knock out the teeth of a member of the middle class, which would ordinarily require a payment of ten *soladi*,[76] he would remain responsible in composition for one half of that amount. As is obvious, the rule differs from the modern one that permits a man to take reasonable measures to defend himself, although the privilege ceases at the time the assailant no longer poses a threat, i.e., has been subdued or has fled. It is quite possible that even though the provision is introduced by confining its applicability to defensive acts "from necessity," the realm concluded that there would be additional value in the minimization of injury if the man defending himself operated under a norm that protected him from half, but not all, liability, to wit, the Code can (not must) be interpreted as a response to a concern that having the privilege of self-defense operate as a complete defense would insufficiently dissuade the man attacked from the enticement to respond more violently, or for a longer period of time, than was, strictly speaking, necessary,

*Trespass to Home and Land*

The Burgundians placed great value on the sanctity of their homes, and the king, in turn, considered violent entry into a home an intolerable disruption of the public peace. This is evidenced in the *lex Gundobada* section governing one's entry into another's home for the purposes of starting a fight. In a provision applicable to Romans and Burgundians alike, the perpetrator would pay six *soladi* to the owner of the home and another twelve *soladi* to the king's treasury.

As with Justinian's Code before it and all notable civil code and common law provisions that would follow, redress was provided for trespass to land without the need for showing actual harm. Indeed, under the *lex Gundobada*, the matter was made a matter of private composition and also payment to the crown, signifying the awareness within the realm that quasi-criminal fines were an appropriate means of emphasizing the seriousness of such defalcations. A

---

[76] *lex Gundobada* (First Constitution) Sect. XLVII at *id.* par. . If the assailant who lost his teeth was a member "of the lowest classes," the gross composition set at five *soladi* ( Lex Gundobada (First Constitution) Sect. XLVIII at *id.*) and the man defending himself would remain responsible for one half of that amount etc.

trespass to land that involved breaking into the close obligated the wrongdoer to pay three *soladi* to the owner and a fine of six *soladi* to the king.[77] If the breaking of a fence was for the purpose of providing pasture for an intruder's horses, he would pay one *solidus* for every animal as composition for the damage to the crops or meadow.[78]

Entry to another's vineyard by day could entail payment of "three *soladi* for his presumption[,]" while the landowner encountering a trespasser entering by night into "a vineyard bearing fruit" could kill him in defense of his vineyard (and its grapes), with no composition due to the trespasser's family or master.[79] A communitarian approach was taken in regard to Burgundians and Romans who did not possess forest and trees. They would be permitted to enter another's forest and to take the wood of fallen trees without penalty. But if the entrant cut down fruit bearing, pine or fir trees in another's forest, he would be obligated to pay to the owner one *solidus* for each such tree.[80]

If by mistake, which is to say, without the objection of others, a Burgundian or a Roman planted a vineyard on another's land, he would be required to satisfy the true owner with a "like field[.]" If, however, a man after "prohibition" (notice) persisted in doing so, he would be required to cede the improved property to the true owner and recover nothing for his labor.[81]

*Damage by Fire*

The *Burgundian Code* treats *in extenso* the liability that follows damage caused by a fire that is either transmitted accidentally to another's property, or that is set deliberately on another's property. One who set a fire in a clearing, and the fire subsequently and unaided by wind traveled to another's land, was required

---

[77] *lex Gundobada* (First Constitution) Sect. XXV par. 1. The provision speaks in terms of one who "enters a garden with violence," but the implication is not one of violence against man or animal, but rather the pushing aside or the breaking of a fence of or a gate to enclosed land, as distinct from trespassory entrance into another's open field.

[78] *lex Gundobada* (First Constitution) Sect. XXVII par. 4.

[79] *lex Gundobada* (First Constitution) Sect. XXVII par. 8.

[80] *lex Gundobada* (First Constitution) Sect. XXVIII par. 2.

[81] *lex Gundobada* (First Constitution) Sect. XXXI par. 1, 2.

to make composition by replacing anything burned.[82] It is possible that the application here of a composition standard of replacement in kind rather than in either liquidated or value-based damages in *soladi* reflects considerations of administrative cost and judicial competence, as well as pragmatic necessity. First, it is fairly straightforward to assign a liquidated value in *soladi* in composition, with or without an additional fine to be paid to the king's treasure, for injury to or even theft of a more or less fungible chattel, such as a plowshare, a horse or an ox. Once the universe of damaged or destroyed property is enlarged to include damage by fire to, for example, the contents of a house, and the almost limitless categories of personalty that might be contained therein, an accounting in money damages for the items would be both difficult and inherently unreliable. Second, and in terms of pragmatic necessity and the limited numbers of vendors accessible to them, it may have been though better to place the burden of acquisition and replacement on the wrongdoer.

*Injuries Caused by or Trespass of Animals*
Generally the *lex Gondobada,* as did the other Germanic codes, followed a rule of strict liability for damages caused by a horse or other agricultural animal.[83] These types of incidents are to be distinguished from the common law rules regarding, for example, innocent trespass onto adjoining land by animals being herded upon a public way. In a departure from strict liability for the acts of animals, should a pig damage a vineyard or a tilled field, and if the owner had been warned twice of this, the owner of the property that was damaged was entitled "to kill the best from the herd and turn it to his own use."[84] A like provision is found in the later *Lex Gondobada (Constitutioines Extragantes)* XVIII par. 1, for pigs found in another's vineyard. A potential rationale for having an explicitly self-help remedy for foraging pigs but not for farm animals such as horses or oxen is that among these animals only the pig is a comestible.

---

[82] *lex Gundobada* (First Constitution) Sect. XLI par. 1.

[83] For statements of similar rules of law in Great Britain and in the United States, *see* Tillett v. Ward, L.R. 10, Q.B.D. 17 (1882); Wood v. Snider, 79 N.E. 858 (N.Y. 1907).

[84] *lex Gundobada* (First Constitution) Sect. XXIII par. 4.

If a man penned animals that had entered his property and had caused damage, the owner seeking to recover them was required to pay a *trimissis* for each animal, and a fine of three *soladi*. In a humane vein regarding the protection of wandering horses, one section declares a predicate observation that horses wandering at large have sometimes been subjected to mistreatment. The Code provides that any such horse found must be turned over to the king where, pending establishment of ownership, "they may be guarded with zeal and diligence."[85]

Concerning all animals that are wont to wander off, one was not permitted to seize a horse "wandering at large through the countryside." If, on the other hand any such animal was found to be doing damage to property, the property owner could pen up the animal, and bring "suit" (in this context, give notice) of the whereabouts of the animals. If the owner did not arrive within two days, the possessor was permitted on the third day, and "in the presence of witnesses," drive the animals off.[86] Should the original owner reveal himself, another section of the Code provides for only partial composition regarding damages caused by animals,[87] a remedy, it can be seen, that falls short of reestablishment of the *status quo ante*.

In another provision limiting to partial composition an owner's remedy for damage caused by animals, let us say that one settler's (*vicini*) animals are causing damage to their enclosure, and for this reason another man drives the animals to enclosures on his own property. If, thereafter, if the animals are killed by "mischance (i.e., without fault). . . before he can send a messenger and bring immediate notice to their owner," the man last in possession of the animals is responsible in composition for only half of the animals' value.[88]

It would seem sensible that a man should be permitted to, without incurring liability, drive another's animals from his land, without the predicate of notice, etc., even if the animal was injured in the course of being driven. And

---

[85]  *lex Gundobada* (First Constitution) Sect. XLIX par. 4.

[86]  *lex Gundobada* (First Constitution) Sect. XLIX par. 4.

[87]  *See also* the rule relating to self-defense. *See lex Gundobada* (First Constitution) *id.* at par. 4.

[88]  *lex Gundobada* (First Constitution) Sect. XLIX par. 1.

indeed the *lex Gundobada* so provided.[89] For any animals driven justifiably into the enclosure of another, if the man so doing fails to give notice to the true owner that he must retrieve them, and if any mishap causes death to the animals, the possessor would be liable for their entire value. If, conversely, the possessor did give notice and the true owner fails to regain possession, and the animals die, the possessor would not be liable.[90]

Both the visible and the potential for different outcomes under these several rules is most likely due to the fact that the *lex Gundobada*, as was characteristic of all Gothic codes, was the subject of ongoing revision, executed by appointees of the realm, and that such revisions were often not accompanied by careful scrutiny for conflicts.

## Injuries to Animals

A man killing a dog "without apparent cause" was required to make composition of one *solidus*.[91] If an animal, presumably a beast of burden or a horse, should be killed in the course of a harvest, the man responsible would be responsible for "the value of the animal"[92]

Perhaps the term horseplay derived from pranks, sometimes cruel, that adults and children alike have, over time, worked upon horses. If a man should clip the tail of another's horse, he would be responsible for turning over to the owner a horse of the same value.[93]

## Dignitary Harms

The Burgundians do not seem to have treated with any breadth what might be described as the conventional dignitary torts, such as defamation. One provision nonetheless addresses the effrontery of cutting a woman's hair

---

[89] *lex Gundobada* (First Constitution) Sect. XXIII par. 2.

[90] *lex Gundobada* (First Constitution) Sect. XLIX par. 2.

[91] *lex Gundobada* (First Constitution) Sect. LVIII par. 1.

[92] *lex Gundobada* (First Constitution) Sect. LXIV par. 1, 2.

[93] *lex Gundobada* (First Constitution) Sect. LXXIII par. 3.

"in her courtyard." The perpetrator would be liable for thirty *soladi* in composition to the woman and fined twelve *soladi* to the benefit of the king's treasury.[94]


## Hospitality

In more primitive times, travel entailed substantial risks, both from the elements and also from persons of ill will. As a consequence of this, the *Burgundian Code* recognized duties of hospitality to travelers to provide the "roof and hearth." A Burgundian refusing this to a traveler would be required to pay to the traveler three *soladi* "for the neglect." If the denial of hospitality were less overt, such as a Burgundian directing the traveler to the house of a Roman, the Burgundian would be liable to both the Roman and the traveler in the amount of three *soladi*.[95]


## False Imprisonment

Provision was made for at least a subset of the acts that today would be named false imprisonment. If a freeman bound against his will an innocent freeman, he would be required to pay twelve *soladi* to the one bound and a fine of twelve *soladi* to the crown. The *lex Gundobada* followed a continuum of examples in which native inhabitants were favored over immigrants or visitors. The rule for false imprisonment represents one such example. For binding a non-native freeman, the composition would be six *soladi*, with the same amount payable to the king's treasury,[96] a varied treatment that probably reveals nothing more than a political tropism towards the rights of established Burgundians and Romans over the protections afforded an immigrant, even if a freeman.

---

[94]  *lex Gundobada* (First Constitution) Sect. XCII par. 1.

[95]  *lex Gundobada* (First Constitution) Sect. XXIX par. 7.

[96]  *lex Gundobada* (First Constitution) Sect. XXXII par. 1, 2.

*Perjury and False Oaths*

The authors of the Code were sagacious in their understanding of human vulnerability to manipulation of facts in any setting in which they might consider it to be in their self-interest so to do. The *Burgundian Code* introduces the sections on perjury and false oaths with language that could be mistaken for both legislative findings of fact and a statutory statement of purpose, and states: "We know that many of our people are corrupted through inability to establish a case and because of instinct of greed, so that they do not hesitate frequently to offer oaths about uncertain matters and likewise perjure themselves about known matters." To deter these practices the *lex Gundobada* outlines the potential outcomes when a claim is brought: (1) if a claim is brought and supported by oaths, and it is found that the accused committed the wrong, the matter is resolved in favor of the claimant; (2) if the accused is confronted with a claim that is supported by oath takers, but declines to receive the oaths, he is free to demand trial by combat, but the combat on behalf of the accused is to be made by an oath taker who supported the accused, letting "God be the judge." If the accuser's proxy is killed, the remaining oath takers must pay the man originally accused the sum of 300 *soladi*. If, though, the accused is killed, the accuser shall be paid ninefold the value of the harm initially alleged. "[A]s a result" of this means, the section concludes, "one may delight in truth rather than in falsehood."[97]

*Dangerous Instrumentalities*

One section of the *Burgundian Code* addresses the then contemporary means of trapping wolves, and imposes specific precautionary duties upon those who would use them. In one means of trapping, a bow would be set that if triggered would kill the wolf by arrow. Naturally such a trap also created a risk of killing other persons or domestic animals. Thus the trapper was required, on any path thus selected, to leave two other triggers at different locations that man or animal would encounter prior to encountering the true zone of danger, so that triggering either of the prior triggers would similarly loose the arrow, except

[97] *lex Gundobada* (First Constitution) Sect. XLV par. 1.

that it would strike harmlessly. Should a person be killed, a trapper conforming his practices to the prescribed methods would be liable in composition for the comparatively modest sum of twenty-five *soladi*. If, in contrast, the trapper did not so safeguard his traps and a man was killed inconsequence, he would be obligated to pay in composition the entire *wergeld* of the deceased.[98] More generally, a different rule applied for one who set "a trap for wild animals outside of cultivated land." If he did so in a "deserted spot" and a man or an animal was injured thereby, "no blame shall be attributed to him who owned the trap."[99]

### Deceit and False Witness

All customary law and early law codes contained provisions regarding deceit or false witness. Not every one treated perjury. The Laws of King Liutprand did so, and provided that "if any freeman advises another freeman to perjure himself[,]" he is liable to pay 100 *soladi* "for that illegal advice which he offered contrary to reason."[100]

# V. THE LAW OF THE LOMBARDS (ROTHAIR'S EDICTS)

With the Lombards in Italy as was true of all Germanic occupation of Roman territory, *realpolitik* obligated the Germanic kings and their minions to recognize that they were the minority population in a largely Roman land. Upon assumption of the administration of Roman territory, the barbarian kings recognized that they were required to play "a dual role."[101]

The ends of the Ostrogothic and the Western Empires provided the cul-

---

[98] *lex Gundobada* (First Constitution) Sect. XLVI par. 1, 2, 4.

[99] *lex Gundobada* (First Constitution) Sect. LXXII par. 1.

[100] *Laws of King Liutprand* 72.III.

[101] THE LOMBARD LAWS 11 (Katherine Fischer Drew, trans.)(U. Pa. Press.1973).

tural and political window for the new Lombard state.[102] To northern Italy the Lombards brought peace and a helpful lack of antagonism towards the papacy. Rothair's 643 A.D. Edictum was written in Latin, within a context of a society in its transition from pre-literacy to literacy. The Lombards did not destroy the Western Empire. Indeed, the law codes of Rothair and those that followed employed Latin, made discriminating use of *Justinian's Code*, and Lombard leaders enlisted Roman lawyers to advise Lombard judges.

While not so deferential to Roman culture, law and the church as had been the Ostrogoths, increased Lombard trade with western territories yet under Roman rule led by the Seventh Century to an "orientalization" of parts of Italy. Noteworthy was the introduction of Greek and Syrian clergy, as well as reciprocal visits of Byzantine Emperor Constans to Italy in 663 A.D. and the Pope to Constantinople in 710 A.D. The Lombards gradually turned from Arianism to Christianity.

From the Fifth to the Seventh Centuries, the sources of post-Justinian law as they persisted in the Italian peninsula are limited, but included both local charters and edicts of greater territorial scope from Naples, Verona, Milan and other smaller municipalities. From the Seventh Century onwards, the record is fuller. As would be expected, the laws of Rothair revealed a marked move away from rules that incorporated kinship considerations. Those provisions that did reference kinship were limited to legal questions in which family or family of origin might sensibly bear. For example, reference is made to extended family groups (*farae*) in the rules relating to migration within the kingdom. Lineage (*parentilla*) was a proper consideration in matters of inheritance, and a confined kinship group (*parentes*) was denied for purposes of oath helping and feud. Rothair's Edict is apparently otherwise oblivious to kinship.[103]

As with other Germanic groups, in earlier times of the Lombards resolution of serious wrongs might be "resolved" by blood feud (*faeda*). This corporal

---

[102]  *See* notes above and accompanying text. Nevertheless, some sixty years would pass between the end of the Ostrogothic kingdom and the ascension of the Lombards. THE LOMBARD LAWS xvi (Katherine Fischer Drew, trans.)(U. Pa. Press.1973).

[103]  EARLY MEDIEVAL ITALY, *supra* at 116-17.

and even lethal answer to grievances, which might be wrought against the offending individual, his family, or both, was characteristic of ancient eras in which it fell to the family or the kinship group to obtain justice. By the time of Theodoric, the state's influence was sufficiently strong, and its structure for provision of remedies of an apparently just nature had become sufficiently accepted, that resort to blood feud became increasingly rare. To be distinguished was trial by combat, referenced below.

While increasingly less prevalent under the Lombards, resolution of selective disputes by feud did persist. This can be explained by several factors. The threshold observation is that feud was a social institution that was very ingrained in Germanic custom. Thus neither the people nor their leaders were likely to consider feuds a material threat to public peace, much less to the state. Also, most feuds did not last for long, and within the custom itself were interwoven various means for nonviolent resolution with honor.

Lombard law made no distinction between criminal and civil delicts. As a consequence, actions were not brought by the state for criminal penalties, incarceration or physical punishment. Modern scholarship suggests several potential explanations for this are insightful, at least as they apply before medieval times. James Lundgren points to (1) the private law remedies available to early peoples, often quite strict and even brutal; (2) the great likelihood of detection in early and smaller societies without the help of the government; and (3) the adoption by many of these groups of liquidated amounts that might be paid in composition for the loss of a life (a full *wergeld*) and for lesser injuries.[104] Taken

---

[104] James Lundgren, *Why the Ancient Systems May Not have Needed a System of Criminal Law*, 76 B.U.L. REV. 29, 31-32 (1996). *See also* Richard A. Posner, *An Economic Analysis of Criminal Law*, 85 COLUM L. REV. 1193, 1203-04 (1985), in which the author writes:

> Primitive and ancient societies (including Anglo-Saxon England) have relied more heavily than has our society on a form of tort damages (usually fixed in amount rather than assessed individually in each case) – "bloodwealth," "wergeld," "composition," – to control crime, apparently with some success. Among other things that makes this approach feasible are lack of personal privacy, which makes probabilities of apprehension and conviction high, and the principle of collective responsibility, which makes the offender's kinship group liable for his damages, thus enabling the society to set fines that exceed the individual's ability to pay.

together, Lundgren suggests, these private law approaches go a great distance in obviating the need for state enforcement in the form of criminal law and penalties, including incarceration.

The final piece to the puzzle is probably that of institutional capacity. The Romans had not only the authority to identify and separate private wrongs from public ones, but also the resources to support both quasi-judicial and penal confinement systems. Thus the capacity of the Romans to create a bright line between civil and criminal wrongs was both unprecedented (at least in the Western world) and also dependent upon the nature and power of their governance. It would not be an approach that would either appeal to, or be feasible for, societies with less structure, fewer resources, or both. Even so, conviction for many wrongs in the time of the Lombards might result in what today would be terms quasi-criminal penalties, with the court imposing a fine, half of which would escheat to the state, and the other half to the injured party.

Importantly, because, with the exception off a judgment of a full *wergeld* for a death, such judgments were ordinarily in the form of fines, and payable only in the proportion of perhaps one-half to the victim or his family, the quasi-criminal nature of these remedies for delict would frequently fall short of compensating the injured parties for the true extent of the harm. Still and all, the opportunity to receive substantial if incomplete pecuniary redress for a delict, as determined before an impartial magistrate, represented an advancement in certainty over the prior practices of blood feud.

The Lombard Laws were codified and published in a succession beginning with the most influential of them, that of Rothair, the seventeenth King of the Lombards. As noted, *Rothair's Edict* was published in 643 A.D.[105] The *Laws of King Grimwald* would follow in 668 A.D.,[106] with the *Laws of King Liutprand* published in 724 A.D.[107] The *Laws of King Grimwald* contained no provisions germane to tort-like wrongs, but as will be discussed, those of King Liutprand did, while often incorporating by reference *Rothair's Edict*.

---

[105]  The leading translation of these several codifications is found in THE LOMBARD LAWS (Katherine Fischer Drew, trans.)(U. Pa. 1973), and the provisions of *Rothair's Edict* contained therein will be cited hereinafter to the edict itself.

[106]  THE LOMBARD LAWS 131 (Katherine Fischer Drew, trans.)(U. Pa. 1973).

[107]  *Id.* at 137.

In general it can be stated that what Lombard Law lacked in systemization it made up for in particularity. Nowhere in Lombard law is the legal taxonomy of provisions into categories such as "wrongs to persons" or "wrongs to property," categorizations that Justinian's Code, for example, would leave as an enduring legacy in western law. Yet at least as it pertained to liability for delicts both *Rothair's Edict* and the *Laws of King Liutprand*, and particularly *Rothair's Edict*, were not surpassed in its seeming devotion to recording a comprehensive recitation of the sprawling array of wrongs for which remedies might be sought.

Under *Rothair's Edictum*, to gain redress for a wrong, the aggrieved must bring an action for damages. Similar to the approach taken by other non-Latins, the Lombards employed two means of judicial proof: compurgation and trial by combat. Resort to the latter, trial by combat, was infrequent. Trial by compurgation relied not upon evidence presented by witnesses, but rather upon the party's reputation. "Oathtakers" (*sacrementales*), whose numbers might be as many as twelve, and who might include relatives, would take an oath vouching for the integrity of the party. This collective oath would be taken into account by the magistrate in determining if the party's account of events was truthful.[108]

In overview, for a wrong resulting in another's death, the Lombards adopted the common Germanic concept of *wergeld*, with the value of the deceased's life to be paid to the victim's family.[109] For personal injury not resulting in death, the penalty would vary depending upon the seriousness of the injury or incapacitation. For harms to property, compurgation might be in the form of the property lost or damaged, e.g., crops or animals, or in coin. The Lombard Laws also took into account instances in which the physical harm might be slight but the dignitary harm great.[110]

---

[108]  Edward Peters, The Lombard Laws 26, 27 (Katherine Fischer Drew, trans.)(U. Pa. 1973).

[109]  *Id.* at 27. *See also* explanation of *wergeld* and *wergild*.

[110]  *E.g., Rothair's Edict*, discussed below.

*Public Nuisance*

One of the original and most important objectives of law has been the maintenance of order. While threats to such order can arise in an almost limitless number of ways, the most classic among them has been breach of the public peace (*scandulum*). *Rothair's Edict* adopted a gender-based treatment for redress of any injuries sustained in a public brawl. If a woman were to participate in a brawl in which men were involved and she is injured or killed, composition would be due to her or her family as though the injury had been sustained by a man in her family. With apparent reference to an actual decision rendered by the court, however, *Rothair's Edict* No. 378 continues by explaining that even though the gravity of the harm might warrant a payment of 900 *soladi*,[111] the woman should recover nothing, as "she had participated in a struggle in a manner dishonorable for women."

*Assault and Battery*

The penalty for the injurious striking of another would vary depending upon the loss sustained. Rothair's Edict No. 377 governed the blinding of a man with only one good eye, and set the composition at two-thirds of the amount that would be due if the man had been slain.[112]

*Laws of King Liutprand* No. 124.VIII states that a man who by striking a slave left him or her crippled must pay the master one half the composition that would be due had the slave been slain.

---

[111] The value of a *solidus*, or its multiple in *soladi*, is described above at note 43 and accompanying text, as used by the Burgundians. I do not here compare the value differentiation as might have occurred between and among the Burgundians, the Lombards and the Salacian Franks.

[112] If the same injury should be sustained by a one-eyed slave, the composition to be paid would be as though the slave had been slain. *Id.* The logic of this is probably found in the fact that it might be considered that there was no value in a sightless slave.

*Unintentional Homicide*

For homicide generally, be it unintentional or intentional, *Code of King Liutprand* describes the means of calculation of the appropriate composition for another's life. This measurement is to be made "according to the quality of the person," a concept that is consistent with the calculation of *wergild* as used throughout this discussion. It was nonetheless seemingly decided that the process would profit from some higher degree of predictability, and *Laws of King Liutprand* 62.VIIII give it just that. It states that it should be recognized as "custom" that "a lesser person (*minima persona*) who is a freeman (*excercitalis*) shall have a wergild of 150 *soladi*, and he who is of the first class (*primus*) shall have a *wergild* of 300 *soladi*.

For cases of unintentional homicide, *Rothair's Edict* proposes composition and discourages blood feud. Composition for the death is pursuant to *wergild*, which is to say, "the price at which the dead man is valued." And, the *Edict* concludes with language encouraging composition over feud, and reads: "feud shall not be required since it was done unintentionally."[113] It is obvious that the composition in the amount of *wergild* adopted throughout Germanic law represents a lineal juridical predecessor to the wrongful death statutes that would follow and many of which are in force today.

As with all Germanic groups adopting agricultural societies, the clearing of land and the felling of trees was an essential part of the endeavor. It is inevitable that many injuries, even deaths, would result. *Rothair's Edict* No. 138 pertains to the unintended (happening "without design") killing of a man by a tree cut down by several men. It provided: "If two or more men cut down a tree, and another man coming along is killed by that tree, then those who were cutting the tree, however many they were, shall pay composition equally for the composition or for the damage." Thus whatever sum might be assigned as *wergild* for the life of the victim, *Edict* No. 138 states that the perpetrators shall share equally in the payment of the total, an early example of comparative responsibility.

Should one of the tree cutters be accidentally killed, *Edict* No. 139 provided, by way of example, that "if there were two colleagues, half the *wergild*

---

[113] *Rothair's Edict* No. 387.

would be assessed to the dead man and the other half shall be paid to the relatives [of the dead man]." Should more than two cutters be involved, liability would be assigned congruently, with "an equal portion...assessed to the dead man and to those who still live," with each paying an equal share of the *wergild*. By this means of composition in resolution of the accident, *Edict* No. 138 concludes, the risk of feud is extinguished.

*Intentional Homicide*

The *Laws of King Liutprand* set forth dire penalties for the unexcused slaying of another, with the penalties to be exacted not only upon the perpetrator but also upon his heirs. The party responsible must turn over all of his property to the family of the victim. If the value of the property exceeds that value which would be assigned as composition for the lost life, then the victim's family keeps the proportion as is of a value equivalent to an appropriate *wergild*, and any excess goes half to the king's treasury and half to the victim's family. If, on the other hand, the value of the property were less than that which would be a fair composition, the assailant would lose all of his property and is turned over himself to the "nearest relatives of the dead man."[114] While the laws do not elaborate, the signification of the turning over of the perpetrator seems to be that the victim's family would be free to exact revenge.

*Self Defense*

If one killed a "mad man" in self-defense, *Rothair's Edict* No. 323 dispensed with liability, although it required that "he not be slain without cause." King

---

[114] *Laws of King Liutprand* No. 20.II. It may be presumed that the man turned over to the victim's family may be treated as a chattel slave. The section ends curiously with language following that providing that if the value of the perpetrator's land exceeds that sufficient to award composition, half goes to the victim's family and half escheats to the king. It states that "in this way the man who committed the homicide may redeem his life." Yet according to the earlier language even if the assailant's property exceeds wergild for the victim's life, the perpetrator keeps nothing. This leaves if unclear how or with what the wrongdoer may redeem his life.

Liutprand develops the defense more broadly to state that a freeman killing another in self-defense should be liable in composition for the lost life of the other, but should not otherwise be punished.[115]

*Negligence*

As was earlier shown in the *lex Gundobada*,[116] the several Gothic groups were practiced in assigning social expectations of care, and in imposing liability upon those whose duties of care were breached. *Rothair's Edict* No. 148 provided: "He who makes a fire beside the road should extinguish it before he goes away and not leave it negligently." Any damage cause by such a fire would require composition only in the amount of the value of what was damaged, as the act was not done intentionally. Potential liability for harm caused by such a fire would be limited to harm occurring within twenty-four hours after the fire was abandoned. Potential liability would also be extinguished should any damage be caused after the fire crossed an open road or a stream.

This is a marvelous provision to parse, as it illuminates early concepts of duty, liability for negligence, proximate cause, and pure compensatory damages. The duty of reasonable care is clearly defined by the statement that a man should extinguish a fire before leaving it. Similarly, the breach of that duty is characterized as negligence. Limitations of liability should the fire cross an open road or a stream tracks its concordance in modern concepts of proximate cause, as the damage on the far side of the road or the stream is clearly caused in fact by the negligence, but for policy reasons liability is determined not to extend that far.[117] Lastly, the composition owed for accidental harm is set at the actual value of the damaged property.

---

[115] *Laws of King Liutprand* No. 20.II.

[116] *See* discussion above at *Burgundian Code*, "Negligence and Accidental Harm."

[117] The common law would come to reach similar conclusions in decisions such as Atlantic Coast Line R. Co. v. Daniels, 70 S.E. 203 (Ga. App. 1911); Palsgraf v. Long Island R.R. Co., 162 N.E. 99 (N.Y. 1928).

*Trespass to Land and Interference with Boundary Markers*

Numerous provisions of *Rothair's Edict* and also the *Laws of King Liutprand* address matters that would today sound in trespass to land. Under *Rothair's Edict*, if a man, even by innocent mistake, plows another man's field, or seeds it, he has no recourse for any improvement or harvest from the land against the true owner.[118] If he plows over another's seeded field he must return any fruits he destroyed and also "pay six *soladi* as composition for his heedless presumption."[119] The *Laws of King Liutprand* provide that one who digs a ditch on another's land must pay to the rightful owner six *soladi*,[120] and that one putting a fence on another's land must pay the same amount.[121]

As sensible to any rules governing and agricultural society, a sequence of provisions address interference with the boundary markers of another's land. The penalty was quasi- criminal, for such interference was considered an effrontery not only to offended property owner but also to the king. *Rothair's Edict* No. 236 provided a substantial penalty for a freeman who is "proved" to have destroyed an old boundary marker will be fined eighty "*soladi*," with one half to the king and the other half to the property owner.[122] Markings on trees were apparently also employed as boundary markers, and a freeman cutting down such designated trees would likewise be fined eighty *soladi*, with half going to the king and half to the landowner. Should a slave cut down such trees at the instigation of his "lord" (master), the lord would be liable for eighty *soladi* as composition, to be apportioned similarly.[123]

---

[118] *Rothair's Edict* No. 354.

[119] *Rothair's Edict* No. 355. A like section, with the same required composition, addresses the reaping of another's meadow. *Rothair's Edict* No. 356.

[120] *Laws of King Liutprand* 46.XVII.

[121] *Laws of King Liutprand* 47.XVIII.

[122] Should the actor be a slave, he might be killed unless he is "redeemed" for forty *soladi*. *Rothair's Edict* No. 237. It is apparent that the rarely employed penalty of death would be applicable only if the slave was acting of his own initiative, rather than at the order of his master, in which latter case the penalty would most probably be only one for money damages. *See* discussion below of *Edict* No. 238 and 239.

[123] *Rothair's Edict* No. 238. If the slave were to do so "on his own authority," he could be killed unless "redeemed" for forty *soladi*. *Edict* No. 239. As might be expected, "justice" for transgressing slaves was generally harsh. *E.g.*, marking a tree in another's

Since the earliest of times societal custom and law have discouraged unjust enrichment. The reasons are multiple, but a section of the *Laws of King Liutprand* addresses the specific issue of wrongful possession of another's property, and the reaping of rewards thereby. Section No. 90.VII describes a man who wrongfully possesses another's property, including houses, land, animals or servants. Upon this man's eviction from the premises, he is required to "render back the time and the fruit of the labor he has unlawfully gained."

*Intentional Arson*

*Rothair's Edict* No. 146 provided treble damages for one "who deliberately and with evil intent burns another's house[.]" "Restoration" would be made "according to the value of the burned house and its contents as determined by men of good faith from the vicinity." This provision is significant for at least three reasons. First, it distinguishes what today is meant by "intent" in tort, i.e., where one knows of or subjectively desires the consequences of their action, from specific, or deliberate and evil, intent. Second, it reflects a super-compensatory or punitive role of a damage action where the wrong is intentional in this sense. And third it represents a departure from the then general rule that responsibility for an injurious occurrence will be assigned by exclusive reference to oath taking and oath takers as to the probity of the party. Instead, *Edict* No 146 describes a role for "men of good faith in the community" in the valuation of the damaged property.[124]

*Injuries or Damage Caused by Animals*

Several provisions of *Rothair's Edict* pertain to injuries caused by dogs. No liability would attach if one's "dog or horse or any other animal" were to go "mad" and injure another person or his animals, nor would any penalty be im-

---

wood, unless ordered by his master; penalty: loss of a hand. *Edict* No. 241.

[124] *Rothair's Edict* No. 149 provides similarly for the man who "deliberately and with evil intent" burns a mill, who is required to "pay as composition a sum equal to three times the value of the property and its contents.

posed on one who killed such animal.[125] If someone incited another's dogs to injure another man or his animals, the owner of the dogs would bear no responsibility, but instead the one who incited them.[126] Absent madness or incitement, if a dog bites a man the owner is liable in composition.[127] This last section is at a seeming variance with the dominant "dog" rules in modern western law, to wit, one is not responsible for the actions of their dog – presumably if properly confined or leashed – unless and until they have notice of its dangerous propensities.

The rules for damage or injuries cause by horses or beasts are different, as is true too in modern tort law. If a beast injures a man or another's animal, the owner must pay composition.[128] Should a horse kick a man, or an ox injure him with its horns, or a pig with its tusks, the owner is responsible in composition for the killing or injury.[129] That section concludes, as do several others similarly, with the admonition that upon payment of composition, that "the feud, and] the enmity, shall cease[.]"[130]

A variation on monetary composition is found when one man's animal kills another's. Referencing the killing of an oxen, *Edict* No. 328 would require that upon receiving the dead animal, the owner of the animal that caused the death must replace it with "another animal of the same kind and value as the injured one was at the time it was hurt." There are at least two significations of this *Edict*. First, it departs from composition in the form of money damages in favor of replacement. It is possible that this choice has to do with the role of oxen in agricultural society, i.e., more or less continuous work as a beast of burden. A man whose oxen were killed would be faced with the immediate and serious dilemma of replacing the animal. In such a case, a replacement animal would be a restitutionary remedy superior to the payment of money. Second, the requirement that the provision of the replacement oxen be the turning over of

---

[125] *Rothair's Edict* No. 324.
[126] *Rothair's Edict* No. 322.
[127] *Rothair's Edict* No. 326.
[128] *Rothair's Edict* No. 325.
[129] *Rothair's Edict* No. 326. Compare Sandy v. Bushey, 128 A. 513 (Me. 1925).
[130] *Id.*

the dead oxen to the owner of the offending animal, can reasonably be seen as a confinement of the remedy only what is necessary to put the owner of the dead oxen in the position he enjoyed before the wrong. A dead beast would have the residual value of its hide, its meat, its horns, etc., and in modernity it might be considered unjust enrichment to permit the complainant to receive both a new oxen and also retain the dead one.

*Edict* No. 344 continues the theme of redress for injuries caused by animals, and again distinguishes between wrongful and innocent conduct by the owner. Several rules of this type can be visualized as arising from the acts of animal herders who either intentionally or carelessly let their animals enter the close of another. If the land is devoted to pasturage, the damage will be that caused by grazing. If the land is dedicated to crops, the result might be damage to the crops and also to any land as it might have been prepared for crops. *Edict* No. 433 provides that if one deliberately causes his horse or oxen to cause damage to the property of another, he is responsible in composition for the damage caused, and additionally is fined one *solidus*.[131] If the animal owner or herder does swear that the harm was not intentional, he is relieved of the payment of one *solidus*, but must still pay composition for the damage done.

In some instances the treatment *Rothair's Edict* gives to damages caused by animals resembles an intricate minuet between the aggrieved party and the owner of the wandering animals. *Edict* No. 342 declares that if a landowner finds another's animal doing damage on his property, he is permitted to pen it up. If the owner of the animal does not come to claim it, the possessor may take the matter before a judge, or "bring it before a gathering in front of a church four or five times[,]"[132] a means of obtaining public notice that resembles later practices in medieval times of posting notices on the doors of a church. Once it has been "made known to all by public proclamation that he has found the horse [or other animal]...[i]f the owner of the horse does not come, "the finder is permitted to keep the horse."[133] The *Laws of King Liut-*

---

[131]   The monetary equivalent of the damage caused is to be decided by an appraisal "according to the custom of the place."

[132]   *Rothair's Edict* No. 342. Presumably "it" refers not to the animal but rather to the issue.

[133]   If the animal later dies, the new owner must keep the hide to show it if the original

*prand* No. 86.III refines parts of *Edict* No. 342 by stating that the man who finds another's horse doing damage to his property is only to be permitted to keep it penned up until a resolution of ownership can be had. If instead the man "presumes to do to the horse anything more,"[134] the man so doing will liable for composition in the measure of half of the value of the horse."

Similar themes are discernible in *Rothair's Edict* No. 346. According to that section, if a man discovers another's animal causing harm to his land, he may bring an action in composition, and the owner of the animal must pay composition for the damage plus one *solidus*. If the animal's owner requests the return of the animal before this remedy is executed, the holder of the animal may request 'three *soliquae* as a pledge for the ultimate redemption" of the amount owed. There is an apparent presumption that in the orderly course of events the complainant should accept the pledge, and if he does not and instead keeps the animal for more than one night, he will owe its owner one *solidus*. What if the original owner simply declines to reclaim the animal? Here the *Edict* takes an inexplicable course of countenancing punishment of the animal as a proxy for penalizing the wrongdoer. In what a modern psychologist might today term a displacement reaction, the possessor is permitted to keep the animal for nine nights and give it only water, and "if anything is killed by that animal it shall be imputed to the negligence of him who neglected to disengage his pledge."

*Human Injuries to Animals*

*Rothair's Edict* includes sections on human depredations upon or injuries to animals. The lesser among these, such as the penalty exacted when a man "cuts off the tail of another man's horse to the very bristle," provide for payment of as little as six *soladi*,[135] a provision practically indistinguishable from

---

owner arrives eventually If the new possessor fails to do this, he must return a horse "ninefold.[.]" *Id.*

[134] By the indeterminate "anything more" is probably meant, on one end of the spectrum, injuring the animal, or on the more likely end, exploiting the animal by riding or other service.

[135] *Rothair's Edict* No. 338.

that regarding molestation of a horse by cutting its tail found in the *Burgundian Code.*[136]


### Trespass to Chattels

As is true today, the wrong of trespass to chattels was considered a lesser offence than conversion.[137] If a man were to meddle with another's property, knowing that the property was that of another, he would be fined minimally, at least insofar as such a fine might be compared with the penalties for other delicts.[138]


### Theft or Conversion

Regarding theft in an amount greater than ten *silequae*, a freeman, if caught in the act (*fegangi*), was required to "return that stolen ninefold" and further to "pay eighty *soladi* composition for such guilt[.]"[139] Thieves not discovered in the act but rather through an informant (*proditor*) received a lesser punishment of simple restoration.[140] The graded elevation of penalties as tied to the value of the property stolen parallels today's distinctions between misdemeanor theft and felony theft.

Edict No. 281 provided that theft of wood from another's woods would result in the exaction of six *soladi* from the owner. The lack of a restoration remedy arguably reveals a logic that as the wrongful taking is in the woods, and might only be discovered after the passage of time, at such time an action is brought the wood may have been consumed as fuel or used as timber.

---

[136] *See id.*

[137] *See* above and accompanying text.

[138] *E.g., Rothair's Edict* No. 342, declaring that if, "after [a man] has announced that [a horse] is not his own, he mounts it, he shall pay two *soladi*" as composition.

[139] *Rothair's Edict* No. 253. If the thief was unable to make such composition, "he shall lose his life[,]" although there is no reliable indication of how frequently this alternative penalty was imposed.

[140] *Rothair's Edict* No. 255.

By the time of the *Laws of King Liutprand*, thievery was apparently thought of as sufficiently pernicious as to warrant imprisonment. Judges were instructed to "make a prison underground" in their respective districts. Thieves would be required to pay composition for the value of the theft, and then could be placed in prison for two to three years. The doubly unfortunate thief who did not have the resources to pay composition could be handed over to the victim, and the victim was permitted to "do with [the thief] as he pleases."[141] Recidivists could be shaved (*decalvit*), beaten or branded on the forehead and face. For a further offense the thief could be sold "outside the province," which is to say, sold into servitude.[142]

To be distinguished from purposeful theft, an asportation of another's animal might be due to the innocent mistake of the actor. If a man "takes someone else's horse or other animal believing it to be his own," and was accused by the owner of wrongdoing, the respondent was permitted to "offer an oath that he did not take it with evil intent or with the purpose of causing contention, but because he believed it to be his own." Upon returning the animal unharmed, he could be absolved of any claim of theft. If, on the other hand, he is not prepared to so swear, it would be interpreted as an admission of wrongdoing, and he would be liable to "return the horse eightfold."[143]

*Maintenance of Dangerous Instrumentality*

If a man constructed a fence and left the head of a pole extend above the rest of the fence, and should a man be injured or die after impaling himself on that pole, he would be required to pay composition.[144] Here, presumably, the composition for death would be in the amount of *wergild*, while the composition

---

[141]   *Laws of King Liutprand* 80.XI.

[142]   *Id.* As to this lattermost remedy, the provision suggests that a higher burden of proof should be required, stating that selling a man should be "a proved case for the judge ought not to sell the man without certain proof." This concluding language is probably best interpreted as meaning "proof to a certainty," as would befit a penal sanction of this order.

[143]   *Rothair's Edict* No. 342.

[144]   *Rothair's Edict* No. 303.

for injury short of death would be determined with reference to the severity of the injury.

## Responsibility for the Insane

*Edict* No. 323 provides: "If a man, because of his weighty sins, goes mad or becomes possessed, nothing shall be required from his heirs." This rule represents a treatment of responsibility for the wrongs of the mentally infirm that departs from the modern standard holding that an insane person (more likely his guardians or insurers) will be liable for his torts.[145]

## Deceit, Fraud and Perjury

All customary law and early law codes contained provisions regarding deceit or false witness. Not every one treated perjury. The *Laws of King Liutprand* did so, and provide that "If any freeman advises another freeman to perjure him-self[,]" he is liable to pay 100 *soladi* "for that illegal advice which he offered contrary to reason."[146]

*Rothair's Edict* No. 192 treated an issue that seems unlikely today but would have been more plausible in days when young and marriageable women were unemancipated. A "girl" could be betrothed to another through the actions of her father, a brother, or by other relatives. Any family member who participated in the betrothal and who later "for some strange reason" entered into "a secret agreement" that the girl be betrothed to another, or who consented to another man's "taking the woman to wife forcefully even with her consent, would be bound to pay the original putative husband "double the marriage portion which was agreed to on the day of the betrothal." "Afterwards," *Edict* No. 192 concluded, "the [originally] betrothed man may not seek more from the prosecution of them or their sureties."

This provision is notable in more than one respect. First and most ob-

---

[145] *E.g.*, McGuire v. Almy, 8 N.E.2d 760 (Mass 1937).

[146] *Laws of King Liutprand* 72.III.

viously, it enunciates the subordinate, even chattel-like status of women in that era. Second, it seeming provides a remedy for fraudulent deprivation of prospective advantage. And third, by describing a monetary limitation on the defrauded suitor at "double the marriage portion [dowry]," and precluding any further attempt to exact more, it is an early example of liquidated damages.

*Dignitary Wrongs*

Since time immemorial, it has been recognized that defamation, in addition to being a wrong, carries with it a substantial risk of physical retaliation. *Edict* No. 381 provides in effect a safety valve for the avoidance of the escalation of potentially injurious enmity, and states: "If anyone in anger calls another man a coward" he may absolve himself of blame, and simultaneously reduce the sting of the insult, by taking an oath that he spoke in anger and does not know the other man in fact to be a coward. He nevertheless would be obligated to pay twelve *soladi* in composition. Should the man "persevere" in the inflammatory comment, "he must prove it by combat, if he can[.]"[147]

From the time of the Lombards through and including the years leading to 1000 A.D., the kingdom that comprised much of modern Italy saw a succession of Carolingian rulers. One of the most notable was Louis II (844-75). He was the last king to truly rule the realm. From 875-962 A.D., autonomy migrated increasingly from the kings to the localities, such that by the opening

---

[147] *Id.* The provision concludes, incongruously, by stating that the man persevering in the claim may, as an alternative to trial by combat, pay twelve *soladi* as composition. This last language cannot be readily reconciled with the proposition that the twelve *soladi* in composition was attendant upon swearing that the man uttered the charge in anger and did not know of its bona fides, i.e., the original provision for composition is in the context of the man backing down from the claim, and permitting both men to save face. It seemingly makes no sense that where the man does retract the claim, and indeed continues to traffic in it, that the Edict provision directs the disputants in the direction of trial by combat or the payment of the same amount in composition. Put another way, if the provision is read literally, the verbal aggressor is permitted resolve the matter with the payment of damages without having taken any steps to calm the situation.

of the new millennium, popular dismissal of central authority signified an Italian state that could no longer truly claim that mantle.[148]

# VI. THE LAWS OF THE SALIAN FRANKS

## A. FRANKISH LAW, GENERALLY

By the early Fifth Century, the Burgundians, the Visigoths, and the Franks had settled in Gaul, in agricultural communities. The Franks comprised two primary populations: the Salians and the Rippuarians. Their laws were named. Respectively, the *Pactus legis Salicae* and the *lex Ripuaria*. The Salian law reflected no real attempt at organization or systemization, even though it was rendered in Latin. Attributed often to the work of Clovis (476-496 A.D.)[149], who brought Christianity to his people, the *Pactus legis Salicae* showed little Roman influence and no Christian influence at all. It was more or less a recitation of Salian Frank customary law.[150]

---

[148]  Historian Chris Wickham writes:

> "By the late tenth century, being a count was no longer very different from being an ordinary landowner; the state bureaucracy was dissolving; the concerns of the ecclesiastical and lay aristocracies were directed towards their own power bases, and barely towards the state at all....In 1024, the inhabitants to Parvia revolted and burned down the royal palace there; after that, Italy barely existed as a state."

EARLY MEDIEVAL ITALY, *supra* note at 168.

[149]  DECLINE AND FALL, *supra* note at 523.

[150]  The *lex Ripuaria*, in contrast, revealed many similarities with the earlier Burgundian Code. A recitation of some of the Frankish laws, those comprising the *lex Ripuaria*, and their Burgundian Code counterparts, was prepared by historian Theodore John Rivers: *lex Ripuaria* 48 (46) par 1, 2 (an animal killing another man or another animal; *lex Burgundia* Sec. 18 par. 1) *lex Ripuaria* 49 (47) sect. 1, 2 (following the trail of a stolen animal; *lex Burgundia* Sect. 16 p. 1-8); *lex Ripuaria* Sect. 68 (65) par. 3 (declining to offer hospitality; *lex Burgundia* Sect 38); and *lex Ripuaria* Sect. 91 (88) Sect. 1 (court officials taking bribes; *lex Burgundia* preface, cap. 5). LAWS OF THE SALIAN AND RIPUARIAN FRANKS 9 (Theodore John Rivers, transl.) (AMS 1986). Professor Rivers

Among both Frankish tribes, the king's original duties were the protection of the realm and the keeping of the domestic peace. With regard to the latter, which we have encountered above, feuds were discouraged by means of a feud fine, called a *feudus*, that would be imposed, with two thirds devolving to the realm and one third to the magistrate who decided the matter. If the laws proved inadequate to the king's purposes he could issue an edict (*bannum*) that operated as today's injunction, and the failure to do or cease to do what the crown ordered would subject a fairly steep fine of 60 *soladi*.[151] The Franks followed the pattern of the other German tribes in the perpetuation of blood feud as one means of resolving a slaying. At the same time they also adopted the more progressive option of the payment of *wergeld*, as has been defined earlier. Acceptance of the offered *wergeld* by the victim's kinship group would resolve the feud. As might be imagined, some greater inducement for the victim's family to not respond violently might be needed, and this would only come in the Eighth Century. [152]

Had the Frankish hegemony lasted long enough, it is possible conceptually that there would have developed a unitary pan-European body of law. But this would not be the case, and the European collectivity would pass several centuries with no central lawmaking and with such law as was developed governed by municipal or regional law, which in turn reflected most closely a region's customary law.

Putting aside Visigothic law[153] for the purposes of this section, I will discuss the law of the Franks, and the Salian Franks in particular.

---

continues by commenting that many other similarities could be catalogued, but the reliability might tail off due to uncertainty as to whether the *lex Burgundia* and the *lex Ripuaria* were themselves influenced by yet a third source or sources. *Id.* at 9, 10.

[151] A definition of a *solidus* and of multiple *soladi* can be found above at p. 106, n. 43 and accompanying text.

[152] Laws of the Salian and Ripuarian Franks 13, 14 (Theodore John Rivers, transl.) (AMS 1986).

[153] *See generally* P. D. King, Law and Society in the Visigothic Kingdom (Cambridge 1972).

## B. THE SALIC LAWS OF THE SALIAN FRANKS

We turn now specifically to Salic law, as found in the *Pactus legis Salicae.*[154] We will see it, as we have seen the other Gothic codes, to be a work of substantial organizational achievement.

*Theft and Conversion*

The *Pactus legis Salicae* opens with six provisions regarding, in the main, farm animals: the theft of pigs, cattle, sheep, goats, dogs, together with birds and bees.[155] The penalty for the theft of a pig varied upon the circumstances. Should it be an unweaned piglet from the "first enclosure" (the perimeter enclosure) or the middle one, the composition would be three *soladi*. If the piglet was stolen from the third enclosure, i.e., the most protected enclosure, the composition would be fifteen *soladi*, plus additional composition in the amount of the piglet's value and a fine for loss of use. Lastly, the theft of a piglet from a locked pigsty would be liable in composition for forty-five *soladi*. It is evident that the level of liability increased on the basis of two factors: (1) the thief's industry, i.e., his culpability; and (2) the level of the intrusion or penetration onto the owner's property. The provisions continue with great particularity to describe the offenses and the penalties therefor, leaving nary a doubt as to the centrality of pig-raising to the Salic agricultural community.

For the theft of cows, increasing penalties, from three to thirty-five *soladi* would be imposed depending upon whether the animal was an unweaned calf, a one-year old, a two-year old, a cow without a calf, or a cow with a calf. For theft of an ox, the penalty might range from thirty-five to

[154] The references to follow are from the translated Salic and Ripuarian laws as found in LAWS OF THE SALIAN AND RIPUARIAN FRANKS (Theodore John Rivers, trans.) (AMS 1986). In the pursuit of brevity, I will from this point forward employ only references to the sections of the laws themselves.

[155] *Pactus legis Salicae* Sect. 2 par. 1-3. As to other related offenses, for example, stealing and injuring a sow with such severity so that she cannot give milk the actor would be required to make composition of seven *soladi*, plus a payment in the amount of the value of the sow, "and a fine for the loss of its use." *Id.* at par. 5.

forty-five *soladi*, the latter liability being imposed if the ox was "a bull that leads the herd."[156]

A similar hierarchical approach was taken for the theft of sheep. For the theft of an unweaned lamb, the penalty was less than one half a *soladus*, as measured in *denarii*, in addition to its value and a fine for the loss of its use."[157] Theft of a one or a two-year old sheep would bring a requirement in composition of three *soladi.*, with the highest level of penalty imposed for theft of "forty, fifty, sixty or more" adult sheep, for which the penalty would be sixty-two and one half *soladi*.[158] A like set of rules, differing only in the description of the animal, was taken regarding theft of goats, dogs, birds, and bees.[159]

Protection of agricultural industry and possessory rights continue throughout the law. Comparable provision is made for, and different designated mount in composition are assigned to, a wide variety of other thefts, ranging from theft from another's garden, theft of the graft from a fruit bearing tree, flax from another's field, the mowing of another's meadow,[160] grazing of one's animals on the land of another, plowing another's field without sowing it (and, alternatively, plowing it *and* sowing it), theft of services, and specifically the services of another's slave,[161] harvesting another's grapes, cutting another's lumber, stealing another's firewood, theft of an eel net, and theft of a woman's bracelet,[162] the lattermost perhaps showing that the Franks were not naked utilitarians.

When the theft was by a freeman, the liability was a hybrid of compensatory and quasi-criminal. The theft of something with a value of two

[156] *Pactus legis Salicae* Sect. 3 par. 7, 8.

[157] Throughout the *Pactus legis Salicae* provisions, in addition to setting fixed monetary composition in *soladi* the paragraphs add language to this effect: "in addition to its value and a fine for the loss of use." Unless otherwise noted, for brevity the reader may assume the inclusion of such extra penalties.

[158] *Pactus legis Salicae* Sect. 4 par. 1-5.

[159] *Pactus legis Salicae* Sect. 5,6,7,8.

[160] Technically trespass, but also theft of the opportunity of the rightful owner to profitably exploit his land.

[161] Specifically, a fine of fifteen *soladi* for "anyone [who] does business with another's slave without the knowledge of his master." *Pactus legis Salicae* Sect. 27 par. 33.

[162] *Pactus legis Salicae* Sect. 27 par. 6, 7, 8, 13, 17, 19, 23, 24, 25, 27, 28, 34.

*denarii* would be responsible for 600 *denarii* (or fifteen *soladi*). Sterner penalties were imposed when the thief broke into the house by breaking a lock or using a skeleton key, in which event his liability would be forty-five *soladi*.[163]

Depriving a man of his horse was a matter of special gravity. Even the simple mounting and riding of another's horse, irrespective of intent to steal, could carry with it liability of thirty *soladi*.[164] Separate attention was devoted to theft of boats, and of theft committed in a mill. As to boats, taking another's boat and crossing the river with it imported a penalty of three *soladi*. But if the boat owner can prove that the man actually intended to steal the boat, the penalty would be fifteen *soladi*. More serious still would be the composition required of the man who broke in to steal a vessel "that is locked up," and an even greater penalty would accompany proof that a man stole a boat was both locked up *and* suspended within a shelter.[165]

Regarding mills, if a freeman stole grain from another's mill, he would be liable in the amount of fifteen *soladi*, "in addition to its value and a fine for the loss of its use." The thief who took an iron tool from that mill would incur a penalty of forty-five *soladi*. One who "breaks a sluice in another man's water mill" would be held liable for the same amount.[166]

The centrality of barnyard animals to the Frankish economic welfare led logically to special treatment for their theft. For the theft of the bell of a herd of pigs the penalty was fifteen *soladi*; for the theft of the bell of a cow three *soladi*; for the bell from a horse fifteen *soladi*; and for the hobble of a horse three *soladi*.[167]

---

[163] *Pactus legis Salicae* Sect. 11 par. 5.

[164] *Pactus legis Salicae* Sect. 23 par. 1.

[165] *Pactus legis Salicae* Sect. 21 par. 1 (three *soladi*); par. 2 (fifteen *soladi*); par. 3 (thirty five *soladi*; and par. 4 (forty five *soladi*).

[166] *Pactus legis Salicae* Sect. 22 par. 1, 2, 3.

[167] *Pactus legis Salicae* Sect. 27 par. 1 (pigs), 2 (cow), 3 (horse bell); 4 (horse hobble). For the bell to a herd of pigs and also the horse hobble the paragraphs also include penalties for "its value and a fine for the loss of its use." It is probable that such additional penalties originally accompanied each animal and each type of theft.

*Breaking and Entering*

The laws of the Salian Franks identify a variety of wrongs for which intruders may be found liable, with distinct amounts in composition liability assigned to each. They range from tearing down another's enclosure;[168] to breaking into an unlocked workshop;[169] to breaking into a locked workshop;[170]

*Harm Caused by Animals*

The liability provisions regarding crop damage caused by barn animals seem less concerned with composition than with (1) the penalties that attached to false denials; and (2) the protection of the animals from harm at the hands of the landowner. Regarding first the penalties for false denials, we turn to *Pactus legis Salicae* Sect. 9 par. 1, 4, 7, and 8. Each of these sections relate to injury to an animal that has trespassed upon another's land, and set a fine for any landowner who injures the animal of another that has come under his control. The provisions also condemn and punish specifically anyone who with another's animals in his possession injures it.

*Theft by Force*

In matters of punishment for ambush and robbery, the *Pactus legis Salicae* favored the Salian Franks over the Romans. Any man robbing a freeman would be liable in sixty-two and one half *soladi*. If a Roman robbed a Salian Frank, and the proof was not definite, the Roman could try to absolve himself with twenty-five oathtakers. Should this number of oathtakers not be found, the accused had a choice between the above-noted money penalty and "the ordeal of boiling water."[171] If, on the other hand, the Frank should rob the Roman,

---

[168] *Pactus legis Salicae* Sect. 27 par. 22 (fifteen *soladi*).

[169] *Pactus legis Salicae* Sect. 27 par. 29 (fifteen *soladi*).

[170] *Pactus legis Salicae* Sect. 27 par. 30 (forty-five *soladi*, plus "in addition to the value of what is stolen" and "a fine for the loss of its use."). Should the burglar steal nothing, he would still be liable for fifteen *soladi*.

[171] *Pactus legis Salicae* Sect. 14 par. 1, 2. The ordeal of boiling water entailed having

and there was no definite proof, the accused could summon twenty oathtakers. Absent this number, he could discharge his liability with the payment of thirty *soladi*. Noticeably absent was the boiling water alternative.

*Arson*

Several sections of the *Pactus legis Salicae* carefully parsed the types of arson and the appropriate penalty for each. For the very serious wrong of setting fire to another's house in which others were known to be sleeping, he would be liable for 2500 *denarii*, or sixty-two and one half *soladi*. If a man were to perish in the blaze, the arsonist would be liable for sixty-two and one half *soladi*, plus a fixed *wergeld* of two hundred *soladi*, and if the house was destroyed, another sixty-two and one half *soladi*.[172]

Composition in the same amount (2500 *denarii*) would be imposed for setting fire to an adjoining house made of wicker, a granary or a barn with stored grain, or a pigsty. Lesser liability would be imposed for setting fire to or cutting down another's fence or hedge.[173]

*Assault and Battery*

The particularity of the *Pactus legis Salicae* regarding battery and wounds caused thereby might lead the reader to think that they had imagined and written corresponding rules for every corporeal wrong man can inflict on man, and the reader would not be far off.

One seeking but failing to kill a man with a blow would be liable for 2500 *denarii*, or sixty-two and one half *soladi*. A missed endeavor to kill a man with a poisoned arrow wound result in the same monetary penalty.[174] If the wrong-

---

the accused place his hand in boiling water. If within a time certain after doing so his hand was uninjured, he was considered innocent, etc.

[172] *Pactus legis Salicae* Sect. 16 par. 1.

[173] *Pactus legis Salicae id.* at par. 2, 3, 4, 6, 7.

[174] *Pactus legis Salicae* Sect 17 par. 1. For computations to follow, if the penalty in *dinarii* does not equal a whole number, I will use only the amount of *dinarii*.

doer wounded a man so that "blood spurts on the ground," the penalty was fifteen *soladi*. One inflicting a head wound "so that the brain appears" would be liable in a like amount.[175]

A head wound sufficiently serious as to cause "the three bones that cover the brain [to] protrude would incur liability of thirty *soladi*, as would one in-flicting a wound that "is between the ribs and...penetrates as deep as the in-testines." If the latter wound failed to heal and continued to bleed an additional liability of 2500 *dinarii* would be imposed, plus nine *soladi* for medical treat-ment.[176] Other provisions draw distinctions between striking with a stick and either causing or failing to cause blood to flow, and striking "another three times with a clenched fist" irrespective of injury.[177]

Other wounds were addressed with a specificity one might encounter in a schedule of modern workers compensation laws. An incomplete but repre-sentative selection of the injuries and the composition associated therewith might include: mutilation of another's hand or foot, the knocking out of an eye, or cutting off an ear or a nose, 100 *soladi*;[178] cutting of another's hand so that it "dangles maimed" or cutting it altogether through, or cutting off an-other's thumb or foot, 2500 *denarii*; cutting off another's thumb that it "dan-gles maimed," thirty soladi; cutting off the second finger, "with which one shoots an arrow," thirty-five *soladi*; cutting off two fingers, thirty-five *soladi* (if three fingers, forty-five soladi); knocking out another's eye 2500 *dinarii*; cutting out another's tongue "so that he cannot speak," 100 *soladi*; breaking another's tooth, fifteen *soladi*; castrating a freeman, 100 *soladi* (or if the entire genitalia, 200 *soladi*).[179]

---

[175] *Pactus legis Salicae* Sect 17 par. 3, 4.

[176] *Pactus legis Salicae* Sect 17 par. 6, 7.

[177] *Pactus legis Salicae* Sect 17 par. 8, 9, 10.

[178] *Pactus legis Salicae* Sect 29 par. 1.

[179] *Pactus legis Salicae* Sect 29 par. 2, 3, 4, 5, 6, 7, 8, 10, 12, 15, 16, 17, 18. Other para-graphs within the same section, specifically par. 1, 1, 13, and 14, designate other monetary damages, for nose, ear, and foot injuries, but the differences are only in degree. They most likely reflect amendments or revisions to the *Pactus legis Salicae* that were layered in over time without the corresponding redactions of the earlier versions. *See also Pactus legis Salicae* Sect 29 par. 1.

*Public Nuisance*

A cluster of the provisions of the *Pactus legis Salicae* address the classic public nuisance scenario of the unprivileged blocking of a public way. The blocking or driving away of a "freeman from his way" would be liable for fifteen *soladi*. To do so to a freewoman or girl would be penalized by a fine of forty-five *soladi*. And the barricading of a road that goes to water, fifteen *soladi*.

As to the steeper liability imposed for blocking or impeding a freewoman or a girl, when compared to the penalty for the same offence against a man, it is possible to imagine whimsically that this shows some germinal stage of chivalry in the Frankish culture. It is more probable that chivalry aside, women and children turned away from the public road and forced in some instances to travel less public paths were, as compared with men, put a greater risk of violence.

*False Accusation and Defamation*

If a man accused before the king an innocent man who was not thereby able to counter the claim, the accuser would be liable for 2500 *dinarii*.[180]

One who hurled insults of several different types might find himself liable. For calling another a louse, the penalty was fifteen *soladi*; a skunk, three *soladi*; a freewoman a prostitute, forty-five *soladi*; a fox or a hare, three *soladi*.[181]

These initial examples prompt some observations. First the identification of certain statements as being *per se* defamatory bears a close resemblance to the common law's later segregating certain slurs, such as impugning unchastity, as slander *per se*. Also, regarding calling a man or a woman yet another living thing would not today be defamatory, as its impossibility of truth would be evident to any observer. For this reason, it may be that the primary objective of the liability rule was to prohibit what today are called "fighting words," which, notwithstanding the First Amendment, a state can permissibly forbid, in order to interdict breaches of the peace.

Also of interest, the consequence of calling another a louse was a fine greater than that for any other animal, which might be explained that of the

180  *Pactus legis Salicae* Sect 18 par. 1.
181  *Pactus legis Salicae* Sect 30 par. 1, 2, 3, 4, 5.

several animals, having lice is an extremely communicable condition that puts all associating with the target of the insult at risk of contracting it, and, it follows, unfair ostracism if the accusation is not true. Lastly, a remedy for being called a prostitute was only available to a freewoman, a reiteration of the rule that slaves owned nothing, not even the right to their reputation.

Finally, a freeman who imputed that another had "thrown away his shield and...taken to flight," and who was unable to prove this, would be liable in the amount of three *soladi*. And one unable to prove the truth of an accusation that another was an informer or a liar would be required to pay fifteen *soladi*.[182]

# VII. CONCLUSION

As summarized by Prof. Edward Peters, "the study of the Germanic law codes has much to contribute to the comparative history of law and society."[183]

Beyond this, I advance two thoughts. The firsts pertains to the relative significance of Justinian's work in the time following its promulgation and imposition. The second relates to the importance of the Gothic peoples', here most specifically the Burgundians, the Lombards and the Salian Franks, legal and societal advancement upon achieving control over most of the former Western Empire.

As to the enduring significance of Justinian's work, it has never been disputed that the form, the substance, and the multiple adumbrations of Justinian's Code and the *Corpus Juris Civilis* are, taken together, a highly accurate representation of Roman customary law and legislative enactment at the time of their mid-Sixth Century promulgation. The question remains this: What were the reach and the depth of the influence of this work in the centuries that followed first the fall of the Western Empire and later that of the Byzantine

---

[182]   *Pactus legis Salicae* Sect 30 par. 6, 7.

[183]   THE LOMBARD LAWS xix (Katherine Fischer Drew, trans.)(U. Pa. Press.1973)(Introduction by Edward Peters).

Empire. I suggest here that to scholars and observers from the early Middle Ages through approximately 1000 A.D., Justinian's contribution has always been larger than life, or put another way, that it was only through its hybridization with Gothic law that it would attain a substantial measure of its enduring influence on European law. The *Corpus Juris Civilis* was only promulgated during Justinian's short-lived (seventeen year) re-consolidation of the Western Empire with that of the East. In none of these territories was Roman law banned, it is true. Rather in each the customary law of the territories of origin of the usurpers would hold the edge, while countenancing Roman law but not advancing it. Indeed, even if Burgundians, the Lombards and the Salian Franks had rulers intended continued, particularized application of Roman law, it would have been extremely difficult to do so. After the fall of the Western Empire, large parts of the *Corpus Juris Civilis* were simply unavailable, and would not reappear until the time of the Crusades.

It is true that upon the discovery of a sufficient part of the original texts Roman law would thereafter become an important theme in the studies in Bologna and elsewhere. But by this time in continental Europe and elsewhere centuries had passed, even including centuries before the fall of the Western Empire, in which Roman law had already been ineradicably altered by contact with the customary law of Germanic populations.

Upon the fall of Justinian, the Romans themselves would not be the conquerors of any of the several Gothic groups.[184] However it was the coming to Christianity of those peoples and the inexorable reconfiguration during the later Middle Ages of the kingships into nations that came to resemble modern Europe, and the reintroduction of Roman-Hellenic structure to the praxis of such states, that commended to observers description of the Goths, at least prior to their conversion, as barbarians. And yet as has been described, in Italy and elsewhere, many Germanic contributions to the law can be correctly called progressive.

What were the principal contributions of the Gothic codes? We must look beyond some scholarly critiques that would characterize the Germanic adum-

---

[184] Nor, for that matter, would there be any Roman resurgence in Britain over the Celtic, Saxon, or Scandinavian groups.

bration of new law codes based reflecting both their own customary law and also Roman law as a simple aping of the Roman model.[185] This assessment is misleading, because the Germans came about their published codes by a far more textured means. For many, the codes were preceded by decades in which the tribes either occupied land upon the perimeter of the Western Empire, taking on the obligation of defending the Empire against more dangerous threats. In the course of this symbiotic relationship, the Germanics of necessity had commercial and cultural intercourse with Romans and their laws. By another means described above, that of the extension of hospitality, Germans in Gaul, modern Italy and elsewhere actually partnered with Romans, further stirring the potlatch that would become the law codes. The codes themselves represented free standing recitations of the law that would govern a multicultural people comprised of Romans and Germanics. Their original content furthered and by their constant revision represented new law for newly organized political states. That the Franks, the Burgundians and the Lombards adopted a written presentations, most often in Latin, with an organization with which the Romans had enjoyed success, was simply astute and does not by any stretch make their contributions derivative.

The Goths were largely successful in turning their culture away from its kinship origins of violent justice, and to systems of composition for injury. At this they developed subtle economic incentives to put away feud and adopt economic compensation or compensation in kind. The adoption of *wergeld* and also the widespread use of codified tables of composition to be associated with particularized wrongs, in addition to presaging in some way, modern workers compensation, sent an understandable message of deterrence to those who might turn to mayhem to solve disputes. Apart from feud, many ancient Germanic practices, such as trial by boiling water, were tamed or eliminated in the pursuit of new agricultural societies. And the codes adopted distinctions between accidental and intentional harm, as well as evaluations for negligence liability employing approaches uncan-

---

[185] ESTHER COHEN, THE CROSSROADS OF JUSTICE: LAW AND CULTURE IN LATE MEDIEVAL FRANCE 16 (E.L. Brill 1993): "the greatest influence of Roman law lay in the act of codification, which provided the impulse for Germanic leaders to ape the emperor in writing down the laws of their people."

nily similar to modern standards of duty and proximate cause. The list could go on.

When the legal and social history of the period is read in its entirety, it becomes clear that the Goths neither destroyed Roman law, nor were they its caretakers. Instead they created an entirely new society, adapted to their new needs. The rejected any old practices, be they Roman or Gothic, that did not advance their new societies. And they developed and codified new law and a new social order the progressiveness of which, when seen relative to its time, stood on an equivalence with any other populations of the early Middle Ages.

# CHAPTER 4

# MYTH, FOLKLORE,
# AND ANCIENT ETHICS

## I. INTRODUCTION

Myths and folklore[1] have been born, adopted, adapted, and passed on for perhaps 10,000 years of Man's recollected past.[2] Mythic characters have been personified as beings who have dwelled in the sky in manlike form with fantastic powers; sea serpents or other fantastical creatures; keepers of the afterlife, or Hell, residing in the bowels of the earth; and as benign or malign, corporeal or incorporeal, actors roaming on land. In sharp contrast, folk tale protagonists ordinarily possess no such fantastic attributes. Rather, they tend to possess the "standard folk-tale qualities of intelligence, courage, kindness, and luck."[3]

From prehistoric time onward, social groups have hewn to myth and story for two principal reasons: (1) to permit them to give logic, however primitive,

---

[1] As will be seen, there are important distinctions between myths and folktales. However, in this Chapter, when the reference is made to generalized imagined being or phenomenon, I will use "myth" to include folklore.

[2] Epic poems have, by one estimate, been dated only as far back as 4,000 years. ROBERT E. ANDERSON, THE STORY OF EXTINCT CIVILIZATIONS OF THE EAST, 44 (George Newnes, Ltd. 1898).

[3] Alison Lurie, THE PASSION OF C.S. LEWIS, 53 N.Y. REV. BOOKS 10, 12 (2006) (reviewing *The Chronicles of Narnia: The Lion, the Witch and the Wardrobe*) (Walt Disney Pictures 2005).

to nature and natural forces;[4] and (2) to reinforce norms the common weal has wished to promote as consistent with an ordered, safe, and productive community. As such, the effect of myth and folklore on social systems is the primary focus this Chapter. More specifically, the objective is to identify a representative selection of myths and folk tales, and to explain their obvious- or arguable-relation to communities' norms of deterring bad behavior and creating incentives for good behavior.

The mind of primitive and ancient man turned to themes, stories, and myths that seemed to be realistic explanations of, or rationalizations of, the external world. As it happens, primitive man, and to a lesser extent ancient man, could not readily distinguish between his life or being and the forces of the external world. Without this latter and fairly modern capacity, man's interpretations of the forces of nature, as well as the behavior of other humans or human collectives, were likely to be projections of his own wishes, fears and experience. When rain would fall beneficially, or the sun would shine seasonally, or combatant groups or cultures would not interrupt the safety and progress of the group, and justice and fairness governed man's activities with others, these stories would explain these phenomena as consistent with the will of nature and nature's gods. When, alternatively, the rain caused floods, or the crops failed due to an erratic climate, or internecine conflict interrupted the ordinary patterns of life, man's myths would assign the reason to the will of a malevolent, capricious, or displeased natural force and its gods. The forceful psychological projection afoot in the adoption of these myths is revealed in the fact that a very large proportion of them involve powerful presences in human form.

In the Preface to his influential BULFINCH'S MYTHOLOGY,[5] mythologist Bulfinch suggests in the language a patrician might employ that' a core value to the study of mythology[6] is that "without a knowledge of mythology much of the elegant literature of our own language cannot be understood and ap-

---

[4] For the purposes of this article, I will use "primitive man" to mean preliterate human social groupings. "Ancient man", in turn, is used to describe ancient literate societies, such as the ancient Egyptians or Greeks.

[5] THOMAS BULFINCH, BULFINCH'S MYTHOLOGY OF GREECE AND ROME WITH EASTERN AND NORSE LEGENDS ix (1968).

[6] In Bulfinch's case, particularly Greek mythology.

preciated."[7] However, as this Chapter will argue, Bulfinch assigns much too modest a role for mythology in both yesterday and today's world because myths, as first envisioned, were a very sincere evocation of how Man interpreted himself in relation to the natural world.

Additionally, and of greater significance here, myths should be seen as a means of expressing and passing from generation to generation a particular society's cultural self image, from matters ceremonial to substantive.[8] And as would be inevitable, a body of myth among primitive and ancient man has always been devoted to concepts of morality, ethics, and notions of right and wrong. In other words, bodies of myth have forever included many of the initiating stories of the rewards of the just life and the penalties that follow the unjust life. Myths may also, from time to time, equip their adherents with the pessimistic expectation that the just result will not always be reached.

# II. MYTH, FOLKLORE, AND SOCIAL MEDIATION

## A. MYTH, GENERALLY

WEBSTER'S THIRD NEW INTERNATIONAL DICTIONARY provides this definition of myth: "a story that is usu[ally] of unknown origin and at least partially traditional, that ostensibly relates historical events usu[ally] of such character as to serve to explain some practice, belief, institution, or natural phenomenon."[9] The definition continues by assigning a principal signification of myth to its role in religious rites.[10] However, as this Chapter will address, the reach of myths as stories, the guidance and uncritical acceptance of which affects a culture, is not confined to a group's sacred rites.

---

[7] *Id.* at 5.

[8] PETER FITZPATRICK, THE MYTHOLOGY OF MODERN LAW 65 (Maureen Cain & Carol Smart eds., 1992).

[9] WEBSTER'S THIRD NEW INTERNATIONAL DICTIONARY 1497 (16th ed. 1971).

[10] *Id.*

There are several telling aspects to this definition. First, the mythical story is usually of unknown origin.[11] This aspect is ordinarily true inasmuch as myths did not spring from the art of individual sooths or visionaries but from collective creativity that certainly spanned generations, as the story underwent adaptation after adaptation in order to render a myth as intelligible to the task as possible. That myths "ostensibly relate historical events" is seen in the form and content characteristics of myths. They entail a story that may begin as simply as a boy walking in a glade or as a god betrayed by a member of his court. However, the portrayal, which seems fantastic to the modern reader, was subjectively thought to be true in its time.[12] Finally, myths serve to explain or rationalize things. As to the natural world, a myth may explain the origin of thunder, the turning of the seasons, or the behavior of game animals. Or, it may explain the origins of the practice of hospitality between and among primitive peoples,[13] or why telling the truth is commendable, but not necessarily gainful.

It has been claimed that mythology and theology are "fundamentally alike in philosophic conception and point of view" in that "[b]oth are supernaturalistic interpretations of the world and of human experience."[14] "In theology, as in myths of primitive peoples, we find the same kinds of stories of gods, demons, and heroes."[15] This Chapter will for the most part avoid discussing religion or sacred texts. As such, it will not treat sacred religious themes as either myth or as fact, although it gives brief treatment elsewhere to representative examples of harmony between Judeo-Christian writings and the subsequent law of torts.[16]

---

[11] *Id.*

[12] *See* FITZPATRICK, *supra* at 17.

[13] *See generally*, M. Stuart Madden. The Cultural Evolution of Tort Law, 37 ARIZ. ST. L.J. 831 (2005) (surveying examples of ancient and primitive cultural responses to torts and remedies).

[14] LESLIE A. WHITE, THE EVOLUTION OF CULTURE: THE DEVELOPMENT OF CIVILIZATION TO THE FALL OF ROME 354 (1959).

[15] *Id.*

[16] *See* EXPLORING TORT LAW 11-51 (M. Stuart Madden ed., 2005); *see also* MADDEN, *supra* at 831 (surveying examples of ancient and primitive cultural responses to torts and remedies). It remains nonetheless an irresistible attraction to point out that the

Conceptually, civil defalcations, such as common torts could be distinguished from outright sins by the application of a simple test in which sins are offenses against God (or more broadly, deities) while torts are offenses against one's neighbor. However, it is necessary to note that this distinction between legal proscription and sin is often indistinct, and that sacred texts have, with frequency, assigned to religious figures the role of law giver. Curiously, although Hoebel suggested that, among primitive groups, it would be rare for the twain between religious strictures and private delict to meet,[17] he also described the Ashanti as a "par excellence" example of "law controlled by religion."[18] By way of a better known example, the author of EXODUS, the second book of the Pentateuch and also of the Christian First Covenant (or Old Testament), places Moses at the foot of Mount Sinai and records the Hebrew leader as the first interlocutor of God's law.[19]

## B. THE MYTH-FOLKLORE DIVIDE

How are we to distinguish myth from folklore, and what does such a distinction signify? Put simply, myth differs from folklore in at least three ways. First, in terms of temporality, myths and mythic figures are conventionally imagined as arising at or before the presence of Man. In other words, myths and mythic figures are believed to have appeared in a time before time. To be distinguished, while many folk tales suggest the most ancient of origins, others allow for an interpretation that they might have taken place in an indeterminate time, or a time that can be counted in generations,[20] with the most familiar of introductions: "Once upon a time."

---

Judeo-Christian depiction of creation set forth in Genesis enjoys, to all but literalists, a singular position among mythic tales.

[17] "I believe [that] a review of the evidence will show that primitive criminal law coincides with certain notions of sin with remarkable frequency, albeit not exclusively. Private law, which predominates among primitives, rarely if ever undertakes to add its sanctions to tabu [sic: taboo]: E. ADAMSON HOEBEL, THE LAW OF PRIMITIVE MAN: A STUDY IN COMPARATIVE LEGAL DYNAMICS 259 (Antheneum 1979) (1954).

[18] *Id.* at 264.

[19] EXODUS 19-23.

[20] For example, someone's father's father's father's father's father's father.

155

Second, in terms of sheer cultural reach, the gods, or other fabulous and powerful creatures of myth, most commonly fight only among themselves for some right or prerogative, as no ordinary mortal is a match for them. Also, the effect of their successes or failures is applicable to the known world, even if it is merely a subpart thereof, such as the phenomena of the sea, the sky, or the land. In contrast, in folk tales the protagonists ordinarily possess only the "standard folk-tale qualities of intelligence, courage, kindness, and luck."[21] The tales are typically parables that reinforce extant community wisdom or norms.

Third, in terms of plain of generality, myths most frequently set a physical or moral rule, or at least an expectation, of general applicability. Also, members of the pertinent social group actually and subjectively believe in the truth of the mythic tale. Accordingly, Man only acts in defiance of such a standard at his peril. Readily distinguishable are folk tales, which do not ordain any particular conduct, but instead invite consideration of the merits and demerits of a course of conduct. Additionally, the audiences of folk stories usually have an inkling that the tale consists of equal parts imagination, history, custom and culture, and admonition. This is to say, folk stories have typically been interpreted to be read with a dollop of circumspection. In addition, fables, even when essaying a similar theme, e.g., harm by force, theft, etc., offer only a parable supporting the theme or tenet already adopted by the community. Put another way, myths, often in overwhelming ways, set the norms, while folk stories, more often employing ordinary persons, operate to reinforce rules.

## C. MYTH AND SOCIAL MEDIATION

Because myth flowed from ancient Man's yet unborn capacity to imagine himself as an agent operating independently of nature and other men, it follows that in its identification, cultural goals, norms, and strictures, myth antedates any law or norm of any society.[22] This is so because to cause a law or norm to

---

[21] Lurie, *supra* at 2, 10, 12.

[22] *See generally* Mark P.O. Morford & Robert J. Lenardon, Classical Mythology 1-8 (Longman Inc. 3d ed. 1985) (1971) (discussing definitions, theories, and

be in effect, man would have had to develop the capacity to imagine himself as distinct from others in his hereditary group, from his possessions, and from his personal or individual prerogatives.[23] Thus, the members of any culture's mythmaking era were, by definition, not yet capable of creating law, and this is true whether the law or norm was written, unwritten, or customary.[24] This is not to say that a culture's commitment to a structure of myths precluded its later adoption of norms or laws, as in the case of the ancient Greeks, but rather that the former simply preceded the latter.[25]

As hunter and gatherer cultures came to adopt agriculture, their myths also evolved. The hunter and gatherer groups, accustomed as they were to a very risky and often dangerous life, possessed myths inhabited by giants and titans.[26] The newer agricultural societies weaned themselves from many of these myths and created myths more harmonious with lives of reasonable predictability associated with the seasons, harvest, and, if successful, surplus.[27] Consistent with this idea, many new agricultural societies developed newer myths in which the older, more violent giants and ogres were defeated and often buried by peace-loving figures.[28] Further, with the passage of multiple millennia, Man would be drawn to the logic of natural law in which certain universally beneficial rules would become accepted as suitable to at least all free men. From natural law, it was but a short step to man-made law.

For each affected social group, primitive and ancient myth constituted an original and synthetic revelation of social order.[29] As such, three features would come to characterize myths pertaining to man's relation *inter se* to others. First,

---

interpretations of myths).

[23] *See id.*

[24] *See id.*

[25] *See* FITZPATRICK, *supra* at 1. In recognizing that the myth had its origins long before that of any law, Fitzpatrick states, "[m]odern law, after all, was formed in the very denial of that mythic realm which had so deluded the pre-moderns." *Id.*

[26] *See* MORFORD & LENARDON, *supra* at 15-23.

[27] *See id.*

[28] *See id.*

[29] *See id.* at 1-8.

such myths or fables either explicitly or implicitly revealed norms and expectations that influenced individual or group behavior. Second, the instruction of these myths would vary in no significant way from such norms, customs, and laws as might in time follow. Third, these myths would enjoy great similarity in their identification of normative values consistent with the healthy growth and prosperity of the respective primitive and ancient groups. As taken from populations from six of the seven continents, these fables provide stories of tribulations, rewards, achievements, and failures that serve as a roadmap through time towards numerous precepts of modern justice, which include, perhaps most centrally, self-discipline, forbearance and fairness.

Thus, a culture's matured mythological philosophy informs every part of its existence, including its goals, the control of group or individual behavior, morality, the integration into and the uniformity of social processes, and indeed, the group's very way of life.[30] The sum total of any peoples' beliefs is its philosophy, which may be naturalistic or supernaturalistic, which is to say, mythical.[31] A people postulating a spiritual reason for natural phenomena impose their logic of observation upon the natural world without distinguishing their existence in an external world independent of themselves. As Leslie A. White wrote, "[w]hile we recognize a significant naturalistic component in the philosophies of primitive peoples, their over-all [sic] complexion appears to be predominately supernaturalistic-mythologic in character."[32]

This Chapter opens this discussion by proposing that myth has operated in two principal ways: first, to assign reasons for the activities of nature, which would be otherwise incomprehensible to ancient Man, and second, to mediate normatively between conflicting perceptions of the human or group behavior, which again is incomprehensible without explanation or rationalization.[33] Of

---

[30]  *See* White, *supra* note 15, at 263-64.

[31]  *Id.* at 261.

[32]  *Id.* at 262.

[33]  *Cf.* Fitzpatrick, *supra* at 16, in which Professor Fitzpatrick, in describing the practical effect of the sacred-mythological text of Genesis, writes: "Such mediations transcend what would otherwise be the insuperable limits and contradictions of the profane world." *Id.*

particular relevance to the latter is that myth, as is also true of norms and customs, can be seen to represent deontic logic, or the "logic of imperatives,"[34] which is to say that myth identifies "necessary relations of opposition and concomitancy.[35] Choosing here for example only the concepts as they might be expressed in the law of torts, a particular myth or fable might provide a society with a means of distinguishing the idea of acting from duty from the idea of "delict."[36]

As to both natural and social mediating roles governing conflicts between expectation and phenomenon, it is generally accepted that ancient myths were born and not made. This is to say that primitive or ancient Man did not as a matter of course objectify a certain external event or sequence of external events and then consciously proceed to construct a mythic structure responsive thereto. Rather, as generally indisposed to or incapable of disassociating the external world from himself, primitive Man projected his own binary mental faculties upon the natural world, imposing mythological explanations for events that without such projection would be inexplicable. Thus myth would serve to explain human interaction if the normatively optimal— or rational— conduct actually occurred. Myth would also make contrary or irrational conduct comprehensible by providing a rationalization for it, i.e., by describing a god who was generally good and predictable but whom was sometimes given to capricious or erratic behavior.

The overarching significance of this mediating role of myth is further revealed in the understanding of a particular man's psychological relationship with the external world and with the actions of others: Man needs an explanation for things. As put by Langer, "[man] can adapt himself somehow to anything his imagination can cope with; but he cannot deal with [c]haos."[37] Myth

---

[34] *See generally*, GEORG HENRIK VON WRIGHT, NORM AND ACTION (Ted Honderich ed., 1963) (discussed in M.D.A. FREEMAN, LLOYD'S INTRODUCTION TO JURISDICTION 205 n.36 (7th ed. 2001)).

[35] Jeremy Bentham, *Of Laws in General* in COLLECTED WORKS OF JEREMY BENTHAM 97 (J.H. Burns ed., 1970).

[36] JOSEPH RAZ, THE CONCEPT OF A LEGAL SYSTEM 94 (1970).

[37] SUSANNE K. LANGER, PHILOSOPHY IN A NEW KEY 287 (1951) (quoted in CLIFFORD GEERTZ, THE INTERPRETATION OF CULTURES 99-100 (1973)).

is one means of avoiding such chaos, as it "provides a 'logical model by means of which the human mind can evade unwelcome contradictions and so provides a means of 'mediating' between opposites that would, if unreconciled, be intolerable."[38]

Primitive and ancient Man's adoption and perpetuation of mythological stories and structures, therefore, reveals his "obsession with the real, his thirst for being."[39] In the analytical structure of Claude Levi-Strauss, human societies throughout the world have evidenced "certain unchanging patterns" and a "consistent structure."[40] Levi-Strauss explained that "[m]yths are part of the working of this social machine and are derived ultimately from the structure of the mind."[41] The structure of the human mind, the reasoning goes, is binary, e.g., life/death, hunter/hunted, just/unjust. Thus, myth mediates between and resolves such "conflicting opposites."[42] As suggested, such binary opposites most often present themselves naturalistically. Of greater interest for present purposes, some of the opposites, such as truth/falsehood or justice/injustice, confront man in his dealings with other individuals or social groups. Whether the myth's instructive value is natural or societal, it is certainly labile and malleable, and may change in time.[43]

For example, one of the repeating patterns of myths from culture to culture and from age to age is that upon his death, a man's good deeds will be weighed against his bad deeds. If the good deeds outweighed the bad, the man would travel to a heaven-like place. If not, a version of hell awaited. Similarly, in Egyptian mythology, Thoth, the god of letters, dwelled in the underworld, where he recorded the weight of each man's soul, and delivered them to Osiris, the stork-like bird. The sum total of a man's good deeds, in

---

[38] MORFORD & LENARDON, *supra* at 10.

[39] MIRCEA ELIADE, MYTHS, DREAMS, AND MYSTERIES: THE ENCOUNTER BETWEEN CONTEMPORARY FAITHS AND ARCHAIC REALITIES 1 (Philip Mairet trans., Harper & Row 1960) (1957); *see* comment on the relation between myth and man's existential realization, below.

[40] MORFORD & LENARDON, *supra* at 7 (synopsizing the work of Levi-Strauss).

[41] *Id.*

[42] *Id.*

[43] *See* FITZPATRICK, *supra* at 26.

comparison to his sins, were measured in a negative confession in which a man's heart (morality) was finally weighed, and which account would become part of a The Book of the Dead. In Greek culture and in many others, a belief in reincarnation held that one who had lived a meritorious life would be reincarnated into some noble beast, such as a horse, whereas the unethical or unjust man would be reincarnated as, let us say, a dung beetle. To be sure, it is elementary to ask what bearing these observations have on myth and ancient ethics. This Chapter suggests that at its core, a belief in a final accounting, irrespective of wealth or moral judgments, is a strong incentive to peaceful, ethical behavior.

A societal belief in a myth or in a norm derived therefrom need not have the force of law in order to effectively regulate behavior. Indeed, some norms seem to have controlled social activity even more effectively than laws on the same or similar themes. Oftentimes characterized as "ruling ideas," myth's "exemplary" ideas "dra[w] a distinction between society and that which lies below it, in an underworld of seedy chaos."[44] In this latter role, even without a society's means of enforcement, myth, as well as norms and customs, can be seen to represent deontic logic, or the logic of imperatives,[45] which is to say the myth identifies necessary relations of opposition and concomitancy.[46] Understood as such, myth is not simply "the preserve of story tellers and performers of ritual," but rather and more importantly "an accessible and regular mode of being in the world, as a mode of making the deepest truths of life generally operative."[47]

Myth has always been imparted by two means: language and symbol. Put another way, myth has historically been conveyed by symbolic or oral story telling. Mythological thought "builds structured sets by means of a structured set, namely, language."[48] Regarding oral story telling, evaluation of the societal

---

[44] J. B. THOMPSON, Introduction to C. LEFORT, THE POLITICAL FORMS OF MODERN SOCIETY: BUREAUCRACY, DEMOCRACY, TOTALITARIANISM 17 (1986), quoted in FITZPATRICK, *supra* at 38.

[45] *See* VON WRIGHT, *supra*.

[46] BENTHAM, *supra* at 97.

[47] FITZPATRICK, *supra* note 9, at 22.

[48] CLAUDE LEVI-STRAUSS, THE SAVAGE MIND 21 n. *(1996) (unnumbered footnote

role of myth cannot be complete without reference to its primary means of transmission—the oral tradition. Anthropologist A. Raphaël Ndiaye explains that "[t]here are multiple suitable definitions of oral tradition; despite numerous nuances, it represents the complete information deemed essential, retained and codified by a society, primarily in oral form, in order to facilitate its memorization and ensure its dissemination to present and future generations."[49] Ndiaye continues, "[o]ral tradition appears then as a heritage which displays the many dimensions of humanity, including reason, intelligence and spirituality; a willingness to live on, allowing Claude Levi-Strauss in particular to affirm that there are no children among people—all are adults."[50] In preliterate societies, although deference was owed great men and village elders—or in matriarchal societies, their female equivalents—decisions were arrived at communally, or horizontally. "Within such societies, oral tradition guarantees its own reproduction by spreading in two directions, vertically and horizontally: vertically from the elders and the past to the present; horizontally, in a synchronous process between members of the contemporary society."[51] As one means of this reproduction, children played an essential role in the nurturing of the governing myth from one generation to another, in that they seemed to be as infused with a recognition of their participation in the collective as were their adult counterparts. Thus, the oral transmission of myth reinforced the horizontal aspects of primitive societies, including their horizontal decision making and law giving.

To some, a culture's adoption of mythic ideation is a function of primitive or ancient Man's incapacity to analyze reality. However, Claude Levi-Strauss, C. Leach, and others have rebuffed attribution of myths and rites to a proto-analytical "myth-making faculty," in which mankind "turn[s] its back on reality."[52] Instead, these thinkers have posited that a culture's myths

---

on page 21

[49] A. Raphaël Ndiaye, Oral Tradition: From Collection to Digitization, available at http://www.ifla.org/IV/ifla65/65m-e.htm

[50] Id.

[51] Id.

[52] A. Raphaël Ndiaye, Oral Tradition: From Collection to Digitization, available at http://www.ifla.org/IV/ifla65/65m-e.htm

are the fruits of a methodology that, taking into account the limitations of natural science available to any given era, seem perfectly in step with many of natural and social "truths" generated by many later societies.[53] Even though primitive Man's exploration and explanation of the natural world pre-dated the development of modern natural science, Levi-Strauss suggests, it is not for this reason "less scientific," nor are its postulates "less genuine."[54] However, as later explained by Clifford Geertz, there is reason to disagree that Man's mental disposition was essentially fixed prior to the development of culture, and that his current rational capabilities are merely extensions thereof. To these social scientists, "[t]ools, hunting, family organization, and, later, art, religion, and 'science' molded man somatically; and they are, there-fore, necessary not merely to his survival but to his existential realization." To these social scientists, the "principal value" of a culture's myths has been "to preserve until the present time the remains of methods of observation and reflection which were (and no doubt still are) precisely adapted to dis-coveries of a certain type: those which nature authorized from the starting point of a speculative organization and exploitation of the sensible world in sensible terms." Thus to Malinowski, far from the product of unsophisticated and credulous minds, myths have typically represented "a hard-worked active force[,] a pragmatic charter."[55]

In the end, it is probably most circumspect to assign both scientific and nonscientific attributes to myth. As Levi-Strauss concedes: "Mythical thought for its part is imprisoned in the events and experiences which it never tires of ordering and re-ordering in its search to find them a meaning. But it also acts as a liberator by its protest against the idea that anything can be meaningless with which science at first resigned itself to a compromise.[56] Any examination of myth, therefore, reveals myth and corresponding phenomena in a dialectic

---

[53]  *See id.*

[54]  MIRCEA ELIADE, MYTHS, DREAMS, AND MYSTERIES: THE ENCOUNTER BETWEEN CONTEMPORARY FAITHS AND ARCHAIC REALITIES (Philip Mairet trans., Harper & Row 1960); *see* comment on the relation between myth and man's existential real-ization, below.

[55]  B. MALINOWSKI, MAGIC, SCIENCE AND RELIGION AND OTHER ESSAYS 101 (1954).

[56]  LEVI-STRAUSS, *supra* at 22.

minuet.[57]

All myths relate a story. The form of the myth's conveyance may be a story, dance, or song; the myth may employ symbol, totem, or almost invariably, ritual. The choice and manner of utilizing such forms can greatly affect the power of the message and even the message itself. Whatever the form chosen, a myth's ritual, symbolism, totemism or otherwise "function[s] to synthesize a people's ethos—the tone, character and quality of their life, its moral and aesthetic style and mood—and their world view—the picture they have of the way things in sheer actuality are, their most comprehensive ideas of order."[58] Accordingly, the relation between law—either ancient or modern—and the myths of antiquity is best understood when one evaluates not only the content of the story but also the form of its portrayal. For example, the dress of the participants might provide a subtext, as exemplified by the Navajo elders to represent the myth of their original people by garb recollecting the original animals chosen to guide them. Further, they might involve ceremony, dance, or the erection of totems or even buildings.[59] Ceremonial representation, story-telling and, accompanying ritual represent a sum that is greater than its parts in terms both of believability and indelibility, a phenomenon that is true to this day.[60] It is no surprise that so many of today's binding "legal" actions

---

[57]  *Id.* at 230-31.

[58]  Geertz, *supra* at 89.

[59]  A remarkable feature of the religion of the Chaldeans has been used to explain the shape of their palaces and temples. They "lifted their eyes to the hills" on the northeast, 'the Father of countries,' and imagined it the abode of the Gods, the future home of every great and good man The type of the holy mountain was therefore reproduced in every palace and temple, sometimes by building it on an artificial mound with trees and plants watered from above [.] ." Anderson, *supra* at 34.

[60]  Of this phenomenon in modern popular culture, *see* Richard K. Sherwin. Law in Popular Culture, in The Blackwell Companion to Law and Society, 95, 99 (Austin Sarat ed., 2005):

Images do not simply 'add' to the persuasive force of words; they transform argument and, in so doing, have the capacity to persuade all the more powerfully. Unlike words, which compose linear messages that must be taken in sequentially, at least some of the meaning of images can be grasped all at once. This rapid intelligibility permits visual messages to be greatly condensed (it takes a lot less time to see a picture than to read a thousand words),

are enveloped in ceremony. For example, one need only consider the sacra-ment of marriage. Indeed, Scandinavian Realist Axel Hagerstrom sought to prove that, prosaic as the oral exchanges of purchase and sale under the Roman system of jus civile may have been, they were still part of "a system of rules for the acquisition and exercise of supernatural powers[,]"[61] and that the words and rituals had a "magical effect."[62] And, as M.D.A. Freeman paraphrases Fred-erick Pollack, "ritual is to law as a bottle is to liquor; you cannot drink the bot-tle, but equally you cannot cope with liquor without the bottle."[63]

Natural law, to Bertrand Russell, "decides what actions would be ethically right, and what wrong, in a community that had no government; and positive law ought to be, as far as possible, guided and inspired by natural law."[64] How-ever, the diplomacy that leads away from analyzing religion qua religion-as-myth does not preclude taking note of the frequent correlations diverse religions have made between natural law and the belief in one or more partic-ular gods. Such an analysis seems to step off the diplomatic tightrope with the expectation of distinguishing fact from fiction within a particular faith, for al-though most religious followers credit their sacred texts and stories as largely factual, they are typically inclined to assess the beliefs of others as fantastic. Therefore, it can arguably be said that at least from the perspective of a sub-stantial minority of persons, the sacred underpinnings of faith is footed in myth or fantasy.

What does this approach, if credited, permit us to do? To be sure, it urges thinkers to examine a pattern among faiths of assigning God's will as respon-sible for, or at least consistent with, natural law or natural rights.[65] The basic

---

and allows the image creator to communicate one meaning after another in quick succession. Such immediacy of comprehension enhances persuasion.

[61]  FREEMAN, *supra* at 857 (referencing AXEL HAGERSTROM, DER ROMISCHE OBLIA-TIONSBERGRIFF (1927).

[62]  *Id.*

[63]  *Id.* at 857-58.

[64]  BERTRAND RUSSELL. A HISTORY OF WESTERN PHILOSOPHY 628 (1945).

[65]  This inquiry puts aside Jeremy Bentham's legendary dismissal of natural law as "nonsense upon stilts." Jeremy Bentham, Anarchical Fallacies, Being an Examination of the Declaration of Rights Issued During the French Revolution, in NONSENSE

structure of natural law proposes that (1) the plan for man in society is the pursuit of what is good, just, and moral; (2) a perfect God is responsible for this plan, from which man deviates only at his peril; and (3) there is an unbreakable teleological connection between God's will and natural law.[66]

If this much is true, then the conclusion is almost inescapable—where diverse and heterogeneous faiths co-exist, one faith's perception of goodness, justice, and morality is based upon myth. This can be true even if the compared faiths share essentially similar sacred conclusions.

As suggested earlier, when a society has believed in myth, that myth has remained a means of social control, despite the fact that it has not been officially recognized as law.[67] Myth has long existed in societies that simultaneously adhered to independent social norms, or even written law.[68] Indeed, examples abound in which the power of myth to regulate a society's behavior has equaled or exceeded the power of its laws. As systematic significance along these lines, the mythological trappings of equality among mortals does not mean that primitive civil justice was immune to considerations of status or personage. For example, when discussing the legal tradition of the Plains Indian, Hoebel writes: "By the very reason of their special characters and social status the litigious behavior of such personages does not give a full picture of law at large. Justice may wear a blindfold and every man be equal before the law, but in every society—primitive and civilized—personality and social status color and influence every legal situation.[69]

---

Upon Stilts: Bentham, Burke and Marx on the Rights of Man 53 (Jeremy Waldron ed., 1987).

[66] *See* Mark Murphy, *The Natural Law in Ethics* Stan. Encyc. Phil. Sept. 23, 2002, available at http://plato.stanford.edu/entries/natural-law-ethcs (citing Saint Thomas Acquinas and his "moral theorizing" in natural law tradition) (last visited September 25, 2006).

[67] *See* Freeman, *supra* at 205.

[68] An important distinction between societies governed by law versus those governed by value or custom has been that "value judgments do not state facts but indicate choices or preferences." and therefore can be "so vague and subject to so much qualification, as to be vacuous" where as societies governed by law characteristically have the power of physical coercion which in effect create value and custom. Lord Lloyd of Hampstead Introduction to Jurisprudence 106-07 (M.D.A. Freeman ed., 4th ed. 1979).

In the next section, this Chapter will visit a variety of mythical stories that reveal the approach individual cultures have taken to rendering comprehensible the second type of myth referred to throughout; stories that pertain not to man's life in nature, but rather to man's life in his culture. In each of these stories it will be possible to see a normative message as to optimal behavior within that society. Without variation the stories are honest and industrious encomiums about individual behavior that show the preservation of a peaceful, just, and prosperous community. At the same time, in many of these myths the outcome is contrary to that which the individual or the society might fairly aspire. When this happens, as often as not, the result is attributable to the acts of a capricious, willful, or displeased deity or spirit. As unfortunate as this result may seem in absolute terms, it is by virtue of this latter type of story that primitive and ancient man could, when phenomena did not seem to align themselves intelligibly with results, locate a rationalization.

Put another way, although a central role of myth is to advance a cultural ideation that explains the external world, it follows that this explanation will provide that fairness, justice, comfort, and prosperity ought to prevail from time to time. However, perhaps just as often, those noble ideals will not prevail. This again is part and parcel to the rationalizing, mediating role of myth. An example of this role is the East African tale of Fire and Water that speaks of the "eternal struggle between truth and falsehood."[70] The tale recounts Truth, Falsehood, Fire, and Water journeying together, only to discover a herd of cattle. They decide it will be just to divide the herd into equal shares. This however, is not enough for greedy Falsehood. He seeks to set his fellow travelers upon themselves by first turning to Water and claiming that Fire intends to burn all nearby vegetation, thus driving the cattle away. Falsehood advises Water to extinguish the fire right away. Water unwisely heeds Falsehood's counsel and does so. Falsehood approaches Truth and claims that on the basis of what Water has done, he is not to be trusted and that he and Truth should flee with all of the cattle and head into the mountains. Truth is fooled, and

---

[69] HOEBEL, *supra* at 44.

[70] *See* THE BOOK OF VIRTUES FOR YOUNG PEOPLE: A TREASURY OF GREAT MORAL STORIES 277-79 (William J. Bennett ed., 1997).

agrees. As Truth and Falsehood take the cattle uphill, Water cannot follow. Atop the mountain, Falsehood reveals his mendacity and claims Truth as his servant. Truth defies him and the two fight amidst the rumble of thunder. Neither can destroy the other. They both call in Wind to decide the conflict but Wind responds that it is not for him to decide. In language that conveys a clear, normative preference for Truth, Wind states:

> Truth and Falsehood are destined to struggle. Sometimes Truth will win, but other times Falsehood will prevail, and then Truth must rise up and fight again. Until the end of the world. Truth must battle Falsehood, and must never rest or let down his guard, or he will be finished once and for all.[71]

With stories such as these in mind, the focus of this Chapter will be myth and folk tale, not as they interpret natural phenomena, but rather as they illuminate beliefs or customs of ethics, morality, and justice. As such, this Chapter will recite representative selections of myths and fables that illustrate many matters central to these evolving standards of conduct. Thus, the organization of this Chapter will avoid a formal separation of myth and folklore. Rather it will follow the paths of both through discussions of their substantive subject matter.

## III. ANCIENT MYTHO-DELICTUAL PRECEPTS

The universality of myths and folk tales is evidenced by the central role they play in giving cultural guidance, particularly when such stories or beliefs pertain to themes of justice, or notions of right and wrong. The myths and folklore of virtually all cultures contain a rich vein of such stories.

---

[71] *Id.* at 279.

## A. GOOD AND EVIL

The roads to many delicts are paved with bad intentions, and thus it is no surprise that primitive mythology contains variations on the most infamous story of the introduction of intentional violence into the world. The story, of course, is that of Cain and Abel, or the tale of the Good Twin and the Evil Twin.[72] Unsurprisingly, in other cultures, the intentional killing of a member of one's own family, clan, or tribe has always been considered the most horrific of evils.[73] For example, in a Native American context, the killing of one Cheyenne by another Cheyenne "was a stain on the tribal 'soul'..." revealing itself by a "miraculous appearance of blood on the feathers of the [Medicine] Arrows[,]" one of two important sacred totems (or fetishes) of the Cheyenne.[74] "While the blood remained on the feathers "bad luck dogged the tribe['s]" hunters and war parties.[75] The perpetrator was thought—by Judeo-Christian analogue— to bear "the mark of Cain," his internal organs rotting with such a stench as itself to drive away the game.[76]

A common mythic thread is that of evil being portrayed as a trickster. This is true in the following Aztec myth of Quetzalcoatl, and in the Norse myth of Balder thereafter. In the Aztec tradition, we find that the myth of Quetzalcoatl, in fact, may be "a combination of fact and myth."[77] In history, Quetzalcoatl may have been "Topilitzin (Our Prince)," who brought ethics and laws to the Toltec nation. In one version of the Quetzalcoatl myth, his counterpart, Tezcatlipoca, is not characterized as the Evil Twin of Quetzalcoatl, but for all intents and purposes he might as well be. Tezcatlipoca "represent[s] all the evils that test the moral fiber of human beings." Fittingly, "Tezcatlipoca is invisible" and has no corporeal presence. The themes of the principal Quetzalcoatl/Tezcatlipoca in-

---

[72] *Id.* at 279.

[73] *See, e.g.,* Molly Moore, In Turkey. 'Honor Killing' Follows Families to Cities, WASH. POST, August 8, 2001, at A01 (stating "[i]n Turkey, the killing of a family member draws the most stern penalty allowable: death or life in prison.").

[74] HOEBEL, *supra* at 156-57.

[75] *Id.*

[76] *Id.*

[77] DONNA ROSENBURG, WORLD MYTHOLOGY: AN ANTHOLOGY OF THE GREAT MYTHS AND EPICS 609 (1999).

clude the tensions between temptation and forbearance, temperance and excess, and reason and emotion. In this version, Tezcatlipoca holds a mirror to Quetzacoatl's face, and persuades him that his image "is wrinkled like that of an ancient creature."[78] Tezcatlipoca convinces the now insecure Quetzacoatl that he can regain his vitality and handsomeness by adopting a ridiculous raiment of quetzal bird feathers, a red and yellow painted face, a feathered beard, and a turquoise mask. He then urges Quetzacoatl to drink an inebriating beverage, of which he and his followers partake in excess. When he is again sober, Quetzacoatl realizes that among other immoral acts, he has committed incest with his sister. Even though he is ashamed, Quetzacoatl rationalizes temporarily that with his new wisdom of himself, he can lead his people. However, Tezcatlipoca continues his evil work by imposing illness and privation upon the tribe of Quetzacoatl, and ultimately Quetzacoatl leaves in a self-enforced exile and dies alone.

Again, against the backdrop of a Good Twin and an Evil Twin, an Iroquois creation myth develops the origins of the divide between good and evil. In the story of the Iroquois early people, there existed an Upper World that was inhabited by the Divine Sky People, and a Lower World covered by Great Water.[79] The Great Darkness comprised the world between the Great Water and the Upper World. In the myth of The Woman Who Fell From the Sky, the great chief of the Divine People had a daughter, Atahensic, who became gravely ill. A great corn tree provided food to the people. While sleeping, the chief dreamed that if he placed his daughter at the base of the corn tree, and then dug the tree up by its roots, she would be made well. He did so, but the only consequence was that the tree fell thunderously. A member of the sky people, horrified to see their source of food jeopardized, kicked Atahensic into the hole and she fell towards the Great Water. To save her, the water animals formed a raft of their bodies, but they eventually tired. These animals, Great Turtle, Muskrat, Beaver and Otter, then attempted to each dive to the bottom of the water and to return to the surface with earth. Only Muskrat succeeded, although he died in the effort, and Atahensic spread the earth about the edges

---

[78]   *Id.* at 611 (the text following the footnote recounts the myth of Quetzalcoatl).

[79]   *Id.* at 627 (the text following the footnote recounts the myth of The Woman Who Fell From the Sky.

of Great Turtle's shell, more and more, until the shell became so broad that it became Great Island, which would be inhabited by Earth People. There Atahensic dwelled, and eventually gave birth to a child, called Earth Woman.

Some time thereafter, Earth Woman became pregnant by the West Wind and gave birth to Good Twin and Evil Twin. Evil twin was so competitive in desiring to be born before Good Twin that he burst from Earth Mother's side, killing her. As time passed, for each beneficial act Good Twin sought for Great Island, Evil Twin would seek to sabotage them. Evil Twin shrunk Good Twin's fruit bearing Sycamore into a tree bearing only shrunken and inedible pods, and used his evil imagination to create the great mountains and the sharp rocks that hurt people's feet. Evil Twin then made huge predators, such as Bear, Wolf, and Panther, and game animals so large that they could not be safely hunted; however, Good Twin made the predators smaller, and the game animals of such a size that they cold be hunted by man. This was intolerable to Evil Twin, who sought to capture the abundance of beneficial animals and hide them in a cave, closing the cave with a boulder. Aware of this act, Good Twin pushed the boulder away, freeing the animals.

Eventually, Evil Twin concluded the obvious—that he and Good Twin could not coexist. Thus, Evil Twin proposed a fight. Good Twin, wishing to avoid violence, proposed a race. Then, Evil Twin asked Good Twin what could hurt him, and the Good Twin answered: "the wild rose." Asked the same question, Evil Twin answered: "Buck's thorns." Thus, along the proposed racing courses, Evil Twin placed the branches of the wild rose that he had taken from the garden of his grandmother, Atahensic. Good Twin gathered Buck's thorns from the forest and strew them along Evil Twin's side of the race path. The race began, and as it progressed, whenever Good Twin tired, he stopped, picked a wild rose, and ate it for renewed energy. Evil Twin had nothing to refresh himself, and was increasingly hobbled by the thorns in his feet. Upon his collapse, Evil Twin begged for mercy, but Good Twin resolved to treat him as he would have been treated had Evil Twin prevailed, and beat Evil Twin to death with a branch of Buck's thorns. Evil Twin's spirit left to become the spirit of the dead, and would eventually become the Evil Spirit.

One Norse tale of Balder also exemplifies this genre, and emphasizes the punishment that the treacherous may expect. To the Norse, Balder—the son of Odin and Frigg—represented the apogee of purity and virtue.[80] Inevitably therefore, evil, in the personage of Loki, would seek a way to kill him. Traveling the world, Balder's mother sought and received a covenant from all living things not to harm her son, save the little mistletoe bush, which she thought too young to bring harm. In disguise, Loki interrogated Frigg, who conceded this omission. Fashioning a mistletoe twig into a weapon, Loki joined a group engaged in a game in which Frigg's success was tested by having the participants hurl objects at Balder, only to find them bounce off harmlessly. Through trickery, Loki persuaded Hoder, Balder's blind brother, to take the mistletoe and throw it at Balder, and as a result, Hoder killed Balder with the mistletoe. With all of the gods in shock, Frigg asked Hermod the Bold to enter Niflheim, the kingdom of the dead, to confer with Hel, Loki's daughter, to seek conditions of Balder's release. Hel required proof that all creatures and forms in nature weep over Balder's death. Only one giantess refused, but it turned out that the giantess was Loki in disguise. Loki then fled for his life by taking the form of a fish. Thor, engaging in the search, captured him. Loki was bound to three huge rocks with his slain son's intestines, beneath a giant venomous snake. When drops of the venom touched Loki's skin, he writhed in such pain that the earth shook.

## B. VIRTUES

### 1. The Wages of Vice

Vanity and envy are the subjects of the Celtic tale "Gold-Tree and Silver-Tree."[81] In this tale, a particularly prideful Silver-Tree—the wife of the king

---

[80] *Id.* at 468 (the text following the footnote recounts the myth of The Death of Balder).

[81] Joseph Jacobs, Celtic Fairy Tales 88 (1968) (the text following the footnote recounts the myth of Gold-Tree and Silver-Tree).

and mother of Gold-Tree—returns time and again to a trout in a well and asks if she is "the most beautiful queen in the world." The trout, no thrall of the Queen, responds consistently that she is not, and says that the most beautiful is Gold-Tree. The Queen then devised a plan in which she feigned illness, and told her King that the only way for her to recover would be to eat the heart and liver of her daughter. Unprepared to so provide her, the King sent out hunters who killed a he-goat, and presented it to the Queen, who ate its heart and liver and declared herself well. When the Queen again questioned the trout a year later, she was alarmed to learn that Gold-Tree was still alive, had married a prince, and lived abroad. At her request, the King prepared a long ship to permit Silver-Tree to voyage to the land in which Gold-Tree now dwelled. Upon her mother's arrival, Gold-Tree hid in a locked room; however, Silver-Tree successfully importuned her daughter to at least put her finger through the keyhole so that she might kiss it. Of course, Silver-Tree did no such thing, and instead stabbed it with a poisoned point. When her husband, the Prince, found her dead, rather than begin burial rites, he placed her in a room and locked it. He eventually remarried. One day, the Prince's new wife gained access to the room and discovered the beautiful Gold-Tree. Noticing the poisoned stab in her finger, she removed it and Gold-Tree arose, as alive and as beautiful as ever.

At the end of the year, Silver-Tree returned to her trout in the well, and was again enraged to learn both that she was not the most beautiful Queen in the world, and that Gold-Tree was alive. Again Silver-Tree set out for the land of Gold-Tree, her Prince, and the second wife (as the Prince had decided to keep them both). The three went to the shore to greet her. Silver-Tree offered Gold-Tree a special drink, which was poisoned of course, but the second wife reminded the Queen that the custom of the land was for the person offering a draught to drink first. When Silver-Tree put the goblet near her mouth, the second wife struck the goblet, causing some of the drink to go down Silver-Tree's throat. The vain and covetous Queen fell dead, and the Prince with his two wives lived peacefully thereafter.

## 2. The Rewards of Virtue

Honesty has always been a mainstay of cultural virtues as well. Accordingly, in myth and folklore, there is no want of examples of good befalling the truth teller and ill befalling the deceiver. In the Celtic folktale of King O'Toole and His Goose, a happy and good King O'Toole has grown old, and has resorted to buying a goose as his sole diversion.[82] Eventually, the goose is stricken by old age and the King is left feeling utterly alone. One day St. Kavin, appearing simply as a young man, greets the King by name. The King repeatedly asks the young man questions such as his identity and the basis of the man's knowledge of the king's regal status, but St. Kavin answers only: "I am an honest man." St. Kavin does, however, state that his trade is that of "makin' old things as good as new," and adding, "what would you say if I made your old goose as good as new?" The King is overjoyed, and after a brief negotiation, agrees to give the young man "all the ground the goose flies over." The agreement settled, St. Kavin makes the sign of the cross over the goose, holds it up in his hands, tosses it into the air, and the goose flies like a swallow.

At this point St. Kavin asks, "[W]ill you gi`e me all the ground the goose flew over?" to which King O'Toole answers he will, "though it's the last acre I have to give." St. Kavin then replies: "It's well for you, King O'Toole, that you said that word for if you didn't say that word, the devil the bit o' your goose would ever fly ag'in."

Only now St. Kavin reveals his saintly origin, and that he came to the King to "try" him.[83] Having shown his honesty, the King lived out his days with his goose. Even afterwards, the goose was blessed, in a sense, in that one day in diving for a trout, it instead struck a horse eel, which killed the goose; however, the eel would not eat the goose because "he darn't ate what Saint Kavin had laid his blessed hands on."

---

[82]  *Id.* at 93 (the text following the footnote recounts the myth of King O'Toole and His Goose).

[83]  *Id.* at 98.

## C. DECEIT

A linchpin of all justice systems has been the elevation of truth over falsity. A Hebrew saying states that "[t]he worst informer is the face,"[84] suggesting the near impossibility of being able to facially conceal a deceit. Predictably, numerous primitive myths support the ethos of honesty. A myth of certain Eastern Woodlands Indians fortifies a moral that truth is rewarded.[85] This myth has sometimes received the anglicized title of The Indian Cinderella. It begins on the shores of a bay, where there lived a great warrior, who had once been among the helpers of Glooskap, a Native American mythic hero. This warrior, who was known as Strong Wind, the Invisible, had the power to make himself invisible. He used this skill to sneak among enemies and learn of their plans. The warrior lived with his sister, who could see him when others could not. Many maidens wished to wed this warrior, and as sisters are wont to do, Strong Wind's sister helped him evaluate the candidates. In the early evening, she would walk to the beach with any girl wishing to wed him. The warrior would approach in his invisible form, and the sister would ask the suitor: "Do you see him?" The girl would invariably respond falsely: "Yes." The sister would indulge herself with further questions, such as: "With what does he draw his sled?" to which she would receive other fabricated replies. The village chief, a widower, had three daughters. The youngest was beautiful, and for this reason the two older sisters were jealous. Thus, they dressed her in rags, cut her hair, and burned her face with coals. Lying to their father that their younger sister had done these things to herself, the two older maidens naturally wanted to win the hand of Strong Wind, and like so many others, they lied that they could see him, but went home disappointed. One day, the youngest patched her tattered clothes and adorned herself in such modest ornaments as she had, and went to visit Strong Wind's sister. "Do you see him?" the sister asked, and the young maiden answered: "No." Again Strong Wind's sister asked: "Do you see him now?" This time she answered: "Yes, and he is very wonderful." "With what does he draw his sled?" The maiden responded: "With the Rainbow."

---

[84] A Treasury of Jewish Folklore 638 (Nathan Ausubel ed., 1948).

[85] The Book of Virtues for Young People, *supra* at 259-62 (the text following the footnote recounts the myth of The Indian Cinderella

"Of what is his bowstring?" She answered: "His bowstring is the Milky Way." It was now that Strong Wind's sister knew that the maiden had spoken the truth when she had said that she had seen him, as he had made himself visible after her first truthful answer. The warrior's sister took her to their home and bathed her. Her scars disappeared and her hair grew long and beautiful. Thus, she took the wife's seat next to her new husband. As for the cruel daughters, Strong Wind learned of their acts and turned them into aspen trees. The story concludes:

> And since that day the leaves of the aspen have always trem-
> bled, and they shiver in fear at the approach of Strong Wind,
> it matters not how softly he comes, for they are still mindful
> of his great power and anger because of their lies and their
> cruelty to their sister long ago.[86]

## D. UNJUST ENRICHMENT

Deceit is a frequent subject of Hebrew folk tales. Together with conspiracy, it is the subject of a certain Hebrew folk tale concerning a Jewish tenant farmer living in a Polish village, who was a pious and good man.[87] One day a young nobleman entered the village, and after wasting his money on wine, women, and song, he determined that he should displace the Jew from his land and till it himself. Despite all of the young nobleman's fruitless efforts first to cajole and then to menace the farmer into abandoning his land, the nobleman eventually persuaded several peasants by offering them money and drink to lay in wait for the farmer as he passed through the woods. On the farmer's trip through the woods, the tenant farmer was full of foreboding. Rain fell as night closed in, and he could not see his way. Yet he continued, and repeated the psalm. "God is our refuge and strength Therefore we will not fear."[88] Eventu-

---

[86]   *Id.* at 262.

[87]   A Treasury of Jewish Folklore, *supra* at 581 (the text following the footnote re-counts the myth of Caught in His Own Trap).

[88]   *Id.* at 582.

ally, the way cleared, and the Jew continued on his journey home.

In the meantime, the nobleman grew impatient to receive word from his hirelings that they had set upon the farmer, but no word came. Impatient, the nobleman set out by horse and wagon through the woods. Suddenly, he was attacked by many men and beaten until he lost his voice. Only after the men had grown tired of beating him did they realize their mistake. The nobleman never again showed his face in the village for fear of being ridiculed.

## E. THE GOLDEN RULE

Since prehistory, the goal that one should treat another man as one would expect to be treated has remained one pole star of man's cultural evolution. Stated most famously by Jesus of Nazareth in what would become the vernacular "Golden Rule," one African myth masterfully conveys both the concept and the operative effect.[89] In a folktale simply entitled Gratitude, from the Nupe of the Sudan, a hunter in the bush kills an antelope. Boaji, a civet, asks the hunter for some of the meat, and the hunter complies. The following day, the hunter encounters a crocodile that is lost and unable to find its way back to the River Niger. The crocodile offers the hunter five loads of fish if the hunter will show him the way, and the hunter agrees. He ties a thong around the crocodile's foot and leads him to the river's edge. He loosens the thong to permit the crocodile to make good on the bargain, but after bringing up several loads of fish the crocodile snaps the hunter's foot and drags him underwater. The crocodile presents its catch to his brother crocodiles, at which point the hunter explains the circumstances and pleads, "Is th[is] fair?" The crocodile relents somewhat and agrees to solicit the views of four others. The first is a colored oval mat called an Asubi, which was floating down the river. The Asubi, old and torn, recounted its experience at the hands of man. The Asubi spoke of how man holds the Asubi in high regard until it is old, at which time he throws it away into the river. The Asubi concludes that the crocodile should be free

---

[89] LEO FROBENIUS & DOUGLAS C. FOX, AFRICAN GENESIS: FOLK TALES AND MYTHS OF AFRICA 163 (1999) the text following the footnote recounts the myth of Gratitude).

to do with the man as it wishes. The next item consulted, also floating down the river, is an old dress, which reaches the same conclusion as the Asubi. An old mare that has come to the river to drink then gives the same advice. Next, the hunter and the crocodile meet Boaji, the civet.

The civet replies that it cannot properly respond until it is able to understand the entirety of the circumstances that led to the hunter's plight. He has the hunter tie the thong around the crocodile's foot as it had been initially. He then has the hunter lead the group back into the bush to the place where the hunter had first encountered the crocodile. The civet asked of the crocodile if it had been satisfied once it had been led by the foot to the water, and the crocodile replied: "No, I was not satisfied." Boaji said: "Good. You punished the hunter for his bad treatment of you by grabbing his foot and dragging him to the sandbank. So now the matter is in order. In order to avoid further quarrels of this kind the hunter must unbind the thong and leave you in the bush." The civet and hunter left, leaving the crocodile lost, hungry, and thirsty. The crocodile could not find the way back to the river. The tale concludes, "[t]here comes a time for every man when he is treated as he has treated others."[90]

## F. HOMICIDE AND SENILICIDE

Even among subsistence societies there exist strong social strictures against killing, be it by commission or omission, and as often as not these social norms are rooted in myth. For example, there has been much misunderstanding about the practices of the ancient Inuit. Among the Inuit, claims of countenanced senilicide are both true and untrue. There was widespread, if not general, acceptance that the aged individual could decide that he or she could no longer contribute effectively to the collective, and ask that a family member or friend end her life.[91] However, Iglulik myth reveals a social antipathy towards the involuntary killing of the elderly, "generally provid[ing] [for] some miraculous form of rescue with a cruel and ignominious death for those who abandoned them."[92]

---

[90] *Id.* at 170.

[91] HOEBEL, *supra* at 76-77.

Among the Plains Indians, this part of the law was driven by religion while other segments were not.[93] For the Cheyennes, a killer was supernaturally punished.[94] The killer's punishment was in accord with the group's taboo against such acts and thus represented a "pollution" of a universal communal taboo.[95] Thus, the tribe would exile, or "got shed," the individual so as not to be tainted by the deed.[96]

## G. MISCELLANEOUS

### 1. QUASI-JUDICIAL DECISION MAKING

The horizontal consensus approach to primitive decision making, be it for defalcations or otherwise, has mythological antecedents. For example, the creation myth of the Navajo, The Emergence, tells of four gods appearing before the First People, who lived in the Yellow World, who, upon experiencing a shortage of food that imperiled their very existence, dispatched messengers to the North, South, East and West in search of one who might lead them.[97] From the West returned the Mountain Lion, who was strong and wise; from the East the Wolf, as he was strong and clever; from the South, the Bluebird, who was kind and wise; and from the North, the Hummingbird, who was swift and just. The First People recognized that to ensure peace, plentitude, and justice, they needed the counsel and leadership of each gift that the four proposed leaders possessed. To this day, the legend continues as the Navajo are led by a council of wise men representing each gift: "Wolf wears a silvery white coat, Bluebird a blue-feathered coat, Lion a coat of yellow fur, and Hummingbird a coat of many colors."[98]

---

[92]  *Id.* at 77 (quoting KNUD RADMUSSEN, INTELLECTUAL CULTURE OF THE IGLULIK ESKIMOS: REPORTS OF THE FIFTH THULE EXPEDITION, 1921-1924 160 (1929).

[93]  *Id.* at 262-63.

[94]  *Id.* at 263.

[95]  *Id.*

[96]  *Id.* at 263.

[97]  ROSENBERG, *supra* at 616 (the text following the footnote recounts the myth of The Emergence).

If a principal instruction of the law of civil justice in any age is the avoidance of bloodshed and the adoption of peaceable means of resolving discord, the story of Penelope's Web seems on its face to be the exception that tests the rule.[99] Perhaps this is true, at least in the view of Michael Gagarin:

> [T]he dispute between Odysseus and the suitors seems to validate the rejection of a peaceful settlement in favor of the use of self-help to obtain one's desired compensation. The dispute itself stems from the conflicting set of rules guiding the behavior of both the suitors and Penelope in the ambiguous situation of Odysseus's extremely long absence. As legitimate suitors of a woman who has indicated that she will soon decide to select one of them to be her new husband, they have a right to be entertained in Odysseus' house until she makes this decision. In several respects, however, their behavior in the house is clearly improper; moreover, most of them obviously violate the norms for proper treatment of a beggar, and their plan to kill Telemachus is a clear violation of several norms.[100]

## 2. INJUSTICE GENERALLY

With literary flair, Dinka legend reveals the mediating role myth can play for a person or a people who must see some reason for their confrontation with hardship or injustice.[101] The Dinka rationalize injustice through the myth of the Departed Divinity.[102] As characterized by Clifford Geertz, in a less homiletic than descriptive account, the Sky (wherein dwells the Divinity) and the Earth were once connected by a rope. There was no death or suffering,

---

[98]   *Id.* at 618.

[99]   The Book of Virtues for Young People, *supra* at 313-19.

[100]   Michael Gagarin, Early Greek Law 104 (1986).

[101]   Geertz, *supra* at 108.

[102]   *Id.* at 107 (the text following the footnote recounts the myth of Departed Divinity).

and the first man and woman were able to subsist on a single grain of millet each day. Eventually, greed overtook the woman,[103] who planted more than her aliquot share. In her haste, her hoe struck Divinity. Divinity thereafter severed the rope and retreated to the Sky, leaving man to the evil and injustice in which he suffers to this day. As can be recognized, without the myth of the Departed Divinity, the Dinka would be hard pressed to find any "moral coherence" in a world of suffering, injustice, and inequity.[104]

## 3. MAN'S INNER STRENGTH

Within the genre of African folk tales or myths, numerous stories address a polycentric array of human strengths and foibles, and in so doing reveal norms and cultural expectations very similar to those recognized in modern law throughout the world. One Soninke legend from the Sudan, entitled Gassire's Lute, tells of a mythical Wagadu, "not of stone, not of wood, not of earth[,]" but of "the strength which lives in the hearts of men."[105] Wagadu would disappear (or "sleep"), and the strength in men's hearts, when overwhelmed by man's vanity, falsehood, greed, or dissension (the four pillars of man's "guilt"), would disappear with her.[106] In one of many tales centering upon Wagadu, she appears not as a mythical person, but as a town.[107] The forces of Wagadu, led by Wagana Sako, go to war against a rival group led by Mamadi Sefe Dekote.[108] One night, Mamadi Sefe Dekote secretly leaves the battle lines and enters Wagadu, seeking an audience with Wagana Sako's wife and another woman. On the same night, Wagana Sako leaves the lines and returns to see his wife. As he approaches his hut, he silently observes his wife and Mamadi Sefe Dekote. As Mamadi Sefe Dekote addresses Wagana Sako's wife, the two of them wit-

---

[103] Geertz points out the obvious similarities to the Creation Story in the Judeo-Christian Book of GENESIS.

[104] *Id.* at 108.

[105] FROBENIUS & FOX, *supra* at 97.

[106] *Id.* at 98.

[107] *Id.*

[108] *Id.*

ness a mouse running along a beam above them. The mouse sees a cat below it, and is so frightened that it falls and is killed by the cat. Mamadi Sefe Dekote says, "[j]ust as the mouse fears the cat, so do we fear your husband."[109] Hearing this, Wagana Sako knows he cannot confront his enemy and remounts his horse and leaves, for "[i]t was considered unchivalrous for a Soninke to challenge a man who admitted that he was afraid."[110]

## 4. Disturbing the Peace

All societies for all times have valued a peaceable and prosperous community. For example, one embodies the premium placed upon peace in the community and the deterrence of those who contribute to wrongful conduct or unrest. It notes, "Be a disciple or promoter thereof." This folk-saying sounds in the original goals of a peaceable community.

## 5. Invasion of Privacy

Long before Samuel D. Warren and Louis D. Brandeis staked claim to one of the earliest expositions of a right to be left alone,[111] that right, and a particularly harsh punishment for its violation, were described in a story about Actæon, his hounds, and the virgin goddess Diana. Thomas Bulfinch records how the virgin goddess Diana punished Actæon, the son of King Cadmus, upon Actæon's inadvertent invasion of her privacy.[112] One day under a warm midday sun when Actæon his companions, and his hounds were hunting stag in the mountains, Actæon announced to the others that, because their hunting had already brought sufficient success for one day, they should take their rest.

---

[109] *Id.*

[110] *Id.*

[111] Samuel D. Warren & Louis D. Brandeis, *The Right to Privacy*, 4 HARV L. REV. 193 (1890).

[112] BULFINCH, *supra* at 42-44 (the text following the footnote recounts the myth of Dianna and Actæon

Nearby in a small body of water fed by a stream, Diana—the huntress queen—also took her rest as her nymphs—Crocale, Nephele, Hyale, and the others—attended to her bow, javelin, quiver, clothes, and sandals. Actæon, having left his companions with no direction, encounters Diana, whose screaming nymphs rush to cover her.[113] Unable to locate her arrows to slay the intruder, Diana utters instead, "[n]ow go and tell, if you can, that you have seen Diana unapparreled."[114] At once, stag horns began to grow from Actæon's head, and the rest of his body began to assume the form of a stag. He fled, and although he admired his new speed, when he paused to see his reflection in some water, he wept in fear and shame. As he paused, Actæon was seen by his own hounds, and Malampus—a Spartan dog—together with Pamphagus, Dorceus, Lelaps, Theron, Nape, Tigris, and the others gave chase. Over cliffs and through gorges, Actæon fled until his dogs closed in. He attempted to command them, declaring, "I am Actæon; recognize your master!" But he was unable to speak any human words, and was felled by his own hounds to the cheers of his hunting companions.[115]

## 6. Alienation of Affections

Another Greek myth seemingly instructs that if one is intent upon alienating the affections of a woman, it is best that the woman not be the wife of

[113] *Id.* at 43. Bulfinch writes that Actæon was "led thither by his destiny." *Id.*

[114] *Id.*

[115] *Id.* at 44. In his poem Adonais, Shelley wrote of the story of Actæon:

> Midst others of less note came one frail form,
> A phantom among men: companionless,
> As the last cloud of an expiring storm,
> Whose thunder as its knell; he, as I guess,
> Had gazed on Nature's naked loveliness
> Actæon-like, and now he fled astray
> With feeble steps o'er the world's wilderness;
> And his own Thoughts, along that rugged way,
> Pursued like raging hounds their father and their prey.

*Id.* (Stanza 31). Bulfinch surmises that "[t]he allusion is probably to Shelley himself." *Id.*

Ulysses.[116] In the tale sometimes referred to as Penelope's Web, Ulysses,[117] King of Ithaca, is at first reluctant to join the war against Troy, but does so at the insistence of his wife, the beautiful Penelope. Ten years pass; Troy is in ruins, and the Greek warriors return. However, there is no sign of Ulysses. Even Laertes tells Penelope that Ulysses must have lost his life in a shipwreck. Another ten years pass for the faithful Penelope, and inevitably, others seek the love of Penelope, asking that she choose from among them. She resists:

> Give me a month longer to wait for him In my loom I have a
> half-finished web of soft linen. I am weaving it for the shroud
> of our father. Laertes, who is very old and cannot live much
> longer. If Ulysses fails to return by the time this web is fin-
> ished, then I will choose, though unwillingly.[118]

Penelope's suitors took her at her word, taking lodging in her palace and par-
taking of all of the attendant luxuries. Penelope, in turn, showed them each
day how her weaving was progressing, but at night she unraveled what she had
woven. Eventually, however, her ruse was discovered, and her rude suitors demanded that she make a decision. Those gathered arranged once more for a
feast, and it was larger and more uproarious than those before.

Scarcely noticed, an old beggar entered the courtyard. He first approached
Argos, Ulysses' favorite hunting dog, who had grown old and toothless, and
was mistreated by the interlopers. The beggar patted the dog's head, and whispered "Argos, old friend."[119] The dog stood, and then fell dead with a look of
joy upon its face. The suitors noticed the beggar and ridiculed him, ordering
him out. But the beggar offered news of Ulysses, and Penelope bade that he
stay and receive refreshment. An old lady, who had been Ulysses' nurse,
washed the beggar's feet, but sprang back in alarm upon noticing a scar upon

---

[116] See generally THE BOOK OF VIRTUES FOR YOUNG PEOPLE, supra at 313 (the text
following the footnote recounts the myth of Penelope's Web).

[117] Ulysses is the Roman name for the Greek hero Odysseus.

[118] Id. at 314-14.

[119] Id. at 317.

his knee—a scar that seemed distantly familiar to her. The beggar whispered to her, "Dear nurse you were ever discreet and wise. You know me by the old scar I have carried on my knee since boyhood. Keep well the secret, for I bide my time, and the hour of vengeance is nigh."[120] The suitors grew more demanding and Penelope responded by pointing to a great bow hanging on the wall, saying: "Chiefs and princes let us leave this decision to the gods. Behold, there hangs the great bow of Ulysses, which he alone was able to string. Let each of you try his strength in bending it, and I will choose the one who can shoot an arrow from it the most skillfully."[121]

Each chief and prince tried his hand but each failed until one said derisively: "Perhaps the old beggar would like to take part in this contest."[122] The beggar approached the bow, and stood tall, revealing himself. Penelope cried Ulysses' name. The suitors fled in panic, but Ulysses, with his arrows, killed every one. Penelope returned to Ulysses with the soft, white cloth of her web, and declared: "This is the web, Ulysses. I promised that on the day of its completion I would choose a husband, and I choose you."[123]

## 7. Children's Folklore

Lest children be left out of the cultural message that life can be harsh and unfair, many folk songs and folk games include what might be described as truly appalling results. As stated by one scholar, many children's games reveal "something of the stern, hard rules of society in an early day."[124] For example, in a Swiss version of the game-song of "Judge and Jury," a thief who has fled from capture is caught, and is brought back to the king who orders his execution by beheading.[125] Another example is a German game-song, carried out in

---

[120] *Id.* at 318.

[121] *Id.*

[122] *Id.*

[123] THE BOOK OF VIRTUES FOR YOUNG PEOPLE, *supra* at 319.

[124] Paul G. Brewster, *Traces of Ancient Germanic Law in a German Game-Song,* in 1 FOLK LAW 408 (Alison Dundes Renteln & Alan Dundes eds., 1994).

[125] *Id.*

verse and pantomime, in which a young girl[126] sits on a stone in the center of the game, "combing her golden hair."[127] Her assailant approaches undetected, until such time as she notices him, and sees him to be her "wicked brother" Karl.[128] As she begins to weep, he pulls an imaginary knife, stabs her, and then flees.[129] Some in the circle then rush to her aid.[130] Her good brother Benjamin then appears, lifts her in his arms, and carries her from the circle.[131] Several variations on this game-song exist, but in none of them are the good brother, family members, or others able to protect her or, for that matter, apprehend the villain.[132]

# IV. CONCLUSION

A dominant but not exclusive tenet of myth is that the story conveyed by the myth was at first thought to represent real events. Only later would it become, among certain quarters, fantastic. In modern times, it might be unlikely that young persons would be told of Zeus, Athena, or any part of classical mythology with the purpose or expectation that either the teller or the audience would take the story to be anything but fantastic. Yet in our post-modern age, numerous modern myths play roles very similar to those played by ancient myths. Several modern tales that may be termed myths may have always been thought fantastic, and yet, even when tempered with this modern insight, the role they have played in society's concept of itself is still forceful. Among such modern myths (or sagas or fables) are included in such stories as that of Superman and

---

[126] As in this era boys and girls did not play together, at a gathering of boys the part would be played by a boy.

[127] *Id.* at 409.

[128] *Id.*

[129] *Id.*

[130] *Id.*

[131] Brewster, *supra* at 409.

[132] *Id.* at 410.

Spiderman. As this Chapter suggests, a central feature of mythical and totemic adherence is the "mediation between nature and culture."[133] The Chapter references the former role of myths as the assignment of reasons for environmental uncertainty, be they benign or ruinous, including among others, sun, rain, drought, and plentiful game. The Chapter, however, strongly focuses on the mediation—often strongly normative—between conflicting perceptions of the external world, such as the idea that generosity and honesty are to be rewarded.[134] In these ways, myth and folklore have directly or indirectly provided early and ancient man his sense of social cohesion and social order.

As the opening reference from Bulfinch suggests, the study of mythology is an important exercise in that it gives the reader an understanding of tales, metaphors, and references that are part of day to day parlance.[135] Additionally, myths and folklore are often simply a marvelous read. Interestingly, while it is true that most myths and folk stories were adopted in the past, there remains an occasional modern demonstration of man's desire to fantastically portray the heights of human experience and the depths of human emotions and troubles. For example, folktales are still created today, even if their dissemination is limited. At a law school that I visited, the Departments of Art and Art History assigned students the task of creating oversized masks of a sin or a virtue of their choosing to present in a parade of "Gigantes y Cabezudos." Representations included one student's sculpture of a giant hamburger to represent gluttony; another's representation of "suicide" intending "to comment on the moral issues surrounding suicide;" anger, portrayed by a "hot head;" and sin, generally, portrayed by Satan's head, replete with horns.[136]

---

[133]  CLAUDE LEVI-STRAUSS, THE SAVAGE MIND 91 (University of Chicago Press 1966).

[134]  Among primitive peoples, such hospitality (or generosity) would ensure that all in the community, including infants not yet able to contribute to any communal work, would be provided for adequately:

> [F]or example, the [primitive] Australian hunter who kills a wild animal is expected to give one certain part of it to his elder brother, other parts to his younger brother and still other parts of the animal to defined relatives. He does this, knowing that [the other brothers] will make a corresponding distribution of meat to him.

[135]  Robert Redfield, *infra* n. 136 at 81.

At a formal level, modern law shares many similarities with the myths of antiquity. Indeed, Professors Goodrich and Hachamovitch suggest that the law is a "presence which implies the totality of its history, but this implication is not logical or historical; rather, it is traditional and mythic."[137] Law has also been plausibly described as magical; that is, it represents society—the effects of which are imposed magically—through "a method of supporting endeavor to control the environment and social relationships by means where the connection of effort with achievement cannot be measured."[138] And so, it is perhaps arbitrarily dichotomous to inquire as to the effect of myth on primitive and modern justice, when myth and justice are so closely interrelated.

However, it is observable that myth and fable have performed a role that differs from that played by religion, and they did so a millennia before organized faith. In terms of timing, myths and fables were adopted as socio-cultural interpretive means at times when their appurtenant cultures were pre-theistic or pan-theistic. Myths and fables also served the smaller and more insular constituencies of clans and tribes, while a more fully developed society was the typical social predicate for organized faith.

Of greatest importance, myth and fable, unlike religion, have always enjoyed the malleability that would permit them to change, if only incrementally, to respond to the new externalities that might face a social group. If after untold years of fruitful existence, in a region of deciduous forests, changes in climate made the availability of game less predictable, then mythic figures were ready to mold themselves into forms with personal traits that were displeased with the affected climate. Further, if guiding cultural tenets of honesty (or generosity, or other estimable characteristics) were sometimes put to the test by the injustice or greed of others, myth or fable could render such unpredictable results susceptible of rationalization, if not even agreeable.

---

[136] Robert Redfield's *Ancient Law in Light of Primitive Societies*, in C. Smith & David N. Weisstub, The Western Idea of Law 81 (1983).

[137] Peter Goodrich & Yifat Hachamovitch, *Time out of Mind: An Introduction to the Semiotics of Common Law*, in Dangerous Supplements: Resistance and Renewal in Jurisprudence 74 (Peter Fitzpatrick, ed., 1991).

[138] M. Gluckman, Magic, Sorcery and Witchcraft, in A Dictionary of Sociology 111 (London: Routledge & Kegan Paul, 1968).

None of this is to suggest that myth and fable hold a monopoly on the social self-image of any particular culture, or on the instruction of behavior that should be or must be. There is no doubt that religion's sacred texts include copious behavioral instruction. Yet myth cannot be displaced as a fundamental source of social history, and as such, an ongoing cultural influence throughout the world. Myth gave to primitive and ancient man at least as much to hope as to fear, which is, after all, the function of progressive modern justice systems.

# CHAPTER 5

# THE VITAL COMMON LAW:
# ITS ROLE IN A STATUTORY AGE

## I. INTRODUCTION

> "[T]he common law is not static; its life and heart is its dynamism—its ability to keep pace with the world while constantly searching for just and fair solutions to pressing societal problems."[1]

This Chapter discusses the common law, the judge-made law of property, contracts, torts and beyond. Common law observers and commentators have been rightly jarred by the claim of professional, academic and judicial authors who state that the common law is dead, or at least in retreat;[2] that we live in a "statu-

---

[1] Harrison v. Montgomery County Bd. of Educ., 456 A.2d 894, 903 (Md.1983) (internal citation omitted); Kelley v. R.G. Indus., Inc., 497 A.2d 1143, 1150 (Md.1985).

[2] See, e.g., Calvin R. Dexter & Teresa J. Schwarzenbart, Note, City of Milwaukee v. Illinois: The Demise of the Federal Common Law of Water Pollution, 1982 WIS.L.REV. 627; Gary T. Schwartz, The Beginning and the Possible End of the Rise of Modern American Tort Law, 26 GA.L.REV. 601 (1992); Martha Middleton, A Changing Landscape, 81 A.B.A.J. 56, 57 (Aug. 1995), quoting Prof. David G. Owen as observing that "tort law has been changed in a variety of significant ways in many states," and noting particularly "substantial alteration" to the basic doctrines of products liability and medical malpractice. The author states further that "[m]any reformers claim that

tory era";[3] and that the "orgy of statutemaking,"[4] state and federal, since 1960 effectively occludes the common law horizon.[5]

This pessimistic vision is that of a common law marginalized, relegated to the desuetude of a secondary role inAmerican jurisprudence; the common law as a test track for eventual statutory solutions[6] or a lexicon for statutory terms;[7] the common law as background music for a modern statutory lyric.

Most would describe this as an ignominious path for the once dominant common law tradition, one that for 800 years has woven together the custom and morality of English speaking nations into the fairest dispute resolution mechanism ever devised. Even so, advocates of the robust common law role must concede that (1) the common law, with its "principles...embedded in masses of report[ed] cases, is not always to be reconciled with another,"[8] does not rise to the level of a rudimentary or even proto-science; (2) the system of common law judging vests enormous power in presiding judges, a power that can lead to unseemly subjectivity in interpreting law to apply that may be at quite a remove from, although frequently more progressive than, contemporary societal perceptions of justice;[9] and (3) a jury's prerogatives on such im-

---

federal legislation is the only way to bring uniformity to the patchwork structure of 50 different state tort systems." *Id.* at 58.

[3] Daniel A. Farber & Phillip P. Frickey, *In the Shadow of the Legislature: The Common Law in the Age of the New Public Law*, 89 Mich.L.Rev. 875 (1991).

[4] Guido Calabresi, A Common Law for the Age of Statutes 169 (Harvard 1982) [hereinafter Calabresi, Age of Statutes] (*citing* Grant Gilmore, The Ages of American Law 95 (1977).

[5] The vigor of statutory development is not exclusively a twentieth century phenomenon. At least as early as the late nineteenth century, "utilitarian" jurists "concentrate[d] on codification as the instrument of legal reform." Richard A. Cosgrove, Our Lady the Common Law: An Anglo-American Community 1870-1930 39 (1987) [hereinafter Cosgrove, Our Lady].

[6] *E.g.*, Ohio Admin.Code 3745-15-07(A) (1995) (public nuisance).

[7] *E.g.*, Comprehensive Environmental Response, Compensation and Liability Act of 1980 (CERCLA), 42 U.S.C. § 9601, 9607(b)(3) (1994) (due care standard for third-party defenses regarding hazardous waste disposal).

[8] Cosgrove, Our Lady, *supra*, at 39.

[9] *Cf.*, Mary J. Davis, *Individual and Institutional Responsibility: A Vision of Comparative Fault in Products Liability*, 39 Vill.L.Rev. 281, 330 (1994) (judge's decisions may be "subject to influence by his or her own personal predilections").

portant issues as damages can lead to results not easily squared with proven loss, and can occasionally be openly hostile to business.[10]

There is no substantial dispute that common law adjudication experienced a "revolution" in the Twentieth Century.[11] The issue is whether that revolution has been prudent and progressive, or nihilistic. Has the common law itself become more scientific, or are efforts to assign a science to it, as one critic put it, "crude Baconianism at best,"[12] a supernal *ipse dixit*? Has the common law of the latter century ratified or repudiated Roscoe Pound's admission that "a composite of the law of then forty-eight American states cannot, in the nature of things, be the logical unity in which Langdell believed"?[13]

This Chapter opens by summarizing the historical role of the common law, and in so doing describe the accepted common law doctrinal goals—some moral, some economic, but each in its way pragmatic. The discussion will not attempt to assign ascendancy, much less victory, to one or more of the common law objectives, as each, and all together, are essential to gaining an integrated understanding of the common law's modern contribution.[14]

The Chapter continues by giving some detail to common law decision making, a process the author describes as one of *enlightened gradualism*, re-

---

[10] *See, e.g.,* Charles Allen, *Lawsuit Fight Over More Than Spilled Coffee*, PHOENIX GAZETTE, March 29, 1995, at B-9.

[11] Justice Ellen Ash Peters, *Common Law Judging in a Statutory World: An Address*, 43 U.PITT.L.REV. 995 (1982). Justice Peters estimated that only ten percent of the cases before her Connecticut Supreme Court were "purely common law," with statutes being "relevant [to] if not determinative" of the balance. *Id.* at 996.

[12] "[T]he Baconian scientists of the first part of the nineteenth century believed that their research revealed truth. Indeed, their work was a revelation. The principles they adumbrated were real and true because, in the end, they were expressions of the Creator." WILLIAM P. LAPIANA, THE ORIGIN OF AMERICAN LEGAL EDUCATION 32 (Oxford 1994).

[13] COSGROVE, OUR LADY, *supra* at 37 (quoting Roscoe Pound to Pollack (May 23, 1934), *in* ROSCOE POUND PAPERS, Harvard Law School Library).

[14] *See, e.g.,* James A. Henderson, Jr., *Process Constraints in Tort*, 67 CORNELL L.REV. 901 (1982) ("Fierce debates have raged in recent years over the objectives reflected in the tort-law system. A growing number of observers insist that tort law reflects efforts to achieve allocative efficiency and wealth maximization. A somewhat smaller, but no less intensely committed number insist that tort law primarily reflects fairness concerns." (citations omitted)). *Id.* at 901.

sourcefulness and adaptability. Specific examples of this process at work will be drawn from the common law of contract, domestic relations, torts, criminal law and evidence, including development of the distinctions between common law and statutory approaches, and also including their respective strengths and the weakness, in policy objectives and in application.

# II. THE MODERN INTERFACE OF STATUTORY AND COMMON LAW

## A. GENERALLY

The common law represents the largest proportion of the law of property, contracts[15] and torts.[16] The common law is often called "judge-made" law, to distinguish it from statutes, regulations and ordinances, which are enacted by state and federal legislatures, agencies and political subdivisions. Richard Posner describes common law broadly as "anybody of law created primarily through judges by their decisions rather than by the framers of statutes or constitutions,"[17] and "the body of English and American judge-made rules, many of great antiquity, governing torts (civil wrongs that result in personal injury or property damage), contracts, property, crimes and many other fields

---

[15]  This observation depends in part upon acceptance of the characterization of the Uniform Commercial Code as a crystallization of the common law of sales, negotiable instruments, secured interests, and the like.

   *See discussion of* Charles Fried's "moral institution" theory of contract doctrine as "based on the moral obligation to keep one's promises ... and that contract's doctrines reflect that obligation[,]" in Vincent A. Wellman, *Conceptions of the Common Law: Reflections on a Theory of Contract,* 41 U.Miami L.Rev. 925, 926 & n. 9, 970 (1987); *see also* Charles Fried, Contract as Promise: A Theory of Contractual Obligation (1981).

[16]  New Jersey v. Culver, 129 A.2d 715, 720 (N.J.1957) (quoting Heise v. Earle, 35 A.2d 880, 885 (N.J.1943)).

[17]  William M. Landes & Richard A. Posner, The Economic Structure of Tort Law vii (1987) [hereinafter Landes & Posner, Economic Structure].

of private conduct."[18] In 1821, Maryland's Chief Judge Chase described it more elegantly as "a system of jurisprudence founded on the immutable principles of justice, and denominated by the great luminary of the law of England, the perfection of reason."[19] Lastly an functionally, Arthur Corbin suggests that the common law is not so grand, luminescent or sacred as some state. To Corbin, common law is not a body of rules; it is a method. It is the creation of law by the inductive process."[20]

Whatever individual or aggregate definition you accept, today you cannot understand American law regarding a broad subject, be it privacy, employment relations or environmental harm, by looking solely at statutes, or solely at the common law. The symbiosis between common law doctrine and statutory law pervades our jurisprudence. In most circumstances, the state or federal statute is concerned only with enforcement of state public policy, civil or criminal, and leaves individual pursuit of monetary or injunctive relief to existing common law.[21] In many settings, such as privacy,[22] products liability,[23] or public nuisance,[24] state statutes essay to codify common law causes of action, con-

---

[18]  Allen v. State, 605 A.2d 960, 966 (Md.App.1992), (quoting State v. Buchanan, 5 H. & J. 317 362 (1821) (Chase, C.J., separate opinion)).

[19]  *Id.*

[20]  COSGROVE, OUR LADY, *supra* at 33 (quoting ARTHUR L. CORBIN, WHAT IS THE COMMON LAW? 75 (1912)).

[21]  *E.g.*, Clean Water Act of 1972, 33 U.S.C. § 1319(c)(1)(B) (1994).

[22]  *E.g.*, N.Y.CIV.RIGHTS LAW §§ 50, 51 (McKinney 1995) (statutory right of privacy) *discussed in* Haelan Lab., Inc. v. Topps Chewing Gum, Inc., 202 F.2d 866 (2d Cir.1953) (involving defendant's alleged invasion of "plaintiff's exclusive right" to use photographs of baseball players).

[23]  For example, state statutes in Delaware, Idaho, Iowa, Kansas, Kentucky, Maryland, Minnesota, Missouri, North Carolina, North Dakota, Ohio, Tennessee and Washington "bar an action for strict [products] liability depending on whether jurisdiction may be obtained against the manufacturer and whether the manufacturer is able to satisfy a judgment." RESTATEMENT OF THE LAW (THIRD) TORTS: PRODUCTS LIABILITY § 1 cmt. e. Reporters' Note (Tentative Draft No. 2, 1995) [hereinafter Tentative Draft No. 2].

[24]  *E.g.*, ARIZ.REV.STAT.ANN. § 36-601(A) (1995) (setting forth "conditions" that constitute "public nuisances dangerous to the public health"); OHIO ADMIN.CODE 3745-15-07-(A) (1995), stating as follows:

[T]he emission or escape into the open air from any source or sources what-

serving them, either conservatively or progressively, as the vehicle for personal actions for money damages or injunctive relief. In still other matters, a defendant's conformity with a statutory standard may either hinder or preclude a plaintiff's common law claim;[25] while noncompliance with a statutory standard may all but vouchsafe a plaintiff's suit for damages.[26]

## B. DISTINCTIONS BETWEEN STATUTORY AND COMMON LAW

For their frequent coalescence, there exist important distinctions between statutory law and common law. I will describe some of the prominent discriminating markers.

From the beginning, customary law or common law operated independently of the development of political rights, which give rise to "public law." In the Nineteenth Century, the "jurisprudential roots" distinguishing the common law from statutory law, a conceptual segregation of so called "private law" from "public law," permitted the conclusion that common law pertained to protection of pre-political rights, such as those involving property or autonomy interests, against personal injury or property loss.[27] Public law, in turn, "consisted of government compulsions *restricting* private freedom,"[28] while the common law identified and *protected* private freedom and autonomy. Over time, we will see preservation of individual freedom and autonomy as the pole star of the developing common law.

Accordingly, although in application statutory and common law ap-

---

soever, of smoke, ashes, dust, dirt, grime, acids, fumes, vapors, odors, or any other substances, or combination of substances, in such a manner or in such amounts as to endanger the health, safety or welfare of the public, or cause unreasonable injury or damage to the health, safety or welfare of the public, is hereby found and declared to be a public nuisance.

*Id.*

[25] Tentative Draft No. 2, *supra* at 7(b) ("Effects of Compliance and Non-compliance with Applicable Products Safety Statutes or Regulations").

[26] Tentative Draft No. 2, *supra* at 7a.

[27] Indeed, aspects of common law tort are thought to antedate not only early statutes but even the modern state. LANDES & POSNER, ECONOMIC STRUCTURE, *supra* at 1.

[28] Farber & Frickey, *supra* at 886 (emphasis added).

proaches sometimes converge, blurring the distinctions between the two,[29] the roles of statutory and common law are differentiable. Conventionally, legislatures have been considered responsible for effecting public policy through the passage of *ex ante* rules, while courts have occupied themselves with entry of *ex post* justice between private litigants.[30] By *ex ante* legislative rules rules is meant rules of prospective application, such as a statute requiring a manufacturer to report a product that creates or may create a substantial product hazard.[31] *Ex post* rules of law entered by judges applying the common law typically evaluate disputes, injuries or losses already suffered, and resolve the issue of where the loss should finally rest—with the injured party or the actor. In common law matters, prior to acting it may not be crystal clear to individuals whether their actions will incur liability, for example, whether their statements are defamatory, whether they may peaceably repossess property, or whether they may erect a fence that obscures their neighbor's view. This uncertainty has given rise to acerbic observations like that of Jeremy Bentham; who wrote: "Common law judges make law as a man makes laws for his dog. When a dog does anything you want to break him of, you wait till he does it, and then you beat him for it."[32]

Another distinguishing characteristic of common law is that it is conceptual, while statutory law can be described as textual.[33] This distinction is played out in the markedly different tasks before the court applying statutory law as opposed to applying common law. In Posner's words, "just as statutory concepts must be justified by demonstrating their provenance in statutory texts, so common law concepts must be justified by demonstrating their provenance in sound public policy.[34]

---

[29] *Id.* at 876. The authors comment upon the increased and confessed policy encouraging and *ex ante* approaches of common law courts.

[30] *Id.*

[31] Consumer Product Safety Act § 15, 15 U.S.C. § 2064 (1994).

[32] Jeremy Bentham, *quoted* in Lawrence M. Friedman, American Law 93 (1984).

[33] Posner, Problems, *supra* at 247.

[34] Posner, Problems, *supra* note 17, at 249. By way of example, there are salient differences between the structure and workings of the common law system pertaining to environmental torts and the structure of statutory environmental laws.

Accordingly, unlike a statute, the common law permits a contextual evaluation of conduct. This is to say that the judge's inquiry does not end at reaching an answer as to whether the defendant's conduct was prohibited, or permitted, by the state. Rather, the inquiry involves evaluation of whether the conduct conformed with, or exceeded, the developed and normative standards of the common law. In property law the contextual inquiry might be whether a landowner's use of her property is compatible with customary neighboring uses. In tort law the question might be whether the defendant acted as we would expect a reasonable man, or whether the injured plaintiff took ordinary precautions to protect himself from harm.

To hypothesize, if we were to have a statute, or a regulation pursuant to a statute, defining the proper method of taking one's seat when operating ride-on farm equipment, an operator injured after falling off equipment while operating it from a standing position would, we can suppose, find any potential tort recovery reduced or eliminated because of this departure from the statutory standard of care. Under the common law of torts, however, the evaluation of the operator's conduct would be contextual.[35] A contextual approach would permit, though not require, a fact finder to conclude that

---

As summarized by Professor Gerald W. Boston and the author:

> The law of nuisance consists of general, broad and abstract principles of unreasonable interferences, applicable to any activity. The regulatory structure, in contrast, is highly particularized, detailed and expected to govern well-defined kinds of activity. In nuisance, plaintiff's rights are exclusively determined by courts of general jurisdiction. To be contrasted, the regulatory structure is drafted, enforced and adjudicated within regulatory agencies and under the supervision of officials commanding technical expertise in particular, and often quite specialized, areas of regulation.

Gerald W. Boston & M. Stuart Madden, The Law of Environmental and Toxic Torts: Cases, Materials and Problems 213-214 (West 1994).

[35] "The question what a prudent man would do under given circumstances is then equivalent to the question of what are the teachings of experience to the dangers of this or that conduct under these or those circumstances; and as the teachings of experience are matters of fact, it is easy to see why the jury should be consulted with regard to them." Oliver Wendell Holmes, Jr., The Common Law 150 (1923) [hereinafter Holmes, The Common Law].

it was unreasonable for a middle-aged Brookfield, Connecticut ophthalmologist to operate a rider-mower in a standing position, but perhaps reasonable for an experienced thirty-year-old Iowa farm employee to do so on a thresher.

An additional distinction between common law and statutory regimes is their respective responsiveness to development, amendment, or withdrawal. A trial court's entry of an improvident common law interpretation is subject to one or often two tiers of appellate review. A judge's unwarranted constriction or enlargement of rules can be corrected. Where a state's high court has countenanced a new rule, the political process provides for a legislative veto.[36] Because of their prerogatives to turn aside rules whose former utility cannot be demonstrated in a modern setting, common law judges can discard outdated rules with far greater ease than outdated legislation can be set aside.[37]

# III. STATUTORY AND COMMON LAW FOIBLES

## A. STATUTORY SHORTCOMINGS

There are demonstrable limitations to both statutory and common law

---

[36]  Kelley v. R.G. Indus., Inc., 497 A.2d 1143 (Md.1985).

[37]  As Wheeler, J., *concurring*, wrote in Dewy v. Connecticut Co., 92 A. 883, 891 (Conn.1915):

> The court best serves the law which recognizes that the rules of law which grew up in a remote generation may in the fullness of experience be found to serve another generation badly, and which discards the old rule when it finds that another rule of law represents what should be according to the established and settled judgment of society, and considerable property rights have become vested in reliance upon the old rule. It is thus great writers upon the common law have discovered the source and method of its growth, and in its growth found its health and life. It is not and should not be stationary. Change of this character should not be left to the Legislature.

*Id.*

approaches. I begin with observations about the limitations of statutory approaches.

Statutes do not readily distinguish hues. As a general proposition, a statutory solution is confined by the four corners of the statute's language. As the British authority, Craies, put it in STATUTE LAW, "a statute may not be extended to meet a case for which provision has clearly and undoubtedly not been made."[38] As conduct is either approved or forbidden, generally there is no opportunity for equitable adjustment of the conflicting interests, or for consideration of the comparative responsibility of opposing parties for the harm or inequity.

A concomitant limitation is that where a statute specifically describes an approach or remedy to be taken by the court, it will admit of no departure from it. The problems with the inflexibility of such an approach have been manifest in the application of the Federal Sentencing Guidelines,[39] requiring sentences of definite ranges to be given defendants filing certain bright line criteria. The appalling inappropriateness of some of the required sentencing, and the incapacity of the sentencing judge to consider the exigencies of particular cases in fashioning a sentence, have led at least one federal trial judge to deflect statutory sentencing restrictions.[40]

Statutory responses to societal problems are also vulnerable to what Locke

---

[38] P.S. Atiyah, *Common Law and Statute Law*, 48 MOD.L.REV. 1, 8 (1985) (quoting CRAIES ON STATUTE LAW 102) [hereinafter Atiyah, *Common Law*].

[39] *See* The Comprehensive Federal Crime Control Act of 1984, 18 U.S.C. §§ 3551-3693 (1994), 28 U.S.C. §§ 991-998 (1994). The underlying Senate Report stated the goal of the statute as the elimination of "unwarranted dispar[ities]] and uncertainty" in sentencing. S. Rep. No. 225, 98th Congress, 1st Sess. 49 (1983) (discussed in Symposium, *The Tennessee Supreme Court: Judicial Activists?*, 24 MEM.ST.U.L.REV. 297 & n. 2 (1994).

[40] Peter Bowles, *Judge Ignores Ruling*, NEWSDAY. Dec. 3, 1994, at A-26 ("Utilizing a loophole in the law, U.S. District Court Judge Jack Weinstein this week ignored a higher-court mandate to sentence an admitted heroin addict to 10 years in prison and instead imposed the 26 months she already had served."). *Id.*

In a June 4, 1994 column, journalist Nat Henthoff quoted District Court Judge Jack Weinstein as stating that the sentencing guidelines "require, in the main, cruel imposition of excessive sentences." Nat Henthoff, *Judge Breyer: Lots of Room for Dissent*, THE WASHINGTON POST, June 4, 1994, at A-19.

called "the dangers of enthusiasm,"[41]and the invariable fellow traveler of enthusiasm, haste.[42]

In contemporary terms, what better example of the perilous "enthusiasm" described by Locke is available than in the realm of recent hastily-considered and unseasoned limitations upon the government's ability to promulgate land use restrictions in the public interest? A growing number of states have passed legislation requiring that the state or governmental subdivision provide compensation to landowners for restrictions on their use of land, in many settings where the landowner's use historically has been proscribable under the doctrine of public nuisance.[43] Representative is the Florida statute, entitled the

---

[41]  Locke wrote:

> Enthusiasm, though founded neither on reason nor divine revelation, but rising from the conceits of a warmed or over-weening brain, works yet, where it once gets footing, more powerfully on the persuasions and actions of men than either of those two, or both together, men being most forwardly obedient to the impulses they receive from themselves; and the whole man is sure to act more vigorously, where the whole man is carried by a natural motion. For strong conceit, like a new principle, carries all easily with it, when got above common sense, and freed of all restraint of reason, and check of reflection, it is heightened into a divine authority, in concurrence with our own temper and imagination.

JOHN LOCKE, LOCKE SELECTIONS 17 (Sterling P. Lamprecht ed.. 1956).

[42]  In THE EDUCATION OF HENRY ADAMS, in the chapter titled "A Law of Acceleration," Adams writes, "In every age man has bitterly and justly complained that nature hurried and hustled him[.]" HENRY BROOKS ADAMS, THE EDUCATION OF HENRY ADAMS 493 (1946) [hereinafter EDUCATION OF HENRY ADAMS].

A corollary of haste is inattention to detail. Richard Posner writes:

> The basic reason why statutes are so frequently ambiguous in application is not that they are poorly drafted—though many are—and not that the legislators failed to agree on just what they wanted to accomplish in the statute—though often they do fail—but that a statue necessarily is drafted in advance of, and with imperfect appreciation for the problems that will be encountered in, its application.

Richard A. Posner, *Statutory Interpretation—in the Classroom and in the Courtroom*, 50 U.CHI.L.REV. 800, 811 (1983).

[43]  *E.g.*, ARIZ.REV.STAT.ANN. §§ 9-500.12, 9-500.13, 11-810, 11-811 (1995); COLO.REV.STAT.ANN. § 24-68-105(1) (1995); FLA.STAT. ch. 163.3184 (1995); IDAHO CODE § 67-8001-8003 (1995); 1995 Kan.Sess.Laws 2015; LA.REV.STAT.ANN. §

"Private Property Rights Protection Act," providing sweepingly that "when a specific action of a governmental entity has inordinately burdened an existing use of real property * * * the property owner * * * is entitled to relief, which may include compensation for the actual loss to the fair market value of the real property caused by the action of government."[44]

Such statutes provide an alarming example of the risks of the sometimes hasty legislative and political process, as they hobble the effectiveness of land use regulation by levying upon the state a monetary cost to what was previously a simpler public interest predicate for such restrictions. Let us imagine a Maryland state environmental agency contemplating a public nuisance initiative against a Chesapeake Bay marina operator whose jet ski rentals cause shore erosion, damage oyster beds, and disturb the serenity of migratory fowl. Regulations pursuant to historical public nuisance authority would not require compensation to the marina operator.

If, in contrast, Maryland had a law such as Florida's, the agency could no longer be guided solely by considerations of whether requiring the marina operator to moderate this land use will serve the public interest, or is in furtherance of state public nuisance authority to enjoin activities corrosive to the public health, welfare and safety, a conventional zoning and public nuisance balancing of individual hardship and public interest. Under such new land use regulations, the regulator's pragmatic concern will be largely financial, for example, whether the state of Maryland is prepared to pay the marina operator the $1 million or more her attorneys will demand in just compensation. It requires no elaboration to recognize that such legislation acts as a strong disincentive to those charged with protecting the environment.

What are the legislative enthusiasms that permit such laws to be passed, and how is it that they prevail over widespread public commitment to environmental protection? The answer is found in simple principles of political

---

3:3621-3624 (1995); N.D.CENT.CODE § 42-01-06 (1995); TEX.GOV'T CODE ANN. § 2007 (West 1995); VA.CODE ANN. § 9-6.14:7 (Michie 1995); WYO.STAT.. § 9-5-301 to 9-5-305 (1995).

[44] H.B. 863, 1995, Reg.Sess., 1995 Fla.H.B. 863, *available in* LEXIS Legis Library. Sttext File. The statute defines "existing use" as including "reasonably foreseeable" uses. *Id.* at § (2)(b).

economy. In the Florida setting, a large proportion of Florida residents own or aspire to own property. They can readily imagine land use initiatives, by the law of public nuisance, a clean water act or otherwise, that will trammel their prerogatives to use their land as they wish. In contrast to this sprawling, politically alert, and anxious proportion of the electorate, only a small and politically inefficient number of Florida residents have reflected deliberately upon the predicament such compensation statutes create for this generation and the next.

Another example of improvident legislative enthusiasm was the push during the 104th Congress for a so-called "loser pays" approach to civil litigation. For years tort reform proponents have discussed various "loser pays" approaches, whereby a losing plaintiff, or one who rejects a settlement offer that turns out to be more generous than his ultimate reward, if any, would be liable for some measure of the opposing party's marginal counsel fees. H.R. 10, the Common Sense Legal Reform Act of 1995, had such a provision, applicable to suits brought in state courts and alleging violation of state liability laws. Apart from the gross overinclusiveness of such approaches, in that they would deter frivolous litigation only by means of discouraging much meritorious litigation, a loser pays protocol represents a "fee shifting" approach which has been demonstrated repeatedly to be ineffective, inefficient, and unfair in working its purported goal.[45]

While statutory solutions may be improvidently hasty, they may also arrive too late in the day. A statutory answer is not normally sought until a problem has erupted in the public consciousness, when a societal dilemma has achieved

---

[45] *See* Keith N. Hylton, *Fee Shifting and Incentives to Comply With the Law*, 46 VAND.L.REV. 1069 (1993); Judith L. Maute, Peevyhouse v. Garland Coal and Mining Co. *Revisited: The Ballad of Willie and Lucille*, 89 NW.U.L.REV. 1341, 1439 (1995); Peter Charles Coharis, *A Comprehensive Market Strategy for Tort Reform*, 12 YALE J. ON REG. 435, 525 & n. 142 (1995); Clinton F. Beckner, III & Averly Katz, *The Incentive Effects of Litigation Fee Shifting When Legal Standards are Uncertain*, 15 INT'L REV.L. & ECON. 205 (1995) ("Our analysis shows that when legal standards are administered imperfectly, the efficiency of fee shifting is a problem of the second best.... We conclude that just as there is no reason to believe that the British rule generally reduces the procedural costs of litigation, there is also no good reason to think that it generally promotes efficient substantive' behavior.").

such a level of gravity and tenacity that "social convention" demands "community voting."[46] As Benjamin Cardozo observed, "All history demonstrates that legislation intervenes only when a definite abuse has disclosed itself, through the excess of which public feeling has finally been aroused"[47] In contrast, the common law judge is not encumbered by any political need that a critical mass of public concern have been reached before justice can be entered in an individual case. The common law judge will consider and resolve a societal conflict when presented early in its maturation. With neither a governing statute nor a controlling common law rule, the judge can nevertheless enter a judgment illuminated by the refracted light of parallel or related common law principles. In so doing, in Professor Marshall Shapo's words, the common law judge "semiconsciously captures society's ideas about justice in legal issues framed by specific disputes."[48]

A related shortcoming of the statutory approach is that statutes typically have no provision for the subtle and particularized application of accepted principles to individual circumstances, a model Professor John Siliciano describes as one of "individualized justice."[49] Dean John Wade wrote that unlike common law tort decisions, which "require a careful and judicious balancing of the conflicting interests of the various parties," legislation typically involves "tradeoffs" which "can produce varying results that may combine to establish a reasonably fair average, but the average often comes from many specific instances in which one or the other party is treated unfairly."[50] Accepting the necessity of such tradeoffs, statutes are notorious for omitting to state clearly

---

[46] Marshall S. Shapo, *In the Looking Glass: What Torts Scholarship Can Teach Us About the American Experience*, 89 NW.U.L.REV. 1567, 1569 (1995).

[47] Benjamin N. Cardozo, The Nature of the Judicial Process 144 (Yale 1921) [hereinafter Cardozo, Judicial Process].

[48] Shapo, *supra* at 1569.

[49] John A. Siliciano, *Corporate Behavior and the Social Efficiency of Tort Law*, 85 Mich.L.Rev. 1820 (1987) [hereinafter Siliciano].

[50] John J. Wade, Book Review, 47 LA.L.REV. 691 (1987) (reviewing Wex S. Malone, Essays on Torts (1987)). In Washington v. Davis, 426 U.S. 229, 253 (1976) (Stevens, J., concurring), Justice Stevens corroborated Dean Wades's assessment of the legislative process, describing "governmental action" as "frequently the product of compromise, of collective decision making, and ... of mixed motivation."

their rationale, and thus attorneys and judges are often left adrift in determining a statute's applicability.[51]

Finally, it is not by any stretch clear that increased codification of the common law gains the commonality, uniformity or predictability that its proponents desire.[52] In the words of tort observer Victor E. Schwartz: "The fact is that over the past twenty years state tort law has grown further apart, not closer together. The advent of so-called 'tort reform'... augumented this trend. This year alone, approximately one dozen states have enacted tort reform statutes; yet none of them are the same. A nuance in any one of them could be major and outcome determinative."[53]

In the end, as Professor Lawrence M. Friedman writes, "the legislative process is neither as good at accommodating everybody as some have thought, nor as elitist and undemocratic as the worst of the cynics has described it. Rather, it is rough, complex and imperfect."[54]

## B. COMMON LAW SHORTCOMINGS

What is a clear-eyed look at the inherent limitations of common law jurisprudence? A primary objection to modern common law development, and an impe-

---

[51] McNollgast, *Legislative Intent: The Use of Political Theory in Statutory Interpretation*, 57 L. & Contemp.Probs. 3, 13 (1994).

[52] *Cf.*, Saul Levmore, *Rethinking Comparative Fault: Variety and Uniformity in Ancient and Modern Tort Law*, 61 Tul.L.Rev. 235 (1986).

[53] Victor E. Schwartz, 'Class Action' Reform: Endless Clashes of Values of Constructive Results?, Mass Tort Litig.Rep., Aug. 1995, *3. Schwartz stated:

> As someone who has studied the law of torts for a while, I am troubled by generalizations about tort law being 'in common' throughout the United States. The pressure to more litigation forward for the 'round-up' tend to lead even the most thoughtful of judges to see American tort law as somehow capable of being placed in a Cuisinart (TM), where differences of law are lost in a blended product that somehow represents both plaintiff and defendant interests.

*Id.* at *3.

[54] Lawrence M. Friedman, American Law 106 (1984). Professor Friedman continues: "Blacks and consumers have, for example, a much greater chance to win the ear of legislators than was true some fifty years ago."

tus for its statutory modification, is that, in crafting a remedy, the common law judge has no meaningful disincentive to the temptation to subtly gratify his or her own philosophical or social predilections. An element of this is unassailably true,[55] and it may be that in the natural law foundation of the common law we will find the basis for the modern criticism that judicial tinkering with common law principles invites, or even requires, manipulation of policy objectives, rules, and outcomes in order to harmonize results with the views of individual judges. After all, what could be more problematic than the question of what rights and obligations are the original and inalienable of modern men and women?

As has been suggested, the common law is ideally suited to resolving claims arising at the borders of societal and business dynamics, whether the issue is promissory estoppel or damages for emotional distress. Ironically, it is just this role of deciding cases at the margins of modern experience that enlarges the vulnerability of common law adjudication to the individual views of the sitting judge. A judge's own ideological gloss, the argument goes, is most likely to be detected where "preexisting doctrinal propositions do not provide a clear answer."[56] Examples of modern causes of action in which unsettled doctrine stimulated and will continue to stimulate the normative orientations of sitting judges are the developing law affecting the old, but now eroding, doctrine of employment at will, and the gestational rights of children *in utero*.[57]

Common law courts are also criticized for the sometimes seemingly cav-

---

[55] As Cardozo wrote:

> There is in each of us a stream of tendency, whether you choose to call it philosophy or not, which gives coherence and direction to thought and action. Judges cannot escape that current any more than other mortals. All their lives, forces which they do not recognize and cannot name, have been tugging at them—inherited instincts, traditional beliefs, acquired convictions; and the resultant is an outlook on life, a conception of social needs, a sense in James' phrase of 'the total push and pressure of the cosmos,' which, when reasons are nicely balanced, must determine where choice shall fall.

Cardozo, Judicial Process, *supra*, at 12.

[56] Stephen M. Bainbridge, *Social Propositions and Common Law Adjudication*, 1990 U.Ill.L.Rev. 231, 232 (reviewing Melvin A. Eisenberg, The Nature of the Common Law (1988)).

[57] *See infra* 230-244 and accompanying text. *See also* Terrence F. Kiely, Modern Tort Liability: Rocovery in the '90's § 6.6 (1990).

alier approach taken to the doctrine of *stare decisis*, i.e., the rule that courts should ordinarily follow the substantive rule of law recognized to that point by previous holdings of equal or higher courts in that jurisdiction. For its seemingly plain and overarching imperative, implementation of *stare decisis* has perplexed the finest legal minds in common law history. Considering the role of *stare decisis*, Benjamin Cardozo pondered:

> What is it that I do when I decide a case? To what sources of
> information do I appeal for guidance? In what proportions do
> I permit them to contribute to the result? If a precedent is ap-
> plicable, when do I refuse to follow it? If no precedent is ap-
> plicable, how do I reach the rule that will make a precedent
> for the future? If I am seeking logical consistency, the sym-
> metry of the legal structure, how far shall I seek it? At what
> point shall the quest be halted by some discrepant custom, by
> some consideration of the social welfare, by my own or the
> common standards of justice or morals?[58]

Consistent with Cardozo's implicit thesis that common law decisions bear the stamp of judicial individualism, much of the modern common law vulnera-bility to statutory "correction" can be attributed to common law rules that are arguably, to use a baseball metaphor, "ahead of the curve" of the "com-munity's sense of justice."[59] For example, Professor Martin Kotler character-ized recent and ongoing state and federal products liability reform as a

---

[58] CARDOZO, JUDICIAL PROCESS, *supra* at 10. Jurists have long recognized that prece-dent is a necessary, but not sufficient, source of the law. Cardozo wrote:

> I do not mean that precedents are ultimate sources of the law, supplying the
> sole equipment that is needed for the legal armory, the sole tools. Back of
> precedents are the basic juridical conceptions which are the postulates of
> judicial reasoning, and farther back are the habits of life, the institutions of
> society, in which these conceptions had their origin.

*Id.* at 19

[59] Martin A. Kotler, *Utility, Autonomy and Motive: A Descriptive Model of the Development of Tort Doctrine*, 58 U.CIN.L.REV. 1231, 1240 (1990) (citations omitted).

statutory rebuff to so-called "strict" products liability, with the reform statutes showing a consistent commitment to returning liability rules to the older predicate finding of fault.[60]

Further to Professor Kotler's point, common law approaches may also be subject to statutory correction where there is neither public nor legislative consensus that the common law rule satisfies an instrumentalist objective—an objective either to encourage worthy conduct, or to deter harmful or wasteful conduct. An example of a common law rule with a precarious instrumentalist basis might be the widespread common law rule that nonmanufacturing sellers are subject to liability without fault, or strict products liability, even though most wholesalers and retailers are not parties to the design process or the crafting of warnings or instructions for products, and thus are not in a position to efficiently remove unsafe products—at least not prior to an accident—or to influence better behavior on the part of their manufacturing suppliers. One cannot, therefore, be surprised that recent proposed products liability reform legislation would in most circumstances return the negligence standard to products liability for nonmanufacturing sellers.[61] The bills then before both

---

[60]  *Id.* at 1239. Using the example of statutory abrogation of strict liability rules in products liability, Kotler explains:

> Given that there probably has never been a social consensus in favor of the instrumentalist values underlying strict liability in tort for defective products, the wave of product liability reform legislation proposed or enacted within the past few years was probably inevitable. Although some features of this body of legislation appear to be solely a product of industry lobbying, it is worth noting that the most important features serve to immunize defendants from liability where the harm caused cannot fairly be said to have been their fault. This legislative insistence on the existence of fault as a condition for the imposition of liability is serving to bring tort doctrine back into line with the community's sense of justice.

> *Id.* at 239-40.

[61]  S. 565, Product Liability Fairness Act of 1995 § 5(a)(2), 104th Cong., 2d Sess.1995 [hereinafter Fairness Act]. The Fairness Act adopted three liability standards for non-manufacturing sellers. There was liability where the claimant proves that: (1) the product causing the harm was sold by the defendant; (2) the defendant failed to exercise reasonable care; and (3) this failure to exercise reasonable care was a proximate cause of the claimant's harm. There would also be liability if the seller has given an express warranty, and, far less frequently, if the seller has engaged in inten-

the House of Representatives and the Senate recognized the unfairness and illogic of imposing "strict" liability upon retailers and wholesalers who neither participate in the design process for products they sell, nor create warnings or instructions for a product.

Noteworthy is the parallel readjustment occurring in the American Law Institute's draft RESTATEMENT (THIRD) OF TORTS: PRODUCTS LIABILITY, a reinterpretation taking place a mere thirty years following publication of its strict products liability provision, RESTATEMENT (SECOND) OF TORTS § 402A. The proposed Restatement tethers finding of design or informational (warnings) defects to a risk-utility analysis that fully examines the prudence, foresight, and vigor of a manufacturer's conduct.[62] In all settings but the primitive manufacturing defect, liability would no longer be "strict" in any important sense, but rather tied to a manufacturer's failure to conform to society's expectation of a manufacturer's professionalism, or conversely the manufacturer's substandard, blameworthy or culpable conduct.

While common law responses may have been ahead of the curve in a doctrine such as strict products liability, elsewhere the common law has been behind the curve, or tardy, in its incremental response to changing conditions.

---

tional wrongdoing.

The Fairness Act stated that liability cannot be based solely upon "an alleged failure to inspect a product if the product seller had no reasonable opportunity to inspect the product that allegedly caused harm to the claimant." *See generally* Products Liability: Hearings on S. 565 Before the Senate Comm. on Commerce, Science and Transportation, 104th Cong., 2d Sess., 1995 WL 152027 (1995) (testimony of M. Stuart Madden.

These observations are not intended to address potential liability issues raised by private labelers, such as Sears, who engage manufacturers to produce products under the Sears trademark or other trademarks proprietary to Sears.

[62] Reporters James A. Henderson, Jr. and Aaron D. Twerski explained the adoption of a risk-utility analysis for design defects and for warnings defects in §§ 2(a) & (b) in a Note comment reading in part: Scholarly commentary agrees overwhelmingly with the ... risk-utility approach adopted.... *See, e.g.,* MADDEN, PRODUCTS LIABILITY vol. 1 at 299 (2d ed. 1988) ("[T]he majority rule posits that plaintiff cannot establish a prima facie case of defective design without evidence of a technologically feasible, and practicable, alternative to defendant's product that was available at the time of manufacture.")

Tentative Draft No. 2, *supra* at 2, commentary at 83.

Professor David R. Hodas provides the illustration of the special injury rule for bringing a claim in public nuisance. Describing the public nuisance private claimant's obligation to show a harm qualitatively different from that suffered by the public at large,[63] Hodas states the while the special injury rule "may have made sense in an era when misuse of existing technology affected only people in the immediate vicinity," such concerns "pale in comparison to modern worries about an accident at a chemical plant ..., or an oil spill."[64] These modern risks, which can cause severe and sprawling damages and which "prompted a revolution in statutory environmental law," Hodas notes, have spurred no similar reexamination of the restrictive special injury requirement,[65] which indeed has been adopted in numerous state statutes treating public nuisance.[66]

This review would not be complete without mention that while the common law has sometimes developed a right or a remedy that has yet to command significant public approval, it has also sometimes worked in seeming conflict with the development of progressive jurisprudence. Indeed, common law doctrine has often "worked ... as a tool for those with sufficient resources to influence the legal system."[67] During the 1950s and the early 1960s, the common law was

---

[63]  See Restatement (Second) of Torts § 821C(1) (1979), which provides that "[i]n order to recover damages in an individual action for a public nuisance, one must have suffered harm of a kind different from that suffered by other members of the public exercising the right common to the general public that was the subject of interference."

[64]  David R. Hodas, *Private Actions for Public Nuisance: Common Law Citizen Suits for Relief From Environmental Harm*, 15 Ecology L.Q. 833, 884 (1989).

[65]  *Id.* at 884-85.

[66]  *E.g.*, Cal.Civ.Code § 3493 (West 1993) ("A private person may maintain an action for public nuisance if it is specially injurious to himself, but not otherwise."); Ala.Code § 6-5-123 (1993) ("If a public nuisance causes a special damage to an individual in which the public does not participate, such special damage gives a right of action.").

The tendency towards stasis of judge-made common law may also stem from the processes in which judges are appointed, a process in which "the normal criteria of judicial fitness have been an eager acceptance of the American past rather than an eager interest in the American future." Harold J. Laski, The American Democracy: A Commentary and an Interpretation 31 (1949) [hereinafter Laski, American Democracy].

[67]  Abner J. Mikva, *The Shifting Sands of Legal Topography*, 96 Harv.L.Rev. 534. 540

employed by certain states "to sanction ... discriminatory treatment."[68] Moreover, many Twentieth Century statutory modifications of the common law were motivated by a desire to ameliorate the harshness of common law rules perceived as unfair to plaintiffs. An example is the Federal Employer's Liability Act of 1908, [69] which eliminated such common law barriers to railworker claims as assumption of the risk, contributory negligence, and the fellow servant rule.[70]

# IV. ANTECEDENTS AND HISTORICAL ROLE OF THE COMMON LAW

## A. NATURAL LAW AND CUSTOM

The origins of the common law can be traced at least from Aristotle[71] and Cicero[72] through the BOOK OF EXODUS.[73] It is generally supposed that much

---

(1982) (reviewing GUIDO CALABRESI, A COMMON LAW FOR THE AGE OF STATUTES (1982)).

[68] Bell v. Maryland, 378 U.S. 226, 308 (1964).

[69] 35 Stat. 65 (1908) (current version at 45 U.S.C. § 51-60).

[70] Peter L. Strauss, *On Resegregating the Worlds of Statute and Common Law*, 1994 SUP.CT.REV. 429, at 430.

[71] ARISTOTLE, THE NICOMACHEAN ETHICS, Book V (350 B.C.) (1947), classics. mit.edu/Aristotle/nichomachean.html

[72] Cicero wrote in DE LEGIBUS II: Of all these things about which learned men dispute there is none more important than clearly to understand that we are born for justice, and that right is founded not upon opinion but in nature. There is indeed a true law, right reason, agreeing with nature and diffused among all, unchanging, everlasting, which calls to duty by commanding, deters from wrong by forbidding ... It is not allowed to alter this law nor to deviate from it. Nor can it be abrogated. Not can we be released from this law either by the senate or by the people. Nor is any person required to explain or interpret it.

BENJAMIN FLETCHER WRIGHT, JR., AMERICAN INTERPRETATIONS OF NATURAL LAW: A STUDY IN THE HISTORY OF POLITICAL THOUGHT 5 (1931) [hereinafter WRIGHT, INTERPRETATIONS] (quoting CICERO, DE LEGIBUS II, 4, 10).

[73] *See, e.g.,* James J. Restivo, Jr., *Insuring Punitive Damages*, NAT'L L.J., July 24, 1995,

of the animating basis for early common law derived from an innate, elemental, and sometimes theocratic concept of justice often termed "natural law."[74]

What is "natural law"? Conceding the lack of a single and generally agreed to definition,[75] Benjamin Fletcher Wright, Jr. offered three alternative definitions: (1) "rules which are statements of the basic laws of the universe, or of man's constitution, or of social and political relationships"[76] (2) "principles of right, principles which are established or which should be established if justice is to prevail";[77] and (3) "either a set of standards or ideals, or a set of limitations imposed upon men by some superhuman power."[78]

For those persons ascribing to a power greater than themselves as the giver of natural law, Thomas Aquinas offered this theocratic description:

> [G]ranted that the world is ruled by Divine Providence,... that the whole community of the universe is governed by Divine Reasons. Wherefore the very Idea of the government of things in God the Ruler of the universe, has the nature of a law. And since the Divine Reason's conception of things is not subject to time but is eternal, according to Prov. viii. 23, therefore it is that this kind of law must be called eternal.[79]

With expected succinctness, Richard Posner, in turn, has offered the secular observation that equates natural law to "basic political morality."[80]

Such rights as were recognized as "natural" to man, and thus cognizable

---

at C-1 ("[I]n *Exodus* 22:9 ... it is prescribed that one found guilty of taking another's property be required to pay back double what was taken.").

[74] Wright, Interpretations, *supra* at 33-35. *See also* Surya Prakash Sinha, What is Law?: The Differing Theories of Jurisprudence 92-106 (1989).

[75] Wright, Interpretations, *supra* at 3.

[76] Wright, Interpretations, *supra* at 3.

[77] Wright, Interpretations, *supra* at 3.

[78] Wright, Interpretations, *supra* at 3.

[79] St. Thomas Aquinas, *The Summa Theologica, Part II*, in Readings in Jurisprudence 29 (Jerome Hall ed., 1938) [hereinafter Readings in Jurisprudence].

[80] Posner, Problems, *supra* at 230.

to English common law, were not limited by those recognized by Roman Law or English Royal law. As explained by the thirteenth century British jurist, Brackton, a nuisance imposes a servitude upon the land of another. It is "an attack upon the ordinary amenities of land-holding, or, in the now established if optimistic phrase, upon 'natural rights.'"[81]

Of course what an age has considered to be a right "natural" to society is doubtless affected by custom. Custom too has long been considered a building block of the common law.[82] In modern common law, the role of custom is recognized not as a reference principally to custom of the community, as it was in earlier times, but rather to the doctrinal custom of hundreds of years of common law, developed by accretion like a coral reef.

Nevertheless, societal and professional customs still play a recognizable role in the development of common law doctrine. For example, the custom of an industry may be referred to for determination of whether a brewery owner would, in the exercise of ordinary care, place mats upon slippery floors, even though such evidence would not preclude a finding of negligence if the *laissez faire* approach, even if generally countenanced, of no mats were concluded to be negligent.[83] Likewise, such concepts as the prudent man standard for evaluating the conduct of a fiduciary is, of course, pregnant with consideration of customary investment and related practices.[84]

---

[81]  C.H.S. FIFOOT, HISTORY AND SOURCES OF THE COMMON LAW: TORT AND CONTRACT 8 & n. 26 (1970) [hereinafter FIFOOT, HISTORY] (citing HOLDSWORTH, HISTORY OF ENGLISH LAW VII 328-33 Methuen 1925).

[82]  RICHARD A. POSNER, THE ECONOMICS OF JUSTICE 25-26 (1981).

[83]  *See* The T.J. Hooper, 60 F.2d 737, 740 (2d Cir.1932) (Hand, J., dictum), *cert. denied.* ([A] whole calling may have unduly lagged in the adoption of new and available devices."); Richard A. Epstein, *The Path to the T.J. Hooper: The Theory and History of Custom in the Law of Torts*, 21 J.LEGAL STUD. 1, 38 (1992) ("There are many competitors for this questionable honor, but Hand's famous bon mot is perhaps the most influential, and mischievous, sentence in the history of the law of torts.").

    *See also* Clarence Morris, *Custom and Negligence*, 42 COLUM.L.REV. 1147 (1941); Mayhew v. Sullivan Mining Co., 76 Me. 100, 112 (1884) ("If the defendants had proved that in every mining establishment that has existed since the days of Tubal-Cain, it has been the practice to cut ladder-holes in their platforms, ... without guarding or lighting them, and without notice to contractors or workmen, it would have no tendency to show that the act was consistent with ordinary prudence.").

## B. EARLY ENVIRONMENTAL TORTS

Long before the modern rapture with comprehensive statutory schemes, common law courts weighed costs and benefits, and mediated disputes between private interest and societal goals. Not surprisingly, much early common law rights balancing concerned the reconciliation of competing property interests. The societal commitment to a freeholder's liberty to develop his land was early limited to development that did not impair the rights of neighboring landowners to quietly or profitably enjoy their own property. As Bracton wrote:

> If a servitude is imposed upon a man's land by the law, though not by the grant of a man, whereby he is forbidden to do on his own land what may harm his neighbor, as if he should raise the level of a pond on his own land or make a new one whereby his neighbor is harmed, as for example if his neighbor's land is thus flooded, this will be an injurious nuisance of his neighbor's freehold unless his neighbor has given him permission to do it.[85]

Solicitude for the rights of the ordinary landholder as against development by more economically powerful neighbors continued into this century. The early New York decision of *Whalen v. Union Bag & Paper Co.*[86] reinstated an injunction against a pulp mill, employing hundreds of persons and representing a then substantial $1 million investment that was polluting the waters of a downstream neighbor whose actual annual damages the jury calculated at $312 per year. Rejecting defendant's claim that the injunction should not stand in that plaintiffs alleged actual injury was "small as compared with the great loss which will be caused by the issuance of the injunction,"[87] the Court of Appeals stated:

---

[84]   Salem v. Central Trust Co., No. C-930932, 1995 WL 238936, at *3 (Ohio Ct.App. 1995).

[85]   FIFOOT, HISTORY, *supra* at 8 (citations omitted).

[86]   101 N.E. 805 (1913).

[87]   *Id.* at 805-06.

Although the damage to the plaintiff may be slight as compared with the defendant's expense of abating the condition, that is not a good reason for refusing an injunction. Neither courts of equity nor law can be guided by such a rule, for if followed to its logical conclusion it would deprive the poor litigant of his little property by giving it to those already rich.[88]

# V. THE COMMON LAW IN THE TWENTIETH CENTURY

## A. MODERN COMMON LAW GOALS

### 1. Social Utility; Wealth Maximization

From the earliest jurisprudential writings through and including modern law and economic theorists, there has existed consensus that a proper goal of law, common law and statutory law alike, is the reconciliation of the public welfare with private rights. In modern terms, this measurement has been termed alternately as one of social utility and wealth maximization.[89] This inclusive analysis of the role of law measures a law's justice by the answer to this question: "Has the law worked the greatest good for the greatest number?"

---

[88]   *Id.* at 806.

[89]   Although complementary, the two concepts enjoy an important distinction. According to Richard A. Posner, the utilitarian analysis may essay to calculate the benefit to society of a general good, such as equality of economic opportunity, or preservation of green space in urban areas, without reference to the presence or absence of the proponents' willingness to pay for such objectives. A "wealth maximization" efficiency approach, on the other hand, counts only those "preferences backed by a willingness to pay." Richard A. Posner, *The Ethical and Political Basis of the Efficiency Norm in Common Law Adjudication*, 8 Hofstra L.Rev. 487, 499 (1980) [hereinafter Posner, *Ethical and Political Basis*].

## a. Social Utility

Essentially, a social utility or utilitarian approach posits that conduct is acceptable, if not salutary, if its expected benefits to the actor and to society together outweigh its expected hardship upon another in particular or society more generally.[90] Demonstration of this principle is found in the legal disputes following the death of Elvis Presley, involving the issue of whether the designees of Presley's estate could control the singer's "right of publicity" as against all others—or, more prosaically, could the estate's designees forever profit from others' use of his likeness.[91] The Sixth Circuit decided to leave undisturbed the traditional common law rule that heirs may not retain exclusive control over an ancestor's name or likeness, commenting in words redolent of economic concerns:

> It does not seem reasonable to expect that [changing the common law rule] would enlarge the stock or quality of the goods, services, artistic creativity, information, invention or entertainment available. Nor will it enhance the fairness of our political and economic system. It seems fairer and more efficient for the commercial, aesthetic, and political use of the name, memory and image of the famous to be open to all rather than to be monopolized by a few.[92]

The rest is history. As readily as if they had set up a card table with Elvis paraphernalia on Manhattan's Lexington Avenue, the Sixth Circuit anointed the modern Elvis industry, an American apotheosis of wealth maximization.

Such litigation illustrates that a guiding principle of modern economic analysis of the law is that the public good is enhanced when the expected benefits derived by a rule—benefits to the actor together with benefits to society

---

[90]   Cf. David C. Owen, *The Moral Foundation of Product Liability Law: Toward First Principles*, 68 NOTRE DAME L.REV. 427 (1993), discussed in Products Liability Restatement Tentative Draft No. 2, at 48; David G. Owen, *Products Liability: Principles of Justice for the 21st Century*, 11 PACE L.REV. 63 (1990).

[91]   Memphis Dev. Found. v. Factors Etc., Inc., 616 F.2d 956 (6th Cir.1980), *cert. denied.*

[92]   *Id.* at 959-60.

more broadly—outweigh the expected costs, both monetary and social. A rule of law achieving this goal is termed "efficient." The economic analysis of law to evaluate its efficiency is often called "utilitarian."[93]

What is meant by social utility, or a utilitarian role of law?[94] In a general sense, it may be described as law's role in promoting what is just, with the implicit expectation that what is just promotes the general welfare. Aquinas states the idyllic proposition that "we call those legal matters just, which are adapted to produce and preserve happiness and its parts for the body politic; since the state is a perfect community."[95] James Barr Ames expressed the apogee of the utilitarian ethos in these words: "The law is utilitarian. It exists for the realization of the reasonable needs of the community. If the interest of an individual runs counter to this chief object of the law, it must be sacrificed."[96] Writing that law is "forward looking," a "servant of human needs,"[97] Richard Posner and others call for a scientific ethic of wealth maximization, a so-called "efficiency norm."[98] Many have responded to this call, with one influential commentator concluding that "much (though by no means all) of modern tort law is at least roughly consistent with a Posnerian economic analysis."[99]

Arguing the point, Posner enlists the law of battery—the common law rule concerning liability for harmful or offensive touching. Quite apart from the corrective justice, moral, and fairness attributes of the doctrine of tortious battery, the law and economics argument states that an efficient doctrine should "dete[r] persons from engaging in activities that a reasonable person

---

[93] See generally James Barr Ames, Law and Morals, 22 HARV.L.REV. 97, 110 (1908); Henry T. Terry, Negligence, 29 HARV.L.REV. 40 (1915).

[94] Cf., John C. Goodman, An Economic Theory, of the Evolution of Common Law. 7 J.LEGAL STUD. 393 (1978).

[95] READINGS IN JURISPRUDENCE, supra at 28. See generally DAVID G. OWEN, PHILOSOPHICAL FOUNDATIONS OF TORT LAW (1995). Early "scientific" utilitarian analyses "drew upon several trends in Victorian intellectual history for [their] roots." COSGROVE, OUR LADY, supra at 39.

[96] Ames, supra, at 110.

[97] POSNER, PROBLEMS, supra at 29.

[98] See, e.g., Posner, Ethical and Political Basis, supra at 89

[99] Gary T. Schwartz, Reality in Economic Analysis of Tort Law: Does Tort Law Really Deter?, 42 UCLA L.REV. 377, 381 (1994).

would view ... socially wasteful."[100] Thus in *Garratt v. Dailey*, [101] remembered as the case in which the nearly six-year-old Dailey pulled away the lawn chair as his, until that point, affectionate aunt was sitting down, tort liability in battery would serve efficiency principles irrespective of whether Dailey received any psychic or material benefit from the act. If the harm to the aunt exceeded any benefits to Dailey, a simple utilitarian analysis would support imposition of liability. If, on the other hand, Dailey derived benefits that exceeded any physical or psychological injury to his aunt, pulling out the chair was wasteful or inefficient. Why wasteful? Because the transaction (the act and the harm) without the aunt's consent would, and did, generate a laborious lawsuit in which great expense, or transaction costs, were unnecessarily devoted to determining liability. In Posner's words:

> [T]orts like simple battery ... involve a ... coerced transfer of wealth to the defendant occurring in a setting of low transaction costs. Such conduct is inefficient because it violates the principle ... that where market transaction costs are low, people should be required to use the market if they can and to desist from the conduct if they can't. [I]t is inefficient to permit the market to be bypassed in this way.[102]

Numerous analysts have identified a common law tropism towards efficiency.[103] Importantly, scholars have also concluded that efficient rules of law actually predict efficient litigation strategies, including settlement strategies. As stated by Ramona L. Paetzold and Steven L. Willborn, "where both parties to a dispute have a continuing interest in precedent, the parties will settle if

---

[100] James A. Henderson, Jr. et al., The Torts Process (4th ed. 1994) (discussing Richard A. Posner, Economic Analysis of Law 191-195 (3d ed. 1986)).

[101] 279 P.2d 1091 (Wash.1955).

[102] Richard A. Posner, Economic Analysis of Law 192-193 (2d ed. 1977) [hereinafter Posner, Economic Analysis].

[103] *E.g.*, George L. Priest, *The Common Law Process and the Selection of Efficient Rules*, 6 J.Legal Stud. 65 (1977); Ramona L. Paetzold & Steven L. Willborn, *The Efficiency of the Common Law Reconsidered*, 14 Geo.Mason.U.L.Rev. 157 (1991).

the existing precedent is efficient, but litigate if the precedent is ineffi-cient."[104] Wes Parsons, even while disputing these premises, collected schol-arship revealing, in fact, the broad range of cost internalization achievements of evolving common law doctrine.[105] Included in Parsons's review was scholarly attribution to the common law of accidents as promoting "efficient resource allocation;"[106] the efficiencies of the common law of rescue, salvage, and Good Samaritan assistance;[107] the efficiency of the common law damages rule for an-ticipatory repudiation of a contract;[108] and the efficiency of the economic loss rule in tort.[109]

A primitive but greatly influential evaluative standard was offered in a neg-ligence context by Judge Learned Hand in the opinions in *United States v. Car-roll Towing Co.*[110] and *Conway v. O'Brien.*[111] In those two cases, the court stated that "the degree of care appropriate to a situation is the result of the calculus using three factors: the likelihood that the conduct will injure others, multi-plied by the seriousness of the risk if it happens, balanced against the burden of taking precautions against the risk." In formula, the calculation is known to many as B (Burden) < P (Probability of Harm) x L (Magnitude of Loss Should It Occur).[112] The Learned Hand approach can be conformed to more modern utilitarian analysis by visualizing B, or the Burden upon the actor, as encom-passing not only the particular burden of precautionary measures upon the

---

[104] Paetzold & Willborn, *supra* at 157.

[105] Wes Parsons, Note, *The Inefficient Common Law*, 92 YALE L.J. 862 (1983).

[106] William M. Landes & Richard A. Posner, *The Positive Economic Theory of Tort Law*, 15 GA.L.REV. 851, 852 (1981).

[107] William A. Landes & Richard A. Posner, *Salvors, Finders, Good Samaritans and Other Rescuers: An Economic Study of Law and Altruism*, 7 J.LEGAL STUD. 83, 128 (1977).

[108] Thomas H. Jackson, *"Anticipatory Repudiation" and the Temporal Element of Contract Law: An Economic Inquiry into Contract Damages in Cases of Prospective Nonperformance*, 31 STAN.L.REV. 69, (1978) ("Compensating the aggrieved party for its entire expec-tation loss, without overcompensating it, is an economically sound principle in that it facilitates the movement of goods and services to their higher value user.").

[109] W. Bishop, *Economic Loss in Tort*, 2 OXFORD J.LEGAL STUD. 1, 2-3 (1982).

[110] 159 F.2d 173 (2d Cir.1947).

[111] 111 F.2d 611, 612 (2d Cir.1940), rev'd 312 U.S. 492 (1941).

[112] *Id.*

actor, but also the burden upon society if the conduct must either be eliminated due to liability rules, or made more expensive, and therefore beyond the economic reach of many, and then asking would the precautionary measures be undertaken.[113]

A leading exponent of the efficiency role of the common law of tort was Guido Calabresi, who argued persuasively that in matters of compensation for — accidents, civil liability should ordinarily be laid at the door of the "cheapest cost avoider," the actor who could most easily discover and inexpensively remediate the hazard. Together with A. Douglas Melamed, Calebresi stated persuasively that, particularly in the setting of environmental harm, considerations of economic efficiency dictate placing the cost of accidents "on the party or activity which can most cheaply avoid them."[114] Validation of this approach came in the Ninth Circuit decision in *Union Oil Co. v. Oppen*,[115] a California coastal oil spill case in which the court allowed commercial fishermen to recover their business losses caused by lost fishing opportunity during a period of pollution. The court followed Calabresi's suggestion that it "exclude as potential cost-avoiders those groups/activities which could avoid accident costs only at extremely high expense,"[116] a consideration militating against the conclusion that the cost of preventing or repositioning the loss be borne directly by consumers (fishermen or seafood purchasers) in the form of precautionary measures (whatever they might hypothetically be), or by first party insurance. Rather, the court found justice and efficiency were served by placing responsibility for the loss on the "best cost avoider," in this setting the defendant oil company, reasoning:

---

[113]  Guido Calabrese & A. Douglas Melamed, *Property Rules, Liability Rules, and Inalienability: One View at the Cathedral*, 85 HARV.L.REV. 1089, 1096-97 (1972). *See also* MARK C. RUDERT, COVERING ACCIDENT COSTS: INSURANCE, LIABILITY AND TORT REFORM 29, 32-33 (1995).

[114]  Likewise in keeping with a utilitarian view that transcends the concerns of the individual plaintiff and defendant, consideration of the factors P (Probability of Harm) and L (Magnitude of the Loss should it occur) would be enlarged to contemplate the likelihood of harm to others, and the magnitude of the potential harm, not only in terms of the individual plaintiff but also to the population exposed to the risk.

[115]  501 F.2d 558 (9th Cir.1974).

[116]  *Id.* at 569.

[T]he loss should be allocated to that party who can best correct any error in allocation, if such there be, by acquiring the
activity to which the party has been made liable. The capacity
"to buy out" the plaintiffs if the burden is too great is, in
essence, the real focus of Calabresi's approach. On this basis,
there is no contest—the defendants' capacity is superior.[117]

A utilitarian analysis also influences modern rules governing issuance of injunctions, but here the accepted standards have in effect forced a marriage of
utilitarian principles with those of corrective justice. Again in the setting of
environmental harm, notions of corrective justice and utilitarianism have coexisted uneasily for decades. Put most simply, courts then and today must wres-
tle with choices between (1) corrective justice (putting remediation of plaintiff's
wrongfully-caused harm as the most prominent objective); or (2) utilitarian
justice, pursuant to which the court may permit defendant to continue all or
part of the injurious conduct, most often accompanied by a requirement that
plaintiffs be indemnified for their involuntary hardship.

Originally, and due in some measure to the sanctity in which the common
law of property held interests in land, even the most economically powerless
landholder could seek and secure an injunction against a neighboring activity
that interfered substantially with the plaintiff's use of his property. Against a
defendant's argument that its smelter, or its pulp mill, employed hundreds of
people and brought great wealth to the community, in deciding whether or
not to issue an injunction an early court responded that it was unwilling to
"balance" injuries. The court would not weigh the defendant's cost and the
community hardship in losing the industry, against the often modest provable
harm to plaintiff's ordinarily small and noncommercial property. As the New
York Court of Appeals stated in *Whalen v. Union Bag & Paper Co.*,[118] to fail to
grant the small landowner an injunction solely because the loss to him, in absolute terms, is less than would be the investment-backed loss to the nuisance-
creating business and lost employment of the community, would "deprive the

---

[117] *Id.* at 570 (citing GUIDO CALABRESI, THE COST OF ACCIDENTS (1970)).
[118] 101 N.E. 805 (1913).

poor litigant of his little property by giving it to those already rich."[119] By "giving it," the court of course means "requiring plaintiff to endure ongoing environmental servitudes imposed by defendant."[120]

*Whalen*,[121] together with *Madison v. Ducktown Sulphur Copper & Iron Co.*,[122]
in a mirror image judicial response, pose the dilemma presented by a plaintiff's
environmental claim against the conduct of an entity enjoying economic influence in the community. Contrasted with the *Whalen* court's unabashedly
populist sentiment, the modern rule of environmental injunctions might seem
coldly utilitarian. The RESTATEMENT (SECOND) OF TORTS section 936 factors
for injunction issuance expressly include weighing of "the nature of the interest
to be protected,"[123] thus, presumably inviting an elevation of plaintiff's bona
fides where the court considers the activity meritorious, perhaps a Camp Fire
Girls campground, and a devaluation where the court deems it less valuable,
perhaps an automobile scrapyard. Along similar lines, hardship to the defendant of ceasing or changing its activity and "the interests of third persons or
the public" are proper considerations.[124] To this observer, Mr. Whalen would
have difficulty today in obtaining his injunction.

*Boomer v. Atlantic Cement Co.*[125] involved a widescale and conceded industrial nuisance in the form of airborne cement dust emanating from an upstate
New York cement plant. In the lower court, a nuisance was found, and tem-

[119]  *Id.* at 806.

[120]  *Id. See also* McCleery v. Highland Boy Gold Mining Co., 140 F. 951 (D.Utah 1904)
(reaching a comparable corrective justice conclusion, and granting the injunction
against defendant's mine and smelter).

[121]  101 N.E. 805 (1913).

[122]  83 S.W. 658 (Tenn.1904). *Ducktown Sulphur* involved a state supreme court's reversal
of a trial court's injunction, where the high court assigned great weight to defendant's
showing that an injunction would render useless defendant's property, valued at many
multiples the value of plaintiffs property and representing the largest single contribution to county revenues, as well as turn out of work hundreds of employees. The
court observed that it is often true in a case of conflicting rights, "... that neither party
can enjoy his own without in some measure restricting the liberty of the other." *Id.*
at 667.

[123]  RESTATEMENT (SECOND) OF TORTS § 936(a) (1979).

[124]  RESTATEMENT (SECOND) OF TORTS § 936(e), (f), (g) (1979).

[125]  257 N.E.2d 870 (N.Y.1970).

porary damages awarded, but plaintiffs' application for an injunction was denied. Before the New York Court of Appeals, Judge Bergen's opinion early identified the policy issue most troublesome to the court: to what extent should the court in deciding a justiciable controversy between private litigants simultaneously decide broad policy issues (in this case air quality) often thought the proper province of legislation?[126]

Recognizing that to deny the injunction would depart from *Whalen's* corrective justice—no balancing approach, discussed above, the court nevertheless adopted a utilitarian approach that weighed the hardships imposed upon plaintiffs against the economic consequences, for Atlantic Cement and for regional employment, of the requested injunction:

> The ground for denial of injunction, notwithstanding the finding both that there is a nuisance and that plaintiffs have been damaged substantially, is the large disparity in economic consequences of the nuisance and of the injunction.[127]

## b. Corrective Justice

The moral authority of natural law, and its successor the common law, turns upon the perception and the reality that its tenets lead to "just" results.[128] What is meant

---

[126] *Id.* Even without resolution of the question of whether or when it is appropriate to exercise "judicial power to use a decision in private litigation as a purposeful mechanism to achieve direct public objectives greatly beyond the rights and interests before the court," Judge Bergen observed that the resolution of air quality issues is likely to require massive public expenditure and to demand more than any local community can accomplish and to depend on regional and interstate controls." *Id.* at 871.

[127] *Id.* at 872. Authentic questions may be raised about the reach of *Boomer.* It is possible that *Boomer* is an anomaly in that Atlantic Cement was a big economic contributor to the region and, for the purposes of the suit, the conduct of its business operations was Simon pure. *Cf.* Little Joseph Realty v. Town of Babylon, 363 N.E.2d 1163, 1167 (N.Y.1977), in which the same New York Court of Appeals issued an injunction against an asphalt plant operating contrary to zoning ordinances, and distinguished *Boomer* as a case involving "no zoning violation, or for that matter, [no] violation of any other statute."

[128] As Augustine says (De Lib. Arb i.5), "[t]hat which is not just seems to be no law at

by "justice?" In Aquinas's words, "a thing is said to be just, from being right, according to the rule of reason."[129] Most contemporary observers would agree that a core consideration in any modern contemplation of "justice" is the goal of "corrective" justice, i.e., a result that, to the extent money damages can, deprives the wrongful party of their gain, and restores the injured party to the position they enjoyed before the harm.[130] Holmes, contemplating torts, explained:

> Be the exceptions more or less numerous, the general purpose
> of the law of torts is to secure a man indemnity against certain
> forms of harm to person, reputation, or estate, at the hands
> of his neighbors, not because they are wrong, but because they
> are harms.[131]

In Book Five, chapter two of NICOMACHEAN ETHICS, Aristotle is credited with laying, the cornerstone of the corrective justice principles of the common law.[132] Under the Aristotelian corrective principle of *diorthotikos*, or "making

---

all: wherefore the force of a law depends on the extent of its justice. Now in human affairs a thing is said to be just, from being right, according to the rule of reason. But the first rule of reason is the law of nature.... Consequently, every human law has just so much of the nature of law, as it is derived from the law of nature. But if in any point it deflects from the law of nature, it is no longer a law but a perversion of law." READINGS IN JURISPRUDENCE, *supra* at 37. *Cf.*, Randy E. Barnett, *Getting Normative: The Role, or Virtual Rights in Constitutional Adjudication*, 12 CONST.COMM. 93, 105-113 (1995).

[129]  READINGS IN JURISPRUDENCE, *supra* at 37.

[130]  I say "to the extent possible" because the majority of common law remedies involve the award of money damages, and money damages do not restore to their pre-incident condition a person who has suffered personal physical injury, or the dignitary injury of a defamation or an invasion of privacy. Likewise it is only by flight of the imagination that we suppose the payment of money damages deprives a defendant of a "gain" achieved by a tortious battery or medical malpractice. In these settings, the justification of common law remedies will depend heavily upon connections with other goals, such as deterrence, individual autonomy and liberty, and instrumentalism.

[131]  HOLMES, THE COMMON LAW, *supra* at 144.

[132]  Considered synonymous with the terms "rectificatory" or "commutative." POSNER, PROBLEMS, *supra* at 313. "[T]he law ... treats the parties as equal, and asks only if one is the author and the other the victim of injustice or if the one inflicted and the

straight," at the remedy phase the court will attempt "to equalize things by means of the penalty, taking away the gain from the assailant. For the term 'gain' is applied generally to such cases, even if it be not a term appropriate to certain cases, e.g., to the person who inflicts a wound—and 'loss' to the sufferer.... The judge restores equality."[133]

## 3. Instrumentalism and Morality

### a. Instrumentalism

The instrumental role of common law doctrines comprises its effect upon social and business behavior. A rule having a successful instrumental role will convey simultaneously an exhortative, hortatory message, lauding behavior deemed beneficial, together with a message intended to discourage or deter behavior deemed bad by whatever measure (utilitarian or rights-based). As an abstract proposition, a just and effective common law rule will encourage positive and productive behavior and discourage negative activity.

Often the instrumental objectives of a rule may not be apparent on its face, and are evident only upon their salutary realization in risk reduction, loss prevention or the like.[134] The empirical failure of a common law doctrine may likewise manifest itself.

---

other has sustained an injury. Injustice in this sense is unfair or unequal, and the endeavor of the judge is to equalize it." ARISTOTLE, NICOMACHEAN ETHICS 146 (J. Welldon trans., 1912), *discussed in* DAVID G. OWEN, THE PHILOSOPHICAL FOUNDATIONS OF FAULT IN TORT LAW (1995).

[133]   2 ARISTOTLE, THE COMPLETE WORKS OF ARISTOTLE 1786-87 (Jonathan Barnes ed., 1984). "It is for this reason," Aristotle continues, "that it is called just [dikaion], because it is a division into two parts [dika]... and the judge [dikastes] is one who bisects [dichastes].... Therefore the just... consists in having an equal amount before or after the transaction." *Id.*

See generally Richard W. Wright, Substantive Corrective Justice, 77 IOWA L.REV. 625 (1992).

[134]   The instrumentalism of law was recognized by Aquinas: "A thing may be known in two ways: first, in itself; secondly, in its effect, wherein some likeness of that thing is found: thus someone not seeing the sun in its substance, may know it by its rays." READINGS IN JURISPRUDENCE, *supra* at 31.

*i. Discouragement of Harmful Conduct*

Imposition of an external standard of conduct, it has been argued, serves less to buy, affect or co-opt the moral position of the population than to put persons on notice of the behavior expected of them to avoid liability. In Holmes' words:

> The true explanation of the reference of liability to a moral stan-
> dard... is not that it is for the purpose of improving men's hearts,
> but that it is to give a man a fair chance to avoid the harm before
> he is held responsible for it. It is intended to reconcile the policy
> of letting accidents lie where they fall, and the reasonable free-
> dom of others with the protection of the individual from injury.[135]

Just what is Holmes' "fair chance to avoid" behavior before being held responsible for it? In tort, for example, the triggering event for imposition of responsibility for another's loss takes "knowledge" as the "starting point," followed
by examination of the "circumstances" that "would have led a prudent man to
perceive danger, although not necessarily to foresee the specific harm."[136]
What are such circumstances? Holmes answers "experience."[137]

The goal of deterrence has seemingly been torts' perpetual and faithful
companion. As early as 1890 an academic author wrote of the goals of the negligence action in these words:

> The really important matter is to adjust the dispute between
> the parties by a rule of conduct which shall do justice if pos-
> sible in the particular case, but which shall also be suitable to
> the needs of the community, and tend to prevent like acci-
> dents from happening in [the] future.[138]

---

[135] Holmes, The Common Law, *supra* at 144.

[136] *Id.*

[137] *Id.*

[138] William Schofield, Davies v. Mann: *Theory of Contributory Negligence*, 3 Harv.L.Rev.
263, 269 (1890).

Even those who question whether tort law, for example, "does in fact deter as thoroughly as economic models suggest"[139] concede it delivers a "moderate amount of deterrence."[140]

### ii. Encouragement of Useful Conduct

The instrumental quality of law, be it positive (statutory) law or common law, lies in its capacity to influence behavior. Thus, by hypothesis (1) following the notorious verdict involving the woman scalded by McDonald's coffee, it might be predicted that fast food restaurants would serve coffee at lower temperatures; (2) following the English decision in *Lumley v. Gye*,[141] a rival theater owner might be disinclined to importune a leading singer away from her existing contractual obligations; and (3) after the verdict arising from the spill of the Exxon Valdez, tanker owners might be more probing in their evaluation of the fitness of vessel captains.

### b. The Moral Promontory: Mores and Morality

Ronald Dworkin has been called a "chief evangelist" of the proposition that judges should advance a right-based jurisprudence rooted in moral precepts,[142] a proposition that begs the question: "To whose moral precepts do we refer?" In periods of our country's past in which populations were less heterogenous and political power less pluralistic, the guiding precepts were those of white Christian males. Many academic analyses have concluded that Nineteenth Century judges unabashedly used tort law as a device for inducing morally suitable behavior.[143]

---

[139] Schwartz, *supra* at 379.

[140] *Id.*

[141] 118 Eng.Rep. 749 (1853).

[142] Vincent A. Wellman, *Conceptions of the Common Law: Reflections on a Theory of Contract*, 41 U.MIAMI L.REV. 925, 925 n. 1 (1987) (citing RONALD DWORKIN, TAKING RIGHTS SERIOUSLY 1-130 (1977)).

[143] *E.g.*, Robert J. Kaczorowski, *The Common Law Background of Nineteenth Century*

Does morality remain an identifiable fixture of modern common law doctrine? Ernest J. Weinrib answers affirmatively, pointing to tort doctrine as common law in which wrongdoing is a necessary, if not by itself sufficient, component of liability.[144] How is a moral position to be determined? Rawls claimed that "one of the aims of moral philosophy is to look for possible bases of agreement where none seem to exist. Moral philosophy must attempt to extend the range of existing consensus."[145]

To some, the modern surge towards strict tort liability, even though receding in some settings, is reflective of a moralistic conception of indemnity obligations, i.e., behavioral and compensatory obligations unaffected by utilitarian weighing or even, when taken to the extreme, comparative causal contribution. Richard Posner explained the shift (until quite recently at least) from negligence based criteria for accident compensation to strict liability in these words: "The need for compensation is unaffected by whether the participants in the accident were careless or careful[,] and we have outgrown a morality that would condition the right to compensation upon a showing that the plaintiff was blameless and the defendant blameworthy."[146]

---

*Tort Law*, 51 OHIO ST.L.J. 1127, 1128 (1990).

[144] Ernest J. Weinrib, The Morality of Tort Law, Address at the Tort Law Section, Association of American Law Schools Annual Meeting (Jan. 9, 1988), discussed in Kotler, *supra* n. 59 at 1231 n. 2, 1240.

[145] JOHN RAWLS, A THEORY OF JUSTICE 582 (1971). As Holmes explained, describing the common law antecedents of the modern law of misrepresentation:

> [t]he common law ... preserves the reference to morality by making fraud the ground on which it goes. It does not hold that a man always speaks at his peril. But starting from the moral ground, it works out an external standard of what would be fraudulent in the average prudent member of the community, and requires every member at his peril to avoid that.

HOLMES, THE COMMON LAW, *supra* at 137.

Holmes likewise identified a moral basis for the common law action in malicious prosecution. "The legal remedy here, again, started from the moral basis, the occasion for it, no doubt, being similar to that which gave rise to the old law of conspiracy, that a man's enemies would sometime seek his destruction by setting criminal law in motion against him." HOLMES, THE COMMON LAW, *supra* at 141.

[146] Richard A. Posner, *A Theory of Negligence*, 1 J. LEGAL STUD. 29, 29-30 (1972).

## 4. Individual Autonomy and Liberty

What do we mean by the terms autonomy and liberty? "Autonomy" has been defined as "independence or freedom."[147] Liberty, in turn, is defined as "freedom from external control of interference, obligations, etc., freedom to choose."[148] Some have argued that among the first tasks of a common law doctrine such as torts "is to define the boundaries of individual liberty."[149] The "justice" rationale of private property, in turn, "is that it enhances the owner's reasonable autonomy."[150]

In THE MORALITY OF FREEDOM, Joseph Raz writes that "[a]utonomy requires that many morally acceptable options be available to a person."[151] Our society's commitment to a legal system vouching safe individual autonomy and liberty is expressed in the earliest interpretations of its organizing principles in the Constitution. In his dissent in the *Slaughter-House Cases*,[152] Mr. Justice Field described the import of the Privileges and Immunities Clauses of Article IV, Section 2 and Section 1 of the Fourteenth Amendment as ensuring that "which of right belongs to the citizens of all free governments. Clearly, among these must be placed the right to pursue lawful employment in a lawful manner, without other restraint than such as equally affects all persons."[153] As our society recognizes a fundamental right to pursue lawful activity without wrongful interference of others, it likewise has recognized the right to do so with relative safety from personal physical harm. Another's autonomy or liberty interest extends, as it were, to the tip of your nose and no further. As Professor Richard Epstein has explained: "The law of tort does not end with the recognition of individual liberty.

---

[147]  THE RANDOM HOUSE COLLEGE DICTIONARY 92 (rev. ed. 1975).

[148]  *Id.* at 772.

[149]  Richard A. Epstein, *A Theory of Strict Liability*, 2 J. LEGAL STUD. 151, 203 (1973).

[150]  JOHN FINNIS, NATURAL LAW AND NATURAL RIGHTS 173 (1980), *discussed in* David G. Owen, *Products Liability: Principles of Justice for the Twenty-first Century*, 11 PACE L.REV. 63, 65 & n. 4 (1990).

[151]  JOSEPH RAZ, THE MORALITY OF FREEDOM 378 (1986).

[152]  83 U.S. (16 Wall.) 36 (1872).

[153]  *Id.* at 97 (Field, J., dissenting).

Once a man causes harm to another, he has brought himself within the boundaries of the law of tort."[154]

Economists, in turn, might cast the sentiments of individual autonomy and liberty in terms of avoiding involuntary or coerced transfers of wealth. A manufacturer of amplified sound systems who loses customers as a result of a trade libel[155] or a theater owner whose premier singer under contract is lured away by a rival theater,[156] each suffers lost profits. The rival theater owner may actually realize a money profit from the wrongful interference with the singer's contractual obligations. The author of the trade libel may gain increased sales of his or her business commentary, or may merely realize a nonpecuniary increase in wealth—whatever satisfaction one might derive from having harshly and erroneously criticized a large corporation. The economist argues that the theater's suit for interference with contractual relations, or the manufacturer's suit for trade libel, operate simply to correct a coerced transfer of wealth. If those lost profits are left unmediated by a remedy for money damages, they represent an involuntary and inefficient transfer of wealth from the injured party to the injurer.

## C. THE PROCESS OF ENLIGHTENED GRADUALISM

Let us now turn to a broader consideration of the systems, mechanisms and means by which the common law effects its goals of justice and efficiency. By trial, error, experiment, expansion, and correction, the common law has hewn to an objective of advancing the public welfare. Making obeisance in turn to principles of corrective justice, individual autonomy, instrumentalism and efficiency, courts hearing common law claims receive and resolve disputes that ordinarily are not the subject of statute or regulation. Reconciling the nomi-

---

[154] Epstein, *supra* at 208. Professor Epstein continues: "It does not follow, however, that he will be found liable in each and every case in which it can he showed that he caused harm, for it may still be possible for him to escape liability, not by an insistence upon his freedom of action, but upon a specific showing that his conduct was either excused or justified." Epstein, *supra* at 208.

[155] Bose Corp. v. Consumers Union of United States, Inc., 446 U.S. 485 (1984).

[156] Lumley v. Gye, 118 Eng.Rep. 749 (1853).

nally divergent goals of corrective justice and efficiency—the incongruity between which is more formal than real[157] —the common law proceeds along a course of enlightened gradualism. I use the term enlightened to describe common law judges' identification and consideration of evolving societal needs, examined through the lens of developed principles of modern justice, sociology and economics. The term gradualism connotes recognition of the common law court's constant reference in existing doctrine and precedent, providing it with a genuine but moderated capacity to mold new doctrine.

What have been the principal methodologies of the common law capacity for growth? This section discusses but a few.

## 1. Conditional Stare Decisis

An original assessment of a court's obligation to follow germane prior decisions, or precedent, of its own or superior courts, commonly called the rule of stare decisis, left some common law judges with the perception that theirs was a limited charge of the application of precedent to new disputes.[158] As early as 1833, English Jurist Baron Parke stated the theory of case law in these words: "It appears to me to be of great importance to keep this principle of decision steadily in view, not merely for the determination of the particular case, but for the interests of law as a science."[159]

Unlike legislatures, which may shed prior policies as a snake sheds its skin, courts applying common law principles are at least nominally constrained by

---

[157] LANDES & POSNER, ECONOMIC STRUCTURE, *supra* at 9. "[I]n the absence of a more precise specification of fairness we find no necessary incompatibility between a positive theory [of torts] that stresses fairness and one that stresses efficiency." LANDES & POSNER, ECONOMIC STRUCTURE, *supra* at 19.

[158] In 1890 one author described a modest court prerogative: "The office of the judge is not to make [the law] ... but to find it, and, when it is found, to affix to it his official mark, by which it becomes more certainly known and authenticated." JAMES C. CARTER, THE IDEAL AND THE ACTUAL IN THE LAW 231, *quoted in* COSGROVE, OUR LADY, *supra* at 32.

[159] ARTHUR R. HOGUE, ORIGINS OF THE COMMON LAW 231 (1966) [hereinafter HOGUE, ORIGINS] (quoting Mirehouse v. Rennell, I Cl & F., 527, 546 (1833)).

stare decisis.[160] Professor Eisenberg, in THE NATURE OF COMMON LAW offers this modern description of the doctrine and its contemporary role, emphasizing support and replicability as its central tenets:

> Under [the principle of stare decisis,] as it is traditionally formulated, the 'ratio decidendi' (ground of decision), 'holding,' or 'rule' of a precedent is binding in subsequent cases, within broad limits.... Under the principles of *support* and *replicability*, the courts must establish and apply rules that are supported by the general standards of society, ... and must adopt a process of reasoning that is replicable by the profession. Reasoning from precedent satisfies both those principles.[161]

For Professor Eisenberg's distillation of stare decisis into the twin goals of support and replicability, stare decisis has always represented more of an aspirational goal than a rule of any rigidity. Perhaps the bloom of stare decisis was off the rose when Lord Gardner, Lord Chancellor of England, was reported in the New York Times as announcing the Law Lords' abandonment of a rule observed for six decades that the body was powerless to alter its own decisions. Henceforth, Lord Gardner stated, the Law Lords would be free to "depart from a previous decision when it appears right to do so."[162]

---

[160] *See* RUPERT CROSS, PRECEDENT IN ENGLISH LAW 103 (3d ed. 1977); ABNER J. MIKVA, THE SHIFTING SANDS OF LEGAL TOPOGRAPHY (reviewing CALABRESI, AGE OF STATUTES, *supra*). *See also* HOGUE, ORIGINS, *supra* at 231:

> Our Common Law system consists in the applying to new combinations of circumstance those rules of law which we derive from legal principles and judicial precedents; and for the sake of attaining uniformity, consistency, and certainty, we must apply those rules, where they are not plainly unreasonable and inconvenient, to all cases which arise; and we are not at liberty to reject them, and to abandon all analogy to them, in those to which they have not yet been judicially applied, because we think that the rules are not as convenient and reasonable as we ourselves could have devised.

HOGUE, ORIGINS, *supra* at 231 (quoting *Morehouse*).

[161] MELVIN A. EISENBERG, NATURE OF THE COMMON LAW 47 (1988) [hereinafter EISENBERG, NATURE OF THE COMMON LAW] (emphasis added).

[162] N.Y. TIMES, July 31, 1966, § E. at 6, *quoted in* White & White v. King, 223 A.2d

Our own courts have repeatedly confirmed that stare decisis imposes no more than a rebuttable obligation, which obligation is released when competing public policy beckons persuasively. In one court's words,

> [n]otwithstanding the great importance of the doctrine of stare decisis, we have never construed it to inhibit us from changing or modifying a common law rule by judicial decision where we find, in light of changed conditions or increased knowledge, that the rule has become unsound in the circumstances of modern life, — a vestige of the past, no longer suitable to our people.[163]

And as a Maryland Court of Special Appeals stated: "[t]his Court has manifested a willingness to change common law rules which have 'become unsound in the circumstances of modern life.'"[164] Thus the animating principle for abandoning an established rule of common law is that where the reasons for a rule have changed, the law too should change.[165]

---

763, 766 n. 1 (Md.App.1966).

[163] Boblitz v. Boblitz, 462 A.2d 506, 526 (Md.1983) (abandoning spousal immunity bar as applied to a vehicular tort claim brought by a woman against her estranged husband).

[164] Jones v. Maryland, 486 A.2d 184, 188 (Md.1985) (abrogating common law rule precluding conviction of an accessory before the fact of a higher crime than that for which the principal has been convicted). The court in Jones noted further that another common law rule discarded once it became "obsolete" was that of precluding trial of an accessory until the principal was tried. *Id.* at 188 (citations omitted).

[165] New Jersey v. Culver, 129 A.2d 715, 724 (N.J.1957) ("As long ago as 1609, in Milborn's Case, 7 Coke 7a (K.B.1609), Lord Coke stated that the reason for the law is the soul of the law, and if the reason for the law has changed, the law is changed.") Along similar lines, Mr. Justice Holmes wrote "[i]t is revolting to have no better reason for a rule of law than that so it was laid down in the time of Henry IV. It is still more revolting if the grounds upon which it was laid down have vanished long since, and the rule simply persists from blind imitation of the past." OLIVER WENDELL HOLMES, JR., COLLECTED PAPERS 187 (1920).

*Cf., in re White,* 223 A.2d 763 (involving an automobile guest statute and a choice of law issue). While declining appellant's request that the court abandon Maryland's *lex loci delicti* rule the court nevertheless stated:

Whether or not a given common law rule will be scrutinized for modification or rejection is a function of the whether the court considers the rule just. The enduring "justice" of a given common law rule is revealed in the degree of acceptance accorded it in ensuing decisions, for it will be the decisions that follow which reveal the community's adoption or rejection of the rule. Cardozo identified the paradox that it is the very reality that a judge's expansion or contraction of existing doctrine may be rejected on appeal or in later decisions should liberate the court to apply its independent reasoning to the case before it. In Cardozo's words: "I sometimes think that we worry ourselves overmuch about the enduring consequences of our errors.... In the endless process of testing and retesting, there is a constant rejection of the dross.[166]

Have courts succumbed to the heady recognition that they can depart from established precedent seemingly at will? The decisions suggest that they have not. For example, courts have rejected invitations to decree new public policy judicially, particularly where a new policy would fly in the face of manifest legislative intent. In one Maryland decision, *Felder v. Felder*,[167] a drunk driving case, the court was asked to countenance a claim against a tavern owner who sold liquor to a visibly intoxicated person, who was later involved in an accident. Rejecting the invitation, it concluded: "We should virtually usurp legislative power if we should declare plaintiff's contentions to be the law of Maryland.... On few subjects are legislators kept better informed of legislation in other states."[168]

> The doctrine of stare decisis, important as it is, is not to be construed as preventing us from changing a rule of law if we are convinced that the rule has become unsound in the circumstances of modern life. While it is important, in our legal system, that persons should know the probable consequences of their acts, that consideration has little bearing on the commission of unintentional torts.... It is characteristic of our legal system that the emergence of a new doctrine depends for its clarification on the case-to-case decisions, as its application to different factual situations presents new difficulties to be resolved and new factors to be weighed.

*In re White*, 223 A.2d at 766.

[166] CARDOZO, JUDICIAL PROCESS, *supra* at 179.

[167] 438 A.2d 494 (Md.App.1981).

[168] *Id.* at 496 (quoting State v. Hatfield, 78 A.2d 754 (Md.Ct.App. 1951)).

Does such a malleable interpretation of stare decisis doctrine throw the common law and broader jurisprudential goal of predictability, or Professor Eisenberg's support and replicability, into a cocked hat? Are the interests of those engaged in or contemplating business or private pursuits disserved for being denied a clear common law expression of what conduct is permitted and what is penalized? Are common law rules truly formed as a man might make rules for his dog, by waiting for an excess or an omission and then punishing defendant for it?

To the argument that the very qualities of flexibility we have ascribed to the common law work unfairly against the actor who may not know in advance he may be liable in reparations for his conduct, Cardozo responds that "even when there is ignorance of the rule, the cases are few in which ignorance has determined conduct."[169] Other courts and commentators have parsed it according to whether potentially affected activity is a private one, or one that is commercial or public. Common law judges are more reluctant to give greater amplitude to an existing law affecting business matters, in reliance upon which investment-based decisions have been made, than upon common law rules affecting personal conduct. Developing this distinction, the court in Woods v. Lancet[170] stated:

> [R]ules of law on which men rely in their business dealings should not be changed in the middle of the game, but what has that to do with bringing to justice a tort-feasor who surely has no moral or other right to rely on a decision of the New York Court of Appeals? Negligence law is common law, and the common law has been molded and changed and brought up to date in many another case. Our court [has] ... not only the right, but the duty to reexamine question where justice demands it.[171]

---

[169] Cardozo, Judicial Process, *supra* at 145.

[170] 102 N.E.2d 691 (N.Y.1951).

[171] *Id* at 694.

## 2. Flexibility and Particularized Determination

One of the most distinctive qualities of common law adjudication is its path of deductive reasoning, i.e., the following or forging of a path from general principles to a conclusion specific to the case before it.[172] In the most liberal sense, the process is scientific. As Cornelius J. Peck explains: "Frequent encounters with a general problem, presented in various contexts that an endless variety of fact patterns provides, give courts a type of experimental program in which they can formulate and test a governing rule."[173]

Where precedent is seemingly sound and the facts presented by a particular case are neither novel nor noteworthy, the process followed by the common law judge is similar in ways to that followed by a judge applying a statute.[174] True, however, to its distinctive role as the forum for resolving conflicts as to which there is not yet consensus, or at least a brokered legislative solution, it is the common law jury to which litigants repair for answers to "complicated and doubtful cases."[175] Using the model of products liability, Professor Marshall Shapo has ably described the fact-sensitive and particularized evaluation that characterizes the incremental development of design defect, informational obligation and other dimensions of the common law of products liability:

> Products liability is highly fact oriented, a phenomenon man-
> ifest in the case law on defect, issues of liability as they pertain

---

[172] "Deduction" is defined as "the act or practice of deducing; reasoning from a known principle to an unknown; from the general to the specific, or from a premise to a conclusion." WEBSTER'S NEW WORLD DICTIONARY OF THE AMERICAN LANGUAGE 383 (College Ed.1962).

[173] Cornelius J. Peck, *The Role of Courts and Legislatures in the Reform of Tort Law*, 48 MINN.L.REV. 265, 297 (1963), *discussed in* Carl T. Bogus, *War on the Common Law: The Struggle at the Center of Products Liability*, 60 MO.L.REV. 1, 65 (1995).

[174] "[U]nless [exceptional] conditions are present, the work of deciding cases in accordance with precedents that plainly fit them is a process similar in its nature to that of deciding cases in accordance with a statute. It is a process of search, comparison, and little more[,]" a mechanistic endeavor comparable to "match[ing] the colors of the case at hand against the colors of many sample cases spread out upon their desk." CARDOZO, JUDICIAL PROCESS, *supra* at 20.

[175] Marshall S. Sharpo, *infra*

to the position of parties in the distributional chain, the problems involving alleged failure to warn, and in questions of proof. In part because of this orientation, and also in this way reflecting the general law of torts, products law requires incremental development. It is a classic of case-by-case construction of lines of precedents, which courts constantly test against their own jurisprudence on the subject and indeed against the bodies of law developing in other states. It is the very model of the cross-country conversation about the law that is a salutary feature of American jurisprudence.[176]

## 3. Adaptive Ability

To Arthur R. Hogue, "[t]he survival of the [English] common law has depended in large part on the ability of its practitioners to adapt the legal system to new conditions—and adaptation has meant growth. Bold judges have created precedents adding new rules to meet new social and economic circumstances."[177] Has the American experience been similar? The Maryland Court of Appeals decision in Kelley v. R.G. Industries, Inc.[178] is emblematic.

*a.* Kelley v. R.G. Industries
A microcosm of the qualities, and the liabilities, of common law growth is Kelley, which involved the painful and modern problem of injury and death caused by criminal use of small, concealable handguns, often called "Saturday-Night Specials." In this suit, a convenience store employee who was wounded in a Maryland holdup sued the West German manufacturer of the Rohm revolver. The complaint alleged that the manufacture and distribution of the gun was

---

[176] Marshall S. Shapo, *In Search of the Law of Products Liability: The ALI Restatement Project*, 48 VAND.L.REV. 631 (1995).

[177] HOGUE, ORIGINS, *supra* n. 159 at 233.

[178] 497 A.2d 1143 (Md.App.1985).

an abnormally dangerous activity, and that the gun itself was defective within the meaning of products liability law because of its negligent or incautious "marketing, promotion, distribution and design."[179]

The Maryland Court of Appeals found itself obligated to reject these two counts. The handgun could not be considered "abnormally dangerous" under the rule in RESTATEMENT (SECOND) OF TORTS §§ 519-520 because Maryland courts, in line with courts of other jurisdictions, had not extended the doctrine beyond its original precincts, i.e., imposition of liability only upon owners or occupiers of land.[180] Neither could the gun be considered defective inasmuch as it functioned precisely as it had been designed to perform, and as the user had expected it to perform.

In terms of conventional dialectic, the thesis accepted by the Maryland court was that the sale of so-called Saturday Night Specials posed a grave and nonreciprocal danger to urban safety, and must therefore be deterred. The antithesis comprised two prongs: (1) extant products liability law posed obstacles to finding such handguns "defective" where they did, in fact, perform as was expected; and (2) existing law governing liability for abnormally dangerous activities had not been extended to encompass products that were, at the time of injury, no longer in the actual or constructive control of the manufacturer.

What avenues, then, were open to the Kelley court? It could not declare "all handguns or handgun usage ... inconsistent with Maryland public policy" as that would be at a clear variance with the state's "comprehensive regulatory scheme concerning the wearing, carrying and transporting of handguns.[181] No such obstacle existed, however, to the declaration of liability for certain gunshot injuries caused by a small subset of firearms used in the course of criminal conduct. In the court's words:

> There is, however, a limited category of handguns which
> clearly is not sanctioned as a matter of public policy. To im-

---

[179]  *Id.* at 1145.

[180]  *Id.* at 1147.

[181]  *Id.* at 1151, 1153 (discussing MD.ANN.CODE art. 27, § 36B-36G (Cum.Supp.1984).

pose strict liability upon the manufacturers and marketers of these handguns, in instances of gunshot wounds caused by criminal use, would not be contrary to the policy embodied in the enactments of the General Assembly. This type of handgun, commonly known as a 'Saturday Night Special,' presents particular problems for law enforcement.[182]

The Kelley crafting of common law liability for manufacturers of inexpensive concealable handguns was soon overturned by the Maryland legislature.[183] Yet the seed planted will doubtless continue to sprout elsewhere until a lasting common law response to this form of urban violence is achieved. Has the Kelley experience prompted courts in any other jurisdictions to refashion common law remedies to respond to these risks? Only recently a California court, weighing the negligence and strict tort liability cases arising from a San Francisco law firm office massacre, found that the victims' claims against the manufacturer of the semi-automatic assault weapon used in the killings could be pursued under California law of ultrahazardous activities.[184]

# C. SPECIFIC DEMONSTRATIONS OF COMMON LAW POLYCENTRIC JUSTICE

Numerous other examples exist of common law developments that successfully redress societal need, and which do so where legislatures have ceded the terrain to common law growth, or have failed to act for want of broad-based political will to do so. These common law developments each manifest, in varying de-

---

[182] Kelley, 497 A.2d at 1153. The court continued with a definition of "Saturday Night Specials" as "characterized by short barrels, light weight, easy concealability, low cost, use of cheap quality materials, poor manufacture, inaccuracy and unreliability. These characteristics render the Saturday Night Special particularly attractive for criminal use and virtually useless for the legitimate purposes of law enforcement, sport, and protection of persons, property and businesses." *Id.* at 1153-54

[183] MD.CODE ANN. art. 3A, § 36-I(h) (1992).

[184] *In re 101 California Street*, No. 959316, 63 U.S.L.W. 2652 (BNA) (Cal.Super.Ct. April 10, 1995).

grees, some or each of the central propositions of judge-made law: corrective justice, morality, instrumentalism, efficiency, and capacity for growth.

## 1. Comparative Fault

The common law rule of contributory negligence precludes a plaintiff from recovery for wrongfully caused harm where the plaintiff's lack of ordinary care for her own safety contributed to that harm.[185] An early and influential expression of both the rule and its perceived logic was given in *Butterfield v. Forrester*,[186] the early Nineteenth Century decision where the plaintiff rode his horse into a pole left in the road by defendant. Lord Ellenborough explained the court's logic in denying judgment for plaintiff:

> A party is not to cast himself upon an obstruction which has been made by the fault of another, and avail himself of it, if he do[es] not himself use common sense and ordinary caution to be in the right.... One person being in fault will not dispense with another's using ordinary care for himself.[187]

The defense's logic and application was widely embraced by a Nineteenth Century judiciary that was solicitous of early industry's desire to avoid hobbling liability rules, as well as by its conceptual reluctance, or incapacity, to contemplate that a harm might have more than one proximate cause.[188]

Whatever might endure of the contributory negligence doctrine's original and facial logic, it can be seen to be in conflict with principles of corrective justice, instrumentalism and efficiency. For a plaintiff to be stripped of any

[185] 2 M. STUART MADDEN. PRODUCTS LIABILITY § 13.1 (2d ed. 1988 & Supp.1995 with K. Northern).

[186] 103 Eng.Rep. 926 (K.B.1809).

[187] *Id.* at 927.

[188] Mary J. Davis, *Individual and Institutional Responsibility: A Vision for Comparative Fault in Products Liability*, 39 VILL.L.REV. 281, 284 & n. 5 (1994) (citing Fleming S. James, Jr., *Contributory Negligence*, 62 YALE L.J. 691 (1953); Wex S. Malone, *The Formative Era of Contributory Negligence*, 41 ILL.L.REV. 151 (1946)).

remedy whatever due to any substandard conduct on his part, however inconsequential, permits considerations of formalism, even scholasticism, to override fairness. The orthodox rule of contributory negligence also fails to serve instrumental goals. It over deters a plaintiff's behavior by seemingly offering only the unilluminating admonition "don't do anything that might later be considered wrong," while providing no intelligible encouragement of useful conduct. For the potential defendant, contributory negligence under deters, by providing the message that for a substantial number of the defendant's wrongfully-caused harms, it will avoid all liability by a mere showing of some incautious conduct of plaintiff. Lastly, the contributory negligence rule is inefficient, as it contains no obligation to apportion the cost of detecting and ameliorating risk along the lines of the parties' comparative causal contribution to the loss. In this way it imposes substantial external costs upon parties who are not, with regard to the totality of the risk, the cheapest cost avoiders.

Today, comparative fault, in either its pure or its modified form, is "firmly entrenched in American law."[189] Where not implemented by statute,[190] the doctrine of pure comparative fault is a model of an efficient common law rule. By levying accident costs upon participants in proportion to their causal contribution to the harm, pure comparative fault fairly apportions the cost of accident prevention, and the burden of failing to prevent accidents, between the actor and the victim. The comparative fault approach also achieves the binary instrumental role lacking in pure contributory negligence in that the rational actor, no longer completely exculpated by even a small level of substandard behavior on the plaintiff's part, will govern her conduct in the knowledge that as the author of an injury-causing activity, she will bear some, and more often than not most, of any indemnification obligation.

---

[189] *See* Michael Steenson, *Comparative Negligence in Minnesota*, 9 WM. MITCHELL L.REV. 299, 303 (1983), for a valuable exposition of the legislative and judicial enactment of comparative fault in Minnesota and other states.

[190] *See* Harrison v. Montgomery County Board of Education, 456 A.2d 894, 906 (Md.1983) (Davidson, J., dissenting) ("In this country, 39 states have abandoned the doctrine of contributory negligence and have adopted the doctrine of comparative negligence—31 by legislative enactment and 8 by judicial decision.").

## 2. Criminal Law

The dynamism of the common law is revealed not only in matters of it litigation, but also in criminal law. Maryland courts have shown particular intrepidity in discarding common law doctrine that has outlived its logic or utility, i.e., law that no longer serves the public welfare. For example, in *Pope v. State*,[191] the court abandoned the common law doctrine of misprision of a felony. While the passage of time without any significant employment of the doctrine does not, without more, require its abandonment, the court conceded that "non-use, we believe, is not without significance. When an offense has lain virtually dormant for over two hundred years, it is difficult to argue that the preservation of society and the maintenance of law and order demand recognition of it."[192] On substantially similar logic, in *Jones v. State*[193] the Maryland Special Court of Appeals abrogated the common law rule "that an accessory could not be convicted of a greater crime than that of which his principal was convicted."[194]

## 3. Immunities

### a. Spousal

The common law rule precluding one spouse from suing the other was derived from the legal fiction that husband and wife were "one person in law,"[195] a fic-

---

[191]   396 A.2d 1054 (Md.1979).

[192]   *Id.* at 1074. The court went on to explain: "[m]isprision of a felony at common law is an impractically wide crime, a long standing criticism which remains unanswered.... It has an undesirable and undiscriminating width." *Id.*

[193]   486 A.2d 184 (Md.1985).

[194]   *Id.* at 185. In so doing, the court offered this reasoning:

> [m]erely because the evidence in the principal's trial may have been different or the principal may have agreed to a favorable plea bargain arrangement, or the jury in the principal's trial may have arrived at a compromise verdict, is not a good reason for allowing the accessory to escape the consequences of having committed a particular offence.

*Id.* at 188.

[195]   "By marriage, the husband and wife are one person in law: that is, the very being or legal existence of the woman is suspended during the marriage, or at least is in-

tion described as an "outgrowth" of "various legal disabilities" that were placed upon women, and which also included the vesting, upon marriage, of a married woman's personal property with that of her husband, a wife's incapacity to make contracts in her own name, and the husband's entitlement to his wife's services.[196]

Courts evaluating the common law question of whether or not to retain the rule of spousal immunity provide particularly revealing examples of courts' interest and willingness to adopt the better rule of law as reflected in the decisions of courts and legislatures of other states. *Shook v. Crabb*[197] was an Iowa general aviation wrongful death claim that followed an accident in which the husband, as pilot, and the wife, as passenger, perished. The suit was brought by the estate of a wife against the estate of her husband, and claimed that while he may have been a good husband, he was a poor pilot. Iowa at that time observed spousal immunity, a doctrine immunizing a spouse from tort actions arising from the non-intentional torts of another, a policy arising from the same legal fiction of husband and wife unity mentioned above.

The Iowa court prefaced its comments with this statement:

> "[W]hen a doctrine or rule is of judicial origin, we would "abdicate our own function, in a field peculiarly nonstatutory, when we refuse to reconsider an old and unsatisfactory court-made rule." An appellate court would be remiss in its duties if it did not from time to time reexamine the analysis underlying its precedents.[198]

Deciding to abrogate the common law doctrine, the court was influenced by its review of the law of other jurisdictions, which "evidence[d] a definite trend

---

corporated and consolidated into that of the husband.... If the wife be injured in her person or her property, she can bring no action for redress without her husband's concurrence." 1 WILLIAM BLACKSTONE, COMMENTARIES 442-43, quoted in Boblitz v. Boblitz, 462 A.2d 506, 507 (Md.1983).

[196]  Condore v. Prince George's County. 425 A.2d 1011. 1013 (Md.1981).

[197]  281 N.W.2d 616 (Iowa 1979).

[198]  *Id.* at 617 (citations omitted).

toward abolishing in toto or limiting in part application of the doctrine of in-
terspousal immunity due to the fundamental policy consideration of providing
judicial redress of an otherwise cognizable wrong."[199]


## 4. Tort

### a. The Common Law Relation to the Due Process and Takings Clauses

Modern tort law is generally agreed to be "the offspring" of the Fourteenth
Century "action on the case."[200] It is a fitting genealogy, for as "action on the
case" freed the ancient remedy in trespass to redress more subtle and indirect
injury in an increasingly interdependent and urbanized English society,[201]
modern tort law continues to mediate claims for civil wrongdoing that are at
the margins of modern life.

The common law role as the engine of corrective justice is seen in bold
relief where Constitutional remedies either fall short or are an incomplete ar-
biter of Constitutionally-addressed liberty or property interests. The common
law's past role, and its future potential as a proxy for claims stymied by interpretation of Due Process rights under the Fourteenth Amendment is evidenced in holdings on Constitutional claims involving such varied settings as
(1) a public official's failure to act permitting injury to a person remanded in
some measure to their care; (2) an official reproval that has defamed a private
individual; and (3) school-administered corporal punishment of a student.

The common law has reflected a societal recognition that new circumstances
require new responses. One such common law initiative is evidenced in *Tarasoff*

---

[199] *Id.* at 618 (collecting authority of 34 jurisdictions). More generally, gender-based
immunities continue to fall by the common law wayside. As Professor Larry Levine
has written, "[i]n many instances, duty determinations reflect a judge's views of society's paramount interests at a specific time. Thus, the duty determination is a dynamic and evolving concept." John L. Diamond, Lawrence C. Levine, M.
Stuart Madden, Understanding Torts § 304[C], 57-59 (1996).

[200] Fifoot, History, *supra* note 81, at 3.

[201] *See* Stanley v. Powell, 1 Q.B. 86 (1891); Joseph W. Little, Torts: The Civil
Law of Reparation for Harm Done by Wrongful Act 14 (1985).

*v. Regents of University of California,*[202] in which the California Supreme Court held that under certain circumstances "a psychotherapist has a duty to protect third parties from a threat of serious harm posed by a patient under his care."[203]

In contrast with Tarasoff are the results reached within the confines of statutory or Constitutional language. For example, in *DeShaney v. Winnebago County Department of Social Services,*[204] brought on behalf of a four-year-old boy repeatedly beaten by his father until he lapsed into irreversible retardation, appointed representatives for the injured child were rebuffed in their suit claiming that the Due Process Clause of the Fourteenth Amendment was violated by social workers' systematic failure to protect the child. The Supreme Court concluded as follows:

> [N]othing in the language of the Due Process Clause itself requires the state to protect the life, liberty and property of its citizens against invasion by private actors. The Clause is phrased as a limitation on the State's power to act, not as a guarantee of certain minimal levels of safety and security."[205]

A like example of the common law of tort's role filling the gaps in Constitutional remedies is shown in private litigation challenging the occasional and churlish municipal practice of using public posting to discourage so-called "active" shoplifters. In *Paul v. Davis,*[206] Davis, the petitioner, sought an injunction against Louisville, Kentucky police to stop their circulation to Louisville merchants of a flier to that effect. Although prosecuted for the offense more than once, Davis had never been convicted of shoplifting. He claimed in his lawsuit that the fliers inhibited him "from entering business establishments for fear of being suspected of shoplifting and possibly apprehended, and would seri-

---

[202] 551 P.2d 334 (Cal.1976).

[203] Alan A. Stone, *The Tarasoff Decisions: Suing Psychotherapists to Safeguard Society*, 90 Harv.L.Rev. 358 (1976).

[204] 489 U.S. 189 (1989).

[205] *Id.* at 195.

[206] 424 U.S. 693 (1976).

ously impair his future employment opportunities,"[207] constituting a deprivation of his Fourteenth Amendment Due Process liberty interest.

The Supreme Court rejected the Due Process claim, holding that a right to one's reputation, standing alone,[208] did not invest in Davis any liberty interest that would trigger procedural Due Process guarantees. Rather, the Court concluded, his remedy, if any, lay in a common law action for libel, explaining that "his interest in reputation is simply one of a number which the state may protect against injury by virtue of its tort law, providing a forum for vindication of those interests by means of damages actions."[209]

Lastly, in circumstances of school-administered corporal punishment, the Supreme Court held that the common-law claim of tortious battery, and the ancient limited privilege of school administrators and teachers to administer corporal punishment, together act as both a shield and a sword. In *Ingraham v. Wright*,[210] a procedural Due Process and an Eighth Amendment "cruel and unusual punishment" challenge to school corporal punishment, the Court conceded that physical punishment involved a "constitutionally protected liberty interest."[211] Even so, the Court concluded, the constitutional claim was obviated by the presence of "common law constraints and remedies."[212] The Court explained "Were it not for the common-law privilege permitting teachers to inflict reasonable corporal punishment on children in their care, and the availability of traditional remedies for abuse, the case for requiring advance procedural safeguards would be strong indeed."[213]

---

[207] *Id.* at 697.

[208] The Court contrasted Wisconsin v. Constantineau, 400 U.S. 433 (1971), granting Due Process relief to a woman subjected to official posting in liquor stores forbidding sale of alcoholic beverages to her for a period of one year, as involving an actionable deprivation of a "right previously held under state law—the right to purchase or obtain liquor in common with the rest of the citizenry." Paul v. Davis, 424 U.S. at 708.

[209] Paul v. Davis, 424 U.S. at 712.

[210] 430 U.S. 651 (1977).

[211] *Id.* at 672

[212] Ronald D. Rotunda, Modern Constitutional Law: Cases and Notes 378 (4th ed. 1993).

[213] *Ingraham*, 430 U.S. at 674.

In *Lucas v. South Carolina Coastal Council*, the Court, evaluating the Takings Clause limitations upon a state's land use authority, held that "[a]ny limitation so severe [as to prohibit all economically beneficial use of land] cannot be newly legislated or decreed (without compensation), but must inhere in the title itself, in the restrictions that background principles of the State's law of property and nuisance already place upon land ownership."[214]

The Court's guideline invited but did not require, the interpretation that continued development of the law of public nuisance as it affects land use will be closely reviewed for Takings Clause concerns, at least where the owner can make the claim that the state's interpretation of permissible land use operates to deprive the owner of all or practically all beneficial use of the land. In so doing, the *Lucas* Court reaffirmed the vitality of the common law of public nuisance as permitting, generally, continued state prohibition of uses historically found to be public nuisances. Without, perhaps, intending to do so, Mr. Justice Scalia simultaneously preserved the role of the common law of nuisance, trespass, and liability for abnormally dangerous activities as pivotal in future land use regulation. By finding constitutionally unobjectionable those land use restrictions footed in ancient public nuisance prerogatives of regulators, the Court ensured for the time vigorous refamiliarization, by regulators and developers alike, with the metes and bounds of these common law doctrines.

### b. The Adaptive Quality of Common-Law Remedies

An exemplary demonstration of the adaptive ability of the common law is in the development of the cause of action for negligently inflicted emotional distress. In an early decision permitting such recovery to a woman who rationally feared future cancer from a severe radiodermatitis that followed excessive radiation treatments for bursitis, the New York Court of Appeals in *Ferrara v. Galluchio*,[215]

---

[214] 505 U.S. 1003, 1029 (1993). Regarding public nuisance, Professor John Humbach has written that "[t]he common law of public nuisance is, if anything, even more indeterminate than private nuisance in the range of behavior to which it can potentially apply." John A. Humbach, *Evolving Thresholds of Nuisance and the Takings Clause*, 18 COLUM.J.ENVTL.L. 1, 12 (1993).

[215] 152 N.E.2d 249 (N.Y.1958).

while conceding the "valid objections" that such a cause of action created the risk of "vexatious suits and fictitious claims," [216] concluded, nevertheless, that "freedom from mental disturbance is now a protected interest in this State."[217]

Courts continue to "exhibit significant concern over whether claims for emotional or mental distress are legitimate."[218] The traditional common law rule provided that damages for emotional distress occasioned by mere negligence required "impact" or evidence of physical injury.[219] As the early decision in *Ferrera* explained, "[n]ot only fright and shock, but other kinds of mental injury are marked by definite physical symptoms, which are capable of medical proof. It is entirely possible to allow "recovery only upon satisfactory evidence and deny it when there is nothing to corroborate the claim, or to look for some guarantee of genuineness."[220]

In many jurisdictions, the "impact" rule has been loosened to permit tort recovery where plaintiff "actually feared for her own safety," the so-called "zone of danger" rule.[221] The watershed decision in *Dillon v. Legg*[222] involved a claim for damages for a mother who witnessed an automobile fatally injure her infant daughter. Rejecting the "zone of danger" rule as "hopelessly artificial,"[223] and denoting "foreseeability of risk" as the paramount gauge of duty,[224] the court announced the following approach:

[216] *Id.* at 252.

[217] *Id.*

[218] Nancy Levit, *Ethereal Torts*, 61 Geo.Wash.L.Rev. 136, 172 (1992).

[219] *E.g.*, Champion v. Gray, 420 So.2d 348 (Fla.Dist.Ct.app. 1982); Little v. Williamson, 441 N.E.2d 974 (Ind.Ct.app. 1982).

[220] *Ferrara*, 152 N.E.2d at 252.

[221] Gnirk v. Ford Motor Co., 572 F.Supp. 1201, 1202 n. 3 (C.D.S.D.1983). In Gnirk, plaintiff, a mother whose son drowned while strapped in an automobile that, due to a defective transmission, shifted from Park to reverse and submerged in a stock dam, was permitted to recover even though she was not in the "zone of danger." The court reasoned that no such restriction ought apply where she was a "user" of a product, under Restatement (Second) of Torts § 402A, rather than a bystander.

[222] 441 P.2d 912( Cal.1968).

[223] *Id* at 915 (noting that "we can hardly justify" permitting recovery to one witness and denying it to another due solely to the "happenstance" of one being "some few yards closer to the accident").

[224] *Id.* at 919.

In determining ... whether defendant should reasonably foresee injury to plaintiff, or, in other terminology, whether defendant owes plaintiff a duty of due care, the courts will take
into account such factors as the following: (1) Whether plaintiff was located near the scene of the accident as contrasted
with one who was a distance away from it. (2) Whether the
shock resulted from a direct emotional impact upon plaintiff
from the sensory and contemporaneous observance of the accident, as contrasted with learning of the accident from others
after its occurrence. (3) Whether plaintiff and the victim were
closely related, as contrasted with an absence of any relationship or the presence of only a distant relationship.[225]

*Dillon* stands as an example of the common law's refraction of social change.
One interpretive ray refracted is modern feminist theory. Specifically, feminist
theorists have argued effectively that an array of inequalities in political
power[226] throughout the common law reflect "male gender bias."[227] Regarding
emotional distress claims particularly, the argument goes, the distinctions,
mandated by the "impact" rule and even its successor, the "zone of danger"
rule "marginalize the interests of women."[228] Thus, *Dillon's* enlargement of recovery for fright-based injury operates to redefine the "reasonable man" standard of tort law to include the reasonable mother. As Professors Chamallas
and Kerber explain, "[w]hen a mother's fear for her child is acknowledged as
a cause of her own physical harm we can glimpse the beginnings of a femi-
nization of tort law. Relational interests become a constituent feature of one's
own physical integrity."[229]

---

[225]  *Id* at 920.

[226]  *See* The Politics of Law: A Progressive Critique 4 (David Kairys ed., rev. ed.
1990).

[227]  Robert L. Rabin, Perspectives on Tort Law 305 (4th ed. 1995).

[228]  Martha Chamallas & Linda K. Kerber, *Women, Mothers, and the Law of Fright: A
History*, 88 Mich.L.Rev. 814 (1990), *quoted in* Rabin *supra* at 307.

[229]  Chamallas & Kerber, *supra* at 862. *See also* Rabin, *supra* at 318.

## 5. Contract

### *a. Employment*

One of the most extraordinary common law transformations of the legal landscape of recent years is that involving employee rights, and the ancient doctrine
of employment at will. At common law, and unaffected by statutory initiative
in most states, an employee serves at the will of her employer.[230] She may be
released for any reason, bona fide or otherwise, or for no reason at all, "even
if such action was purely arbitrary or morally suspect."[231] Where preserved,
the doctrine has been justified in part by the logic that the employee's freedom
to depart from the employment relationship at any time requires bestowal of
a reciprocal freedom to the employer, sometimes referred to as a theory of
"mutuality."[232]

Recognition of a germinal liberty interest in the continuation of employment, absent dismissal for cause or for economic reasons, has led to the
growth of a tort remedy for "unjust discharge."[233] The remedy, a hybrid of
tort and contract, is also referred to as "retaliatory discharge" or "wrongful
termination."[234]

---

[230]   The rule was described in HORACE G. WOOD, TREATISE ON THE LAW OF MASTER
AND SERVANT (1877):

> With us the rule inflexible, that a general or indefinite hiring is prima facie
> a hiring at will, and if the servant seeks to make it out a yearly hiring, the
> burden is upon him to establish it by proof. A hiring at so much as a day,
> week, month, or year, no time being specified, is an indefinite hiring, and
> no presumption attaches that it is for a day even, but only at the rate fixed
> for whatever time the party may serve.

*Id.* at 134

[231]   TERRENCE F. KIELY, MODERN TORT LIABILITY: RECOVERY IN THE '90S § 1.18, at
47 (1990) [hereinafter KIELY, MODERN TORT LIABILITY].

[232]   *Cf.*, Palmateer v. International Harvester Co., 421 N.E.2d 876, 878 (1981) ("Recent
analysis has pointed out the shortcomings of the mutuality theory. With the rise of
large corporations conducting specialized operations and employing relatively im-
mobile workers who often have no other place to market their skills, recognition
that the employer and employee do not stand on equal footing is realistic.").

[233]   St. Antoine, *A Seed Germinates: Unjust Discharge Reform Heads Toward Full Flower,*
67 NEB.L.REV. 56 (1988); Reuther v. Fowler & Williams, Inc., 386 A.2d 119
(Pa.Super.Ct.1978); Sheets v. Teddy's Frosted Foods, Inc. 427 A.2d 385 (Conn.1980).

Only decades ago, employment at will was the practically universal common law rule.[235] Today, judicial decisions in over eight percent of the jurisdictions "have unilaterally, and without legislative sanction, expanded their common law governing the master-servant relationship to limit employers' discretion to terminate employees."[236] These common law modifications have relied variously upon three approaches: (1) public policy; (2) contract theory; and (3) the covenant of good faith and fair dealing.[237]

The most conspicuous fissure in the previously monolithic doctrine of employment at will has been the so-called "public policy" exception. Wisconsin, for example, has redelineated an employee's discharge remedy to "balance employers' needs for 'sufficient flexibility to make needed personnel decisions' against employees' job security interests' and the public interest in protecting employee actions that advance 'well established public policies.'"[238] In that state, the "public policy" unjust discharge remedy turns upon (1) identification of a specific statutory or regulatory policy; and (2) a determination that the employee's discharge resulted from his refusal to violate that policy.[239]

Just what are such "public policies" sufficient to trigger this incremental common law foray? Revealing is *Wilcox v. Niagara of Wisconsin Paper Corp.*,[240] an unjust discharge claim following the firing of Kenneth Wilcox, the company's longstanding director of computer operations. In the five days preceding his discharge, repair exigencies spurred by a computer malfunction caused Wilcox to work some 61 hours, 35 of them on the last two days of the workweek. Wilcox, who had heart surgery less than two years before, left work that Friday at 9:30 P.M. after experiencing angina pains. Later that evening his

---

[234] KIELY, MODERN TORT LIABILITY, *supra* at § 1.18 ("Retaliatory Discharge").

[235] Dennis P. Duffy, *Intentional Infliction of Emotional Distress and Employment at Will: The Case Against "Tortification" of Labor and Employment Law*, 74 B.U.L.REV. 387 (1994).

[236] *Id* (collecting authority).

[237] KIELY, MODERN TORT LIABILITY, *supra* at 48.

[238] Beam v. IPCO Corp., 838 F.2d 242, 245 (7th Cir.1988) (quoting Brockmeyer v. Dun & Bradstreet, 335 N.W.2d 834, 841 (Wisc.1983)).

[239] Bushko v. Miller Brewing Co., 396 N.W.2d 167, 169-171 (Wisc.1986).

[240] 965 F.2d 355 (7th Cir.1992).

manager called and told Wilcox he would be expected to work both Saturday and Sunday. Wilcox explained his situation, and that he still felt ill, but assured his superior the system would be functioning by Wednesday, the first day it would be needed. He warned Wilcox he would be dismissed if he did not work the weekend. Wilcox was hospitalized, and released Saturday with instructions to "take it easy." Returning to work Monday, Wilcox did, in fact, see the computer system to satisfactory functioning by Wednesday. Nevertheless, he was fired the following day.[241]

In his ensuing action for breach of contract, Wilcox alleged that his discharge violated the public policy set out in the Wisconsin statutes,[242] an interpretation the court found to "reflect the public policy of the State of Wisconsin."[243] Finding that Wilcox's claim fell "squarely within the bounds of the public policy exception," the court explained that "compliance with the manager's demand for still more hours over the weekend would have required Wilcox to work 'for such a period of time ... as was dangerous or prejudicial to his life, health, safety or welfare."[244]

The public policy exception to the employment at will doctrine is a clear-cut example of an efficient judge-made rule. In utilitarian terms, in today's employment environment, a discharge based upon an employee's refusal to obey an unlawful command works an emotional hardship upon the employee, together with potentially devastating economic consequences. The benefit to the employer of maintaining such a prerogative is psychological at most, and of no identifiable social value. Thus a rule discouraging such discharges deters wasteful conduct while imposing no material workplace or social cost.

Indeed, the exception to the employment at will doctrine can be considered Pareto Optimal. A rule is Pareto Optimal when its effects benefit all parties, in essence a win-win proposition. The rule discussed is Pareto Optimal,

[241] *Id.* at 357-59.

[242] *Id.* at 358. *See also* Wis.Stat.Ann. § 103.02 (West 1988), which reads in part: "No person may be employed or be permitted to work in any place of employment for such period of time during any day, night or week, as dangerous or prejudicial to the person's life, health, safety or welfare...." *Id.*

[243] *Id.* at 360.

[244] *Id.* at 363.

or win-win, in that the employee gains in economic security and individual autonomy. The employer gains in that it is more efficient to desist in capricious firing practices than it is to defend a regulatory enforcement action brought by a state or federal discrimination or labor standards unit. Lastly, the broader public welfare is advanced as the common law rule works in effective synergy with the statutory goal.

## 6. Evidence

### a. Spousal Privilege

It is in the evidence rules and policies governing the spousal testimonial privilege that we find a noteworthy example of the common law's progressive incrementalism. The law of evidence, at both the state and federal level, has been subject to pervasive codification. In federal courts, the Federal Rules of Evidence specifically excised from their coverage several evidentiary topics, notably the evidence rules concerning testimonial privileges, leaving these subjects to the substantive law of the states.[245] Rule 501 of the *Federal Rules of Evidence* enjoins the federal courts to shepard the evolution of testimonial privilege in criminal trials "governed by the principles of the common law as they may be interpreted ... in the light of reason and experience."[246]

The evidentiary rule that a husband or a wife could, by claim of spousal privilege, prevent their spouse from giving testimony against them in a criminal trial was recited in 1628 by Lord Coke, who stated, "[I]t hath been resolved by the Justices that a wife cannot be produced either against or for her husband."[247] As the Supreme Court has explained, the rule,

> [t]his spousal disqualification sprang from two cannons of medieval jurisprudence: first, the rule that an accused was not permitted to testify in his own behalf because of his interest

---

[245]  FED.R.EVID. 501 advisory committee's note.

[246]  FED.R.EVID.501

[247]  1 E. COKE, A COMMENTARY UPON LITTLETON 6b (1628) (2008 https://archive.org/details/cu319240216616).

in the proceeding; second, the concept that husband and wife were one, and that since the woman had no recognized separate legal existence, the husband was that one. From those two now long-abandoned doctrines, it followed that what was inadmissible from the lips of the defendant-husband was also inadmissible from his wife.[248]

Identified in modern evidence law as a rule of privilege rather than one of disqualification, the modern rationale for a spousal privilege against giving criminal testimony against the marital partner "is its perceived role in fostering the harmony and sanctity of the marriage relationship."[249]

Criticized by no less authority than Professor Wigmore as "the merest anachronism in legal theory and an indefensible obstruction to truth in practice,"[250] the Supreme Court in *Hawkins v. United States*[251] nevertheless turned back a prosecution request that the privilege be modified to vest only in the witness-spouse,[252] although it did emphasize that its decision should not "foreclose whatever changes in the rule may eventually be dictated by 'reason and experience.'"[253]

Two decades later, noting the sea change in state evidence rules, demonstrating a clear conversion to a more limited privilege,[254] and the unquestioned ascent of women in the cultural and political perception,[255] the court in *Trammel v. United States* held that the existing rule should be modified so that the witness-spouse alone has a privilege to refuse to testify adversely; the witness

---

[248]  Trammel v. United States, 445 U.S. 40, 44 (1980).

[249]  *Id.* at 44.

[250]  *Id.* at 45 (quoting 8 John H. Wigmore, Evidence in Trials at Common Law § 2228, at 221 (3d ed. 1961)).

[251]  358 U.S. 74 (1958).

[252]  By the time of the decision in *Hawkins*, the American Law Institute's Model Code of Evidence Rule 215 (1942) had rejected the common law rule, as had the Unif.R.Evid. Rule 23(2). *Trammel*, 445 U.S. at 45.

[253]  *Hawkins*, 358 U.S. at 79.

[254]  *Trammel*, 445 U.S. 40, 49-50 & nn. 9, 10.

[255]  *Id.* at 52.

may be neither compelled to testify nor foreclosed from testifying. This modification—vesting the privilege in the witness-spouse—furthers the important public interest in marital harmony without unduly burdening legitimate law enforcement needs.[256]

The Supreme Court's ruling in *Trammel* evinces a non-normative commitment to principles of justice and fairness, as well as an unspoken obeisance to efficiency. By non-normative commitment to principles of justice is meant that the court is not noticeably stirred by any distaste for felonious, conspiratorial husbands who have embroiled their wives in lawless pursuits—although we might forgive the Court had it been. Rather, the Court seems to have recognized that anterior to just judicial resolution are facts, and that the old rule operated simply as an obstruction of facts.[257] Whether the probandum is criminal culpability or civil liability for money damages, liberal access to evidence is the hallmark of modern adjudication. As the Court stated in *United States v. Bryan*,[258] "'the public ... has a right to every man's evidence.'"[259]

*Trammel* can also be harmonized with principles of efficiency. In all litigation, information costs are considerable. Here, the Supreme Court's holding is consonant with an "informational asymmetry policy" described by Professor Eisenberg, suggesting that "the applicability of a legal rule should not depend upon information that will characteristically be in the hands of only one of the parties."[260] It likewise conforms to Professor Eisenberg's described "opportunism policy," which posits that "legal rules should not encourage exploitative conduct."[261]

---

[256] *Id.* at 53.

[257] *Id.* at 44.

[258] 339 U.S. 323 (1950).

[259] *Id.* at 331 (quoting 8 JOHN H. WIGMORE, EVIDENCE IN TRIALS AT COMMON LAW § 2192 (3d ed. 1961)).

[260] EISENBERG, NATURE OF THE COMMON LAW, *supra* at 28.

[261] *Id.*

# VI. CONCLUSION

Has the common law comprised a resolute, patient, faithful and effective engine of social change for three hundred years? Has the "revolution" in common law judging resulted in a vital, supple common law capable of a continued, integral jurisprudential role, a system of law and judging to which the public will continue to look to resolve the critical case, the case at the perimeters of societal change?[262] In common law is there yet reposed our legal system's best instrument for responding to "changes in social values"?[263] Or has the common law embarked on a course of marginalization and irrelevance that will reduce its contribution in the new century?

The New York Court of Appeals put it well in *Schenectady Chemicals*,[264] approving application of the doctrine of public nuisance against the generator of waste even though the defendant did not own the premises constituting the nuisance: "The common law is not static. Society has repeatedly been confronted with new inventions that, through foreseen and unforeseen events, have imposed dangers upon society."[265]

Particularly in the Twentieth Century, with two global wars, there has been much to belie any "fiction that society [has] educated itself, or aimed at

---

[262]  KARL N. LLEWELLYN, THE CASE LAW SYSTEM IN AMERICA 99 (Paul Gewertz ed. & Michael Ansaldi trans., 1989).

Legal uncertainties arise far more when *non*legal norms in society are in conflict. [Conflicts among interest groups] are *fact situations* that arise because the margins of growth keep shifting in real life, and or that very reason they shift the law's margins of growth too.... The critical case always involves a fact situation not from the stable core but from the growth zone of life waiting to be regulated.

*Id.*(discussed in John R. Nolan, *Footprints in the Shifting Sands of the Isle of Palms: A Practical Analysis of Regulatory Takings Cases*, 8 J.LAND USE & ENVTL.L. 16 (1992)).

[263]  Farber & Frickey, *supra* at 875.

[264]  New York v. Schenectady Chemicals, Inc., 459 N.Y.S.2d 971 (N.Y Sup.Ct.1983), *aff'd as modified* 479 N.Y.S.2d 1010 (N.Y.App.Div.1984).

[265]  *Schenectady*, 459 N.Y.S.2d at 977. In environmental and toxic torts, for example, tort law "has addressed various manifestations of uncertainty" with resultant "movement away from notions of unicausality and toward systemic or multiple causation and accountability." Levit, *Ethereal Torts*, *supra* at 137.

a conscious purpose."[266] In my view, our common law represents just such an example of a sustained societal pursuit of a common purpose. Dispute will always be stimulated by the means selected by a particular common law doctrine— especially new doctrine. Should the waistband be pulled in as to what constitutes trade puffing? Should child psychologists and school administrators be under a duty to report potential child abuse? These questions, at the perimeters of our social and business dealings, will be resolved only with the passage of time, and with the entry of two or three score more common law judgments entered on the basis of individualized facts and able lawyering. The core of the common law, however, represents an unequaled American commitment to personal freedom, business opportunity, dignity, and mutual expectations leavened by two centuries of cultural development.

The debate over the proper goals of the common law continues, with some arguing that its principal objective should be fairness, while others seem to be suggesting that efficiency should reign. In the perception of this author and others, goals of economic efficiency and corrective justice fairness have proved their compatibility as complementary societal commitments supporting the progressive development of common law justice.

What are the potential common law initiatives of the future? Intentional infliction for emotional distress for racial discrimination?[267] A nuisance-based foundation for land use law that responds to Mr. Justice Scalia's instruction that litigants seeking to immunize land use regulation enforcement from Takings obligations find a common law nuisance or trespass-based foundation for the prohibition? An enduring tort response (1) to the unconscionable manufacture and distribution of handguns and automatic weapons with no plausible purpose other than to kill and maim; or (2) to rights of the unborn, with the implications of such doctrine to highly-charged political and religious issues?

---

[266] EDUCATION OF HENRY ADAMS, *supra* at 483.

[267] *See, e.g.*, Curtis v. Loether, 415 U.S. 189, 195 n. 10 (1974). The "contours of the [intentional infliction] tort are still developing, and it has been suggested that 'under the logic of the common law development of a law of insult and indignity, racial discrimination might be treated as a dignitary tort.'" *Id.* (quoting C. GREGORY & H. KALVEN, CASES AND MATERIALS ON TORTS 961 (2d ed. 1969)), *cited in* Rickel v. Commissioner, 900 F.2d 655, 663 (3d Cir.1990).

As the Twentieth Century closes, the common law thrives. Its vitality does not depend upon adherence to the claims of others that any constraint of existing remedies is unjust. Mindful of political pressures, but a thrall to no ideology, the common law enters the next century much as it did the last—representing a conjunction of ancient principles of corrective justice with modern, developed consideration of individual autonomy, social efficiency and fairness.

Observers past and present offer agreement that "in relating law to the totality of social relationships it is difficult to feel that America now has any rival[.]"[268] A partner, with statutory law, in that system of social justice, our common law is more than a legacy of jurisprudence. Progressive, protean and dynamic, American common law is a reflection of our society's better self.

---

[268] Laski, American Democracy, *supra* at 66.

# CHAPTER 6

## A COMPARATIVE ANALYSIS OF UNITED STATES AND COLOMBIAN TORT LAW: DUTY, BREACH, AND DAMAGES

## I. INTRODUCTION

Throughout Europe, South America, and North America there exist systems for extra-contractual reparations for personal physical injury or property damage caused by the substandard conduct of others. The tort law of the United States, and that of other common law countries, derived in a labored but largely undistracted path from the common law of England. In contrast, in continental Europe, Central America and South America, the jurisprudence of such civil liability has developed within the procedural matrix and the cultural expectations of their respective civil codes.[1]

Many observers have quailed at the prospect of identifying similarities between and among the diverse civil code treatments of liability for "negligence," a concededly common law nomenclature. Such observers often note that the civil code maturation through the original Napoleonic Code and the greatly

---

[1] Such civil codes find their rootstock in Roman law and the Napoleonic Code. *See* Richard Azarnia, *Tort Law in France: A Cultural and Comparative Overview*, 13 WIS. INT'L L.J. 471, 471 (1995).

influential adaptation of that code in Chilean law is simply too incongruous a presentation of cultural commitment to justice for victims of unintentional injury to ever be reconciled meaningfully with common law negligence.

An examination of the contemporary Colombian civil code treatment of extra-contractual liability for harm (*daño*) to persons or property in fact reveals a system, similar in many respects to the civil code regimens of other Latin American nations, in which the similarities with the policies of common law negligence actually dwarf the distinctions, or at least reduce most of the distinctions to formalisms.

# II. ANGLO-AMERICAN DEVELOPMENT OF THE LAW OF NEGLIGENCE

## A. GENERALLY

The Anglo-American development of liability for negligent acts causing harm to others or to their property followed a lengthy legal devotion to liability without fault, or strict liability.[2] Some scholars have associated the perfection of fault-based liability with the Industrial Revolution in England.[3] However, observers seem not to have established satisfactorily whether negligence liability was a mechanism of legal benevolence to persons and chattels or instead a legal prophylaxis that reduced the potential liability of businesses by requiring the putative plaintiff to prove not only injury and causation, but also that the actor had proceeded with an absence of due care under the circumstances.[4]

---

[2] *See generally* DAN B. DOBBS, THE LAW OF TORTS 259-63 (2000).

[3] The development of negligence law "was probably stimulated a good deal by the enormous increase of industrial machinery and by the invention of railways in particular." P. WINFIELD, LAW OF TORT 404 (5th ed. 1950).

[4] *Compare* WINFIELD, *id.* ("At that time railway trains were notable for neither speed nor for safety. They killed any object from a Minister of State to a wandering cow, and this naturally reacted upon the law.") with Robert J. Kazorowski, *The Common-Law Basis of Nineteenth-Century Tort Law*, 51 OHIO S.L.J. 1 (1990) (referencing schol-

Modern negligence law is concerned primarily with the provision of reparations to persons suffering personal injury or property loss due to a failure of others to act with due care under the circumstances. It is established that (1) tort law is devoted to the protection of persons and property from unreasonable risk of harm; and (2) the actor's liability in tort is limited by concepts of reasonable foreseeability. Employing as an example the law of products liability, it is possible to state a rule for negligence liability for the sale of an unreasonably dangerous product: A product seller is liable in negligence if he acts or fails to act in such a way as to create an unreasonable risk of harm or loss to the user of a product or to another who might foreseeably be injured thereby, and such act or omission is the legal cause of the claimant's harm.

More broadly, the contemporary United States cause of action for negligence requires the plaintiff to prove that (1) the defendant owed a duty to the plaintiff; (2) that the defendant breached that duty; (3) that the defendant's breach was the cause in fact and the proximate cause of the plaintiff's injury or loss; and (4) that the plaintiff suffered harm compensable in tort. This segment of the Chapter will be devoted only to a discussion of Anglo-American legal treatment of the first three dimensions of the plaintiff's cause of action in negligence: (1) duty; and (2) breach, and (4) compensable damages. Two theoretical models serve as a backdrop for consideration of modern Anglo-American treatment of duty and breach in negligence law. Considerations of corrective justice and economic efficiency each contribute distinctive but largely harmonious analytical threads.

## B. CORRECTIVE JUSTICE

In general terms, corrective justice proponents advance the proposition that the judiciary should promote a rights-based jurisprudence grounded in moral precepts.[5] Even among those observers who would not subscribe wholeheart-

---

arly proponents of theory that negligence liability arose in a court-stimulated effort to moderate the liability of businesses and to permit devotion of industrial capital to production rather than to satisfaction of legal liability).

[5] *See* Vincent A. Wellman, *Conceptions of the Common Law: Reflections on a Theory of*

edly to this proposition, there is probably a consensus that if moral precepts are not to be the primary values supported, justice and morality-based goals still form a necessary if not sufficient foundational element of modern tort law.[6] The moral authority of any law turns upon the perception that its tenets lead to just results.[7] There is widespread agreement that a core consideration in any modern contemplation of "justice" would be the goal of "corrective" justice, i.e., a result that to the extent possible deprives the wrongful party of his gain, and restores the injured party to the position he enjoyed before the harm[8]. Holmes explained: "Be the exceptions more or less numerous, the general purpose of the law of torts is to secure a man indemnity against certain forms of harm to person, reputation, or estate, at the hands of his neighbors..."[9]

---

*Contract,* 41 U. Miami L. Rev. 925, 925 n.1 (1987) (citing Ronald Dworkin, Taking Rights Seriously 1-130 (rev. ed. 1977), in which Dworkin "propound[s] a rights-based theory of law and a corresponding obligation of judges to consider moral precepts when deciding significant cases").

[6] It is agreed generally that only a wrong can transgress a moral imperative, in the sense that a harm befalling a plaintiff with no predicate negligence or violation of some other doctrinal imperative, such as liability for abnormally dangerous activities, creates no rectificatory duty of any actor. Ernest Weinrib might point to tort doctrine as common law in which wrongdoing is a necessary, but not individually adequate, component of liability. *See* Martin A. Kotler, *Utility, Autonomy and Motive: A Descriptive Model of the Development of Tort Doctrine,* 58 U. Cin. L. Rev. 1231, 1240 (1990) ("[W]rongdoing of a party is an essential factor in the decision to impose liability ...." (citing Ernest J. Weinrib, *The Morality of Tort Law,* Address to the Tort Law Section, Association of American Law Schools Annual Meeting (Jan. 9, 1988))).

[7] *See* Readings in Jurisprudence 37 (Jerome Hall ed., 1938) ("As Augustine says (De Lib. Arb i.5), that which is not just seems to be no law at all: wherefore the force of a law depends on the extent of its justice."); cf. Randy E. Barnett, *Getting Normative: The Role of Natural Rights in Constitutional Adjudication,* 12 Const. Comm. 93, 105-13 (1995) (arguing that for constitutional procedures to be legitimate, they must be of such a nature as to bind in conscience).

[8] Jules L. Coleman, *The Practice of Corrective Justice,* in Philosophical Foundations of Tort Law 53 (David Owen ed., 1995) ("[C]orrective justice is the principle that those who are responsible for the wrongful losses of others have a duty to repair them, and that the core of tort law embodies this conception of corrective justice.").

[9] Oliver Wendell Holmes, The Common Law 115 (Mark DeWolfe Howe ed., Little, Brown & Co. 1963) (1881) (emphasis added). In addition, Henry Sumner Maine observed: "Now the penal Law of ancient communities is not the law of Crimes; it is the law of Wrongs, or, to use the English technical word, of Torts. The

## C. ECONOMIC EFFICIENCY

Richard Posner and others call for a scientific ethic of wealth maximization, a so-called "efficiency norm."[10] Many have responded to this call, with one influential commentator concluding that "much (though by no means all) of modern tort law is at least roughly consistent with a Posnerian economic analysis."[11]

Numerous analysts have identified a common law tropism towards efficiency.[12] Importantly, scholars have also concluded that efficient rules of law actually predict efficient litigation strategies, including settlement strategies. As stated by Ramona L. Paetzold and Steven L. Willborn, "[w]here both parties to a dispute have a continuing interest in precedent, the parties will settle if the existing precedent is efficient, but litigate if the precedent is inefficient."[13] Wes Parsons, even while disputing these premises, collected scholarship revealing in fact the broad range of cost internalization achievements of evolving common law doctrine.[14] Included in Parsons's review was scholarly attribution to the common law of accidents as "promot(ing) efficient resource allocation;"[15] the efficiencies of the common law of rescue, salvage and Good Samaritan assistance;[16] the efficiency of the common law damages rule for

person injured proceeds against the wrong-doer by an ordinary civil action, and recovers compensation in the shape of money-damages if he succeeds. ... [All such Torts] gave rise to an Obligation or vinculum juris, and were all requited by a payment of money." Henry Sumner Maine, Ancient Law: Its Connection with the Early History of Society, and Its Relation to Modern Ideas Its Relation to Modern Ideas 370 (1866).

[10] *See generally* Richard A. Posner, The Ethical and Political Basis of the Efficiency Norm in Common Law Adjudication, 8 Hofstra L. Rev. 487 (1980).

[11] Gary T. Schwartz, Reality in Economic Analysis of Tort Law: Does Tort Law Really Deter?, 42 U.C.L.A. L. Rev. 377, 381 (1994) [hereinafter G. Schwartz, Deterrence].

[12] *E.g.*, George L. Priest, *The Common Law Process and the Selection of Efficient Rules*, 6 J. LEG. STUD. 65 (1977); Ramona L. Paetzold and Steven L. Willborn, *The Efficiency of the Common Law Reconsidered*, 14 GEO. MASON. L. REV. 157 (1991)[hereinafter Paetzold and Willborn].

[13] Paetzold and Willborn, *supra*.

[14] Wes Parsons, Note, *The Inefficient* Common Law, 92 YALE L.J. 862 (1983).

[15] William M. Landes & Richard A. Posner, *The Positive Economic Theory of Tort Law*, 15 GA. L. REV. 851, 852 (1981).

[16] William A. Landes & Richard A. Posner, *Savors, Finders, Good Samaritans and Other*

anticipatory repudiation of contract;[17] and the efficiency of the economic loss rule in tort.[18]

# III. DUTY

When it is claimed that an actor owed a duty to a plaintiff, the duty described is that of ordinary care, or care commensurate with that which would be expected of a reasonable man under the same or similar circumstances. The duty is not owed to a public generally, but rather to those whom the actor, looking prospectively with the eye of reasonable vigilance, would perceive to be put at an unreasonable risk of harm or loss should the actor proceed incautiously, or with an absence of due care.[19] The decision of the Massachusetts Supreme Judicial Court in Brown v. Kendall[20] put the proposition in these influential words: "[W]hat constitutes ordinary care will vary with the circumstances.... In general it means that kind and degree of care, which prudent and cautious men would use, such as is required by the exigency of the case."[21]

---

*Rescuers: An Economic Study of Law and Altruism,* 7 J. Leg. Stud. 83, 128 (1977).

[17] Thomas H. Jackson, *'Anticipatory Repudiation' and the Temporal Element of Contract Law: An Economic Inquiry into Contract Damages in Cases of Prospective Nonperformance,* 31 Stan. L. Rev. 69 (1978)("compensating the aggrieved party for its entire expectation loss, without overcompensating it, is an economically sound principle in that it facilitates the movement of goods and services to their higher value user." *Id.* at 69).

[18] W. Bishop, *Economic Loss in Tort,* 2 Oxford J. Leg. Stud. 1, 2-3 (1982).

[19] The proposition .... is that whenever one person is by circumstances placed in such a position with regard to another that every one of ordinary sense ... would at once recognize that if he did not use ordinary care and skill in his own conduct with regard to those circumstances, he would cause danger of injury to the person or property of another, a duty arises to use ordinary care and skill to avoid such danger.

Heaven v. Pender, 11 Q.B.D. 503 (C.A. 1883) (Brett, M.R.).

[20] Brown v. Kendall, 60 Mass. 292 (1850).

[21] *Id.* at 296.

Duty is relational, which is to say that for a duty to exist, it must be associated with a particular person or a particular class of person within which the plaintiff finds himself.[22] (John L. Ranard, Lawrence R. Levine, M. Stuart Madden, Understanding Torts 112 (1996)) Thus as it has been said that negligence "air" does not exist,[23] and neither does its predicate, duty. Returning to the model of products liability law, MacPherson v. Buick Motor Co.[24] secured its position as a lynchpin in the development of products liability by providing persuasive arguments as to three propositions governing the duty of manufacturers.

The opinion of Judge Cardozo is greatly informative in its evaluation of duty as affected by the variability of risk, the foreseeability of that risk should the actor proceed without due care, and the identification of the class of persons to whom duty is owed. The three propositions were these: (1) a manufacturer owes a duty of due care to not only its immediate vendee, but also to remote vendees who in the ordinary course may be expected to purchase the product; (2) the duty is not confined to the manufacture and sale of so called imminently dangerous products, but instead to all products that could be expected to do substantial harm to others if not made with care appropriate to the pertinent risks; and (3) this duty of due care is nondelegable, and thus even if it is a component part of the product that causes its injurious failure, the manufacturer of the overall product may remain liable.

MacPherson stood for the principle that although manufacturers of all products would be held to a standard of ordinary care under the circumstances, the ordinary care expected of a manufacturer of locomotives would logically involve a higher level of scrutiny than would the "ordinary care" that one might expect of a the weaver of fruit baskets, as the risk of harm from a negligently manufactured locomotive is incalculably greater than that created by a defectively fashioned basket. Each of the rules advanced in MacPherson: (1) the injured plaintiff's negligence remedy against the remote manufacturer without regard to privity; (2) the finished product seller's responsibility (or duty) for the prudent design and

22

23   *See* Brown v. Racquet Club of Bricktown, 95 N.J. 280, 471 A.2d 25, (1984), quoting William Prosser, The Law of Torts (5th ed. 1971)(while facts may indicate negligence in the air, "it is still necessary to bring it home to the defendant.").

24   217 N.Y. 382, 111 N.E. 1050 (1916).

the manufacturing integrity of component parts; and (3) the manufacturer's duty to conduct reasonable and necessary tests on the product before its introduction into commerce, represents the established majority rule in tort today.

Further illustrative of modern interpretation of duty in tort law is the New York decision in DiPonzio v. Riordan.[25] That suit involved injuries sustained by a filling station patron when another customer's car, left running as the latter paid his bill inside, slipped either into gear or into neutral and backed into plaintiff, injuring his leg. Plaintiff and his wife sued the car owner and the filling station. As to the filling station, plaintiffs' theory was that it "had been negligent in failing to properly train its attendants and that its attendants had been negligent in failing to comply with [station's] rules requiring that customers be warned to turn off their engines while fueling their vehicles."[26] The Supreme Court denied defendant's motion for summary judgment, in which defendant argued "the lack of any cognizable duty, the lack of a proximate causal relationship between its alleged negligence, if any, and the accident, and the unforeseeability of the accident."[27] The Appellate Division reversed.

The New York Court of Appeals identified the "threshold" inquiry as being "whether [the station] had a legally cognizable duty" to take measures to prevent this accident. Acknowledging that a business proprietor's duty extends to "maintain[ing] their property in a reasonably safe condition[,]" and that the duty "may extend to controlling the conduct of third persons who frequent or use the property, at least under some circumstances[,]" the court observed that these duties are "not limitless."[28] Drawing upon the Palsgraf v. Long Island R.R., the Court reiterated that "[t]he risk reasonably to be perceived defines the duty to be obeyed."[29] Applying this standard, the Court of Appeals concluded there could be no service station liability, as "DiPonzio's injuries did not arise from the occurrence of any of the hazards that the duty would exist to prevent." The Court's reasoning continued: "When a vehicle's

---

[25]   DiPonzio v. Riordan, 89 N.Y.2d 578, 679 N.E.2d 616, 657 N.Y.S.2d 377 (1997).

[26]   Id. at 581-82.

[27]   Id. at 582.

[28]   Id.

[29]   Id. at 583 (citing Palsgraf v. Long Is. R.R. Co., 248 N.Y. 339, 344, 162 N.E. 99).

engine is left running in an area where gasoline is being pumped, there is a natural and foreseeable risk of fire or explosion because of the highly flammable properties of the fuel....It is this class of foreseeable hazards that defines the scope of [the] station's purported duty. The occurrence that led to plaintiff's injury was clearly outside of this limited class of hazards."

Further illustrative of the boundaries that will be imposed upon an actor's duty is one decision requiring the court's consideration of whether a manufacturer's duty, and potential liability, in a DES case should be extended to the generation born not of the mother who ingested the DES, but rather to the second generation, which is to say, the offspring of the DES daughter. The Ohio Supreme Court offered a telling treatment of the logical limits of an actor's duty in Grover v. Eli Lilly & Co.,[30] following a federal trial court certified this issue to the Ohio Supreme Court in the setting of a grandchild's claim, through his representatives, that his severe birth defects were caused by defects in the mother's reproductive system, which defects were earlier caused by the grandmother's ingestion of the drug DES. The court noted that courts in some other jurisdictions, on similar but distinguishable facts, had not permitted actions to proceed for such "preconception" torts.[31] The Ohio high court noted Palsgraf v. Long Island RR. Co.[32] for the proposition that "[a]n actor does not have a duty to a particular plaintiff unless the risk to that plaintiff is within the actor's 'range of apprehension.'"[33] Finding no cause of action inuring to the grandchild, the Grover court explained:

When a pharmaceutical company prescribes drugs to a woman, the company, under ordinary circumstances, does not

[30] 591 N.E.2d 696 (Ohio 1992).

[31] The court noted Monusko v. Postle, 437 N.W.2d 367 (Mich. Ct. App. 1989)(cause of action against mother's physicians for failure to inoculate mother with rubella vaccine prior to child's conception) and Renslow v. Mennonite Hospital, 367 N.E.2d 1250 (Ill. 1977) (negligence action by child against hospital that negligently gave mother Rh-positive blood eight years before, stimulating Rh-positive antibodies that injured the fetus).

[32] 162 N.E. 99, 100 (N.Y. 1928).

[33] 591 N.E.2d 696, quoting Palsgraf, 162 N.E. at 100.

have a duty to her daughter's infant who will be conceived twenty-eight years later. Because of remoteness in time and causation, we hold that the grandchild does not have an independent cause of action, and answer the district court's question in the negative. A pharmaceutical company's liability for the distribution or manufacturer of a defective prescription drug does not extend to persons who were never exposed to the drug, either directly or in utero.[34]

# IV. BREACH OF DUTY

Turning to the left side of the equation, suppose the financial burden to the manufacturer of either using a more sturdy material for the tank, or placing the tank in a more forward position beneath the vehicle, was only a matter of $200 per car. The claimant would argue that such a cost is certainly moderate, and is, in any event, less than the risk of some harm multiplied by the seriousness of that harm (death or serious bodily harm) should the design change not be undertaken. If the assumptions in this hypothetical are accepted, a plaintiff injured in this way should be able to make out a prima facie case that the manufacturer has breached its duty of care.

# V. COMPENSATORY DAMAGES

## A. GENERALLY

Compensatory damages are those damages awardable to a person as compensation, indemnity, or restitution for harm or loss caused by the tortious act of

---

[34] *Id.* at 700-01.

another.[35] One principal goal of compensatory damages is to place the person in the position they were in before the injury or loss, at least insofar as money damages can do so, which is to say compensatory damages "are designed to place [the injured party] in a position substantially equivalent in a pecuniary way to that which he would have been in had no tort been committed."[36] A second goal is that of deterring similar tortious conduct in the future, be it undertaken by the defendant or by others.[37] Restatement Second, Torts § 901 summarizes the purposes of tort damages as: "to give compensation, indemnity, and restitution for harms *** to determine rights *** to punish wrongdoers and deter wrongful conduct *** and to vindicate parties and deter retaliation of violent and unlawful self-help."[38]

A claimant's non-economic harm is ordinarily distinguished from his economic harm. Often also termed pecuniary loss, economic loss includes such loss as to which a monetary value can be assigned with some level of experience-based reliability. Examples of economic harm would be past and future lost wages, or the cost of past and anticipated medical care, physical rehabilitation and the like. Non-economic damages are less susceptible of reliable monetary valuation. Such non-economic damages can include, without limitation, indemnity for a claimant's pain and suffering, emotional distress, a spouse's loss of consortium, and lost quality of life—the latter often referred to as hedonic damages. An endorsement of this evaluation is found in the Analysis to the Model Uniform Product Liability Act which suggests that awards for pain and suffering "have no market value and, thus, are to be contrasted with pecuniary damages which compensate victims for lost wages, medical and rehabilitation costs, and other actual expenditures he has or will incur due to injuries caused by a defective product."[39]

---

[35] RESTATEMENT (SECOND) OF TORTS § 903.

[36] RESTATEMENT (SECOND) OF TORTS § 903 cmt.

[37] *See generally* RICHARD A. EPSTEIN, CASE AND MATERIALS ON TORTS §§ 4.4-.7 (6th ed. 1995).

[38] *Id.* at § 17.2 ("[T]he bywords in establishing the law of damages are compensation, deterrence, and consistency.").

[39] Model Uniform Product Liability Act § 118(D) (Analysis), 44 Fed. Reg. 62746 (Oct. 31, 1979).

## B. PERSONAL PHYSICAL INJURY

All jurisdictions permit the personal injury plaintiff recovery for pain and suf-fering.[40] Restatement Second, Torts § 924 confirms that the prevailing plaintiff may recover damages for past or prospective "bodily harm and emotional dis-tress[;] *** loss or impairment of earning capacity [[;] *** reasonable medical and other expenses; and *** harm to property and business caused by the invasion."[41] Thus, it is agreed generally that the successful plaintiff in a tort personal injury claim can recover provable damage to property, for personal injury, illness, or death, or for mental or emotional harm accompanying plaintiff's placement in direct physical peril by such a the defendant's actions.[42] Plaintiff's personal injury damages are recognized generally to include "medical expenses, loss of future earnings, permanent disability or disfigurement, and damages for past and future mental pain and suffering."[43] The general rule is that the injured plaintiff may be awarded compensatory damages without proof of pecuniary loss.[44]

For personal physical injuries involving a reduction or elimination of the plaintiff's ability to earn a livelihood, the claimant may recover damages for loss of future earnings. Such injuries are recoverable in tort, because, as they are associated with personal injury, they are not precluded by application of the rule ordinarily applied to "pure economic loss."[45] Accordingly, in deter-mining the size of such an award, it is agreed generally that the finder of fact

---

[40] Epstein *supra* note 47, at § 17.2 ("All jurisdictions recognize a right to recover dam-ages for bodily injuries, generally defined to cover 'any impairment of the physical condition, including illness and physical pain." '), quoting Restatement (Second) of Torts § 905 cmt. b. *E.g.*, Lakin v. Senco Products, 329 Or. 62 (Or. 1999).

[41] *See generally* Thomas W. Long, *Economic Impairment in Personal Injury Actions*, 30 So.Tex.L.Rev. 97 1989); Steven G. Schumaier, *Proof of Hearing Loss*, 22 Trial 32 (1986).

[42] *See* N.J.Rev.Stat. § 1(1), Ch. 197.

[43] *E.g.*, Adkins v. Asbestos Corp., Ltd., 18 F.3d 1349 (6th Cir.1994) (asbestos-related personal injury action).

[44] *See, e.g.*, Croteau v. Olin Corp., 644. 208 (D.N.H.1986).

[45] The "economic loss" rule provides generally that economic loss that is not associated with personal physical injury or damage to property cannot be recoverable in tort. Rather, such 'pure' economic loss claims may only be pursued in warranty or other contract claims.

may consider plaintiff's loss of earning ability, loss of future earning capacity, work life expectancy, age, life expectancy, investment income, inflation, predictable productivity increase, prospects for rehabilitation, and probable future earning capacity.[46]

## C. INCREASED RISK OF FUTURE ILLNESS

In some jurisdictions a plaintiff whose exposure to a process, often a process that contaminates the environment, elevates his risk of contracting an injury or disease in the future may seek a monetary award for incurring the increased risk. Where a claimant can show existing illness or disease that is understood by sound medical science to be a precursor of the future injury or disease feared, many jurisdictions will permit recovery in damages for the increased risk of that future disease.[47]

## D. EMOTIONAL DISTRESS

Subject to application of state by state standards, courts in all jurisdictions permit the award of damages for emotional distress associated with plaintiff's personal injury.[48] Such recovery may be secured under any of the conventional doctrines under which the finder of fact determines an award to be allowable, be it negligence, warranty, or strict tort liability.

## E. FEAR OF FUTURE ILLNESS

Distinct questions of recoverability and proof are posed by the emotional distress claims of the plaintiff who is "at risk" of illness due to antecedent exposure to a long latency disease-inducing substance due to another's claimed negligence. The issue posed is how, if at all, may the person exposed to, for example,

[46]  *E.g.*, Lanclos v. Rockwell International Corp., 470 So.2d 924, 934(La. Ct. App.1985); Robertson v. Superior PMI, Inc., 791 F.2d 402 (5th Cir.1986).

[47]  *E.g.*, Martin v. Johns-Manville Corp., 469 A.2d 655, 659 (Pa. Super. 1993).

[48]  *See comment to* RESTATEMENT (SECOND) OF TORTS § 46.

respirable asbestos, or a contaminated water source, or whose mother was pre-scribed a synthetic estrogen during pregnancy, articulate a claim for damages for the reasonable apprehension of future illness.

A claim for increased risk of future disease differs from a claim for fear of such future illness. The former is based solely upon the medical probability of the future illness, and in this sense permits recovery to the plaintiff who has involuntarily been denied a future without an unreasonable risk of harm from defendant's product or process. The latter claim, for reasonable fear or appre-hension of the manifestation of a future illness, represents a claim for emo-tional distress damages.

## F. PROPERTY DAMAGE

In tort suits, including negligence actions, compensatory damages will be con-sidered appropriate for plaintiff's injury or loss due to harm to his property, or for the loss or diminution of individual or business earning capacity, but only upon proof of the actual pecuniary loss.[49] In a products liability claim, to use one model, physical damage the defective product causes to the user's other property should be compensable in a cause of action brought either in negli-gence or in strict liability, or as consequential damages in warranty.[50]

The ordinary measurement for tortious damage to property is the calcu-lation of the value of the property immediately preceding the loss, less the value following the loss, plus appropriate compensation for plaintiff's depri-vation of the property or loss of use.[51] When the loss to plaintiff's property amounts to total destruction, plaintiff will be entitled to damages measured by the difference between the value of the property before the loss and after the harm, or the reasonable cost of repair or restoration, and the loss of use.[52]

---

[49] RESTATEMENT (SECOND) OF TORTS § 906: "Damages for causing a loss of earning capacity are not necessarily based upon what the plaintiff has done or would have done, but are based upon the amount by which the earning capacity of the plaintiff has been reduced through the conduct of the tortfeasor."

[50] See, e.g., Z-J Corp. v Tice, 126 F.3d 539 (3rd Cir. 1997) (allowing recovery in neg-ligence and strict liability for "other" property).

[51] RESTATEMENT (SECOND) OF TORTS § 927(a), (b), (c).

# VI. COLOMBIAN DEVELOPMENT OF THE LAW OF NEGLIGENCE

## A. GENERALLY

As is the case for most Latin American countries, Colombia's jurisprudence is based largely upon its civil code; thus, its approach to tort law liability differs from common law countries, such as the United States.[53] Unlike Anglo-American jurisprudence, which uses case law as primary authority in the development of its legal principles, such as the doctrine of negligence, Colombian jurisprudence does not follow precedent as a primary authority of its laws. Cases are decided based on the particular facts of the case at hand, and the court's ruling is not binding on future decisions even if the facts of the latter case mirror that of the prior case.

This analysis of the Colombian notion of negligence is based on four primary texts written by Colombian legal scholars.[54] They all agree that in its basic form, the term liability suggests a link between individuals. It is a term that suggests a nexus between two people—he who causes the harm and he who suffers it. The term liability is used to describe the duty to assume the consequences of an act, an occurrence or a form of conduct.[55]

Non-contractual duty arises when a person wrongs or harms another or its belongings. This form of liability arises where there is no contractual nexus between the two. Non-contractual civil liability is divided into direct or personal liability and indirect or complex liability. Indirect liability refers to vicarious liability or acts made with the aid of machines that are used in dangerous activities. These forms of liability are codified in the Colombian Civil Code. Personal liability is stated in Article 2341, third-party liability is

---

[52] RESTATEMENT (SECOND) OF TORTS § 928.

[53] M.C. Mirow, *The Power of Codification in Latin America: Simon Bolivar and the Code Napoleon*, TUL. J. INT'L & COMP. L., 83, 83 (2000).

[54] *See* HUMBERTO CUELLAR GUTIERREZ, RESPONSABILIDAD CIVIL EXTRACONTRACTUAL (1983); JUAN CARLOS HENAO, EL DAÑO (1995); GILBERTO MARTINEZ RAVE, RESPONSABILIDAD CIVIL EXTRACONTRACTUAL (10th ed. 1998); JAVIER TAMAYO JARAMILLO, 2 DE LA RESPONSABILIDAD CIVIL (1989).

[55] *See* MARTINEZ RAVE, *supra* note 21, at 3.

stated in Article 2347, liability due to the acts of an animal is stated in Article 2353, liability arising out of the use of machines is stated in Articles 2350 and 2355, and liability arising out of dangerous activities is stated in Article 2356.[56]

The Colombian legislature maintains a division in the treatment of contractual versus non-contractual liability. This differential treatment is shown in the separate codification of these two forms of liability in the Colombian Civil Code.

## B. THE UNICISTAS V. THE DUALISTAS

There are two theories of liability among Colombian scholars. The first theory is the Unicista (unity) theory.[57] This theory reinforces that both types of liability come from a breach of duty or obligation (responsabilidad). The fact that one arises out of a contractual obligation and the other does not should not be a factor in determining liability.[58] The second theory is the Dualista (dual) theory. This is the conventional Colombian theory. It seeks to treat liability in terms of the obligations assumed either by contract or by law in two separate categories.[59]

Irrespective of the theory adopted, in either situation the act that causes the harm or injury does not have to be an illicit act. The trigger to liability lies in the modification or alteration of the previous state of a thing or person. In contractual liability there are different levels of breach. There is only one level for breach non-contractual liability. "Culpa" which translates into fault, is also used when referring to civil liability. Culpa must be proved under Civil code Article 2341 but it is presumed under Articles 2347, 2350, 2353, 2355, and 2356.[60]

The study and development of non-contractual liability in Colombia in the modern times has also looked at risks (riesgos) when identifying the elements of liability. In the past, Colombian law had a subjective approach towards the elements necessary to establish liability. In the study of non-

---

[56] See Martinez Rave, *supra* note 21, at 1-50.

[57] See *id.* at 17.

[58] *Id.*

[59] *Id.*

[60] *Id.*

contractual liability there are two interests at stake: the progress of technology and the welfare of the public in general from the use or misuse of this technology. In this quest, Martinez questions the Colombian legal system's ability to handle these interests and still uphold the rights of the injured.[61]

## C. IMPACT OF SCIENCE AND TECHNOLOGY IN COLOMBIAN JURISPRUDENCE: JARAMILLOS' APPROACH

Jaramillo states that the scientific and technological advances of the past few decades have obligated and permitted that the laws regarding liability for negligent acts undergo a radical change. The scholar posits that most of the principles guiding negligence liability of fifty years ago are not applicable today. In effect, transportation in general and objects used in everyday life have made it almost impossible for the victim to be able to demonstrate the fault (culpa) by the responsible party.[62]

Based on this proposition, Colombian jurisprudence has attempted to mitigate this problem, for example, in cases of dangerous activities, the victim only has to show that the occurrence caused by the defendant was the triggering factor of his injuries and harm. Legislators have tried to free the victim from the procedural burdens of proof that bring the element of fault into the equation for sustaining a negligence liability claim.[63] Social Utility theory is also present in Colombian law as it accepts the harms posed by technology (*tecnología* meaning man-made structures, products, or mechanical fixtures) upon the individual in order to improve society as a whole.

## D. DUTY

Chile's Civil Code, written by Andres Bellos, served as guide to Colombia's Civil Code.[64] Both codes followed the French model regarding non-contrac-

---

[61] *Id.*

[62] *See* TAMAYO JARAMILLO, *supra* note 64, at 1.

[63] *See generally id.* at ch. 2.

[64] *See* MIROW, *supra* note 63, at 83

tual liability, the Napoleonic Code.[65] Both codes, however, left out the following words, which were present in the Napoleonic Code, Article 1384 "we are responsible (liable) of the things that we have under our care (custody)." These few words have had a great impact in the development of Colombian law. Without these words the victim was left with the burden of proving fault or breach when dealing with other than direct or personal negligence cases.[66]

Through the use of technology and scientific development, the role and importance of direct liability as stated in Article 2341 of the Colombian Civil Code has decreased. As potential liability arising out of dangerous activities increases, the interpretation and application of Article 2356 is also elevated. A victim of a civil non-contractual wrongdoing fares best if he can establish that his harm and injuries arose out of defendant's engagement in a dangerous activity defined by Article 2356. If the claimant is successful in establishing the claim, the liability, or breach of due care is presumed by law. This is an important advantage for the victim who now does not have to prove defendant's fault or guilt.[67]

According to Tamayo Jaramillo, the words left out from the Napoleonic Code, Article 1383 "one is responsible (liable) for the things that we have under our care (custody)," while not stated expressly in the Article, are given implicit effect in another article of the Colombian Civil Code Article 669. Thus, arguably, it operates as a means of avoiding the issue of, the predicate showing of which predominated, in the early stages of Colombian jurisprudence. Article 669 of the Civil Code defines the word dominion as follows: "dominion [[that is also called property] is the right to a corporal [material] thing, to enjoy and dispose of arbitrarily, as long as it is not against the law or against the rights of others." These words allow for the interpretation that intruding upon the rights of others does not require the element of fault, thereby negating the proposition that it is needed in non-contractual liability.[68]

---

[65]  *See id.* at 83-4.

[66]  *See* Tamayo Jaramillo, *supra* note 64, at 2.

[67]  *See id.* at 8-9.

[68]  *See id.* at 40-41.

# VII. DANGEROUS ACTIVITIES

In 1938 Colombia was introduced to the theory of civil liability for dangerous activities, which today is codified by Article 2356 and translated below. By dangerous activities (actividades peligrosas) is meant human pursuits that crate a high and unavoidable risk of great harm. Up to 1938, Colombian courts hewed to the principle of fault, which is present in the French legal system. The historical development of this theory arises out of the work of a lawyer by the name of Eduardo Zuleta, who through his arguments in front of the Supreme Court was able to introduce this theory to Colombian jurisprudence. Later, Carlos Ducci Claro, in his doctoral thesis published in 1936, invoked the teachings of Zuleta, and further developed this theory.[69]

Article 2356 presumes the liability of the defendant. He can only be exonerated by a break in the causation link, such as an act of force majeure. There were many debates among Colombian scholars as to whether the use of the risk theory should play a role in this type of liability, or whether the principle should be that of objectivism. Whether the risk theory or the objective theory is applied, one thing remains consistent: the person engaging in the dangerous activity bears the burden of exonerating himself from liability.[70]

The test of Article 2356 demands that there be malice or negligence on the part of the responsible party. This requirement is founded on the notion of fault. The fact that fault is presumed or proved is a matter of legal interpretation. One thing is certain, according to Tamayo Jaramillo, to wit, the risk theory is adoptive in nature and does not have its roots in Colombian jurisprudence. The Supreme Court has debated over the elements needed to pointdown the responsible party to a dangerous activity. The modern trend is to hold liable he who has the "intellectual direction and control over the dangerous activity."[71]

---

[69] *See id.* at 52-53.

[70] *See id.* at 53-54.

[71] *Id.* at 60.

## A. CIVIL CODE ARTICLE 2356

The translation to this Article is as follows:

> Article 2356 Obligations arising out of dangerous activities. As
> a general rule all harm resulting from the malice of negligence
> of another person must be compensated by the obligator.
>
> Particularly obligated to reparation are:
>
> 1) He who imprudently fires a firearm;
>
> 2) He that removes things from a pipe or sewer line, or leaves
> them open in a street or highway, without the precautions
> needed to prevent the injury (falling) of its transients either
> day or night;
>
> 3) He who does construction or reparations to aqueducts or
> fountains that cross roads, has it in a state that could cause
> harm to those traveling the roads.[72]

The Article further states that there is a presumption of guilt on those who
engage in dangerous activities. This is due to the consideration that it is not
the victim but the defendant who creates the danger to third parties by engaging in an activity, which although licit, in its nature implicates risks of such a
nature that the imminent occurrence of harm explains and validates this presumption.[73]

---

[72] Art. 2356: Responsabilidad por actividades peligrosas. Por regla general todo daño
que se pueda imputarse a malicia o negligencia de otra personon, debe ser reparado
por esta.
Son especialmente obligados a esta reparacion:
1) El que dispara imprudentemente un arma de fuego;
2) El que remueve las cosas de una acequia o caneria, o las descubre en calle o en
camino, sin las precauciones necesarias para que no caigan los que por alli transiten
de dia o de noche;
El que obligado a la construccion o reparacio de un acueducto o fuente, que atraviesa
un camino, lo tiene en estado de causar daño a los que transitan por el camino.

[73] *See id.*

## B. AUTOMOBILE ACCIDENTS

Automobile accidents have constituted one of the most abundant sources of Colombian personal injury litigation. Humberto Cuellar Gutierrez summarizes different forms of accidents which contain a negligent act. Some of these examples include, running a red light and speeding. Both of these situations contain both a criminal act and a civil wrongdoing. The modern doctrine, Gutierrez states, finds that there is only one difference between the criminal and civil wrongdoing, that of degree and not of the nature of the wrongdoing itself. As abovementioned, Article 2356 of the Civil Code defines what Colombian law refers to as dangerous activities. To drive an automobile is considered a form of dangerous activity.[74]

The elements for negligence for this type of activity are as follows: First, there must be an accident. Second, the accident must be occasioned by the dangerous activity. Third, the victim is not obligated to demonstrate the culpability of the author of the injurious act. Fourth, the person liable must be responsible for the dangerous activity. Lastly, the accident cannot be the result of force majeure, fault of a third party, or the fault of the victim.[75]

Savatier defines an accident as the "abnormal fact and unforeseeable that has been produced thus bringing with it the injury." Cuellar Gutierrez states that he would complete the concept by adding the words "as a result of a dangerous activity." This addition to the definition allows people to make the first distinction: the responsibility or liability defined in Article 2356, refers to injuries caused by automobiles, and is not applicable when the injury does not come from the accident itself. Injuries must be caused by the exercise of the dangerous activity and thus when liability and duty of care arise from the same activity, not of fault, it is not necessary to prove non-contractual liability.[76]

In many instances, where there is an accident in land transportation, the obligation or liability will be contractual in kind. If a passenger is injured, the legal claim is made pursuant to the Code of Commerce, in particular, Articles 982, 992 and 1003. If the passenger dies before exercising his rights, his family

---

[74]  *See* HUMBERTO CUELLAR GUTIERREZ, *supra* note 21, at ch. 15.

[75]  *See id.*

[76]  *See generally* MARTINEZ RAVE, *supra* note 21.

will be allowed to commence a contractual hereditary claim (hereditaria contractual). The death of the passenger also allows his family to maintain a personal non-contractual negligence claim. This action is based upon the injury they suffered in relationship to the death of their family member, i.e., lost earnings (lucro cesante). If a transporter causes injuries to a pedestrian, however, his liability will be non-contractual and will be applied under Article 2356.[77]

# VIII. BREACH

For an occurrence or act to give rise to civil liability, the act or occurrence (hecho) does not have to be illicit in nature or unlawful (delictivo) or intentional. Traditionally, the act that gave rise to fault needed to be unlawful. Today the law divides these acts into delictivo and cuasidelictivo. Acts, which are considered cuasidelictivo, are those that occur due to a mistake in conduct, which in turn, result in injury, or results that were not sought after. Martinez disagrees with the traditional use of the word delito (crime) when referring to civil liability. In his view, the word delito should only be used in the context for which it was created, criminal law.[78]

There is considerable debate among Colombian scholars as to whether fault should be part of the equation for civil liability. The word fault or guilt translated into Spanish is culpa. The same word is used in describing tortious conduct and criminal conduct. The word culpa was used because there is no uniform definition to describe breach of duty.[79] To some Colombian Scholars the term culpa imports not only fault or guilt, but also breach. Pursuant to such an interpretation, the breach must have an objective factor that refers to awareness or free will of the actor. To this date, however, culpa is based on a subjective standard. It looks at the internal conditions surrounding the breach

[77] *See generally* Tamayo Jaramillo, *supra* note 21.
[78] *See* Martinez Rave, *supra* note 21, at ch. 7.
[79] *See id.* at ch. 10.

of each individual. Martinez's text refers to some of these objectivists scholars' definition of the word breach. Seratier defined breach as the breach of a duty that the actor was aware existed and could not observe. The Mazeud brothers defined breach as a mistake of conduct that a prudent person under similar circumstances would not make. The aforementioned theorists believe that we should look at breach in the abstract light, which they call objective fault. Objective fault looks at the prudent man as its model, the careful man, a "good family man." Martinez cautions that this term should not be confused with "objective liability" or strict liability, which does not require the element of fault or breach.[80]

The objective fault approach is the modern view of liability embraced by Colombian scholars. Notwithstanding this newest view, the Colombian legal system is still based on subjective fault. The subjective fault has criminal liability as its roots. Despite the Colombian attempt to modify its notion to civil liability, Martinez believes that the principle and the required showing of subjective fault will die out. To him, objective fault is the next step in the progress and development of civil liability.

Within the objective fault movement, there are many debates regarding the management of fault. To some, the element of culpa should be eliminated altogether. To others, liability will be proven if the hecho or negligent occurrence is proven together with the injury. Martinez believes that an adequate interpretation for Colombia would be to treat breach as presumed in all cases where the other elements are proven by the injured. In this case, the defendant can escape liability if he can demonstrate that he acted with diligence and due care. In other cases, which are expressly stated in the Civil Code Article 2356, for example, liability should be presumed. The defendant in this situation can escape liability by establishing a break in the causation link. Unlike the American origin of negligence, Colombian negligence principles emerged with the question of "fault" as the first element of the negligence claim. This is of course, an imitation of the Napoleonic Code's treatment of "fault."[81]

---

[80] *See id.*

[81] *See id.*

# IX. INJURY: AS THE FIRST ELEMENT OF LIABILITY

Non-contractual liability in Colombian law has as its goal to deal with the issue of injuries or harm suffered by an individual in a legal and ordered fashion. The incorporation of this notion into the law allows for society to develop rules regarding human risk and the consequences of acts that arise out of the risks.[82] There is no consensus among Colombian scholars as to which element of liability to highlight in the study of non-contractual liability. The Colombian author Juan Carlos Henao states that in dealing with this form of liability, the first element that must be studied is the injury or harm suffered by the victim.[83]

For there to be negligence liability, particularly prior to the 1991 Constitution, one must show that there was a breach. Concurrently, the injury had to be both present and tied or linked to of causation. Today, the focus has shifted to the element of injury, because in some cases, fault is not always an element or requirement for liability to exist. As Dean Hinestrosa states:

> "[T]he injury is the reason liability exists, and that is why, it is
> imperative that it is explore in its distinct aspects and degree;
> for it should occupy the first place in a logical and chrono-
> logical sense, in the minds of judges. If there is no injury, or
> it can't be determined or evaluated, that should be the end;
> any further effort, relative to the act or actor or moral quali-
> fication of the conduct will be futile."[84]

It is accepted that the harm suffered should be the first element to be discussed in the equation of civil liability. If a person has not been injured or harmed, he should not be favored by a judgment that would unjustly enrich him without cause. The injury is the cause for reparation, and reparation or compensation is the finality of civil liability. Henao criticizes judgments by the

---

[82] *See* Henao, *supra* note 21, at ch. 2.

[83] *See id.*

[84] *See id.*

Colombian "Consejo de Estado based on a lack of service or fault. For example, in a judgment dated October 2, 1996, the Consejo de Estado affirmed, "in an event of sub iudice [lack of service], the injury does not have to be proven by the person claiming the harm." Critics suggest that such cases demonstrate the flaw in treating injury as a subsequent element of civil liability. Notwithstanding the importance of first determining the injury or harm suffered by the victim, it should be noted that a showing of injury alone does not give rise to civil liability.[85]

The person claiming the injury or harm must prove the injury exists. As a starting point, Article 177 of the Code of Civil Procedure affirms that "the legislator has established that it is the duty of the parties to prove the claimed tortious act or conduct (hecho) of the norms that allow the judicial effect that they seek." Therefore, it is not enough for the claimant to state that she has suffered an injury; it must be proven in court.

One exception to this rule applies when dealing with lost earnings (lucro cesante) pertaining to an individual who has been injured or has died. The judge will presume an injury when computing lost earnings sought by those who are economically dependent on that individual and have suffered an injury as a result of the victim's injuries. The standard of proof to determine the value of the lucro cesante is not the same standard required to prove an injury was sustained. Nevertheless, this treatment of the element of injury shows a departure from the American treatment of negligence.

# X. DAMAGES

In a personal injury complaint, it is customary for a plaintiff's attorney not to include a money amount for the total damages sought. Instead, the attorney will include generic language in the complaint. This procedure regarding the questions of damages leaves the judge ample discretion in the determination

---

[85]  *Id.*

of damage awards. An example is illustrated in a case where a minor suffered brain damage due to a gunshot, for which he underwent several surgeries. The minor did not fully recover from the injuries suffered. The Consejo de Estado ordered the defendant to pay the minor's health care bills for the life of the minor together with any psychological treatment he may need in the future. It is seen that the court may acknowledge not only the damages that can be proved at the time of the trial, but also the long term damage that may not be assessable at the time of the trial.[86]

Another case pointed out by Henao is the case of a victim of a negligent occurrence (hecho). He became 86% incapacitated and remained in a paraplegic state. The normal equation for damages in lost future earnings would have been based on the aforementioned percentage. Notwithstanding, the Consejo de Estado held that due to the high percentage of incapacity, the percentage to be used in this case should be 100%. This, the Estado noted, was justified by the necessity to cover the continuous damage suffered by the injured and the assistance he will need in living with the injuries sustained.[87]

As stated above, Colombian law deals with the notion of damages or indemnification, based on the proposition that the injured should be put back in the position he was in prior to the negligent act, or as closely to it as possible. Unlike the law of most United States jurisdictions, under Colombian law, injured parties in cases of personal injury awards arising out of non-contractual liability do not include the recognition of punitive damages. It is argued that the unavailability of exemplary damages allows for the injured to be made whole again without unjust enrichment.

While the common law and the civil code systems diverge on the question of punitive damages, both the civil code and common law approaches are in agreement that the objective of such causes of action both is to permit the meritorious plaintiff to be returned, in however imperfect manner money damages can do so, to his or her original condition. Indeed, it is fair to state that corrective justice is part of both Colombia and the United States equation for negligence.

---

[86] *Id.* at 84.

[87] *See id.*

Furthermore, Henao argues that the application of the aforementioned types of punitive damages do not exist "in theory" in the continental system, which system's gravitational pull can be recognized in much Colombian law. The Colombian objective is to indemnify or compensate the injured for the harm sustained. In contrast, by entertaining the potential of an award of both compensatory damages and punitive damages, the law of most United States jurisdictions provides compensation for the wrongfully injured, and further, in instances of extreme misconduct by the defendant, permit a quasi-criminal penalty that serves both to punish the defendant and to make a public statement as to the unacceptability of such behavior.

Under Colombian law, compensation for injuries sustained must be made fully. Nevertheless, according to Henao, compensation should be limited to the injury actually suffered and proved. In the words of the Colombian Supreme Court "payment for damages must directly correspond with the magnitude of the injury suffered, thus cannot be any higher." The explanation of this notion lies in the public belief that there should not be unjust enrichment to the party injured. Again, Henao, in the context of punitive damages, contrasts the United States' public punishment of tortfeasors by the awarding of enormous sums often bearing no discernible relationship to the harm actually suffered. In his discussion of damages, and in relationship to the concept of unjust enrichment, Henao also considers the issue of subrogation under Colombian law. He analyzes the situation in which an injured individual receives compensation from other sources. The compensation by other sources (other than the tortfeasor) lowers the threshold of damages actually suffered. In Colombia, the term used to describe this type of situation is called compensatio lucri cum damno. This issue arises when other parties contribute to the indemnification of the damages. Examples of these forms of compensation are social security and private insurance policies. In the aforementioned situations, the injured can conceivably end up in a better situation, in other words, unjust enrichment may occur as a result of the payment of damages by other and collateral sources. According to Henao, the Consejo de Estado has stated that even though unjust enrichment does not form part of the equation for computing damages, there may be situations where this enrichment may be legally justified.[88]

---

[88] *See id.* at ch. 3.

Payments of employment insurance policies or social security benefits legally belonging to the injured party or his family does not prevent the injured from recovering damages from the negligent party. Henao contrasts this view with that of France. In France, these sources indeed limit the amount of recovery an injured party may receive from the tortfeasor. One exception to this rule occurs with respect to negligence insurance, where it expressly calls for subrogation in accordance with Article 1096 of the Colombian Commerce Code. According to Henao, discrepancies between supplemental indemnification and negligence contracts arise as a result of the Colombian legislature's decision to differentiate the two. This leaves the courts powerless to allow for supplemental compensation where there is an insurance contract, which contains subrogation clauses.

There are different types of damages which entitle the injured to compensation. The first type of damage is material. It presupposes an economic loss. The second harm is moral in nature, and does not contain an economic value. Colombian jurisprudence has sustained that this distinction must be used to guide the analysis of the types of damages in relationship to their compensation. Notwithstanding, the types of damages as outlined above can present confusion. It allows one to think that all damage that does not have an economic or pecuniary nature must be moral. Under Colombian law, the compensation of "physical harm or in relation to life" was added only in 1993. Henao argues that the better classification would be to say that moral damages are a kind of non-pecuniary damage. In light of the foregoing, the classification of damages should be done in terms of economic versus non-economic.[89]

In Colombian law, another distinction is made between damages that are patrimonial versus non-patrimonial. Under the economic damages are two sub-categories: the lucro cesante and daño emergente, both, which are patrimonial. Under the non-patrimonial damages are included the moral injury and physical injury. The judge decides both types. He has the discretion to decide the injury's classification and the amount of compensation the injured will receive for each type of injury. As to personal but non-physical injuries (daños

---

[89] Henao, *supra* note 21, at 191.

morales), Colombian legal scholars refer to as moral injuries can be classified as the equivalent of American damages for pain and suffering.

Economic damages are those that deal with personal property or economic interests, which is to say, they are measurable in terms of money. Colombian law, perhaps due to Articles 1613 and 1614 of the Civil Code, differentiates between lucro cesante and daño emergente. Article 1614 states that daño emergente arises out of "the damage or loss that arises of an obligation that was not fulfilled, or erroneous fulfillment, or tardy fulfillment." The daño emergente encompasses the loss of patrimonial property, the gains that this property would have brought to the individual. Lucro cesante refers to the earnings that stop from accruing due to the damage aforementioned. These types of damages are applicable in both contractual and non-contractual obligations. Henao distinguishes between the two by stating that the daño emergente produces a "desembolso" an out of pocket damage, while the lucro cesante produces a "no embolso" damage, meaning there is nothing being pocketed which would have been but for the injury or harm sustained. The Mazeud brothers refer to lucro cesante as the "perdida sufrida" or loss suffered and "ganancia frustrada" or frustrated earnings.[90]

## A. EL DAÑO EMERGENTE

As previously stated this type of damage presents itself when it is a physical injury suffered by the individual. Examples given by Henao representing daño emergente are as follows: (1) The victim dies as a result of the injury. His family must incur all expenses related to the victim's burial. Those costs are an example of the daños emergentes. (2) If the victim survives, all the expenses incurred in the rehabilitation of the victim are considered daños emergentes. Daños emergentes can also arise out of harm to one's belongings. When the injurious act affects belongings, the judge applies the same logic for reparation of the damage as used in the damage to the physical damage suffered by the individual.[91]

---

[90] *See id.* at 197.

[91] *See id.* at 210-14.

## B. EL LUCRO CESANTE

As stated by Henao, when the integrity of a person is attacked there are effects that must be compensated. When an individual dies as a result of the negligence of another, his family is entitled to compensation for their out-of-pocket losses or expenses (el daño emergente) but also for the losses that will be sustained by the family due to the injury or death of the family's economic provider. Their loss in terms of monetary reparation refers to the economic dependence family members may have had on the decedent. When the daño emergente is a damage done to an object or thing, the courts look to see the amount of earnings lost as a result of the harm or damage.[92]

For a long time, the Supreme Court and the Consejo de Estado held that non-patrimonial damages constituted only moral damages. It was not until the 1990's that non-patrimonial damages were broadened to include more than moral damages. In one case decided on February 14, 1992, the court awarded a judgment of 1.800 grams of gold for moral damages. This amount was higher than the traditional 1.000 gram courts had previously awarded. Despite the fact that the decision only referred to the compensation of moral damages, it was inferred that the judge was awarding damages that were outside the scope of moral damages.[93]

The definitive recognition of non-material damages took place in another case decided on May 6, 1993. A year after the Consejo de Estado amplified "physical damages" as a synonym of "injury to the relationship of life," this case affirmed that "it is necessary to recognize the award for physical damage or to the damage to the relationship to life. This form of damage must be distinguished from material damage, which encompasses both daño emergente and lucro cesante, and also must be distinguished from subjective moral damages."[94] It remains difficult to achieve recognition of this type of compensable harm. When, for example, a boy suffers an injury that will leave him blind for the rest of his life, or limited to a wheel chair, the amount and logic of the award of damages for pain and suffering may become enmeshed in the amount

[92] *Id.* at 223-224.

[93] *See* Tamayo Jaramillo, *supra* note 21.

[94] *Id.* at 265 (trans. from Spanish).

and rationale of the award of material damages. Further employing the above hypothetical, perhaps the blinded boy will require the aid of a guide dog. Should a part of any monetary award be considered an award to compensate for his physical injury, or is it more appropriately considered an award for daño emergente? Is it an award for pain and suffering? Since 1998, there have been 35 cases where the right to an "objective" award for pain and suffering has been given.

# XI. CONCLUSION

In contrast to Anglo-American law, non-contractual civil liability under Colombian law remains burdened by its continued fidelity to the predicate showing of guilt and fault in determining civil liability. As seen above, Colombian legal scholars are unable to identify and clearly define the elements needed to achieve a unified notion of non-contractual liability. This struggle has as one of its components the influence of French law, which Colombia modified in an attempt suit the Colombian needs regarding the structure of civil liability. Another component is exemplified by the need to modernize the terms and the usage of liability to fully compensate victims. Due to the fear of unjust enrichment, Colombian victims are often left without the compensation due for their proved injuries.

A struggle for legality and compensation are reflected in the texts. They are often unclear, and filled with theses with no concrete answers. It was only recently that most courts accepted the concept of pain and suffering awards, and today, many cases contain awards that are not easily differentiated.

Colombian negligence law emerged from the Napoleonic Code, which it modified to comport with the Chilean Civil Code written by Andres Bello.[95] By leaving out the words "under its care" the Colombian Civil Code created negligence laws that used criminal law principles to attain a desired result—a

---

[95] *See id.* at 2.

non-contractual liability tort system, giving rise to the past and continued disagreement among scholars attempting to define a proper metric for the Colombian law of money remedies for daño.

# CHAPTER 7

# TORT LAW'S THEMES
# OF ECONOMIC EFFICIENCY

## I. INTRODUCTION

Tort law represents a society's revealed truth as to the behaviors it wishes to encourage and the behaviors it wishes to discourage.[1] From causes of action for the simple tort of battery to the more elegant tortuous interference with prospective advantage, the manner in which individuals or groups can injure a protected interest of others seems almost limitless. Despite the amplitude of interests protected by tort law, from its earliest exercise in prehistoric groups up to its modern implementation, there have existed a finite number of goals of tort law, whether the "law" referred to be an unwritten norm, a judicial decision, or a modern statute.

There is general agreement that these objectives, however imperfectly accomplished, include: (1) returning the party who has suffered a loss to the position he enjoyed before the wrongful activity; (2) requiring the wrongdoer to disgorge the monetary or imputed benefit derived from his actions; and (3) by the remedy meted out, or by its example, deterring the wrongdoer and others

---

[1] There will be some rarified instances of behavior that tort law would not discourage, such as abnormally dangerous activities, but instead may wish to modify or limit, and in any event, assign strict liability.

in a similar situation from engaging in the same wrongful and injurious pursuit. Another manner of describing tort goals has been to order them as serving either goals of (4) "corrective justice" and "morality"; or (5) "efficiency and deterrence."

Aligning tort rules to be consistent exclusively with any one of these five goals requires some ungainly packaging, as each of the five themes described actually also serves the other four. This is to say, for example, a remedy that focuses on corrective justice will serve simultaneously the goals of disgorgement of unjust enrichment, morality, efficiency, deterrence, and so on. More specifically, the goal of returning the injured party to the *status quo ante*, the objective most closely associated with corrective justice, is ordinarily reached by a decree ordering the wrongdoer to return to the plaintiff in money the equivalent to what the plaintiff lost. But damages calculated in this way also may be seen as an inexact surrogate for what the wrongdoer gained, actually or by imputation, by perpetrating the wrong. Further, whereas the wrongdoer's disgorgement of his gain often provides corrective justice for the claimant, it also, importantly, punishes the wrongdoer for failing to achieve the plaintiff's *ex ante* approval of the transaction – an omission deemed to be inefficient by exponents of efficiency theory.[2] So it is not surprising that although many suggest that tort rules and remedies aligned with economic and efficiency models provide the most deterrence for civil wrongs, most agree that the tort rules recognized by the corrective justice-morality school also deter in measurable ways. Indeed, in the inexact taxonomy employed by tort scholars, there are so many instances of overlap between what tort goals are claimed to serve corrective justice-morality, but that serve simultaneously goals of efficiency and deterrence, that the legal pragmatist would be tempted to characterize them as functionally equivalent.[3] Even conceding the absence of neatness in any at-

---

[2]   When the loss is personal injury or property damage, a rough estimation of this inefficiency (or waste) may often be the combined amount of the claimant's economic and noneconomic damages. Of course the theme of punishment deterrence is but the flip side of a theme of creating an incentive for efficient behavior. As suggested by Professors David W. Barnes and Lynn A. Stout, "Tort law may be viewed as a system of rules designed to maximize wealth by allocating risks so as to minimize the costs associated with engaging in daily activities." DAVID W. BARNES & LYNN A. STOUT, CASES AND MATERIALS ON LAW AND ECONOMICS 85 (1992).

tempt at categorization, the division of tort goals along these or similar lines is nevertheless illuminating and predictive.

Accident law is a model of social expectations, and these social expectations are at once moral and economically efficient. Emphasizing for present purposes the economic aspect, it can be shown that in broad terms, written or unwritten rules pertaining to civil wrongs cleave to an ethos of efficiency. This efficiency norm has, in turn, an organizing principle of waste avoidance, the protection of persons and their property from injury and wrongful appropriation, the preservation of the integrity of individual or collective possessions or prerogatives from wrongful interference, and the prudent marshaling of limited resources. Although the corrective justice-morality objectives of many tort norms will often, for what appears initially, eclipse any apparent underpinnings of efficiency, still and all, subtle economic themes of efficiency and deterrence can be recognized in almost all tort-type customs, expectations, and rules. Indeed, as this Section will demonstrate, the parallel and harmonious impetus for almost all of what today we call tort law today can be found in principles of economic efficiency.

This Chapter examines preliminarily a selection of past and contemporary societal choices regarding identification, assignment, and implementation of remedies for civil wrongs. Rather than exploring each of the five principal themes of tort analysis noted earlier, I devote this examination solely to tort rules revealing economic themes. Although there are only a limited number of such rules that reveal an economic analysis on the surface, in the examples the Section summons the economic goals can be teased readily to the surface.

Evaluation of accident law as it has evolved during the period of written history is by any assessment a prodigious task. Even with modern translation, there are numerous gaps in the historical record. The potential for analytical error in bridging these gaps is compounded by the difficulties legal scholars and legal historians confront in reading the legal-historical record within the

---

[3] Put another way, both corrective justice and efficiency principles must be regarded as "true" in that they hold significant, albeit nonexclusive, predictive value in anticipating the development of tort law. *See* M. Stuart Madden, *Selected Federal Tort Reform and Restatement Initiatives Through the Lenses of Corrective Justice and Efficiency*, 32 GA. L. REV. 1017 (1998) at nn. 297–98 and accompanying text.

only context that may reveal it reliably: the cultural and political circumstances of its origins. As to prehistoric man, no more than a small part of the history of the earliest human societies may ever be scientifically reconstructed, because of natural loss, or frequently deliberate or inadvertent later human meddling. Forever lost are countless ancient remnants that might suggest the societal norms employed to make group decisions based on what behaviors would bring collective benefit and what would not.

The adoption of durable writing or imagery accelerated our modern understanding of ancient legal norms. The discovery and translation of the first integrated legal codes from the sites that were within ancient Babylonia, a codification of what was surely the customary law that preceded it, provided the first written evidence of regularized norms for civil behavior, identification of civil wrongs, and the remedies for such wrongs. However, even anticipating the development of permanent written records, much regarding human norms and customs may be deduced logically. Taking into account the difficulties in identifying the customs of early humans, experts are of one view that the success and survival of early social groupings bore a more or less exact correlation to their adoption of norms that furthered advancement of knowledge, material comfort, and economic stability. For all human groups, achievement of these attributes would, from prehistory onward, be characterized as "good."[4] It follows that early family clans, and the tribes and ever larger social aggregations that would follow, have shared one sentiment: to pursue such "good" for their members.[5]

Philosophers have disagreed as to whether man in his natural state was innately "good," but any original impulse for good stood no meaningful chance for survival as human concentrations grew and evolved. Group order and expectations in the form of norms, and the subscription to such norms by indi-

---

[4] Robert Redfield, *Maine's Ancient Law in the Light of Primitive Societies*, The Western Political Quarterly 3, 586–89 (1950), in which Redfield writes of primitive societies: "[E]conomic systems are imbedded in social relations. Men work and manufacture not for motives of gain. They tend to work because working is part of the good life . . . "

[5] By "members" is meant the collective, for, as Maine observed: "Ancient Law . . . knows next to nothing of Individuals. It is concerned not with Individuals, but with Families, not with single human beings but groups." Henry Sumner Maine, Ancient Law 229 (1861).

viduals and families, became necessary for communal survival. It will be seen that at its core, tort law, together with its unwritten normative antecedents, bears witness to the fundamental social need for self-limitation. To the sociologist Emile Durkheim, the peaceful process of society has always depended on the individual's submission to inhibitions of or restrictions on personal "inclinations and instincts." Whether the "venerable respect" tendered to a collective "moral authority" is faith-dependent or not, Durkheim continues, "social life would be impossible"[6] without general subscription to such limitations. And so by necessity, social groups developed expectations, norms, customs, and, eventually, laws that (1) encouraged behaviors that contributed to the common good and economic success of the community; and (2) discouraged individualistic pursuit of personal aggrandizement to the extent that the same involved disavowal of community responsibility.

Accordingly, human experience of the ages has demonstrated that man as a social animal has turned almost invariably to structures and norms consistent with defined and enforced standards of "good" as would further the innate and overarching instinct for individual and group survival. By virtue of this ascendant sentiment of most societies of all historical epochs to attain both group and individual "good," the collective conclusions as to what constitutes "good" evolved gradually to this: what is "good" has always been, as it is today, what is just, moral and equitable.[7] Encouragement of "good" conduct has been logically accompanied by discouragement of "bad" conduct, which is to say, behavior considered to be unjust, immoral, or inequitable. And all such systems, save the brashest of totalitarian societies, have included standards by which a person might seek the correction of or compensation for harm caused by the wrongful acts of another. Initially established as practices, then as norms and customs, and eventually as law, evolving social strictures would operate to ei-

---

[6]  EMILE DURKHEIM, THE ELEMENTARY FORMS OF RELIGIOUS LIFE 237 (1915) (1965 Ed.).

[7]  Conceding that Socrates wrote from beyond the spheres of governing power, it is telling that Socrates' ethics are suffused with the goal of avoiding doing harm, and with the argument that a principal marker of "justice" is the simple "returning what was owed." ANTHONY GOTTLEIB: THE DREAM OF REASON: A HISTORY OF PHILOSOPHY FROM THE GREEKS TO THE RENAISSANCE 164 (2000).

ther cabin or punish the behaviors of those succumbing to the seemingly irresistible human appetite for bad, wrongful, and harmful behavior.

In this sense tort law, past and present, has operated as the societal super-ego, a generally subscribed-to social compact in which most persons rein in such impulses as might lead them to trammel the protected rights of others, inasmuch as the norms of tort law require rectification operating *post hoc* to restore the wronged person to the position previously enjoyed.[8] This restoration may be perfect, such as when it is in the form of returning goods where there has been a trespass to chattels and there has been no diminution in value, or when there has been a misappropriation. Or it may be imperfect, such as in settings involving a wrongful physical injury, as to which rectification in the form of money can never truly restore the injured party to the *status quo ante*. As suggested initially, whatever the corrective justice limitations of money damages, they do serve other objectives identified with tort law, which include deterrence of the same or similar conduct by the actor or others similarly situated. Money damages also, in an economic sense, command a transfer of wealth that achieves a figurative rectification of the wrongdoer's "forced taking" of the injured party's bodily integrity. The money damages also, at least conceptually, deprive the wrongdoer of the "unjust enrichment" achieved by creating a tear in the fabric of consensual or contract-based social interaction.

The objective in this Section is to examine this question: In the norms, rules, and philosophical bases for early tort law through and including its modern representations, can there be found a continuous vein of the goals of (1) efficiency and (2) deterrence? It will not surprise students of tort law that numerous social, philosophical, and legal systems, from past to present, are redolent of the economic norms of waste avoidance and the discouragement of unconsented-to taking. I will discuss a spare, but illustrative, selection of groups and societies the organization of which followed written and unwritten

---

[8] "The true explanation of the reference of liability to a moral standard . . . is not that it is for the purpose of improving men's hearts, but that it is to give a man a fair chance to avoid doing the harm before he is held responsible for it. It is intended to reconcile the policy of letting accidents lie where they fall, and the reasonable freedom of others with the protection of the individual from injury." Oliver Wendell Holmes, The Common Law 115 (Mark DeWolfe Howe, ed.) (1963).

norms so showing. I also will touch on modern philosophical and legal tenets that inform us regarding the tenacity of economic efficiency themes in tort law and theory. The Section will conclude with observations as to how this abundant history of human recognition of these economic considerations augurs for the future of tort law.

# II. ECONOMIC IMPERATIVES IN EARLY SOCIAL GROUPINGS

## A. GENERALLY

The raw and primal imperative of simple human survival has required of each successful community the ordered pursuit of "good" for its members, including necessarily standards to discourage or interdict activity that interrupted or compromised pursuit of a "good" social order. In the shadow of such overarching needs, the norms or apparatus of "justice" and "morality" would necessarily be subordinate to the collective pursuit of economic stability, growth, and the elevation of human knowledge. Retaining a focus on the three goals of elevation of human knowledge, material comfort, and economic stability, it follows that within the context of pre-history, of particular pertinence to the furtherance of each goal was the creation and preservation of group circumstances in which persons could expect to live peaceably without physical injury at the hands of others. It also was expected that the community would provide congruent protection against wrongful taking or damage of the property justly acquired by its members. It was collectively thought necessary that man would gradually impose on his groups, and eventually civilizations and states, norms and rules that served to protect the personal physical autonomy and security of group members, and also protect their belongings, against wrongful interference. The group visualization of these norms, and their progressive imposition, would assume the aura of inevitability, and the *gravitas* of a cultural imperative. For successful social groupings, principal among such norms was the expectation there would be some form of remediation for an impermissible intrusion on physical or property interests, including common property rights.[9] And, finally, along this line of civilizing thought, the ideation of society was that this remediation ought properly come from the malefactor.

## B. A PRE-SYMBOLIC SCENARIO

At some distant time in the African veldt, the birthplace of modern man, *homo sapiens* formed family-based social groups or clans. From the time of early family groupings to the development of ever-more complex communities, all successful human gatherings developed work specializations *inter se*.[10] For example, a group depending on fishing for its sustenance would need individuals to prepare nets or baskets for the catch. Others in the group would dedicate themselves to the actual fishing, and travel to the water source with, let us say, spherical fishing baskets that contained a hole on one side that lured fish seeking shade. Swift retrieval of the basket would catch the fish and provide food for the community. Naturally, the entire community would not survive if the actual fishing specialists arrogated to themselves the catch, and so there developed norms of allocative efficiency, a so-called "generosity" norm, that would ensure that all in the community, including infants and the aged, would be provided for adequately.[11] This allocation constituted a micro prototype of efficiency-based exchange of goods that recognized duties owed by the community to its individuals, duties owed by community members to oth-

---

[9]  *Dennis Lloyd*, The Idea of Law 49 (1976) (referencing, *inter alia*, Mosaic law).

[10]  "[F]or example, the [primitive] Australian hunter who kills a wild animal is expected to give one certain part of it to his elder brother, other parts to his younger brother and still other parts of the animal to defined relatives. He does this knowing that [the other brothers] will make a corresponding distribution of meat to him." Robert Redfield, *Maine's Ancient Law in the Light of Primitive Societies*, in J. C. Smith and David N. Weisstub, The Western Idea of Law 81 (1983).

[11]  As Darwin pointed out for flora and fauna and as Durkheim noted in the case of human societies, an increase in numbers when area is held constant (*i.e.*, an increase in density) tends to produce differentiation and specialization, as only in this way can the area support increased numbers.

ers, and the common interest in non-wasteful behavior that would characterize all stable societies to follow.

This economic cooperation characteristic of primitive communities was the antithesis of economic self-interest, and understandably, Karl Polanyi writes that in tribal society, "[the individual's economic interest is rarely paramount, for the community keeps all its members from starving unless it is itself borne down by catastrophe."[12] Moreover, in the circumstances of tribal society, past and present alike, exclusive pursuit of economic self-interest was itself contrary to the economic survival of the group. Early task assignment and economic differentiation within a clan or a small social group required, by "code of honor" or "generosity," recognition that each member of the community served the whole. From the earliest hunting and gathering communities to the later agricultural groupings, task allocation was accompanied by mutual expectancies that the bounty in food or materials gathered by one group would be shared with the others. The others would include, nonexclusively, the homemakers, children, and the elderly. For the vital hunting population to forsake its obligation to return from the hunt with food to share with the family, clan, or tribe would sabotage the very existence of the social group. Failure to share with the homemaker and the children would bring about the speedy end of the bloodline. As to elders, with some exceptions, tribal groups recognized that the aged acted as secondary caregivers and essential repositories of the group's oral history and traditions.

In time, with the increase in population and in the course of the proved northward migration of many human groups,[13] early man found that the working norms for family, clan and single community survival would be taxed by contact with other families or groups. For an untold time, the response of the principal family was simply that of preserving territorial integrity, familial safety, or both. An intruder would be frightened away, or if necessary, beaten

---

[12] PRIMITIVE, ARCHAIC AND MODERN ECONOMIES: ESSAYS OF KARL POLANYI 7 (George Dalton, ed. 1968).

[13] Such extraordinary migrations as would take man out of Africa and eventually permit his species' dispersal throughout all but one continent was facilitated by his evolved ability to walk on two feet, to travel long distances, and to carry objects and infants. J. M. ROBERTS, THE NEW HISTORY OF THE WORLD 5 (2003).

or killed. If the intruder or his group prevailed in any contest, the principal family, with its injured or killed, would abdicate its territory.

In a succession of discrete and unidentifiable moments, this motif would change. Increased populations, changes in climate that made one area more hospitable than another, or migratory patterns of available prey, made contact with other groups more frequent. A group's choices were essentially two. They might preserve their reflexive and potentially mortal repulsion of competition. However losses suffered in non-cooperative contact with other groups might have stimulated a group's conclusion that preservation of pristine territorial integrity was perhaps a pearl of too great a price. And so, alternatively, their response to other communities might begin to partake of peaceable aspects. Non-combative resolution of intra-familial allocative tensions might have served as a model for introduction of cooperative behavior in interfamilial matters. As to the latter, cooperation would lessen or eliminate the enormous waste and cost of violent response to intrusion.

Perhaps at the instigation a group elder, families and tribes eventually developed behaviors and expectations that could coexist within the context of available resources in such ways as to achieve a tenable resource-based economic stasis.[14] Should, for example, our hypothesized fishing community come into contact with a hunting community, the sharing of territory, and perhaps even barter, might well become recognized for its very significant benefit in reducing the group's loss of its ablest members to combat, and thus become a common ideal or norm.

Historians have recognized the similar options presented to later agricultural communities, with the permissible inference of the peaceable and efficient resolution of such options. In the description of J. M. Roberts: "As the population rose, more land was taken to grow food. Sooner or later men of different villages would have to come face to face with others intent on reclaiming the marsh which had previously separated them from one another.... There was a choice: to fight or to cooperate. . . .

---

[14]  Of course the genetic significance of intergroup coexistence is inestimable, but would, in any event be unknown to early man until the development of the incest taboos.

Somewhere along the line it made sense for men to band together in bigger units than hitherto for self-protection and management of the environment."[15] Of necessity the norms developed within such larger social groups reflected the wisdom of not only *ex ante* resource allocation but also of strictures intended to discourage disruption of such allocation by forced takings or otherwise.

The above hypothetical yet historically realistic example gives to us our first chance to measure highly plausible human behavior, and attendant norms, by a yardstick of human economic efficiency. Although multiple economic models are available, one that seems well suited is that propounded by Vilfredo Pareto in the early 1900s. The Pareto analysis imagines a setting in which all goods have been previously allocated, and permits an evaluation of different approaches to reallocation of such goods. A reallocation that left one or more individuals better off, but no one worse off, would be considered a Pareto Superior change.[16] Even better, from a wealth-maximization perspective, is a result in which with the reallocation of goods or resources all affected parties are better off – a result described as Pareto Optimal or Pareto Efficient.[17]

Applying the Pareto approach to early man's described movement away from territorial combat to gradually more peaceable allocations of land and other resources presents this question: Is such rational cooperation efficient? A syllogism posed in a coarse correlation between competition and efficiency may be, on these facts, misleading. That syllogism would go: competition is, generally speaking, efficient. The antithesis of competition is cooperation. Therefore, cooperation is inefficient. However in the example given earlier,

---

[15] J. M. ROBERTS, *supra* note 13 at 49–50. These early incentives toward political and economic cooperation weigh in against the more pessimistic vision of Garrett Hardin. Garrett Hardin, *The Tragedy of the Commons*, 62 SCIENCE 1243, 1244 (Dec. 13, 1968) (arguing that "ruin is the destination toward which all men rush, each pursuing his own best interest.").

[16] The Pareto criteria for wealth maximization analysis are summarized in DAVID W. BARNES & LYNN A. STOUT, THE ECONOMIC ANALYSIS OF TORT LAW 11 (1992).

[17] MARK SEIDENFELD, MICROECONOMIC PREDICATES TO LAW AND ECONOMICS 49 (1996). For general description of Pareto optimality principles, *see* ROBIN PAUL MALLOW, LAW AND ECONOMICS: A COMPARATIVE APPROACH TO THEORY AND PRACTICE (1990).

rational cooperation between early human social groups regarding the sharing of limited land resources was not only efficient, it also can be seen to be the only means by which early societies could flourish. The alternative was either the continuation of wasteful combat, or the relegation of some groups to a continued nomadic life, or both. Thus, cooperation, and its concomitant benefits to participants in agricultural communities, was Pareto Optimal.

Furthermore, as to the theme of surplus, and surplus accumulation, it is widely proposed that the development of agriculture and animal husbandry created the first human experience of surplus.[18] This surplus, in turn, accelerated the development of specialization of labor.[19] Specialization of labor affected the reciprocal entitlements and obligations of three principal groupings: (1) those engaged in agriculture; (2) artisans; and (3) those to whom fell domestic and child-rearing obligations. Those engaged in agriculture had, of course, the duty to efficiently and productively produce and to husband the resources and the comestible rewards entrusted to them. Unlike the expectations typical of the hunting and gathering communities, the development of agriculture both permitted and required that what was produced not be consumed immediately, and that when it was consumed, that it not be consumed exclusively by those who produced it. Rather, the expectation for and the duty of those tilling the fields or tending the animals was to harvest the crops and to preserve the harvest, or to slaughter the livestock and to preserve the meat through salting or otherwise, for distribution among the entire community. The artisans were expected to perform such tasks as the creation of the specialized tools that might be associated with chopping, sewing, tilling, the making of clothing, the building of shelter, and more. The artisans' expectation was that, in exchange for their labor, they would partake of the agricultural production of the fields.

The homemakers also might not participate directly in agricultural production, or if they did, they might do so to a lesser extent than those to whom that task would fall principally. The homemakers' primary tasks would include the bearing, raising, and nurturance of children, and the maintenance of a hab-

---

[18] Agriculture and animal husbandry will be referred to collectively as "agriculture."

[19] J.M. ROBERTS, *supra* at 51.

itable home site, thus freeing both the laborers in the field and the artisans to pursue their work unimpeded of at least the most time consuming obligations of home and child. In return for these responsibilities, the homemakers would rely on the sowers and the reapers, and also the artisans, to share on an equivalence what they had produced.

The significance of these simple group structures, duties, and expectations lay in their promise of and similarity to the more complex duties and expectations that would develop as agriculture permitted the development of larger and more concentrated communities. These larger social or societal groupings would, with the advent of writing and symbolic communication, become the earliest instance of what is now called civilization. And it is in the writings of the earliest civilizations that responsibility for wrongdoing, or tort law, were created.

# III. DEVELOPING HISTORICAL EXAMPLES OF EFFICIENT FORM AND FUNCTION

## A. MESOPOTAMIAN LAW

The watershed discovery and translation of approximately three thousand years of law from the cradle of civilization, framed by the Tigris and the Euphrates Rivers, permitted research, evaluation, and legal synthesis of myriad legal matters. Mesopotamian ancients were, many claim, the first to write their laws in an organized and lasting manner.[20] As discovered by later archaeologists, these laws were collected in the Laws of Hammurabi, the Laws of Ur-Nammu, and the Laws of Lipit-Ishtar.[21] The epoch contemplated by these principal bodies of law is approximately 4600 B.C. to 1600 B.C., or three millennia. Although these legal codes were promulgated, published, and repub-

---

[20] RUSS VERSTEEG, EASLY MESOPOTAMIAN LAW 3 (2000). Several of the references to the principal Mesopotamian codes derive from this work.

[21] *Id.*

lished under the aegises of different rulers and over such a long period of time, scholars suggest that the "similarities"[22] in the form of the "academic tradition," and the provisions themselves, "suggest enduring commonalities in the customary law of Babylonia."[23] For present purposes, the legal themes and systems to be discussed will be those of such form and substance as the ancients devoted to systems of customary, normative, and eventually statutory law governing the rights of individuals to be free from wrongful injury, property damage, or coerced takings initiated by others.

For all that is apparent, Hammurabi himself intended that his law reconcile wrongs and bring justice to those aggrieved. His unmistakable goal was the economic stability and enhancement of his people.[24] Before the Laws of Hammurabi there were published the Laws of King Ur-Nami (2112–2095 B.C.). In the Mesopotamian law collections, the provisions characteristically begin with an "if" clause (the *prostasis*), and end with a "then" clause (the *apodosis*). Thus, the *prostasis* identifies a circumstance or activity that the lawmakers concluded needed a legal rule, whereas the *apodosis* describes the legal consequences for the creation of such a circumstance or the engagement in such activity.[25] This approach bears significant markings of code-based law throughout the ages and is widely followed today.

Review by scholars has revealed examples of remedies for civil wrongs in which Mesopotamian law responded to the *delict* by penalizing, by money judgment, the wrongful disposition (or eradication) of another's right or vested expectancy. This approach was of particular and felt economic significance in instances when the wronged individual was in a weaker social or economic position than the wrongdoer. Thus, the Laws of Ur-Nami provided that a father whose daughter is promised to a man, but who gave the daughter in marriage to another, must compensate the disappointed man

[22] *Id.* at 5, *quoting* Raymond Westbrook, *Slave and Master in Near Eastern Law*, 70 CHICAGO KENT L. REV. 1631, 1634 (1995).

[23] *Id.* at 5, quoting Robert C. Elllickson, Charles D. A. Thorland, *Ancient Land Use Law: Mesopotamia, Egypt, Israel*, 70 CHICAGO KENT L. REV. 321, 331 (1995) (internal citations omitted).

[24] *Id.*

[25] *Id.* at 11.

twice the property value of what the promise of marriage had brought into the household.[26]

As was true particularly of early legal formulations, the law of Mesopotamia emphasized the protection of person, property, and commerce from forced divestiture of a right or a prerogative. Regarding navigation, a collision between two boats on a body of water having a perceptible upstream and downstream would trigger a presumption of fault on the part of the upstream captain, on the logic – faulty or not – that the upstream captain had a greater opportunity to reduce avoidable accidents than did his counterpart, as the former would be traveling at a slower speed.[27]

A subtle interplay between norms of duty, nuisance and causation is evident in the following rule: Neighbors were bound by a rule that served to deter letting one's unoccupied land elevate a risk of trespass or burglary to the neighboring property. The Law of Lipit-Ishtar provided that upon notice from one neighbor that a second neighbor's unattended property provided access to the complainant's property by potential robbers, that should a robbery occur, the inattentive neighbor would be liable for any harm to the complainant's home or property.[28] Particularly harsh legal consequences might be visited on the landowner who failed to contain his irrigation canals, as flooding of the water might "result not only in leaving crops and cattle dry and parched in one point, but also widespread floods in another part of the district."[29] In the simple case involving only damage to grain, replacement of a like amount might give sufficient remedy. But an unmistakable deterrence of more severe consequences would be clear to those knowing that should the careless farmer be unable to replace the grain, the neighbors might be permitted to sell his property and to sell him into slavery to achieve justice.[30]

---

[26] *Ur-nami* 9.

[27] DRIVER AND MILLS, BABYLONIAN LAW § 431 –32, referenced in VERSTEEG at 130.

[28] *Lipit-Ishtar* § 11.

[29] DRIVER AND MILLS, BABYLONIAN LAW 50, *from* VERSTEEG at 136.

[30] *Hammurabi* § 54. *See also* Raymond Westbrook, *Slave and Master*, 70 CHICAGO KENT L. REV. 1631, 1644 (1995).

## B. EARLY RELIGION – THE LAW OF THE TORAH

It is accepted that much of modern society was suckled at the breast of faith, and that much of mankind's law and morality "were born of religion."[31] Often this faith partook of earlier myth, and transformed it to suit the extant needs of the time and the place. And, invariably, the adopted faith adopted strictures against conduct that was inconsistent with the bountiful sustenance of the whole.

The Law of the Torah, with its accompanying interpretation in the Talmud, cannot be described as either ancient or modern, as it is both.[32] It represents the longest continuum of international private law that exists. The domain of the Law of the Torah is, strictly speaking, among the population of observing Jews. It is, though, of a piece with the same Mosaic law that is the foundation of Christianity,[33] and thus its influence has always reached and continues to reach populations and cultures greatly exceeding in number its Jewish adherents.

Israel, and its law, did not differentiate "between the secular and religious realms." Rather, all of Jewish life "was to be lived under Yahweh's command, within his covenant."[34] Included among the contributions of Hebraic law to western legal development was the recognition that man-made law must give way to God-given, moral law should the two be in conflict.[35] The Torah and

---

[31] Elementary Forms *supra* at 87.

[32] Fittingly, religious law – including but not limited to the Law of the Torah – continues to this day to be a part of the weave of both customary law and of national legislation. For example, Hon H. W. Tambiah QC, Principles of Ceylon Law 111 (1972) ("Religion is a source of law through custom or legislation. Difficult questions arise as to the relations between general law and special customary law.").

[33] The gravitational interplay between Hebrew scripture and Greek philosophy is well treated in other works. For example, Bertrand Russell, A History of Western Philosophy 326–27 (1945).

[34] Bernard W. Anderson, Understanding the Old Testament 96 (2d ed.) (1966). *See also* Dennis Lloyd, *supra* at 49–50 (explaining that Hebrew law, the revealed law of the Almighty God and embodied in the Law of Moses and later prophets, "showed that merely man-made laws could not stand or possess any validity whatever in the face of divine laws which the rulers themselves were not competent to reveal or interpret."

[35] Lloyd, *supra* at 50.

its interpretations guide Jews in a very broad spectrum of individual and common pursuits. Naturally, this Chapter is devoted only to such strictures as pertain to the identification of (1) civil wrongs to others; (2) the remedies for such wrongs; and (3) the sensitivity of such written or traditional law to norms of economic efficiency, and deterrence.

The Torah includes the word of God as revealed in the books of Genesis, Exodus, Leviticus, Numbers, and Deuteronomy.[36] These writings, the sociolegal bedrock of Judaism, contain copious treatments, sometimes systematized, of how society ought respond to civil wrongs, and the reasons therefore. Whereas much Western law, particularly modern Western law, is phrased in prohibitory terms, Halakhic law is more apt to treat its society of believers in terms of duty, or put otherwise, "The observant Jew should..."[37] Many of these duties are remarkably fuller and more demanding than those recognized in other systematized bodies of law. For example, within the Torah, Leviticus states that a person who stands by while another is put at risk commits a "crime of omission."[38] In the United States and the majority of other legal systems, there is no *ab initio* duty to come to another's aid; rather, such a duty arises only in particular circumstances. The approach stated in Leviticus doubtless describes the higher and more moral road. But might its rationale also resonate in some other social premium important to Jewish society? Apart from obedience to God, another central and seemingly perpetual goal of Jews has been mere survival. It requires no particular boldness to recognize that violence to the persons or the property of members of the Jewish community has always been a closely-held awareness of Jewish communities.[39]

A predicate to the advancement of the welfare, progress, and justice of a social group or a state is of course that the group survive as a human commu-

---

[36] This corresponds to what Christians would later recognize as the first five and similarly named Books of their First Covenant.

[37] J. David Bleich, *Contemporary Halakhic Problems* 204 n. 15, *referenced in* CONTRASTS IN AMERICAN AND JEWISH LAW 226 (Daniel Pollack, ed.) (2001).

[38] CONTRASTS, *id.* at 226 (Ch. 6, Daniel Pollack, Naphtali Harcztark, Erin McGrath, Karen R. Cavanaugh, *The Capacity of a Mentally Retarded Person to Consent: An American and a Jewish Legal Perspective*).

[39] *Compare* Ernest J. Weinrib, *The Case for a Duty to Rescue*, 90 YALE L. J. 247 (1980).

nity. As the chosen people with no property of their own, it is proven that the historical Jews were set on by army after army, and it is quite certain that what behavior, from simply cruel to savage, that was not visited on them collectively was surely inflicted on them in discrete, individual and unrecorded incidents. An interpretation that the Law of God required spontaneous protection of other Jews from danger might be seen as a simple and justifiable requirement of the survival of Judaism and its believers.

The *Code of the Covenant*, set out at Exodus 24: 3 – 8, describes rights and restrictions regarding "slaves, cattle, fields, vineyards and houses."[40] The civil code-like provisions therein are replete with strictures that provide guidance to the community regarding permissible and impermissible community conduct as it affects land, material, and economic transactions. One borrowing another's cloak must return it by nightfall.[41] Should one's bull gore a man, the bull is to be stoned.[42] Even an unworthy thought process that might lead to wasteful bickering or more is enjoined in the admonition "Thou shalt not covet thy neighbor's house, ... nor his ass[.]"[43]

The Talmud and harmonious rabbinical writings are explicit in the condemnation of waste. The "waste of the resources of this universe [are] prohibited because of *bal tashit*."[44] Such prohibitions include the wasting of food or fuel, the burning of furniture, and the unnecessary killing of animals.[45]

---

[40] Roland de Vaux, Ancient Israel 143 (1961), *from* Smith and Weisstub, *supra* at

[41] Exodus 22: 25.

[42] Exodus 18: 28.

[43] Exodus 20: 17.

[44] Contrasts, *supra* at 110 (Ch. 4, Daniel Pollack, Jonathan Reis, Ruth Sonshine, Karen R. Cavanaugh, *Liability for Environmental Damage: An American and a Jewish Legal Perspective*).

[45] Shabbat 67b; 129a; Chullin 7b; Sanhedrin 100b at *id.*

# IV. EARLY PHILOSOPHICAL TENETS FOR
# IDEAL INDIVIDUAL AND COLLECTIVE PURSUITS

## A. HELLENIC

For a philosophical epoch of greater significance than any other, the Hellenists defined virtue, morality, and ethics in terms that remain the foundation of Western philosophy. Putting aside only a few proponents of distracting philosophic anomalies, the Greek philosophers first identified an ideal of individual behaviors that accented study, modesty in thought and deed, and respect of law. Second, the Hellenist thinkers envisioned a society (at that point a city state) of harmony, accepted strata of skill and task, and, naturally again, respect of law.

However utopian may have been the imagination of such a city state as being led by a politically detached, supremely wise Philosopher-King, the more important instruction is that the Hellenist image of a society and its individual participants was one of social harmony, rewards in the measure of neither more nor less than one's just deserts, and subordination to law. Although undemocratic in many respects, and indeed slave-holding, for a pre-democratic, progressive and just ideal evaluated in recognition of its time, the Greece of this era measures up respectably.

As explained in Chapter 2, hints of the political circumstances in which Stoics found themselves can be found in the graphics handed down to us from antiquity that portray the various philosophers either speaking to small groups or, from all that appears, to no one at all. There are no representations of them speaking in political groups, or advising political representatives. The reason for this seeming isolation of the philosophers from the political process is that by the time of much of the enduring work of the most influential Greek philosophers, political power in the Greek mainland had passed over to the Macedonians. This political powerlessness necessarily affected the focus of many of the philosophers from the politically tinted "How can men create a good state?" to such generally moral issues such as "individual virtue and salvation" and the attendant question "How can men be virtuous in a wicked world, or happy in a world of suffering."[46]

---

[46] *Plato's Republic*, Book IV, in PLATO 448–49 (Buchanan, ed.) (2003) (hereinafter

The end sought by Socrates was happiness. How can a philosophy grounded in the pursuit of "happiness" influence its adherents, much less any larger population, in the ways of efficient civil justice, the ostensible theme of this section? The answer is that to Socrates and other mainstream Hellenic thinkers, happiness could only be achieved through pursuit of the virtuous life, and both the vision and the reality of the virtuous life are suffused with themes of justice, waste avoidance, and deterrence of unjust enrichment. The entire structure of Socrates' ethics is permeated by the principle of avoidance of doing harm.[47] In parts of his lectures Socrates hypothesizes that perhaps the identifying marker of all acts of "justice" were simply "returning what was owed."[48] For the individual, justice pertained not to the "outward man" but, rather, to the "inward man." The just man "sets in order his own inner life, and is his own master and his own law, and [is] at peace with himself." For the just man, reason governs "spirit" and "desire."[49]

To Socrates, self-knowledge was the very essence of virtue. Without such self-knowledge, any man's accumulation of wealth or power would leave one "baffled[,] ... disappointed[,]...and unable to profit ..." from any success. Rejecting the Sophists' lax attitudes toward generalizable moral or ethical standards, Socrates thought that to be effective self-knowledge must become so familiar to the adherent that it, and its attendant guidance in virtuous and ethical matters, would be worn like one's very skin.[50] To Socrates, wisdom, or self-knowledge, was to be found, at least in one's early years, through the teaching of wise men. And according to Socrates' account there was a broad-based societal subscription to this goal. As all men "have a mutual interest in the justice and virtue of one another," Plato records, "this is the reason why everyone is so ready to teach justice and the laws[.]"[51]

To Socrates, temperance conveyed a meaning different than the modern

---

PLATO).

[47]  *Id.* at 164.

[48]  *Id.* at 159–60.

[49]  BERTRAND RUSSELL, A HISTORY OF WESTERN PHILOSOPHY 230 (1945).

[50]  NORMAN P. STALLKNECHT, ROBERT S. BRUMBAUGH, THE SPIRIT OF WESTERN PHILOSOPHY 53, 54 (1950).

[51]  Plato, *Protagoras*, in PLATO, at 69, *supra*.

implication of simple forbearance, be it avoidance of alcohol or any other ine-briant. Instead, temperance meant the avoidance of "folly" or acting "fool-ishly." He nevertheless wonders whether virtue was the sum of the parts "justice," "temperance," and "holiness" when he spoke in these words to Pro-tagoras: "[W]hether virtue is one whole, of which justice and temperance and holiness are parts; or whether all these are only names of one and the same thing: that is the doubt which still lingers in my mind."[52]

Further to the question of *why* a man should choose the path of justice over injustice, Socrates termed the tension as one of "comparative advantage." He posed the issue as this: "Which is the more profitable, to be just and to act justly and practice virtue whether seen or unseen by gods and men, or to be unjust and act unjustly, if only unpunished and unreformed?"[53] Socrates hypothesized the "tyrannical" man, one in whom "the reasoning ... power is asleep[,]" and asked "[H]ow does he live, in happiness or in misery?" Here Socrates imagines a man of pure impulsivity, a man capable of any "folly or crime[.]" He follows the sad and desperate path of this man, and states that his "drunken, lustful, [and] passionate" habits will require "feasts and carousals and revelings" to sat-isfy him. Soon such revenues as he may have are spent. In order to continue to feed his uncontrolled desires, the tyrannical man seeks to "discover whom he can defraud of his money, in order that he may gratify [his desires]."[54] If his parents do not voluntarily submit to his demands, he will try "to cheat and de-ceive them[,]" and if this fails, he will "use force and plunder them."[55]

The intemperate and unjust man is doomed to a spiral of ever-worsening degradation, Socrates warns. This tyrannical man, Socrates and Adeimantus conclude, is "ill governed in his own person"[56] knows no true friends, as when they have "gained their point" from another "they know him no more"; and never knows "true freedom," as he is a simple instrument of his desires, and is "the most miserable" of men.[57]

---

[52] *Id.* at 72, 75 - 76.

[53] PLATO'S REPUBLIC, Book IV, in PLATO, *supra* at 451.

[54] PLATO'S REPUBLIC, Book IX, *id.* at 625, 628.

[55] PLATO'S REPUBLIC, Book X, *id.* at 680.

[56] PLATO'S REPUBLIC, Book IX, *id.* at 637.

Socrates' encomium of temperance in all pursuits is of course quite analogous to the recognition in later tort theory of the central role of self-restraint. Socrates characterizes as "invalids" those who "hav[e] no self-restraint, [and] will not leave of their habits of intemperance." In essence, Socrates thought temperance could be achieved by "a man being his own master," which is to say, "the ordering or controlling of certain pleasures or desires," and the avoidance of "the meaner desires."

Socrates compares evil to bodily illness. As a bodily illness can corrupt and destroy bodily health, so, too, can evil destroy a man's soul: "Does the injustice or other evil which exists in the soul waste and consume her?"[58] and do they not "by attaching to the soul and inhering in her at last bring her to her death, and so separate her from the body?"[59]

Socrates subscribes fully to the existence of a heaven and a hell, as is illustrated by the story he tells Glaucon of Er, the son of Armenius, whose body, after he has fallen in battle, is seemingly uncorrupted by death. On the twelfth day, and prior to his burial, he awakens and tells a tale of men being summoned to justice in a mysterious place in which men's deeds are "fastened on their backs." The good and the just are led to a "meadow, where they encamped as at a festival[,]" whereas those found unjust or evil are thrown into a hell in which their punishments are tenfold the average of a man's years, or ten times one thousand in the mythical account.[60]

Plato's Socrates "argued for the identity of law *and* morality."[61] Reverence for the law followed from recognition of an implied agreement, to Dennis Lloyd, "an early form of social contract," for adhering to the law irrespective of the consequences.[62] Morality, by contrast, would never override the articulated law of the State. While morality might persuade the individual to conclude that the existing law was immoral or unjust, when the two were in

[57] *Id.* at 631, 632

[58] Plato's Republic, Book X, *id.* at 680.

[59] *Id.*

[60] Plato's Republic, Book X, in Plato, *supra* at 687, 688.

[61] Dennis Lloyd, *supra* (emphasis added).

[62] *Id.*

conflict, the disputant's "duty" is "confined to trying to persuade the state of its moral error."[63] In the Hellenic dialogues of Socrates, it is evident that justice entails calling into "account" the transgressor, or a pre-Aristotelian expression of corrective justice. As the Sophist Protagoras suggests in Plato's *Protagoras*, the City stands in the shoes of the schoolmaster in giving to "young men" the laws to be followed. "[T]he laws," states Protagoras, "which were the invention of good lawgivers living in the olden time; these were given to the young man in order to guide him in his conduct whether he is commanding or obeying[.]" "[H]e who transgresses them[,]" Protagoras continues, "is to be corrected, or in other words, called into account."[64]

Socrates himself speaks even more forcefully of the corrective importance of the defect of misbehavior, and of the deterrent value of punishment. In Book XI of PLATO'S REPUBLIC, Socrates tells Glaucon, no man "profits" from "undetected and unpunished" wrongdoing, as such a man "only gets worse[.]" To Socrates, it is better that the man be detected and punished in order that "the brutal part of his nature [be] silenced and humanized[,]" and that "the gentler element in him is liberated[.]" The man's "whole soul is perfected and ennobled by the acquirement of justice and temperance and wisdom[.]"[65] Socrates discouraged in the most direct terms individual miserliness, hoarding, and a spirit of contention and ungoverned ambition. To him, these unworthy characteristics in men were "due to the prevalence of the passionate or spirited element," uncontained by temperance and reason.[66]

To Socrates, the ideal "State" was largely an extrapolation of the ideal man. The State should, Socrates states, have "political virtues" of "wisdom, temperance, [and] courage" that could stand on a parity with Socrates' ideal for the individual.[67] For Socrates, however, identification and description of the fourth virtue, "justice," was more rarified and elusive, and Socrates comments tellingly: "The last of those qualities which make a state virtuous must be jus-

---

[63] *Id.*

[64] PLATO'S REPUBLIC, Book IV, in PLATO, *supra* at 432.

[65] PLATO'S REPUBLIC, Book IX, *id.* at 655.

[66] PLATO'S REPUBLIC, Book VIII, *id.* at 592.

[67] PLATO'S REPUBLIC, Book IV, in PLATO, *supra* at 422, 425, 430–31, 434.

tice, if only we knew what that was."[68] A life of virtue and ethics could only be sustained in "a law abiding and orderly society."[69] Whatever such state-sanctioned justice might be, Socrates commended abidance with existing law, a commitment that ultimately led to his rejection of opportunities to flee his death sentence.

Hellenist thinking cannot be reduced to the aphorism "virtue is its own reward." Rather, there were specific rewards associated with a life of virtue, as well as real or imagined disincentives to the adoption of a baser life and the collateral degrading pursuits associated therewith. Time and time again the philosophers stated that a life of excess, be it eating, drinking, or both, incapacitated the actor from realization of the contributions available to and expected of citizens of virtue.[70]

To both Plato and Socrates, the just man would be content, if not happy, and the unjust man miserable.[71] In addition, and more specifically, such excesses invited physical illness and impairment, a certain departure from God's, or a god's, charge to mankind.

For those who might be tempted to depart from a good life, Hellenic writing portrayed strong deterrents, a Sword of Damocles writ large. At an individual level, the writings repeatedly allude to the dissipating results of a life of excess, to wit, personal physical deterioration, coupled with personal and communal moral degradation. At such time as man should shed his mortal coil, Socrates and other believers in reincarnation wrote of another reason why a man should choose the path of good. Incapable of disproof and widely believed, Socrates and others propounded the belief that they had lived before in other forms, and that after their demise they would be reincarnated in some animal form.[72] If a person had led a virtuous life, he would be reincarnated in

---

[68] *Id.* at 434.

[69] *Id.* at 59.

[70] To Protagoras Socrates spoke of the physical dangers of excess, stating that "pleasure for the moment . . . lay[s] up for your future life diseases and poverty, and many other similar evils[.]" *Plato's Lysis*, in Socratic Discourse by Plato and Xenophon 288 (J. Wright transl.) (A.D. Lindsay, ed.) (1925).

[71] Anthony Gottlieb, *supra* at 174.

[72] *See* discussion of the choices for their future reincarnation by a panoply of demigods

the form of an animal respected by man, such as a horse. If in his life a man had strayed from the life of virtue, his just desserts might well be reincarnation as an insect, perhaps even a dung beetle.

In Plato's version of Socrates' words, even if the definition of "justice" might be elusive, that "justice" is efficient is quite clear. Even more specifically, the lasting philosophy of this age stated that individual good and justice were, in fact, more than efficient – they were *profitable*. Socrates states just this: "On what ground, then, can we say that it is profitable for a man to be unjust or self-indulgent or to do any disgraceful act which will make him a worse man, though he can gain money and power?" Happiness and profit inure to the man who, alternatively, "tame[s] the brute" within, and is "not be carried away by the vulgar notion of happiness being heaping up an unbounded store[,]" but instead follows the rule of wisdom and law encouraging "support to every member of the community, and also of the government of children[.]"[73]

A principal means to the end of justice, to Plato, was education to such a level of legal sophistication that the individual would learn understanding of and respect for the legal process, including such legal process as might pertain to the redress of injury. This is revealed in Socrates' dialogue with Adeimantus in Book IV of THE REPUBLIC. Here Socrates states plainly that it is through education that the individual learns "about the business of the *agora*, and the ordinary dealings between man and man, or again about dealings with artisans; about insult and injury, or the commencement of actions, and the appointment of juries[.]"[74]

Returning what was owed, in effect giving up the actual or conceptual unjust enrichment associated with a wrongful taking, is of course a core model for the appropriate remediation of unconsented-to harm, a concept that is the darling of corrective justice and efficiency advocates alike. It is also part and parcel to the analysis of Aristotle, in NICHOMACHEAN ETHICS Book V, Ch. 2, in which "The Thinker" is credited with laying the corner-stone of the cor-

---

by Socrates in his recitation of the story of Er. Book X, PLATO'S REPUBLIC, in PLATO, *supra* at 694–95.

[73] THE REPUBLIC OF PLATO 318–320 (Francis McDonald Cornford, transl.) (1969).

[74] PLATO'S REPUBLIC, BOOK IV, in PLATO, *supra* at 421 –422.

rective justice principles of today's common law,[75] although as suggested the logic has equivalent bearing on economic considerations. Aristotle's understanding was that corrective justice would enable restoration to the victim of the *status quo ante major*, insofar as a monetary award or an injunction can do so.[76] Under the Aristotelian principle of *diorthotikos*, or "making straight," "at the remedy phase the court will attempt to equalize things by means of the penalty, taking away from the gain of the wrong-doer." Whether the wrongdoer's gain is monetary, or measured in property, or the community's valuation of a personal physical injury consequent to the defendant's wrongful act, by imposing a remedy approximating the actor's wrongful appropriation and "loss" to the sufferer, "the judge restores equality.... "[77]

Aristotle classified among the diverse "involuntary" transactions that would invite rectification of "clandestine" wrongs "theft, adultery, poisoning, ...false witness[;]" and "violent" wrongs, including "assault, imprisonment, ... robbery with violence, ... abuse, [and] insult."[78] He proceeds to distinguish between excusable harm and harm for which rectification may appropriately be sought. For an involuntary harm, such as when "A takes B's hand and therewith strikes C[,]" or for acts pursuant to "ignorance," a more nuanced legal response is indicated. Even for such involuntary acts as "violat[e] proportion or equality," Aristotle suggests opaquely, some should be excused, whereas others should not be excused. As to voluntary and harmful acts attributable to ignorance, Aristotle distinguishes between acts in which the ignorance is excusable and acts in which the ignorance is not.[79] The former, which we might today

---

[75] "[T]he law . . . treats the parties as equal, and asks only if one is the author and the other the victim of injustice or if the one inflicted and the other has sustained an injury. Injustice in this sense is unfair or unequal, and the endeavor of the judge is to equalize it." ARISTOTLE, NICOMACHEAN ETHICS 154 (J. Welldon trans., 1987), discussed in David G. Owen, *The Moral Foundations of Punitive Damages*, 40 ALA. L. REV. 705, 707–08 & n.6 (1989).

[76] "Therefore the just is intermediate between a sort of gain and a sort of loss, *viz*, those which are involuntary; it consists in having an equal amount before and after the transaction." *Id.* at Ch. 4, p. 407.

[77] THE COMPLETE WORKS OF ARISTOTLE 786 (Jonathan Barnes ed.) (1984).

[78] ARISTOTLE, NICOMACHEAN ETHICS Bk. 5, Ch. 2 in INTRODUCTION TO ARISTOTLE 402 (Richard McKeon, ed.) (1947).

characterize as innocent, would not prompt remediation, whereas the latter would. Thus, Aristotle describes an act from which injury results "contrary to reasonable expectation" as a "misadventure," and forgivable at law.[80] To Aristotle, an unintentional act[81] that causes harm, but in which such harm "is not contrary to reasonable expectation[,]" constitutes not a misadventure but a "mistake." To Aristotle, "mistake" is a fault-based designation. The example used is redolent of the sensibility of what would be termed "negligence" in today's nomenclature, *e.g.*, a man throwing an object "not with intent to wound but only to prick[.]" This man, although not acting with an intent to wound another in any significant way, would nonetheless be subject to an obligation in indemnity, for to Aristotle, when "a man makes a mistake[;] ... the fault originates in him[.]"[82]

Aristotle's famous "Golden Mean" hypothesizes that virtue analyzed linearly is the mean between two extremes. Either extreme is a vice. So, for example, if appropriate self-sustenance is a virtue, then it follows that, at one extreme, self-denial to the point of ill health is a vice. At the other extreme, gluttony is a vice. Importantly, Aristotle does not propose distributive justice, in the sense that a man may remedy his antecedent unequal position vis-a-vis another.[83] Rather, only the prospect of corrective justice is a tool that is so confined as to provide that the only remedies available to the judge are those that work to rectify the marginal inequality that the wrongdoing has imposed.[84]

---

[79]  *Id.* at 414.

[80]  *Id.* at 415.

[81]  An act that "does not imply vice[.]" *Id.*

[82]  *Id.*

[83]  To Aristotle: "Justice (contrary to our own view) implies that members of the community possess unequal standing. That which ensures justice, whether it is with regard to the distribution of the prizes of life or the adjudication of conflicts, or the regulation of mutual services is good since it is required . . . for the continuance of the group. Normativity, then, is inseparable from actuality." ESSAYS OF KARL POLANYI, *supra* at 83.

[84]  NICOMACHEAN ETHICS, *supra* Ch. 3 at 403 : "[A]wards should be made "according to merit"; for all men agree that what is just in distribution must be according to merit in some sense, though they do not all specify the same sort of merit[.]"

## B. ROMAN LAW

It is recognized generally that the Romans added little to the metaphysics of law. Nevertheless, Roman law represents the watershed between the law of ancient society and that of modern society. As suggested by Sir Henry Sumner Maine, the rights and the duties under law of ancient society derived from status, or "a man's position in the family," whereas under Roman law and thereafter, "rights and duties derived from bilateral arrangements."[85]

Regarding delicts, or harms that were neither crimes nor grounded in contract, it became the special province of Roman lawyers and lawmakers to record and categorize a sprawling array of specific wrongs and consequent remedies. This approach of Roman law would become the origin of code-based law that governs European lawmaking to this day.

Cicero, the Roman orator, wrote of the truth of an ethic that sounded simultaneously in terms of corrective justice and efficiency-deterrence. In *On Moral Duties* he wrote that even after "retribution and punishment" have been dealt to the transgressor, the person who has been dealt the wrong owes a duty to bring a close to any such misadventure by permitting a gesture such as repentance or apology. From the extension to the wrong-doer of the opportunity to apologize or to repent could be reaped the immediate good of reducing the likelihood that he would "repea[t] the offense," as well as the broader and eventual good of "deter[ing] others from injustice."[86]

Cicero further propounded a cluster of maxims that if followed could conduce to Pareto Superior changes, in the sense that the actor would be no worse off and the affected party or parties would be better off. As to persons beyond a benefactor's core family or kinship group, to Cicero there existed a duty to the entire world as to such things "we receive with profit and give without loss." Thus, in order that we may receive such blessings as are identified in the maxims such as "Keep no one from a running stream[;]" or "Let anyone who pleases take a light from your fire[;]" or "Give honest advice to a man in doubt[;]" Cicero writes, it follows that we

---

[85] ESSAYS OF POLANYI, *supra* at 82–83.

[86] *On Moral Duties* 16, in BASIC WORKS OF CICERO 16 (Moses Hadas, ed.) (1951).

must be willing to give likewise of the same in order to "contribute to the common weal."[87]

Two of the *delicts* of greatest importance were damage to property, real and personal, and personal physical harm to others, giving rise to the *action inuriarum*. The victim could bring an action for "profitable amends," or money damages, or "honorable amends," which is to say, a formal and public apology. The latter remedy would most likely arise in a setting of a dignitary tort, such as defamation. Roman jurists and the Roman legal community were committed to the delineation between what is "just and what unjust," and therefore the Institutes of Justinian and other sources of Roman law reflected an endeavor to "give each man his due right," and comprise "precepts" to all Romans "to live justly, not to injure another and to render to each his own."[88]

The Institutes included rules that reveal numerous strictures against the imposition of one's will over the rights of a neighbor, and strong deterrents for the disregard thereof. Specifically as to urban estates, in Book III, Title II Para. 2 there was a prohibition on the obstruction of a neighbor's view,[89] a rule bearing a resemblance to one recognized today that limits a neighbor's liberty to interfere with "ancient lights." In another notable example, pertaining to what would today be called the law of private nuisance or trespass, a provision of Roman law goes so far as to detail a preference that adjoining landowners bargain in advance for agreement as to contemporaneous uses of land that might trigger dispute. In Book III Para. 4, the Institutes provide that one "wishing to create" such a right of usage "should do so by pacts and stipulations." A testator of land may impose such agreements reached on his heirs, including limitations on building height, obstruction of light, or introduction of a beam into a common wall, or the construction of a catch for a cistern, an easement of passage, or a right of way to water.[90]

These last two examples reflect a clear preference for *ex ante* bargaining

---

[87]  *Id.* at 23.

[88]  THE INSTITUTES OF JUSTINIAN, Book I, Preamble; para. 1 ; para. 3, in THE INSTITUTES OF JUSTINIAN 84, 85 (J. A. C. Thomas trans.) (1975).

[89]  The Digest (or *Pandects*) Book III Title II para. 2., para. 3 at *id.*

[90]  THE INSTITUTES OF JUSTINIAN Book III para. 4, at 84, 85.

over economically wasteful *ex post* dispute resolution. The provision permitting the testator to bind his heirs to any such agreement is additionally efficient in a manner akin to the approach that was taken later and famously by Justice Bergen in the cement plant nuisance case of *Boomer v. Atlantic Cement Co., Inc.*,[91] in which the court's award of damages ensured that its disposition of the matter would be indeed a one-time resolution of the dispute by requiring that the disposition of the claim be entered and recorded as a permanent servitude on the land.

# VI. MODERN ASSIGNMENT OF ECONOMIC NORMS

## A. CUSTOMARY LAW

The organized law of the modern state is a fairly recent phenomenon when compared to the existence of effective and nuanced customary law around which pre-modern societies organized. For both ancient and modern societies, and irrespective of whether that society developed a written law, written or unwritten law is affected by "underlying social norms which determine much of its functioning." This customary law has been described as "living law."[92]

In the historical development of tort law, customary law has regularly followed social norms in giving form, context and content to socio-legal principles.[93] That such law must for the most part conform to societal custom was urged by writers as early as Thomas Aquinas. At such later time as a culture or a nation-state has begun to render its law in the form of written adjudicatory rulings, or legal codes, customary law characteristically diminishes in its significance as an engine for resolution of disputes. For example, in England during the period of the conquest of Scotland, approximately 1290-1305, there

---

[91]   257 N.E.2d 870 (N.Y. 1970).

[92]   Dennis Lloyd, *supra* at 227 (citation omitted).

[93]   *Id.* (discussion of the sources and growth of custom).

arose a "lawyer class" that was a moving force in "hardening customary [law] into legal rights[.]" With notable French influence, the theories of Roman law became ascendant,[94] and the recitation of and reliance upon customary norms receded proportionately. And yet it will be seen that in many cultures customary law continued to, it does today, inform legal development. In some settings, customary law sets parameters for later legal development, or even precludes later law that would contradict earlier custom.

The influence of Roman law on the development of European, Latin American, and Anglo-American law is commonly acknowledged. A concise tour of the lasting effects of customary law, Roman law, and its hybrid, Roman-Dutch law, on a particular national community – Ceylon (modern Sri Lanka) – well illustrates the systemic commitment to wealth maximization, avoidance of waste, and deterrence of behaviors inconsistent therewith.

For Celanese customary law to be considered valid for the purposes of modern adjudication, it must be (1) reasonable; (2) consistent with common law; (3) universal in application; and (4) grounded in antiquity.[95] Although the first and second standards might at first glance seem to subordinate customary law into insignificance, an additional look makes this approach appear more sensible. This is so because (1) as with common-law adjudication, as no court is required to apply common law that is unreasonable, it would be illogical to require application of customary law that was not reasonable; and (2) as both common law and customary law claim lineage in a society's reasoned conclusions as to legal standards best suited to societal well-being, customary law that was at war with common law on the same or similar subject would be presumptively defective in either its rationality or in its claimed representational authenticity.

In some legal systems, legal scholars remain oracles of greater or lesser significance. This was true of the Roman-Dutch tradition, in which schools of legal scholarship, or the scholars themselves were influential. There existed two schools of writers: (1) Grotius, van Leeuwen and Voet, who emphasized

---

[94]  J. R. GREEN, A SHORT HISTORY OF THE ENGLISH PEOPLE  204 (1878).

[95]  H. W. TAMBIAH, PRINCIPLES OF CEYLON LAWS 87–89 (1972). *See generally*, T. NADARAJA, THE LEGAL SYSTEM OF CEYLON IN ITS HISTORICAL SETTING (1972).

the Roman law antecedents of the developing hybrid law; and (2) an "historical school" that emphasized custom as the appropriate principal source of the law.[96] Although the Napoleonic Code superseded the Roman-Dutch law in Holland itself in the early Nineteenth Century, the great Dutch East and West Indian Trading Companies carried Roman-Dutch law into their settlements. So strong was the influence of custom in the Roman-Dutch tradition that, in principle at least, a statute could be rendered nugatory or obsolete by sufficient proof of a conflicting custom.[97]

Under the so-called *Lex Aquilia* of Roman-Dutch law, the Aquilian action required the claimant's showing of a wrongful act, patrimonial loss, and the defendant's fault, because of either the intentional nature of the act or negligence. Borrowing from British law applicable to nonintentional injuries, the law courts of Ceylon adopted the British concept that the plaintiff's claim in negligence must include proof that the defendant owed to plaintiff a duty.[98]

In Aquilian actions, no compensation would be awarded in the absence of physical injury, with physical injury classically defined as excluding emotional distress or dignitary harm. Regarding redressable injuries caused by the positive act of the defendant, should a person be in possession of a thing, including a chattel or an instrumentality, that had the potential for causing harm if not stewarded with care, the actor, owner, or manager would have a positive duty to exercise such care. Should another be injured because of the failure to take such care, liability could be imposed. Even a mere omission to act might be a stimulus to liability if the actor's omission was "connected with some prior positive act." Accordingly, a remedy might be available under the *Lex Aquilia* if the defendant had earlier "created a potentially dangerous state of things," and the failure to correct that caused the claimant's harm.

Various dimensions in the Roman-Dutch tradition recognized the society's

---

[96]  H. W. Tambiah, at *id.*; J. R. Green, *supra* note 94 at 148. The opinions most often referenced could be found in Johannes Voet, Commendtarius ad Pandectas (1698, 1704); Hugo Grotius, Inleiding Tot de Hallanesche Rechts- geleertheyd (2d ed.) (R. W. Lee ed.) (1953); and Simon van Leeuwen's Commentaries on Roman-Dutch Law (J. G. Kotze trans.) (1886).

[97]  *Id.*

[98]  *Id.* at 399.

commitment to the integrity of persons and property from forced takings. Assault was an *inuria*, and therefore redressable, on a showing of *contumelia*. For grazing animals that damaged another's property, if the animal's transgression involved the "animal acting contrary to nature of its class," the owner might be required to pay damages, or even be confronted with the potentially stronger deterrent of giving up the animal. Surely, too, a strong message of deterrence is found in the rule that a person finding another's animals on that person's property could impound them.[99]

For "intentional" wrongs, the intentional torts of today, the requisite intent, or *dolus*, was provided by the defendant's desire to accomplish the act, irrespective of whether he was aware that the act constituted an invasion of the plaintiff's rights. "*Culpa*" was interpreted as a "violation of a duty that [is] imposed by law[,]"[100] an approach revealing the influence of the British common law requirement that the tort plaintiff prove duty. The respondent could avoid liability by showing that the injury could not have been avoided even by the exercise of reasonable care. Furthermore, in order to avoid unjust enrichment, persons could not recover for claims arising from acts or activities to which they consented voluntarily.

For intentional torts such as false imprisonment, the third requirement of the *Lex Aquilia*, that of foreseeability, would be satisfied by a showing that the defendant intended the act. Then, as it is today, a reflection of the rigorous economic guardianship of customary law, Roman law, and Dutch law attached primacy to protection of property and economic rights, and imposed an almost automatic requirement of disgorgement of any unjust enrichment associated with the wrongful interference therewith. Trespass, or the willful and forcible entry into another's property, constituted *inuria*. As has been true for any successful socio-economic unit, the Roman-Dutch tra-

---

[99] *Id.* at 392–95, 399, 418, 420. For damage caused by trespassing dogs, the claimant would be required to show scienter. Within this approach there could be seen a strong overlay of moral blameworthiness: "It is doubtful whether Roman and Roman-Dutch writers regarded negligence objectively or subjectively, but partly under the influence of canon law, and its offspring natural law, the modern systems based on Roman law took culpa to imply moral blameworthiness." *Id.* at 39

[100] *Id.* at 397

dition recognized the rights of a person to protect his property from any form of unjust interference.[101]

At the same time, it was recognized that a landlord owed a duty to his tenants to take reasonable steps to protect them from injury caused by unsafe conditions on the land.[102] In what could be loosely styled as a public nuisance proscription, the Roman-Dutch customary law removed earlier Praetorian edicts prohibiting certain animals from sharing public places, and put in place of such strict prohibitions rules requiring the payment of damages.[103] Private nuisance, in turn, was seemingly remediable in an action for damages or for equitable relief.[104]

Roman-Dutch customary law includes at least one example of the law and its official apparatus not being required to stand idly by to await the social costs of an accident that will occur or that will continue to occur in circumstances in which the parties had not reached a prior agreement as to risks and rewards. Should a neighbor come to fear that a dangerous condition existed in his neighbor's house that, left unabated, might cause damage to the property of the complainant, the complainant could bring an action in what might today be called anticipatory nuisance demanding the neighbor's payment of security against such prospective and potential harm.[105]

## MODERN UNITED STATES ASSIGNMENT OF EFFICIENCY-BASED NORMS

The analysis of tort law has long emphasized its original and lasting tenets in the logic of corrective justice and morality. Another model, more recent but already essential to legal analysis, is that of economic efficiency. Economists, political scientists and legal scholars resort with increasing frequency and interest to the examination of economic truths within the function of injury law.

---

[101] *Id.* at 142, 397, 399, 418.

[102] *Id.* at 399.

[103] *Id.* at 422.

[104] *Id.* at 396.

[105] *Id.* at 422.

This examination has included evaluation of evolving decisional law against the measure of whether such decisions adhere, explicitly or silently, to goals of economic efficiency.

Chronologically, the Anglo-American development of the doctrine of liability for negligent acts causing harm to others or to their property followed a lengthy legal devotion to liability without fault, or strict liability.[106] Some scholars associated the perfection of fault-based liability, or negligence, with the Industrial Revolution in England.[107] However, observers seem not to have established satisfactorily whether the availability of negligence liability was a gesture of socio-legal benevolence to persons and chattels or quite the contrary: a legal prophylaxis that reduced the potential liability of businesses by requiring the putative plaintiff to prove not only injury and causation but also that the actor had proceeded with an absence of due care under the circumstances.[108]

It is established that (1) tort law is devoted to the protection of persons and property from unreasonable risk of harm; and (2) the actor's liability in tort is limited by concepts of reasonable foreseeability. Putting aside the cabined domain of truly strict liability, modern accident law is concerned primarily with the provision of reparations to persons suffering personal injury or property loss because of fault, with fault conventionally defined as a failure of others to act with due care under the circumstances.

Numerous analysts have identified a common-law tropism towards efficiency.[109] Importantly, scholars have also concluded that efficient rules of law

---

[106] *See generally* DAN B. DOBBS, THE LAW OF TORTS 259–63 (2000).

[107] The development of negligence law "was probably stimulated a good deal by the enormous increase of industrial machinery and by the invention of railways in particular." PERCY H. WINFIELD, THE PROVINCE OF THE LAW OF TORTS 404 (5th ed. 1950).

[108] Compare WINFIELD, *id.* ("At that time railway trains were notable for neither speed nor for safety. They killed any object from a Minister of State to a wandering cow, and this naturally reacted upon the law.") with Robert J. Kazorowski, *The Common-Law Basis of Nineteenth-Century Tort Law*, 51 OHIO S. L. J. 1 (1990) (referencing scholarly proponents of theory that negligence liability arose in a court-stimulated effort to moderate the liability of businesses and to permit devotion of industrial capital to production rather than to satisfaction of legal liability).

[109] For example, George L. Priest, *The Common Law Process and the Selection of Efficient Rules*, 6 J. LEG. STUD. 65 (1977); Ramona L. Paetzold & Steven L. Willborn, *The*

actually predict efficient litigation strategies, including settlement strategies.[110] Wes Parsons, even while disputing these premises, collected scholarship revealing in fact the broad range of cost internalization achievements of evolving common-law doctrine.[111] Included in Parson's review was scholarly attribution to the common law of accidents as "promot[ing] efficient resource allocation";[112] the efficiencies of the common law of rescue, salvage and Good Samaritan assistance;[113] and the efficiency of the economic loss rule in tort.[114]

A leading exponent of the efficiency role of the common law of tort has been Guido Calabresi. Calabresi has argued persuasively that in matters of compensation for accidents, civil liability should ordinarily be laid at the door of the "cheapest cost avoider," the actor who could most easily discover and inexpensively remediate the hazard. Together with A. Douglas Melamed, Calabresi has written that considerations of economic efficiency dictate placing the cost of accidents "on the party or activity which can most cheaply avoid them [.]"[115]

Ordinary economic rationales also have described the role of compensatory damages as an effective means of discouraging a potential torfeasor from bypassing the market, and by their substandard or risk-creating conduct injuring an unconsenting third party. Such conduct is wasteful, it is both posited and can be proved, in terms of identifiable accident costs. Better, theoretically at least, to pressure the actor into bargaining with any willing and knowing other for the right to expose him or her to risk.[116]

---

*Efficiency of the Common Law Reconsidered*, 14 GEO. MASON L. REV. 157 (1991).

[110] As stated by Ramona L. Paetzold and Steven L. Willborn, "[w]here both parties to a dispute have a continuing interest in precedent, the parties will settle if the existing precedent is efficient, but litigate if the precedent is inefficient." PAETZOLD & WILLBORN, *id.*

[111] Wes Parsons, *The Inefficient Common Law*, 93 YALE L.J. 862 (1983).

[112] Wes Parsons, *The Inefficient Common Law.*

[113] William A. Landes & Richard A. Posner, *Savors, Finders, Good Samaritans and Other Rescuers: An Economic Study of Law and Altruism*, 7 J. LEG. STUD. 83, 128 (1977).

[114] William Bishop, *Economic Loss in Tort*, 2 OXFORD J. LEG. STUD. 1, 2–3 (1982).

[115] Guido Calabresi & A. Douglas Melamed, *Property Rules, Liability Rules, and Inalienability*, 85 HARV. L. REV. 1089, 1096–97 (1972). *See also* MARK C. RUDERT, COVERING ACCIDENT COSTS: INSURANCE, LIABILITY AND TORT 29, 32–33 (1995).

[116] Today, one might think of the newest "*faux*" TV shows and derivatives thereof.

A lucid adoption of Calabresi and Melamed's approach is found in the Ninth Circuit decision of *Union Oil Co. v. Oppen*,[117] a California coastal oil spill case in which the court allowed commercial fishermen to recover from the defendant their business losses caused by lost fishing opportunity during a period of pollution. Noting some difficulties in applying the "best or cheapest cost avoider" approach in concrete circumstances, the court followed Calabresi and Melamed's predicate that it "exclude as potential cost avoiders those group activities which could avoid accident costs only at extremely high expense."[118] This approach, to the mind of the appeals court, militated against the conclusion that the cost of preventing or repositioning the loss should be borne directly by consumers (fishermen or seafood purchasers) in the form of precautionary measures (whatever they might hypothetically be), or by first party insurance. Rather, the court found, justice and efficiency were served by placing responsibility for the loss on the "best cost avoider," in this setting the defendant oil company. The court explained its reasoning:

> [T]he loss should be borne by the party who can best correct any error in allocation, if such there be, by acquiring the activity to which the party has been made liable. The capacity to "buy out" the plaintiffs if the burden is too great is, in essence, the real focus of Calabresi's approach. On this basis, there is no contest – the defendant's capacity is superior.[119]

Referencing a 1991 *American Law Institute Reporters' Study*, Steven D. Sugarman noted tartly "one of the last places to find lucid thinking about the desirable direction of tort law is in the published opinions of state and federal judges."[120] Although his complaint surely represents hyperbole for effect, Sugarman is correct in observing that discussion of tort principles in the decisional law is frequently colloquial, with courts often doing no more than lumping

---

[117]   501 F.2d 558 (9th Cir. 1974).

[118]   *Id.* at 569.

[119]   *Id.* at 569–570.

[120]   Steven D. Sugarman, *A Restatement of Torts*, 44 STAN.L.REV. 1163, 1165 (1992).

together as coextensive such objectives as expeditious claims resolution, reduced transaction costs, and efficiency. In congressional endeavors to normalize diverse segments of tort law, too, the discussion and fact-finding, in turn, frequently have been more polemic than informative.

Explicit judicial adoption of the tenets of either corrective justice or law and economics has been sporadic, and even when mentioned in decisions, either the expression or the application of the two theories is often inexact. Nevertheless, some courts have consciously elevated their jurisdiction's awareness of economic concepts in fashioning tort law. Illustrative is the Third Circuit's decision in *Whitehead v. St. Joe Lead Co.*,[121] a lead poisoning case in which the defendants included the suppliers of lead to plaintiff's industrial employer. Reversing summary judgment for defendants, the court observed:

> [I]t may well be that suppliers, acting individually or through their trade associations, are the most efficient cost avoiders. Certainly it could be found to be inefficient for many thousands of lead processors to individually duplicate the industrial hygiene research, design, and printing costs of a smaller number of lead suppliers.

Of like effect is the decision of the Wyoming Supreme Court in *Schneider National, Inc. v. Holland Hitch Co.*[122] There the court explicitly relied upon Richard Posner's "alternative care joint tortfeasor" evaluation to reach the conclusion that indemnity should not be available "where both actors have a 'joint care' obligation to avoid the injury." The court noted, however, that when the actors' culpability varied, that is, they were not *in pari delicto*, the higher relative fault of one defendant, the "lower cost avoider," would vest indemnity rights in the other tortfeasor.[123]

---

[121]   729 F.2d 238 (3 d Cir. 1984).

[122]   843 P.2d 561 (Wyo. 1992).

[123]   *Id.* at 575. *See also Ogle v. Caterpillar Tractor Co.*, 716 P.2d 334, 342 (Wyo. 1986). There the court stated:

> When a defective article enters the stream of commerce and an innocent person is hurt, it is better that the loss fall on the manufacturer, distributor

In the insurance declaratory judgment context, the dissenting opinion in *Insurance Co. of North America v. Forty-Eight Insulations, Inc.*,[124] proposed a "discoverability" rule for triggering insurance carrier coverage of asbestos claims, asserting that this approach would, relying on a least cost avoider rationale, provide incentives within the insured-insurer relationship that could hold the promise of reducing accident costs. Specifically, the dissent reasoned:

> The more "early" insurers that are liable upon a victim's exposure, the more likely it is that the potential harm will be discovered and the public warned. If an insurer sees that the product poses some risks, he may raise premiums accordingly. This may ultimately cause the manufacturer to remove the product from the market or to give better warnings in order to lower insurance premiums. This in turn reduces accident costs.

Whichever gloss is placed on economic analysis – its deterrent effect, or its ability to reduce accident costs – its concepts can be understood "even at the rudimentary level of jurists," at least according to Judge Patrick Higgenbotham. In *Louisiana ex rel. Guste v. M. V. Testbank*,[125] the renowned vessel collision case involving claims for economic loss not accompanied by physical damage to a proprietary interest, the Fifth Circuit Court of Appeals justified its refusal to permit such recovery and continued its adherence to the economic

---

or seller than on the innocent victim. . . . They are simply in the best position to either insure against the loss or spread the loss among all consumers of the product.

*Ogle* was later described by the Wyoming Supreme Court as an indication of how strict liability "introduced economic analysis to tort law." *Schneider Nat'l, supra* at 580. The *Schneider Nat'l* court proceeded to analogize *Ogle's* "risk allocation" theory to a "cheapest cost avoider" approach. *Id. See also Wilson v. Good Humor Corp.*, 757 F.2d 1293, 1306 n.13 (D.C. Cir. 1985) (identifying but not pursuing cheapest cost avoider analysis in action brought by parents of child fatally injured while crossing street to meet ice cream vending truck).

[124] 633 F.2d 1212 (6th Cir. 1980).

[125] 752 F.2d 109 (5th Cir. 1985).

loss doctrine of *Robins Dry Dock & Repair Co. v. Flint.*[126] The court relied on reasoning that permitting liability for the "unknowable" amounts that might be posed as economic loss claims arising from any substantial mishap would erode the efficient deterrent effect of such a tort rule, as a rational, wealth-maximizing actor would be unable to gauge the optimal precautionary measures for avoidance of a predictable accident cost. In Judge Higgenbotham's words:

> That the [economic loss] rule is identifiable and will predict outcomes in advance of the ultimate decision about recovery enables it to play additional roles. Here we agree with plaintiffs that economic analysis, even at the rudimentary level of jurists, is helpful both in the identification of such roles and the essaying of how the roles play. Thus it is suggested that placing all the consequence of its error on the maritime industry will enhance its incentive for safety. While correct, as far as such analysis goes, such *in terrorem* benefits have an optimal level. Presumably, when the cost of an unsafe condition exceeds its utility there is an incentive to change. As the costs of an accident become increasing multiples of its utility, however, there is a point at which greater accident costs lose meaning, and the incentive curve flattens. When the accident costs are added in large but unknowable amounts the value of the exercise is diminished.[127]

Even without explicit recognition of economic, utilitarian, or corrective justice concerns, other influential decisions have adopted and promoted such precepts, sometimes distending these established tort principles into ungainly hybrids. In the setting of environmental harm, notions of corrective justice and utilitarianism (or efficiency and equity[128]) have coexisted uneasily for decades.

---

[126]  275 U.S. 303 (1927).

[127]  *Testbank*, 752 F.2d at 1029.

[128]  *See* A Mitchell Polinsky, An Introduction to Law and Economics Chap.

Originally, even the most economically powerless landholder could seek and secure an injunction against a neighboring activity that interfered substantially with the plaintiff's use of property. Numerous early decisions evidenced a judicial unwillingness to "balance" injuries, that is, to weigh the defendant's cost and the community hardship in losing the industry against the often modest provable harm to plaintiff's ordinarily small and noncommercial property. As the New York Court of Appeals stated in *Whalen v. Union Bag & Paper Co.,*[129] to fail to grant the small landowner an injunction solely because the loss to him, in absolute terms, was less than would be the investment-backed loss to the nuisance-creating business and lost employment within the community, would "deprive the poor litigant of his little property by giving it to those already rich."

In contrast, the modern rule governing injunctions, including environmental injunctions, might seem coldly utilitarian. The Restatement (Second) of Torts § 936 lists factors for injunction issuance, which expressly include weighing of "the nature of the interest to be protected," thus presumably inviting an elevation of plaintiff's bona fides in cases in which the court considers the activity meritorious (perhaps a recreational area for Alzheimer's patients) and a devaluation in which the court deems it less valuable (perhaps an automobile scrapyard). Along similar lines, hardship to the defendant of ceasing or changing its activity, and "the interests of third persons and of the public" are proper considerations.[130] The reference to third persons and the public represent a clear invitation to introduce concepts of social costs into environmental damage litigation.

Representative of such an approach is the result reached in *Boomer v. Atlantic Cement Co.,*[131] a decision known to legions of law students. *Boomer* involved a large-scale industrial nuisance in the form of airborne cement dust emanating from an upstate New York cement plant. In the lower court, a nuisance was found, and temporary damages awarded, but plaintiffs' application

---

3 (1989).

[129] 101 N.E.2d 870 (N.Y. 1913).

[130] RESTATEMENT (SECOND) OF TORTS § 936(1)(e)–(g).

[131] 257 N.E.2d 870 (N.Y. 1970).

for an injunction was denied. Recognizing that to deny the injunction would depart from *Whalen's* corrective justice – no balancing approach discussed earlier, the court nevertheless adopted a utilitarian approach that weighed the hardships imposed on plaintiffs against the economic consequences of the requested injunction. In what might be described as a split decision, the court denied the injunction and awarded permanent, one-time damages that would be recorded as a continuing servitude on the land. The court explained: "The ground for denial of injunction, notwithstanding the finding both that there is a nuisance and that plaintiffs have been damaged substantially, is the large disparity in economic consequences of the nuisance and of the injunction."

*Boomer* permits examination of modern nuisance law in terms of a cost-benefit or utilitarian rationale, and the decision stands as a vindication of what the New York court concluded were the overall best economic interests of the community. However, other important elements to an economic analysis of nuisance law are at play, to wit, the elements of social cost. In the introductory paragraph to *The Problem of Social Cost*,[132] Ronald H. Coase illustrates the operation of social cost analysis by employing the example of a factory emitting demonstrably harmful pollutants – in this sense an important distinction with *Boomer*. Coase suggests that application of pure economic principles might prompt economists to conclude that it might be desirable to have the factory pay damages, proportionate or otherwise, or even to shut down. Such results, he proposes, may be "inappropriate, in that they lead to results which are not necessarily, or even usually, desirable."[133]

In a pollution scenario, the most efficient course of conduct will be where the polluter and the complainant reach an *ex ante* agreement regarding the level of harm the complainant is willing to sustain in return for the payment of money. This result, reached through cooperation and which avoids litigation, offers the lowest possible transaction costs, and the optimal, or most efficient resolution. It is received wisdom that any tort rule associated with a redressable phenomenon, in this case nuisance, to be efficient, should

---

[132] Ronald H. Coase, *The Problem of Social Cost*, 3 J. L. & ECON. 1 (1960), reprinted in FOUNDATIONS OF TORT LAW 3 et seq. (Saul Levmore, ed.) (1994).
[133] *Id.*

encourage a resolution that keeps the matter out of litigation. Thus, the question arises: What is the tort rule in nuisance that elevates to the highest likelihood the parties' disposition of the dilemma by negotiation, rather than by litigation?

A. Mitchell Polinsky advances Coase's analysis in its nuisance law context.[134] He first employs the methodology of Calabresi and Melamed in which the authors identify two steps in conceptualizing a nuisance claim: first, an *entitlement* must be established; and, second, a conclusion must be reached as to how to vindicate that entitlement.[135] One approach, Polinsky writes, is that of the injunction. Injunctive relief was rejected in its pure form in *Boomer*, as the court permitted the low-level polluter to continue to cause damage, and to "buy off" the property owners holding the entitlement. Using the example of one polluter and one resident, Polinsky describes the pollution in units, the factory's profits, and the resident's damages. For one unit of pollution, the factory's profits are $10,000, and the resident's damages $1,000. If the factory pays $1,000 in damages, its net profit is $9,000. If the factory doubles its production, and its pollution, to two units, Polinsky assigns a net additional profit to the factory of $4,000. Yet, at the same time the resident's damages actually may not rise arithmetically, but rather in multiples, to, say, $15,000. Two conclusions are evident. First, under a "payment of damages–avoid an injunction" approach the factory is best served by maintaining and not increasing either its level of pollution or its level of production. Second, the *Boomer* requirement that the factory pay one-time damages in order to secure the right to continue its operation at current levels is the efficient solution.

Key to the efficient operation of a nuisance remedy is the assignment of nuisance damages that equal the complainant's actual loss. An impediment to this goal may arise when one or both parties engage in "strategic" behavior in which either the polluter or the complainant adopts a litigation or settlement strategy that is inconsistent with the optimal payment of actual loss, that is,

---

[134]   POLINSKY, *supra* at 11, 15.

[135]   *See* Guido Calabresi & A. Douglas Melamed, *Property Rules, Liability Rules, and Inalienability: One View of the Cathedral*, 85 HARV. L. REV. 1089 (1972); POLINSKY, *supra* at 15.

the polluter seeks to pay less than the proved damages, or the complainant seeks to recover more than his actual damages.

Moreover, a tort rule that did *not* limit the complainant to one-time damages, and preclude future recovery by subsequent owners, would be inefficient. Subjecting the polluter to serial recoveries into the indefinite future would constitute over-deterrence on the model of *Boomer*. Indeterminate liability would potentially fail to cap Atlantic Cement's potential financial responsibility at a level that would permit it to continue to conduct business, and would thereby be inconsistent with the rule expressed in Restatement (Second) of Torts § 826(b), which permits the finding of nuisance even when the utility of the actor's conduct outweighs the damage suffered by the complainant, so long as the damages are not set at a level that would prevent the defendant from continuation of its business. Additionally, an absence of the "one-time damages" provision of *Boomer* would unjustly enrich the property owners, as they would recover first from Atlantic Cement, and then recover again by the sale of overvalued property, which is to say, property priced at a level that failed to take into account the chronic low-level future pollution.

# VI. CONCLUSION

An optimal tort rule – and coincidentally one that is both just and moral – is efficient. It advises those behaving under its regimen of what is expected, of what is discouraged, and of the consequences of departure from the desirable. It does not compensate excessively but, rather, in proportion to the harm. Neither does it undercompensate, as only through justifiable compensation is the rule's deterrent value most effective. It stands in the stead of *ex ante* agreements as to condoned or expected behavior in situations where contract would be impossible. As Jules Coleman put it: "The rules of tort liability allocate risk, but they do not do so on the model of private contract. Tort law is not simply a necessary response to the impossibility of contract, but a genuine alternative to contract as a device for allocating risk."[136] At the same time, and by the same means as tort law discourages extra-contractual elevation of risk, tort rules encourage safer behavior.

Tort law has always been apiece with human optimism, and confidence in the capacity of man to improve himself and by so doing, improve society. No other legal, ethical, or moral schema has so consistently hewn to the magisterial human experiment of moderation, fairness, efficiency, equality, and justice in social groupings. Any recitation of the path of tort law identifies objectives consonant with those described in a contemporary self-identification of a major liberal philanthropy, the pursuit of "a just, equitable, and sustainable society."

This history of tort law is the history of the tension between self-aggrandizement and self-abnegation.[137] In this Chapter are found multiple examples, from disparate groups, of both prophylaxes against and responses to wrongful infliction of harm to individuals or to the social collective. In historical contexts, such groupings, and such examples, have ranged from the Babylonian response to the flooding of another's land; to Socrates' and Aristotle's injunctions against unconsented-to taking; to Roman development of the law of nuisance; to Talmudic rules regarding waste. With conspicuous reference to the law of nuisance, modern U.S. decisional law demonstrates the continued fidelity to the goal of mediating between these two extremes.

Moreover, the inexorable and permeating nature of these precepts of economic efficiency, avoidance of waste, and cultivation of circumstances in when persons may preserve and protect their physical autonomy and their property, is by now evident in almost all cultures. These goals have been effected by rules reflecting societal expectations of personal liberty as leavened by personal responsibility. And as is seen, such rules, be they norms or written strictures,

---

[136] JULES L. COLEMAN, RISKS AND WRONGS 203 (1992).

[137] As to the former, see BERTRAND RUSSELL, A HISTORY OF WESTERN PHILOSOPHY 624 (1945), in which is found a 1656 quotation attributed to one Joseph Lee, and which is representative of a *laissez-faire* social construct: "It is an undeniable maxim that everyone by the light of nature and reason will do that which makes for him his greatest advantage. . . . The advancement of private persons will be the advantage of the public."

have been in greater or lesser harmony. This direction of tort law has been and will continue to be its elevation in comprehensiveness, its shedding of error, and its ongoing self-instruction guiding it to what is denominated sometimes as a "right fit" in its time and culture. This ageless improvement of tort law over time would be predicted by Socrates, in his constant references to the imperative of man's path of enhancing the life of the individual and the polity through education, even if simply experiential, self-knowledge, and the inevitable influence of these attributes to the task of political or judicial development of tort law.

To Immanuel Kant, only a norm respecting personal physical integrity and non-wasteful behaviors would be suited to a rule that if applied to all mankind would bring evenhanded good. Tort law's supple receptivity to change in response to ever-perfectible societal norms is fully harmonious with the norm Kant identified as "acting from duty," as distinct from "acting according to duty." The concept of acting *from* duty is captured in the example of the merchant conducting an honest business because of his "purely moral interest in obeying the [duty] of objectively correct behavior[,]" irrespective of what the state may or may not ordain.[138] It is noteworthy that philosophers reaching back to the Greeks proposed similarly that an individual achieved "good" when leading a life in harmony with nature, and that "virtue" was demonstrated by a man's "will" that was "in agreement with nature."[139] Indeed, Bertrand Russell noted the striking comparisons between the philosophical structures of Kant and those of the Stoics.[140]

If it is true that the development of efficient norms and laws for the treatment of civil wrongs characterizes human development to this date, does this alone demonstrate that employment of such methods will continue, through trial and error, into the future? Of course, such a historical showing, available in this Chapter only in selected sketches, does not so prove, in the same way that coincidence

---

[138] Paul Dietrichson, *What Does Kant Mean by Acting From Duty?*, in Kant: A Collection of Critical Essays 317 (Robert Paul Wolff, ed. 1967).

[139] Bertrand Russell, A History of Western Philosophy 254 (1945), referencing, among others, Seneca and Democritus.

[140] *Id.* at 268.

does not demonstrate causation. The evidence here falls far short of a philosophical proof that admits of no contrary conclusion. Yet, there exists a strong basis for a prediction that tort law's development along these lines will, in fact, continue.

Historians attending to broader topics have reached agreement that the path of history is one of steady improvement. The so-called "law of progress," affecting all disciplines from biology to history, is discussed by the influential R. G. Collingswood,[141] who proposes further that progress in history means simply that man builds his knowledge on the incidents of his history and that of others. Man does not and will not know that he participates in this progress, nor is any assumption of this progress predicated on the identification of man as a "child of nature," thus binding the prediction of societal progress to the laws of evolution.[142] Importantly, progress does not necessarily mean improvement, as the former can be gauged objectively, whereas the latter is in the eye of the beholder.[143] Concerning progress *qua* progress, as distinct from progress as improvement, the law of historical progress has been foundational to the development of man's economic life. Successful historical development is achieved when man's construction of societal change is made actual as fully as possible, by knowledge of the past in such measure as will permit him to avoid its errors. It does not necessarily involve replacement of the bad with the good. As often it will be the replacement of the good with the better. This much is true irrespective of whether history is regarded as a transcendental concept, an empirical pursuit, or a mixture of both. And if a seemingly uncontradicted string of proofs of this progress is shown to be applicable to man's economic development,[144] it would be incongruous to fail to recognize the rightful place of economic efficiency in society's development of rules governing the economic stability of individuals, including tort rules.

---

[141] R. G. COLLINGSWOOD, THE IDEA OF HISTORY 322–323 (Jan Van Der Dussen, ed.) (Rev. ed. 1992).

[142] *Id.*

[143] *Id.* at 325, giving the example of a primitive group's development of a more efficient way to catch fish, resulting in the availability of not one, but instead five fish a day. Although this might be considered progress, those in the community content with the availability of one fish per day might not call it an improvement.

[144] *Id.* at 331.

Applying these concepts to tort-type law, we can see that principles of economic efficiency have always been part and parcel of civil remediation of wrongful harm. And yet the strong philosophical and theistic ties to early tort rules retarded a sensible and explicit recognition of the equivalent and largely harmonious efficiency rationales for such rules. In the past, as now, the legal approaches to tort-type remedies is maturing rather than matured. To use only one example, for their philosophical advances in a philosophy of corrective justice and in ethics, the slave-holding Greek culture did not recognize that inequality is inefficient, but, then, neither did other nations for another millennium.

Even so, it can be predicted with confidence that principles of economic efficiency, waste avoidance, repulsion of unjust enrichment, and deterrence will continue to affect tort theory, policy and law. That to date economic analysis plays only an episodic and subordinate role in decisional law should not vitiate this prediction. Moreover, the presence of proto-efficiency arguments, however crude and polemic, in state and federal tort reform initiatives, should presage that more matured efficiency interpretations will hold increasing sway in the proliferation of statutes governing injury law.

The entirety of history's philosophical development has been devoted to the identification and description of a scientific model of human and societal behavior. In injury law today, principles of economic efficiency and correlative deterrence represent the only applied scientific model. It would be anomalous to suppose that injury law, by reason of its ancient articulation in moral terms, ought be immune from scientific deconstruction and reanalysis in the scientific terms of economic efficiency, and it verges on impossibility to propose that it will fail to find greater and greater employment in tort theory, adjudication, and statutory adoption.